SPYCLOPAEDIA

SPYCLOPAEDIA

*An encyclopaedia of spies, secret services, operations, jargon
and all subjects related to the world of espionage*

RICHARD DEACON

Macdonald

A *Macdonald* Book
Copyright © Donald McCormick 1987

First published in Great Britain in 1988
by Macdonald & Co (Publishers) Ltd
London & Sydney

British Library Cataloguing in Publication Data

Deacon, Richard, *1911–*
Spyclopaedia.
1. Espionage — Dictionaries
Rn : Donald McCormick   I. Title
327.1′2′0321   UB270

ISBN 0-356-14600-6

Photoset in North Wales by
Derek Doyle & Associates, Mold Clwyd.
Printed in Great Britain by
Redwood Burn Ltd, Trowbridge.
Bound at the Dorstel Press

Macdonald & Co (Publishers) Ltd
Maxwell House
74 Worship Street
London EC2A 2EN

A BPCC plc Company

Contents

PREFACE

One of the difficulties in compiling a SPYclopaedia is that it is far from easy to decide at what date formalized espionage really began. However, as it was around 510 BC that the Chinese sage, Sun Tzu, produced his celebrated work on the arts of war and espionage, *Ping Fa*, this seemed to be a good starting point.

Bearing in mind the time span, it seemed most practical to divide the book as follows: the first part introducing the various secret services of the world; the second covering a period from 510 BC to the end of World War I; the third from 1919 to the end of World War II; the fourth from 1946 to the present time; and, finally, a glossary embracing the lore and language of the intelligence game, and explaining the significance of such things as ufology research and PSI espionage.

The biggest problem in compiling this book has been the process of selection, for this is a subject which could easily be extended into several volumes. The aim has been to give a comprehensive picture of espionage through the ages and all around the world. Sometimes this has meant omitting spymasters in favour of lesser spies, and occasionally describing minor rather than major operations, as they convey more of the atmosphere of this mysterious world. Quite often the obscure spies prove to be much more interesting than the household names who have gone out in a blaze of publicity. Such surprises may compensate for some omissions.

It will be noted that dates of births and deaths have not been given in all cases. Indeed, in some instances agents have not only come from obscure origins, but have just mysteriously disappeared leaving no trace.

RICHARD DEACON

PART I

The World's Secret Services

ALBANIA

Always the odd man out in the Communist world, Albania regards itself as the custodian of positive Communism, and even today reflects the views of its first Communist chief of state, Enver Hoxa, that 'American imperialism and Soviet social imperialism are the arch enemies of the people'. It remains very much a closed country, allowing in relatively few visitors even for a Communist state. Though the last of the East European countries to recognize the Chinese People's Republic in 1949, Albania was soon to become China's firmest friend in the European Communist world. China urgently needed an ally in Europe and, as relations with the USSR deteriorated, Albania became the ideal place for a listening post for Eastern Europe and the Balkans.

From independent evidence by radio monitors it would seem that China had its own reception and transmission stations in Albania during the 1960s-70s and that Radio Tirana's transmitters were used to broadcast Radio Peking material, some of these broadcasts being beamed to North America. A radio ham analyst stated that in the early 1970s 'there exists between Albania and PR China both RTTY and other code links ... collaboration extends to mutual espionage ... at 21.40 hours on 12 January 1973, Albania radio quoted "Moscow sources" [obviously unofficial sources] as saying that Soviet submarines had been engaged in placing detecting and recording equipment at key points of NATO activities. Their source stated that it was necessary to create and maintain this method of surveillance to offset advantages gained by NATO through breaches made by US espionage of the Warsaw Pact ... They

11

also referred to the fact that East-West defections had been much greater than those going the opposite way, adding that "the Soviet Union and the USA are clearly determined to maintain a state of terror for all the world's peace-loving people." '

Certainly in the past twenty years, Albanian intelligence has kept a close watch on Soviet submarine activities, and Radio Tirana has broadcast some of these findings, including one Albanian explanation for the presence of an unknown submarine on the sea-bed of a Norwegian fiord. The Albanians claimed it to be a Russian submarine on which some of the crew had mutinied, forcing the remaining crew to take over while another Russian submarine towed it to safety.

ARGENTINA

For many years Argentina's Intelligence Service has made neutrality an asset, giving it opportunities to establish useful links with a wide range of foreign intelligence services. In World War II these links included the USA, the UK, Nazi Germany, Italy, Spain and Japan, and since that war the picture has been much the same. While Argentina had been one of the first countries to provide refuge for escaped Nazi war criminals, it had also remained strictly neutral. At the end of Peron's regime there had been a strong demand in police and intelligence circles for a check on the known association of members of 'La Arana', a political organization which included former Nazis and Italian Fascists. Israel's efficient kidnapping of Eichmann, arch-villain of the concentration camps, would not have been quite so smooth without the unofficial cooperation of the Argentinian Secret Service. Eichmann had been flushed out of Argentina into Bolivia, but had returned to Argentina under an alias. In a strictly confidential memorandum from the Argentinian Government to its intelligence service it was made clear that while Argentina preferred not to be asked to extradite Eichmann, notice had been taken of 'the presence of Israeli Commandos in Argentina' and they were to refrain from 'acting against them, except to keep the situation under control'. Diplomacy was conducted not through the diplomatic services, but the intelligence services of the two nations. This resulted in Argentina shadowing Eichmann day and night, but remaining aloof from the political implications. Full control of the situation was taken by Commander Jorge Messina, Director-General of the Argentinian Central Intelligence body.

In the late 1970s and early 1980s Argentinian Intelligence was used as a major weapon of repression and persecution by the governments of the day. In 1984 *El Periodista* published a list of 1351 names mentioned in a secret government investigation concerning those responsible for illegal repression in this period. The majority of those mentioned were members of the intelligence services, the armed forces and police. Since then President Alfonsin has had to contend with an increasing threat to the stability of his democratic government by discontent within the armed forces. This has caused serious doubts as to whether he can control his own security services. A 'bomb attempt' on Alfonsin's life was denounced by the Army as a mock device planted by the Cordoba police to discredit the Generals.

During the Falklands War and just prior to the Argentinian invasion of these islands, the Intelligence Service received help from a number of unexpected sources: Israel, (rather mysteriously, but possibly connected with the quest for Nazi war criminals), South Africa and the Soviet Union, each of which had different reasons for helping. While some of the secrets passed from South Africa can be attributed to their naval traitor, Dieter Gerhardt (q.v. Part IV) – since imprisoned for spying for the Russians – others undoubtedly included a mysterious spy ring based in South Africa, but including a suspected British mole. Meanwhile Moscow was keeping Buenos Aires Intelligence HQ informed by radio of the British fleet's dispositions.

AUSTRALIA

Few British Commonwealth countries prior to World War II took intelligence-gathering seriously. When that war ended and the Cold War began, Australia began to think in national terms rather than relying on intelligence from the USA and Britain.

The threat of a Japanese invasion had already alerted the Australians to the need for some kind of a security service, and so after the war the Australian Security and Intelligence Organisation (ASIO) came into being. Australia found itself confused between the views of the British and those of the American OSS on what sort of a service it needed. Originally it relied upon the advice given by Colonel C.G. Roberts, director of Australian Military Intelligence with the Allied Intelligence Bureau in Melbourne, an organization assisted by a network of Australian spies known as the 'Coast Watchers' who operated mainly from islands already captured by the Japanese. In the end Australia relied mainly upon Britain for advice and guidance in setting up the ASIO. Sir Roger Hollis, then a senior member of MI5, was called upon to provide this, partly because some Australians feared the Americans might seek to make the ASIO a mere agent of the USA. So sound was Sir Roger's guidance and so effective the results, that this alone might be cited in his favour against those who have recently made (unsubstantiated) allegations that he was a Soviet mole.

In 1950 Brigadier Sir Charles Spry became Director-General of the ASIO, having previously been Director of Military Intelligence. It was Spry who surmised that Vladimir Petrov was ripe for wooing away from the Soviet camp several months before he made the decision to defect. When Petrov went to Australia he had only one hobby – chess. Then, suddenly, it was noticed that he had begun to take an interest in local soccer matches in the Canberra area. Unknown to him, two Australian security men shadowed him and reported back to their chief that, in an unguarded moment, Petrov had said to another spectator: 'This is a splendid game. I should be quite happy to stay in your lovely country for ever.' Shortly afterwards, Petrov, a diplomat in the Soviet Embassy in Canberra, defected, revealing considerable details about Russian operations in Australia and how the KGB had infiltrated its agents among immigrants from Eastern Europe.

Spry had established close links with both MI5 and MI6 in Britain, and the value of these was soon proved after the debriefing of Petrov in 1954. All went smoothly with the ASIO until the 1970s when there were rifts with the government of the day. In Tokyo in 1977 a former Australian diplomat claimed that Western powers had been monitoring and decoding Japan's secret and diplomatic cables for years. He was Gregory Clark, a close aide to the former Australian Premier, Gough Whitlam, and whose book, *Japanese Tribe: Origins of Uniqueness,* suggested that the ASIO had intercepted and decoded such messages. (Clark had resigned from the Foreign Affairs Department in 1965 because he was bitterly opposed to Australian policy on the Vietnam War.) Both the Australian Embassy and the Japanese Foreign Office denied Clark's claims. Then in the early 1980s when the ASIO uncovered another major Soviet spy, Valery Ivanov, a Third Secretary at the Soviet Embassy in Canberra, there was more trouble. Ivanov was found to have been in touch with Labour Party officials who were friends of the Prime Minister, Robert Hawke. As a result, a Royal Commission was set up to consider the ASIO's findings and this led to some resignations from the government. In 1983 there was further dissatisfaction with the ASIO on account of a training exercise by intelligence officers in Melbourne which was described by the *Sydney Morning Herald* as an operation of 'stumblebums'. It resulted in the resignation of John Ryan, the chief of the Secret Intelligence section of the ASIO. The chief complaint was that the officers taking part in the exercise had been under the influence of alcohol. Consequently new controls were put upon the ASIO, insisting upon the organization giving full reports to the Cabinet's security committee and the Attorney-General.

The last royal commission into ASIO in 1984 reported that it 'has properly served the interests of the Australian people and government', and in 1987 there was set up both the Inspector General of Intelligence and Security and the Joint Parliamentary ASIO Committee. The new Director-General of ASIO is Mr Alan Wrigley.

BULGARIA

In many respects Bulgaria has the most sinister of all modern intelligence services, a regrettable fact to record because Bulgarians, on the whole, are a likeable people. Undoubtedly this is because Bulgaria's State Security Service, the *Darjavna Sugurnost* (DS), is very much dominated by the KGB. The

USSR has not only used Bulgarian Intelligence for collecting information, but for conducting many of the 'dirty tricks' of the Soviet Union, including terrorism, assassinations, arms smuggling and drug trafficking. The KGB has also used the DS for collecting intelligence on various paranormal experiments, such as mind-control (see *PSI Espionage* Part V) and on new methods of assassination which can escape detection (see *Markov, Georgi* Part IV).

Vladimir Kostov, who was a member of the DS until he defected in Europe in 1977, has described in his book, *La Parapluie Bulgare*, how the DS attempted to murder him in Paris, using the same poison-umbrella technique that was employed successfully against Markov. This proved that Bulgaria has a long arm when it comes to punishing defectors.

The Bulgarian Secret Service was also implicated in the attempted assassination of Pope John Paul II in May 1981. Two Bulgarians were cited as conspirators and the Turkish gunman, Mehmet Ali Agca, who was brought to trial, was said to have been given special training by the KGB.

In 1986 Graham Atkinson, a reporter on the Communist London newspaper, the *Morning Star*, claimed that the Bulgarians tried to recruit him to track down the Soviet defector Vladimir Kuzichkin (q.v. Part IV), who was hiding somewhere in Britain. They also tried to involve him in their efforts to prove that their secret service played no part in the assassination attempt on the Pope. A key figure in Bulgarian intelligence, especially in establishing good relations in Latin American, particularly Columbia, is said to be the President's daughter, Madame Ludmilla Zhivokva, who has also been head of Bulgarian TV. She was, for a time, studying at St Antony's College, Oxford.

Further reading
La Parapluie Bulgare by Vladimir Kostov (Paris, 1986).

CANADA

It comes as a surprise to many people that for a lengthy period Canada's Secret Service and counter-espionage organization was the 'Mounties' – the Royal Canadian Mounted Police.

Admittedly, this was mainly concerned with internal security, but on occasions it was also responsible for assessing intelligence gained from outside the country. The RCMP was highly effective before and during World War II, supplying considerable evidence of espionage from abroad, although it was ignored both by the Canadian and the British Governments.

One of the first defectors from the Soviet Union in that period was General Walter Krivitsky, who spent some time in Canada with his wife and small son, being known in Montreal under the cover-name of 'Walter Thompson'. When he was driven around in Canada he was usually followed by the RCMP for protection, and officers occasionally called at his home to question him. The RCMP warned the British that Krivitsky was being tailed by unidentified foreigners all the time he was in Canada, but this information was ignored.

The greatest triumph of the Mounties was the case of Igor Gouzenko (q.v. Part IV), a code clerk in the Russian Embassy in Montreal who defected in 1945. It was Nicholson of the RCMP, fluent in Russian, who first interrogated Gouzenko and obtained vital evidence from him which pointed to traitors within the British ranks. This was never adequately followed up by Britain, but the RCMP used Gouzenko's evidence to round up the whole Soviet spy network in Canada, including such people as Fred Rose, a member of Parliament, David Gordon Lunan, editor of *Canadian Affairs*, P. Furnford Pemberton Smith of the National Research Council in Ottawa, Kathleen Willsher, Assistant Registrar of the Office of the UK High Commissioner in Ottawa, and Edward Mazarall, of the National Research Council.

In the 1960s problems were raised for the RCMP by the terrorist campaign organized by the Quebec Liberation Front (FLQ), apparently with Soviet involvement. This campaign of terror culminated in the Cross-Laporte kidnappings in 1970 and played a positive role in Rene Levesque's Parti Quebecois coming to power (see *Schouters, George*, Part IV).

In 1977 a Commission of Inquiry was established to probe allegations of illegal acts by the RCMP. This concentrated on RCMP operations against terrorists of the FLQ. As a result, a number of RCMP personnel were convicted of various offences, including illegal wire-tapping and breaking and entering. The inquiry was conducted by Mr Justice David C. McDonald from Edmonton and it found that the RCMP had made surreptitious entries, 'without consent or warrant', that there was 'a willingness on the part of some members to deceive those outside the Force who have some sort of constitutional authority', and that there had been 'widespread incidence of unlawful opening of mail by RCMP members'. The outcome of this inquiry was to separate the Security Service from the RCMP and establish a new agency. Thus in May 1983 legislation was introduced to establish the Canadian Security Intelligence Service (CSIS). Its role was to deal with internal security and counter-espionage, and it was empowered to tap telephones, use electronical listening devices and operate a mail-cover mission. To many people these seemed to be the very things for which the RCMP had been criticized, even though there were stringent controls of such operations. The first Director of the CSIS was Thomas D'Arcy Finn, a Privy Council official and lawyer. Many RCMP members joined the new service, but there were also recruits from the armed forces and universities. The CSIS is reported to have good relations with the American FBI. It reports to the Security Intelligence Review Committee on certain matters.

CHINA

As Chinese espionage dates back several centuries BC when the sage, Sun Tzu, (q.v. Part II), produced a thesis on the subject, it is not surprising that China still has one of the most enigmatic and unusual intelligence services in the world. Its operations are low-key, fewer of its agents are caught and it produces very few defectors.

The Intelligence Services of the People's Republic of China started in a modest way under Mao Tse-tung before World War I, and its creation was largely due to K'ang Sheng (q.v. Part III). When Chiang Kai-shek was driven from mainland China, the service was greatly strengthened under the title of the Central External Liaison Department (CELD).

In China all government and civic departments have their intelligence organizations which contribute to the Central

Control of Intelligence. There are three main channels for this: first, the Party channel, which includes the investigation department; second, the CELD just mentioned, which is concerned with the analysis of foreign intelligence; third, the State Council, which has links with the Ministry of External Trade and the Military Intelligence Department of the General Staff. It has only been in the last twenty years that these various branches of the Secret Service have been developed to a higher degree of efficiency, but the basic concepts of such an all-embracing Intelligence Service were well laid down in the 1950s. By degrees this led to the creation of the *Cheng pao k'o* (Political Security Section), responsible for counter-espionage against enemy agents and the control and investigation of overseas Chinese, and the *Chi pao k'o* (Organizational Security Section), focusing its attention on personnel in government agencies, factories, schools and so on, and finally the Social Order Section, which divides its time between routine administrative duties, such as census registration, traffic control and investigation of crimes linked to espionage.

One of the Service's earliest tasks was keeping watch on both the American CIA and the Taiwan Intelligence Service in their Far Eastern activities, a watch on the South Korean CIA coming much later. In this period, when there was a need to contain moves from Taiwan aimed at 'liberating' China, the shock troops of Chinese espionage overseas comprised largely the disciplined and fanatically patriotic personnel of the New China News Agency (NCNA), the latter becoming in effect an instrument of the Secret Service. One of the NCNA's earliest and ablest directors in this field was Chiao Kuan-hua, later chief delegate to the United Nations. Chiao was head of the NCNA bureau in Hong Kong from 1946-49. When Keng Biao became head of the CELD he made it a firm policy to aim at winning as many defectors as he could from pro-Taiwan supporters overseas, especially in the USA.

Chinese Intelligence's greatest triumph in the 1950-60 period was undoubtedly in securing nuclear secrets, an espionage drive which started in 1944 when K'ang Sheng received a tip-off from one of his spies inside the headquarters of Tai Li, the Taiwanese Secret Service Chief. The tip was about 'a super-bomb' mentioned by an OSS officer and 'top secret research at

Pasadena'. In due course K'ang Sheng pin-pointed the research centre as being at the California Institute of Technology in Pasadena where, by a lucky chance, they had an ally on the spot – Chien Wei-chang, a member of the Communist Party. While K'ang remained the overall director of intelligence he was greatly assisted in this campaign by Li K'o-nung, head of the Social Affairs Department until the latter's death in 1962. The joint research of these two men revealed that at the end of 1949 there were more than 3500 Chinese students at colleges in the USA and that around 100 were engineers, physicists, chemists or mathematicians. It was from these people that the Chinese eventually obtained the key men in their nuclear information quest. Every attempt was made to lure some of these scientists back to China, but it was all done very discreetly. Their supreme catch was Dr Ch'ien Hsue-shen who, after working for fifteen years on US rocket programmes, returned to China to take charge of its nuclear programme.

Chinese espionage in Europe has been extremely cautious. Since a rift with Russia resulted in their being forced out of their chief European espionage headquarters in Prague in 1963, they relied for a while on Albania and made their main listening post in Berne. Both here, as in The Hague and Paris, the Chinese have kept a very low profile, though in April 1966 a Chinese Embassy secretary and a senior Chinese Nationalist (Taiwanese) official at the World Health Organization in Geneva were both expelled from Switzerland, the latter on the grounds that he had been acting as an informant to the People's Republic! From all accounts the Taiwanese in this incident, Dr Tsung Sing-sze, seems to have been one of China's most successful part-time agents. In Vienna China's biggest espionage coup was in winning European nuclear secrets through the Euratom Agency. In many of China's European bases the Embassy interpreter is often the espionage boss and in effect has the edge on his Ambassador.

There is some evidence that the Chinese and Russians were competing – no holds barred – in a period of aggressive espionage in Holland in the 1960s. The master-mind in this was Liao Ho-shu, who was given diplomatic cover at The Hague. In 1966 a Chinese engineer, Hsu-tsai, living at the home of a Chinese diplomat, was found lying on the pavement in great pain. He was taken to hospital and it was alleged that he had fallen out of a window. Shortly afterwards some Chinese arrived at the hospital, led by Liao Ho-shu. While the doctors were kept in conversation by Liao, Hsu was kidnapped from the X-ray department. The Dutch police were sure Hsu was trying to defect. They were informed by the Chinese later that Hsu had died. The subsequent autopsy revealed that Hsu had been the victim of violence. There was a diplomatic deadlock between China and Holland for six months. It ended with other Chinese engineers being allowed to leave without having given any worth-while evidence about the death of their colleague. Three years later Liao Ho-shu himself asked the Dutch Government for political asylum. He was without doubt the most important defector for the Chinese Intelligence Service in twenty-five years. It is suspected that he was in disgrace for mishandling the Hsu affair.

Further reading
A History of the Chinese Secret Service by Richard Deacon (Frederick Muller, London 1973; Taplinger, New York 1979)

CUBA

For a small country, Cuba has an intelligence and security organization which is quite remarkable, not only in its size but in its influence in many parts of the world. Its secret service is known as *Direccton General de Inteligencia* (DGI). Originally, under Fidel Castro, it was not only modelled on the KGB, but General Viktor Simenov, a Soviet adviser on intelligence, controlled its operations and ensured that the new organization acted as an agent of the KGB as and when required. The bulk of the work conducted by the DGI is not so much devoted to the security of Cuba, as to obtaining intelligence for the USSR, training terrorists and actively supporting terrorist organizations in all parts of the world (see *MPAIAC*, Part IV). This has included operations in Ethiopia, India, Jamaica, Guatemala, San Salvador, Nicaragua and even the Canary Islands.

The Cubans have no hesitation in following the Russian pattern in employing their diplomats as spies and spy-controllers. One such was José Perez Novoa, who was ambassador to Ethiopia from 1976-78. He was expelled from Addis Ababa together with his counsellor and the South Yemeni chargé d'affaires when they were all caught out in a plot to put a Moscow-line man in place of Colonel Mengistu as head of Ethiopia's revolutionary regime. The Cubans and the South Yemenis had conspired to smuggle Dr Negede Gobeze, an enemy of Mengistu's, from exile in Paris into Addis Ababa on a false passport. However, Ethiopian security police foiled that operation.

Among terrorist organizations, the DGI has had close connections with the PLO, the Red Brigade, Latin American terrorist groups and the IRA. It was because the Cubans had made Grenada one of their espionage and subversion bases that the Americans felt impelled to invade that island, and the USA had long been aware of Cuba's spy base in New York where for a long period their DGI director was Rolando Salup of the Cuban Mission. Other key DGI officers in promoting both disinformation and indulging in espionage have been Ramon Cesar Cuenca in Caracas and Norberto Hernadez Corbello in Venezuela.

In recent years there have been signs of a rift between Cuban and Russian intelligence chiefs. One KGB report criticized the Cubans unmercifully for inefficiency in espionage and this rankled with the DGI chiefs. The Cubans began to resent being given orders by the Russians. The result was the demotion of the pro-Soviet Sergio del Valle and the reinstatement of Ramiro Valdes, but this worked neither in favour of the Russians nor the Cubans, and it resulted in a report by the KGB that the Cubans were incompetent in gathering and assessing intelligence from Western countries, though it was admitted that they had done much better in Third World countries, especially in Africa.

It would be a mistake to underestimate the DGI's efforts in the Western World, as evidence from both New York and Washington suggests they have achieved considerable success in the USA. Julian Rizo, station chief in the DGI, turned up in New York as a member of the Cuban mission to the United Nations and as such, established contacts with a group of radical Grenadan students. They were supporters of the pro-Cuban group in Grenada led by Maurice Bishop, the 'New Jewel' chief who toppled Sir Eric Gairy and whose coup led to the American invasion.

CZECHOSLOVAKIA

The Czechoslovakian security service *Statni Tajna Bezpecnost* (STB), is totally under the direction of Moscow. In theory it is the First Section of the Intelligence Directorate of the Ministry for the Interior, but in practice it seeks agents and gathers information on targets indicated to it by the KGB. As a result it is one of the most experienced, versatile and effective of all the Eastern bloc intelligence services, and it has probably scored as many, if not more, successful espionage missions against Britain as the Russians themselves. The Soviet invasion of Czechoslovakia in 1968 resulted in a number of defections from the STB, and it was from these that America and Britain eventually learned the extent of Czech infiltration in the west.

One of the chief talent-spotters for potential spies in Britain was the STB spy-master, Karel Pravec, who controlled operations from inside the Czech Embassy in London. So eager was Pravec in the 1960s to recruit influential spies or agents in Britain that he even attended Conservative Party conferences with this in mind! (This plan was not quite as ludicrous as it might seem, for in the 1950s the Czechs had developed some trade relationships with two Conservative MPs.) Since 1969 the STB has been rebuilt and strengthened by the KGB, and the Czechs have conducted a series of cautiously planned support missions for the Soviet Union in various Western countries. Russia has undoubtedly found it useful to draw on Czechoslovakia's high proportion of well-educated people for its Intelligence Service.

The penetration of Britain by Czech agents began in World War II, long before the creation of the STB, but some unofficial agents from those days were later recruited. One such recruit was Vclav Kindl, a former Czech Army lieutenant, who changed sides under threat of death and became a Gestapo agent. Under the direction of Willy Leimer, a Gestapo Communist expert who was also a major in the Russian NKVD, Kindl played an important role in 'Operation Hermelin', a radio game with London which entailed luring Czech paratroop agents into German traps, thus preventing the Czech government in exile from giving aid to the Resistance movement which Leimer and his Russian masters naturally wanted to destroy. It was reported that Kindl had been shot by a trapped agent and that he died. His gravestone recorded that he was shot by the Gestapo, but later it was said that Kindl had merely gone to ground in London and changed his name to Vaclav Nodat. When MI5 were informed of these details long afterwards they searched for Nodat, but apparently never found him.

Another Czech agent, who changed his name to the tautologous 'Charlie Charles', betrayed countless Free Czechs under the code name of 'Light' after the war while running a boarding house in Folkestone. He died of a heart attack in 1962. However, the vital evidence against the STB came from Josef Frolik (q.v. Part IV), a defector from the Czech Service, who gave enormously detailed evidence to the US Congress and Senate sub-committees on intelligence. He revealed that the Czechs had a plan for approaching former Prime Minister, Edward Heath, but that the approach was never made. He did testify, however, that the Czechs recruited at least one British MP (code-name Lee), a London police officer (code-name Markyz) and an RAF serviceman (code-name Marconi). This testimony was taken by a Senate committee investigating internal security and Communist-bloc activity, and it also included evidence from another Czech agent, Frantisek August (q.v. Part IV). The latter, in referring to agent 'Light', said that he was 'a disaster for the British' and that he supplied the names of British agents who worked in Czechoslovakia, the names of informers who worked for the British in the UK, and ... 'the Middle East, Scandinavia and West Germany'.

August said that the going price for 'turning over' a British agent was £5000 to £10,000. When German panzers arrived in Britain in 1962 for the first joint exercise between the British and German armies since World War II, according to August, a Czech agent was told to smear the Germans by spreading rumours locally that many of the officers were former Nazis. When the German troops were stationed in Wales the 'dirty tricks' department of Czech Intelligence organized the painting of swastikas on Jewish graves to blacken the Germans. These events were reported by British newspapers, but 'outside influences' were blamed. Frolik claimed that several key members of the British trade union movement and the Labour

Party were recruited by the Czechs, as well as a man inside the Treasury Department. He also testified that Major Jan Koska, chief of counter-espionage in the Czech Embassy in London, 'was not averse to inventing agents and contacts in order to charge personal expenses to intelligence accounts ... I heard that he had invented a British policeman who cost Prague £1500 in bribes to cover Koska's drinking bills'. (See *Praeger, Nicholas*, Part IV).

In February 1987 Karl Koecher, a Czech, was named as the first East European 'mole' to have infiltrated the CIA. After being caught he and his wife were allowed to leave the USA in exchange for the Soviet dissident Shcharansky.

Further reading
Reports on Hearings before the Subcommittee to investigate the administration of the Internal Security Act of the Committee on the Judiciary U.S. Senate, 94th Congress, November 18 1975 and April 12 1976 (US Govt. Printing Office, Washington DC)

EAST GERMANY

East Germany's Ministry for State Security, the *Ministerium fur Staatssicherheit* (MfS), was established by a government decree of the German Democratic Republic on 9 February 1950. It owed something to the activities of the German Communist Party 'illegals' of the 1920s which had set up its own 'offensive' and 'defensive' intelligence and security network which worked in close cooperation with the Russians. During World War II Wilhelm Zaisser, Ernst Wollweber, Erich Mielke and Richard Stahlman, who had received training in the USSR, helped form the nucleus of the future East German Security organization. Its headquarters were set up at 22 Normannenstrasse, Berlin-Lichtenberg, East Berlin. This Ministry for State Security is the largest and most powerful intelligence apparatus in the Soviet bloc after the KGB. The massive presence of Soviet military forces in East Germany and the fact that Germany is divided into two nations are the main reasons why this organization has grown to become second to the KGB. Cooperation between the two services is close and this is facilitated by the KGB's presebce in East Berlin's Karlhorst district. West Germany and the NATO forces are the primary targets of the foreign intelligence service of the Ministry (*Hauptverwaltung Aufklärung*, which is the main administration for reconnaissance). This section has conducted several successful operations in West Germany, most notably the penetration of the office of the West German Chancellor, Willi Brandt (see *Guillaume, Gunter*, Part IV).

The Ministry of State Security operates in much the same way as the KGB. Prior to its establishment there had been a Kommissariat known as K5, branches of which were attached to all provincial police command stations in East Germany. This had been created by Zaisser and Mielke and its personnel were merely 'assistants' to the Soviets. When K5 was found unable to combat increasing resistance to the Sovietization of East Germany on its own, it was officially disbanded and incorporated into the MfS. Today the Ministry is divided into three divisions: foreign intelligence, internal security and management. The interesting point here is the real meaning of 'management', for the department with this title is responsible for preparing acts of sabotage in West Germany and other NATO countries in Europe.

An outstandingly efficient and enterprising head of the *Hauptverwaltung Aufklärung* has been Lt-General Markus Wolf (q.v. Part IV) who developed this section of the Ministry from an undercover department known officially as the Institute of Economic Research. It was he who concentrated on employing more female agents and using them to infiltrate West German governmental bodies as secretaries. These agents were employed as much to obtain industrial secrets as any other form of intelligence. The true size of the MfS is not easy to assess, as so many of its agents live outside the territory. Some indication of its numerical strength may be gleaned from the fact that in at least three years during the 1950s and 1960s more than 2000 spies a year were uncovered in West Germany alone. The paramilitary force of the MfS is the Felix Dzerhzhinsky Guard Regiment, estimated at 6000 men, which performs specific security and guard duties. This regiment consists of regular and national service personnel.

EGYPT

Before the United Arab Republic was founded and even after it was disbanded, the *Mukhabarat el-Aam* (General Intelligence Agency), paid as much attention to spying on fellow Arab states as to Israel. When Nasser came to power, the Egyptian security and intelligence services were reorganized, but the many changes were not completed until 1955. In the early days of this regime there was a vigilant hunt for any signs of covert British activities in Egypt, and in 1965 a large British network was liquidated. However, it was Israel which became the prime target for Egypt's counter-espionage and intelligence services, the main thrust of which was a campaign of murder and sabotage inside Israeli territory. Other coups included purchasing documents from a sergeant who worked in the Ministry of Defence in London, catching an Egyptian journalist passing information to the CIA, rounding up 700 members of the Moslem Brotherhood for conspiring against the regime, and foiling what Cairo called the 'Restoration Plot' (to restore the monarchy in Egypt). Nasser later revealed that Mahmoud Khalil, with the full knowledge of Egyptian Intelligence, had played along with British Secret Service agents, actually taking money from them, in order to get full details of the plot.

Each of the armed services had their own intelligence directorates, while the Political Police had the role of guarding the regime against enemies from within. Egypt had benefited from the fact that all the early members of Egyptian Intelligence had been trained by British instructors. In the early days of the revolutionary regime some financial help, training and equipment was provided by the CIA. In the drive against Israel an important role was played by the Regional Intelligence Bureau in Gaza (organizing the *fedayeen* unit), and El-Arish. Responsibility for the General Intelligence Agency lies with the President, and the Director of the service is also Director of the President's Office. During the Nasser era the Egyptian Secret Service acquired an enormous amount of power which resulted in many of its officers carrying out torture with impunity. There was a promise to conduct some reforms when Anwar Sadat

27

became President, but very little change was noticed. As to the quality of intelligence the service gleans, it is certainly not as efficient as that of the Israelis: it was wrong prior to the Six-Day War, while the decision to attack Israel in the Yom Kippur War was based at least partly on Soviet information. Its counter-espionage service is more efficient, but then it relies on all the apparatus of the police state with unlimited powers of surveillance and telephone tapping.

Further reading
The Arab Secret Service by Yaacov Caroz (Corgi Books, London 1978)

FINLAND

Finland's development of an intelligence service only really began in any serious form after the Russian revolution of 1917. From this period onwards the State police (*Valpo*) and *Etsiväkeskus*, Finland's secret police, kept a close and efficient watch on any threats to the state's neutrality from overseas. It was probably as well informed on the activities of the British and French Secret Services as those of Russia. However, Finland's intelligence service was primarily aimed at the Soviet Union, and with this in view, close contacts were established with intelligence circles in Britain and Germany. Secret police files for the years 1920-35 also reveal links with a network of White Russian immigrants known to British agents, such as Sir Paul Dukes, Sidney Reilly and Clifford Sharp, together with British Consular officials like Hector Tait and Vincent Carr. As the White Russian network was infiltrated by the Soviet Union, such activities did not help Finland in the long term.

In the late 1930s attempts were made to cooperate with the Germans on intelligence matters. While this did nothing to prevent Russia's invasion of Finland in 1939, despite the German-Soviet Pact, it did much to curtail Soviet aggression. Finnish military intelligence in World War II was of a much higher level than is generally believed. It was well organized, preventing the Russians from obtaining as much information as they wanted, and it gave considerable help to the Germans. In return Finland received a great deal of military aid and equipment from Germany. There was also cooperation between *Valpo* and the Gestapo. In 1944 Finnish Military Intelligence fled with its archives to Sweden with the aim of continuing the war against the Soviet Union at a later date. About the same time a group of Finnish officers defected to the United States Army.

By 1945 *Valpo* was completely transformed: the pro-German faction had gone and they came largely under the influence of Yrjo Leino, the Communist Minister of the Interior. This situation changed by the end of the 1940s and the Finnish Right, together with the Social Democrats, ousted the Communists. The Americans assisted in the creation of Finland's new intelligence organization and the new secret police were renamed the *Suojelupoliisi* (Protection Police).

FRANCE

Of all nations in the world France probably has one of the most effective secret services. It may make mistakes or become involved in more scandals than any other secret service, but it never allows inhibitions or humbug to hamper its work, as so often happens in America and Britain. Compare the muddled handling of 'Watergate' with the calm efficiency with which France handled the *Rainbow Warrior* episode in New Zealand. Though the pre-World War II *Deuxième Bureau* disappeared after the fall of France in 1940, it has been adapted and even improved since 1945 as the service which centralizes and interprets intelligence for the French High Command.

The pre-war *Service de Reseignements* (SR), which had its headquarters at 2 bis Avenue de Tourville, Paris, came directly under the Army and had four divisions: foreign intelligence, counter-intelligence, communications and a central registry. The SR also had stations in Algeria, Morocco and the Levant. Modern French intelligence and security services owe something to the service set up in London during World War II by the Free French under General de Gaulle and Colonel Passy (sometimes known as André Dewavrin), who at one time worked closely with Britain's Colonel Dansey (q.v., Part III). Passy's service was known as the Central Bureau for Information and Military Action (BCRAM), which operated from 3 St James's Square in London. It worked to a limited extent with both the SOE and the American OSS. For a time there were disputes as to who should have control of the intelligence services, the Army or a civilian body, but in the end de Gaulle's views prevailed and in 1943 he established the *Direction Général des Services Spéciaux* (DGSS) under the control of Jacques Soustelle, who ran it from Algiers. After the liberation of Paris, Soustelle moved the DGSS to Paris and the name of the service was changed to *Direction Général des Etudes et Recherches* (DGER).

After the war de Gaulle recalled Colonel Passy to take over DGER and to reorganize it into a new service which became the *Service de Documentation Extérieure et de Contre-Espionnage* (SDECE). Colonel Passy later told *Le Monde*, 'I made the decision to dismiss 10,500 people who were being subsidized by the DGER budget, to remove the requisitions on more than 100 buildings and to retain temporarily only three, and to turn over 400 vehicles requisitioned at the liberation and to retain only twenty needed for the service'. The SDECE has been frequently reorganized during the past forty years, most notably in 1958 when de Gaulle returned to power, and again during President Pompidou's presidency. Under President Mitterand it has undergone further change, being renamed *Direction Général de Sécurité Extérieure* (DGSE). Despite its ups and downs and the fact that the war for independence in Algeria took up a great deal of its time, the service has remained among the best in the world. It has always been exceptionally well informed on the Middle East and all Arab affairs, and its intelligence on the Eastern bloc and Russia should not be underestimated. To its credit, it has also achieved some rapport with the ultra-cautious Chinese Intelligence Service.

Various internal problems have upset the service from time to time ranging from allegations of kidnapping during the Algerian war and reports of a 'mole' in the USSR during de Gaulle's presidency (see *Vosjoli, Thyraud D.*, Part IV) to the more recent act of sabotage against the Greenpeace ship *Rainbow Warrior* by two French agents in New Zealand (see *Greenpeace Affair*, Part IV). The subsequent *brouhaha* was handled with skill and diplomacy probably unmatched in the world.

In recent years the Count de Marenches (q.v. Part IV) has been an admirable head of the service, achieving a great deal in reorganization, but he left under a cloud following allegations of a Franco-American plot to overthrow Gaddafi of Libya, about which even President Mitterand was said to have been kept in the dark. This led to the resignation of the service's deputy chief, Colonel Alain de Gaigneron de Marolles, and then Mitterand appointed Pierre Marion as the new chief. Marion had served in the Aerospace Consortium under the President's brother, General Jacques Mitterand. Prior to that he had spent nearly thirty years with Air France. In 1982, after only eighteen months, he resigned, allegedly because of internal friction. Vice-Admiral Pierre Lacoste was appointed the new chief of DGSE, an unusual choice in that never before had a naval officer been in charge of French intelligence. There have been suggestions that this was an attempt to pacify opinion in the armed forces, but cynics have suggested that the move had much more to do with linking the Intelligence Service to French trade deals, especially in military equipment.

At the same time as Lacoste's appointment Yves Bonnet, a chief commissioner of police, was made head of France's counter-espionage organization, *Direction de la Surveillance du Territoire* (DST). Bonnet had been *Préfet* of police on Mayotte in the Indian Ocean, and in fact, since World War II it has been something of a tradition that holders of this office come from the ranks of *préfets*. The DST has acquired a reputation for unostentatious efficiency, not least in trapping Soviet spy networks, but even more so for its recruitment of talent to the service. The DST is controlled by the Minister of the Interior and its computerized dossiers and filing system are the envy of many other security services. During the trial of four Frenchmen accused of spying for Moscow some years ago, Desire Parent, deputy of the DST, revealed that at least fifty undercover Russian agents were operating inside France and although thirty had been identified, no action could be taken because there was no positive evidence against them. This impasse was resolved in 1983 when France expelled forty-seven Soviet officials, forty of them diplomats, and accused them of spying 'particularly in the military sphere'. According to inside sources in the DST it was admitted that the number of Soviet citizens on diplomatic or other official missions to France had increased from about 200 to 700 over a ten-year period. Shortly before this the DST had successfully outwitted the Romanian secret service in uncovering a plot to assassinate Virgil Tanase, a Romanian dissident writer living in Paris. In cracking this plot the DST induced a Romanian agent named Motu Haiduc to defect.

Though the Greenpeace affair was handled adroitly by the government of the day, it led to the resignation of the Defence Minister and the sacking of Admiral Lacoste, head of the DGSE. He was succeeded by General René Izbot, who appeared on television to make the remarkable statement that he had discovered 'an operation to destabilize and destroy the French Secret Services'. He went on to say that he had 'lopped off some rotten branches' and that he had 'bolted this service tight ... I am its rampart'.

The present head of the DST is M. Bernard Gerard who, in 1987, visited Damascus to discuss terrorist bombings in Paris with the Syrian authorities. It was said at the time that this was evidence of France having conducted a dual policy: on the one hand openly accusing Abdullah, the suspected head of Lebanese terrorism of organizing the Paris bombings, while having 'friendly' relations with Syrian Intelligence with which the Abdullah brothers were known to have had close links. Probably no other country in the world combines intelligence and diplomacy more effectively than the French.

Further reading
Ma vie d'espionage au service de la France, M. Richer, (Ed. France, Paris, 1936)
Le 2nd Bureau au travail '35–'40, General M. Gauché (Amiot-Dumard, 1954)
L'avant guerre: études et documents sur l'espionnage depuis Dreyfus, Leon Daudet (Nouvelle Librairie Nationale, 1913)
Cinq ans à la tête de la DST 1867–72
La mission impossible, Jean Rochet (Plon, Paris, 1985)
La Piscine. Les Services secrets française 1944–84, Roger Faligot (Editions Seuil, Paris, 1985)

HUNGARY

The short-lived Hungarian Soviet Republic of 1919, with its indiscriminate killings under the 'Red Terror', had a deeply traumatic effect on the people of Hungary. Intense hostility to Communism was the political hallmark of the Hungarian state security and intelligence services. They gradually became operational from 1919 after the National Hungarian Army had occupied Budapest under its commanding officer, Admiral N. Horthy. Consequently, the investigation departments of the Hungarian Army and the Royal Hungarian Gendarmerie, and the Political Department of the Hungarian State Police controlled an army of secret agents operating at home and abroad. Special attention was focussed on the USSR because numerous leaders of the 1919 Hungarian Soviet Republic wished to unite with Communist Russia. The Office of the Inner Cabinet and Military Office of the Regent (Admiral Horthy) acted as Hungary's national security council and controlled the National Defence (Intelligence) Service from 1920. This was largely a counter-espionage body, which soon acquired a reputation for great skill in countering Communist subversion through its network of agents which penetrated both left-wing and right-wing organizations. The activities of all these Hungarian intelligence sections ceased after Hungary's occupation by the Red Army in 1945.

It was then that Gabor Peter, a covert Hungarian security agent of the Russian NKVD, established the Budapest HQ of the political investigation and executive branch of the new Hungarian State Police. In 1947 this became the *Államvédelmi Osztály* (AVO), subordinated to the Hungarian Ministry of the Interior and closely cooperating with its Soviet counterpart, the MVD. But in 1949 it became an independent body with ministerial rank, renamed *Államvédelmi Hatósag* (AVH), the State Security Authority. Gabor Peter, who became head of the new authority, was promoted to the rank of lieutenant-general. The AVH had seventeen main divisions, each with a specific function, though only three of them were publicly acknowledged. From a population of $9\frac{1}{2}$ millions, around 80,000 informers were recruited, some forcibly. The work of AVO and

AVH has been assisted by a second force, the Economic Order and Surveillance Department of the Hungarian State Police. AVO has its own armed forces, including the border guard ('green caps') and the much feared internal security troops ('blue caps'), totalling some 36,000 men.

Cooperation with the Soviet Union, especially the KGB, has always been close and was amply demonstrated during the 1956 Hungarian uprising. The AVH was officially disbanded during that period and Hungary is the only Soviet-block country governed without a separately functioning state security and intelligence organization. After 1956 Hungarian leaders decided that social stability and internal security would be better served without a security force reminiscent of the AVH. Present-day state security and intelligence services are partly incorporated into a kind of political branch of the ordinary police. According to 1974 Hungarian legislation, it is the police who protect the security of the State 'against spies and traitors'. However, Hungary has the poorest record of any Soviet-block nation for successful intelligence operations against Western targets. Perhaps one reason for this is that the KGB does not entrust them with much responsibility, but the main reason for minimal espionage activity must surely be the Hungarian Government's desire to maintain good relations with the Western democracies.

IRAN

Under the rule of the Shah the Iranian Intelligence and Security Service (SAVAK) often had to contend with Arab enemies of their regime, particularly Iraq. The Iraqi services did their best to undermine the Shah, even persuading General Teymour Bakhtiar, the head of SAVAK who was exiled in 1961, to collaborate with them. SAVAK was built up with the help of several secret services, including the CIA, the British SIS and Israel's Mossad, and it acquired a reputation for ruthlessness, torture and repression, though it must be admitted that this was partly in response to acts of sabotage and terror perpetrated against Iran. Eventually it was SAVAK who tracked down Bakhtiar and killed him.

Partly helped by the Shah's decision to sell oil to Israel, a remarkable understanding developed between the secret services of the two countries and continues to this day. After the revolution in Iran, Muslim hardliners took over SAVAK and arrested many of its agents. The Komiteh headquarters of SAVAK were destroyed and its records either burnt or flung into the street. General Nematollah Nassiri, then head of SAVAK, was shot without trial. Despite this purge, the new regime's Intelligence and Security Service is as ruthless as its predecessor, but it still gives some help to Israel, not least because the two countries have a common enemy in Iraq. In fact, Israel's attack on the nuclear plant outside Baghdad was made possible with the help of hundreds of reconnaissance photographs taken from Iranian Phantom jets.

IRAQ

In contrast to some other Arab nations, Iraq had concentrated more on external than internal intelligence, perhaps partly because it has always had both a military and a civilian intelligence service. Heads of each in their time – military in 1959 and civilian in 1973 – have attempted to overthrow the established government. The nation's modern secret service, *Al Mukhabarat* (the Listening Post), was set up after the Ba'ath Party gained control in Iraq in 1968, and it combined both military and civilian intelligence services in the mid-1970s.

Iraq's secret service has always been concerned with watching and eliminating its opponents both inside and outside the country, so its need for external contacts has always been vital. On occasion it has linked up with its opposite numbers in Libya and Algeria, as well as with some Arab guerrilla groups in other countries. One of its major functions had been the assassination of political opponents. In July 1978 eleven Iraqis, five of them intelligence officers attached to the Iraqi Embassy in London, were expelled from Britain for involvement in terrorist activities – in this instance, the assassination of Iraq's former Prime Minister, General Abdul Razzak al-Naif.

In 1973 Iraq's Minister of the Interior, Ghaiden Sadoun, was sent to Moscow to discuss possible cooperation between *Al Mukhabarat* and the KGB. A secret intelligence pact between the two countries was negotiated, including a reorganization of Iraq's internal security on KGB guidelines, the supply of certain technical equipment for espionage to Iraq by Moscow, special training for Iraq intelligence officers in Russia, and the sharing of certain intelligence with the Soviet Union. Yet, though there is a strong pro-Soviet faction within the Iraq leadership, Communism is still persecuted in Iraq, and there is a certain amount of Iraqi suspicion about Soviet long-term motives. Nevertheless, when Russia had no embassy in Madrid in the last years of Franco's reign, Iraq helped out by supplying the USSR with intelligence on the American naval base at Rota and the air force base at Torrejon. When Western intelligence officers discovered a directive to Iraqi spies in the mid-1970s, they learned that the head of *Al Mukhabarat*, Brigadier Khalil al-Azzawi, had called for special reports on NATO activities and deployments as well as a quest for Western electronic warfare devices.

Further reading
The Arab Secret Services by Yaacov Caroz (Corgi Books, London 1978)

ISRAEL

Israel's Intelligence and Security Services developed almost entirely from various Jewish underground movements in Palestine in the harrowing years before independence. That experience was invaluable in many way, not least in teaching them the need for 'instant' intelligence (see Glossary) because they would be surrounded on all sides by potential enemies. Though the state of Israel is less than forty years old, for its size, it has one of the finest intelligence services in the world: *Mossad Le Aliyah Beth* (Institution for Intelligence and Special Services) and *Shin Beth* (the Security and Counter-Espionage Service). The Mossad was largely the inspiration of Eliahu Golomb and Shaul Avigur, who in 1940 had founded Shai, an underground intelligence service for the defence unit called Haganah. David Ben-Gurion, who became Israel's first leader, feared the development of a group within a group and one faction seeking to dominate the whole, so for this reason he delayed the establishment of a new Secret Service until 1949 after the total disbandment of Irgun, the powerful terrorist organisation. Early in 1948 there had been evidence that Russia was trying to manipulate some Jewish fanatics in its own interest, so Ben-Gurion made sure that most of the personnel in Shin Beth were recruited from Haganah.

The Mossad came into operation about the same time with Ben-Gurion's own choice as chief, Isser Harel (q.v. Part IV). In 1949-50 the Mossad, which had excellent agents in Teheran and Istanbul, had news of Soviet espionage against Israel. There were attempts by the Russians to infiltrate Israel with a few non-Zionist Jews from Bulgaria and Rumania. In October 1952 Hagop Antaryessian, an Armenian living in the Old City of Jerusalem, was arrested and charged with spying for Russia. Soon the Israelis found they were fighting an espionage war on two fronts – against the Arabs and the Russians.

The Israeli Secret Service had three main branches: Mossad, similar in many respects to Britain's MI6; Shin Beth, primarily a counter-espionage department, but also a collector of military intelligence and linked to the Directorate of Military Intelligence; Aman, an external collector of purely military intelligence. The Mossad and Aman cooperate, especially on armaments, logistics and enemy defence works. The purely counter-espionage section of Shin Beth is *Sheruth Bitakhon Klali*, more usually known as Shabak.

In the plans he laid down for the structure of the Secret Service Ben-Gurion created autonomy for its military and non-military branches, while allowing enough flexibility for effective cooperation. He may not have achieved perfection, but he certainly obtained efficiency. The buck stopped at two men – the Director of Military Intelligence and the Memuneh, who was titular head of the civilian section of the Secret Service (the post Harel filled for fifteen years). In effect the Memuneh, who is directly responsible to the Prime Minister, is chief executive of the Secret Services as well as being head of the Mossad and chairman of the committee comprising all section heads of the Secret Services. To safeguard against abuse of the Memuneh's sweeping power, he remains answerable to the Knesset, the Israeli parliament, who have the power to dismiss him if dissatisfied with his performance.

Shin Beth has three sections: Arab, Eastern European and Anti-Terrorist, but its strength owes a great deal to both the Mossad and the Aman. No counter-espionage service in the world has a harder task, for Israel's immigration policy makes it possible for spies to be infiltrated, and the country is home to nearly half a million Israeli Arabs. Linked to Shin Beth is the *Reshud*, which is similar to Britain's Special Branch at Scotland Yard, as it makes arrests based on evidence gathered by Shin Beth agents.

Israel's desperate need for 'instant intelligence' has resulted in set-backs as well as triumphs. During 1954, for example, a series of Israeli espionage and sabotage operations inside Egypt and Syria ended in total disaster and the complete loss of its Egyptian spy network. Four years' work was almost totally destroyed and new networks had to be built up speedily at enormous cost in time and money. But prior to the Six Day War the Mossad achieved brilliant successes from their spies inside Egypt and Syria (see *Cohen, Elie* and *Lotz, Wolfgang*, Part IV). During the so-called 'Suez Adventure' and despite the hostility of the Eisenhower administration to the drive against Nasser, the CIA secretly sympathized with Israel and gave the Mossad some support. Israeli Intelligence has, in fact, occasionally cooperated with the CIA, the British SIS and the French and West German intelligence services. One CIA executive told the author that 'if the Mossad and Shin Beth were ever destroyed, we should lose our best allies'. Mohammed Hassanein Heikal, editor of *Al-Ahram*, the Egyptian newspaper, declared after the Six Day War that 'the Israelites had a perfect system of intelligence on Egypt. They knew the secret codes of our air force and our armoured corps'.

There was a marked difference at the time of the Yom Kippur War in 1973. Mossad reports were as good as ever, but there was a lack of coordination in dealing with intelligence reports and nothing approaching the same degree of cooperation between the Mossad and Aman as there had been in 1967.

The hunting down of terrorists has always been a problem for Mossad and Shin Beth, and a severe blow was struck in 1985 when three Israelis killed by the PLO in Cyprus turned out to be Mossad agents, one of whom was an ace hit-team leader (see *Rafael, Sylvia*, Part IV). Another blow was the killing by

Palestinian guerrillas of Major-General Yekutiel Adan, who was being groomed to become head of the Mossad. Scandal has also touched Shin Beth, arising from the deaths in custody of two Palestinian terrorists. Two leading officials, one of them Avraham Shalom, head of Shin Beth, resigned after this incident and the affair became a major political issue for several weeks in 1986, when a police inquiry was ordered.

Then in 1987 Israel came under increasing pressure from the United States to punish the two men responsible for recruiting and operating Pollard, the US Navy analyst (see *Pollard, Jonathan,* Part IV), sentenced to life imprisonment for spying for Israel. The two men involved were Mr Rafi Eitan, a former Mossad secret agent, and Colonel Avi Sela, an Air Force officer indicted by an American grand jury on three counts of espionage. Eitan was dismissed from his position in the Israel Premier's office, but was later made head of the nationalized Israeli Chemicals company.

Further reading
The Israeli Secret Service by Richard Deacon (Hamish Hamilton, London 1977; Taplinger, New York 1977)

ITALY

All branches of Italian Intelligence and Security Services have undergone frequent change since the end of World War II, and there have been blunders and failures among the many successes. Titles of sections have been changed from time to time and there has been some confusion externally about SIFAR, SISME and SISMI, all of which have been concerned with both intelligence-gathering and counter-espionage. Such confusion has been made all the greater when one discovers that in the bizarre world of Italian Intelligence some of its chiefs have had links with such diverse groups as the Mafia, the P2 masonic lodges, the Italian Military Intelligence, the French SDECE and the American CIA. One such man was Francesco Pazienza, a member of SISMI (military and counter-intelligence), who actually started his career as an intelligence agent with the French SDECE before becoming an Italian and an American agent. Prior to his flight to the USA after a series of scandals in 1985, Pazienza was described as being the link-man between the Mafia, P2 and the Italian extreme right-wing, or, as author Alain Guerin called him, 'the Super-S of the SISMI'.

One of Italy's biggest spy cases broke in 1967 when counter-espionage agents in Turin arrested Giorgio Rinaldi, a thirty-nine-year-old Italian parachutist and stunt man, his wife and their chauffeur. All three were charged with spying for the Soviet Union on NATO bases in Italy and US Air Force bases in Spain. This spy ring extended to many countries, but though Rinaldi headed the ring, it was his wife, former member of Mussolini's Women's Corps, antique shop owner and self-styled Countess Zarina, who was the brains behind it. Rinaldi, his wife and chauffeur were all sentenced to imprisonment. Soon afterwards a Russian diplomat in Rome, Yuri Pavlenko, was ordered to leave Italy.

The man chiefly responsible for breaking the Rinaldi ring was Admiral Eugenio Henke who, in 1966, and without any previous experience of espionage, had taken over the then poorly regarded Italian counter-espionage service, SIFAR. He quickly recognized its shortcomings, so he reorganized the service from top to bottom, and promptly stamped out two other Soviet spy operations. In fact, since World War II, most of Italy's counter-intelligence has been concerned with Soviet espionage. As recently as 1983 there were three arrests of men said to have passed top NATO secrets to Moscow.

In recent years Italian Intelligence has been considerably troubled by Red Brigade activities and their links with the Palestinian Liberation Organization (PLO). It has also suffered by association from people such as General Pietro Musumeci, a counter-espionage chief and former deputy director of SISMI who formed a parallel organization and recruited Pazienza among its members. Another embarrassing case was that of SISMI director, General Giuseppe Santovito, who was arrested for trafficking arms and drugs between Italy and the Middle East. Italian legal authorities accused members of SISMI with helping to create the 'Billygate' scandal which involved the brother of former US President Carter, of having ties with the Camorra Mafia in the Cirillo case and having links with P2 banker, Roberto Calvi.

JAPAN

Japan's whole history of intelligence, like that of China, dates back to ancient times. The Japanese regard spying as an honourable and patriotic duty, and even in their reference books do not seek to hide the fact that some of their most illustrious citizens have indulged in espionage. In a Japanese edition of *Who Was Who*, for example, there is this entry: 'Ishikawa, Goichi: Spy. Born 1866, died 1894. Sent to China where he travelled to the Mongolian border ... captured by the Chinese and executed in Tientsin.'

By the 1930s the Japanese Secret Service had developed into a network spreading all over the world, and drew on people from all walks of life, not simply those who were members of an intelligence service. Recruits included trade unionists, peasants and *ronins* (romantically-minded adventurers), as well as professional intelligence officers. This policy exists even today, taking advantage of the Japanese people's natural curiosity, a quality that has often led them to being suspected of espionage when they have simply been indulging a desire for legitimate information. After World War II, of course, the whole apparatus of intelligence and counter-intelligence, including the dreaded *Kempei Tai*, was closed down by Allied Occupation authorities. The secret police were abolished, and so too were various secret societies which had been linked to intelligence-gathering. Gradually Japan earned the respect and trust of the Occupation regime and was treated more as an ally than an ex-enemy.

In 1952 *Hoancho*, the new Security Agency, was set up and given jurisdiction over ground and maritime forces, as well as responsibility for internal order. Two years later the Diet passed bills which introduced a new and revised security agency called *Boeucho* (Defence Agency), and the ground, sea and air forces were formally legalized in 1954. A secret service in the old sense of the word was tacitly forbidden under the original Occupation terms, but naturally any self-defence force must have an intelligence-gathering agency. So in July 1942 *Koan Chosa Cho* (Public Security Investigation Agency) was launched as the successor to *Tokushin Kyoku* (Special Investigation Bureau). Two years later *Keibi Bu*, the Guard Division, of the Police

41

Agency, *Keisatsu Cho*, was established largely to keep a watch on subversive groups of the right and the left.

In the early post-war years Japan was mostly concerned with the threat of Soviet espionage, directed mainly from Harbin in Manchuria. Japan's first chance to show some cautious intelligence initiatives came at the end of the Korean War. For the first time since World War II they entered into negotiations with South Korea, but found that lack of information about policymaking in Seoul was hampering them. It was some years before this was corrected by the cryptanalysts in *Naikaku Chosashitsu*, Tokyo's Cabinet Investigation Board. They deciphered the South Korean codes and so gave Japan a chance to be better prepared for negotiations.

The Japanese made swift advances in the field of computerology and code-breaking and this was soon put to effective use in the Prime Minister's own Security service. For a time they had to contend with espionage from both the Soviet Union and Red China. In 1978 a Japanese Defence White Paper summed up the basic requirements for Japanese military and naval intelligence as follows: 'It is extremely important for Japan with its exclusively defence-orientated policy to constantly conduct surveillance on such military trends as ship and aircraft movements in peripheral waters and air space of Japan ... it is equally important to collect information on world trends.' Under the Defence Agency come various sections comprising the Defence Division, Operations Division, First Research and Intelligence Division and Second Research and Intelligence Division. All these are linked to the National Defence Council and the National Security Council. Equally important is the Security Bureau which is comprised of the First, Second and Third Public Safety Divisions, the Foreign Affairs Division and the Security Research division. The Public Security Investigation Division, which copes with subversion, comes under the Ministry of Justice and is in turn linked to the Public Security Commission which makes decisions regarding subversive bodies and controversial problems. There is also a Civil Liberties Bureau. It should be stressed that this is not a reproductive bureaucracy multiplying, but highly efficient intelligence-gathering on a low budget and that each link fits admirably into all others so that, by and large, this conglomerate provides a balanced overall picture to the government of the day. Indeed, naval intelligence progressed so rapidly in the 1960s and 70s that Japan's current underwater surveillance is among the most sophisticated in the world.

In 1978 Japan's Police White Paper stated that 'espionage and other underground activities by agents of foreign countries have intensified with the improvement of Japan's international status'. Studies on the subject of improved security measures were carried out by the Intelligence Services in the mid-1970s. There are now two security-related research institutes set up and supported by both government and business. One was the Institute for Peace and Security Research, launched in 1976; the other was the Japan Security Research Centre. However, the aim of Japanese Intelligence is not merely security; perhaps 80 per cent of it is aimed at improving Japanese prosperity and the quality of life. To this end Japan involves many business and research organizations in intelligence-gathering: the Federation of Economic Organizations, the Institute of Future Technology and the MITI Bureau of Heavy Industries, to name but three. Japan has nearly forty think-tanks, and their research goes far beyond discovering new Western techniques. It also extends to investigating labour relations in other countries and learning lessons from their experiences.

Japan's view of intelligence-gathering is something that the rest of the world might study to advantage. It makes the point again and again that intelligence has every-day applications, as well as far-sighted scientific ones. Japan is already preparing to lead the world in space colonization, and has forged ten years ahead of the United States and Europe in the field of robotics.

Further reading
History of Japanese Secret Service by Richard Deacon (Muller, London 1982)
Kempetai: A History of Japanese Secret Service by Richard Deacon (Beaufort Books, New York 1983)
Shogaikoku ni okeru joho kankei kancho chosa ikken (Library of Congress, Washington DC, Checklist S1.3.1.0-2)

LIBYA

It was only after Colonel Muamar Gaddafi came to power as President that Libya developed a serious intelligence service. This became known as the *Mukhabarat* and, though it has spent considerable sums of money in fomenting revolution in other countries and supporting revolutionary movements, such as the PLO, the IRA and the Red Brigade, it has made little secret of the fact. Some years ago Gaddafi's Information Minister, Muhammad al-Zuwayy, publicly announced that 'we assert to the whole world that we provide material, moral and political support to every liberation revolution in the world'. At various times the *Mukhabarat* has been influenced by the KGB and East German Intelligence who posted officers to Tripoli and used Ahmed al-Shahati, chief of the Foreign Liaison Office, as go-between. Moscow has often been uneasy about Gaddafi's erratic behaviour, but has generally been glad to accept his covert services in various parts of the world. Evidence has shown that, apart from those organizations already mentioned, the Libyan Secret Service has also aided the Basque guerrilla group (ETA), Muslim secessionists in the Philippines, terrorist groups in Cuba, Venezuela and other Latin American countries, as well as the so-called 'freedom movement' in the Canary Islands (see *MPAIAC*, Part IV).

The Libyan and Syrian secret services have also worked closely together, and through this association Gaddafi's 'Green Brigades' cooperated with Syrian commandos to assassinate exiled enemies of their countries. One such killing was that of Issam al-Attar, leader of the Syrian wing of the Muslim Brotherhood, who was shot dead at his home in Aachen, West Germany. The Italian Security Service discovered that the Libyans had contributed large sums of money to various terrorist groups in Italy, including more than two million dollars for Sardinian separatists. Perhaps the Libyan Secret Service's boldest move was when they tried to implicate Billy Carter, the brother of US President Carter, in their schemes. Doubtless with the best intentions in the world, Billy Carter was used by the White House as a go-between in dealings with Tripoli, but the *Mukhabarat* manipulated him to advance Libya's interests in

Washington, with disastrous results for his brother's subsequent election campaign.

NEW ZEALAND

The Security Intelligence Service (SIS) is the name of New Zealand's ultra-discreet intelligence department. In fact, it took the bungled bombing of the *Rainbow Warrior* in July 1985 to make it break years of silence. New Zealanders, long accustomed to total silence by their SIS, were astonished to read a statement issued from its offices. But it was Prime Minister David Lange, not the head of the SIS, Brigadier J.L. Smith, who answered questions at a subsequent press conference, denying that New Zealand Intelligence had any knowledge of French spies in its midst.

Protected by an Official Secrets Act, the New Zealand SIS was set up in 1947. It is attached to the Prime Minister's office and is located in the Ministry of Defence building in Wellington. Unlike Australia, New Zealand has no external intelligence service, although it does have the Government Communication Security Board (SIGINT) established in 1977. Personnel for the SIS are drawn mainly from the Army and the police and they generally do a first-rate job on internal security. Studies of telephone records on their computer network enabled them to detect the presence of the French agents sent to sabotage *Rainbow Warrior*, by noting that they had dialled an official number of the French Secret Service from their hotel room.

For some years New Zealand's external intelligence has relied on information from allies, but this favour has now been put in jeopardy by the New Zealand Prime Minister's decision to withdraw his country from the weekly meetings in London of the Joint Allied Intelligence Committee. This decision was reached following American criticisms of his anti-nuclear stance, Lange claiming that the USA had made it clear they would not be at such meetings if New Zealand was present.

In 1986 New Zealand investigators checked suggestions that Soviet Embassy staff in Wellington were monitoring New Zealand's communications system. This followed claims by an Australian strategic studies expert, Dr Desmond Ball, that the

Russians in Wellington and Canberra spied on sensitive telephone, telex and other communications.

POLAND

Poland has a long history of intelligence operations, largely because it has so often been a target for other nations. Prior to World War II the British Secret Service had close relations with the Polish Intelligence Service, then headed by Colonel Mayer. This service was sometimes referred to by foreigners as the Polish *Deuxième Bureau*, though this was not an accurate description. Britain and Poland exchanged information on cryptography and this led to the vital breaking of the German Enigma code, details of which were obtained from Poland. The Anglo-Polish intelligence relationship remained an excellent one during World War II and the Poles in exile were allowed to use their own radio transmitters at Woldingham in Surrey, in exchange for which Colonel Mayer agreed to share information.

When the Russians marched into Poland after the war and supervised its transformation to a satellite Soviet state, a new intelligence organization was planned from scratch by the KGB, under whose control it remains to this day. The Polish Intelligence Service is known as *Sluzba Bezpieczenstwa* (SB), and according to Zdzislaw Rurarz, a former Polish ambassador to Japan who defected to the West in 1982, 'it is penetrated and guided by the KGB. The SB is strictly forbidden to wage operations without KGB approval, whereas the KGB has a free hand to do whatever it deems necessary in Poland.' Nevertheless the SB has achieved quite a number of espionage coups, not least the obtaining of top-secret microfilms and reports on advanced future US weapons systems and radar developments. This was master-minded by Marian Zacharski, an SB officer, operating as vice-president of Polamco, which was functioning in Illinois and Delaware as a subsidiary of the Polish Government Corporation.

Another successful section of Polish Intelligence has been *Urzad Bezpieczenstwa* (UB), which also operates overseas. One of UB's officers who defected has declared that 'we had persons in our service posing as United States intelligence officers'. In the 1950s the CIA set up an underground espionage organization in Poland with the aim of encouraging an anti-Soviet revolution. It supplied generous and regular finance to this organization, but years later discovered that it had been infiltrated almost from the beginning and that the SB had kept the network going solely to get hold of the American finance which they used for their own purposes.

RUSSIA

After the revolution of 1917 Lenin ordered the liquidation of the Tsarist Intelligence and Security Service, the *Ochrana* (q.v. Part II), and he gave this task to a Pole called Felix Dzerzhinsky (q.v. Part III). There was a nation-wide round-up of *Ochrana* agents, many of whom were executed, but a few were recruited to a new organization – the Extraordinary Commission for Combatting Counter-revolutions and Sabotage (*Cheka*). The *Cheka* seized the *Ochrana*'s files and ordered an immediate probe into all known counter-revolutionary groups. The great majority of people arrested were executed, usually with no semblance of a trial.

Whereas the *Ochrana* had been directly responsible to the Minister of the Interior, and he in turn responsible to the government of the day, the *Cheka* was only directly responsible to the Soviet Government. This gave Dzerzhinsky absolute power. When the Soviet Government moved to Moscow the *Cheka* transferred its headquarters to Lyublyanka Street, while its chief office in St Petersburg was moved to Gorochovaya Street, where the section chief was a bloodthirsty character named Uritsky. He acquired such a tyrannical reputation that he was eventually murdered by a Revolutionary Socialist. This led to the *Cheka*'s own security measures being tightened up and the organization being split into two main divisions – the Counter-Espionage Section and the Secret Operative Section, which was principally an economic espionage unit.

The *Cheka* copied the *Ochrana* in recruiting a nation-wide team of informers, using terror as a means of inducing people to inform. Priests and peasants, men and women from all walks of life were coerced into undertaking such work, and had to report weekly to a section chief. It was an efficient and cheap way of information-gathering.

In 1922 the *Cheka* was changed into the State Political Administration (GPU), and a Foreign Department (INO) was incorporated. With the change of title came a new policy of allowing trials instead of instant execution, but there were few other changes. Quite soon after the revolution Trotsky, who had created the new Red Army, formed the Fourth Department of the General Staff, more generally known as the Chief Intelligence Administration (GRU). This was almost entirely concerned with military intelligence, but the creation of a rival Intelligence Service irked the *Cheka*, and Dzerzhinsky insisted that his own service should have the right to screen GRU personnel. He also demanded to put *Cheka* agents inside GRU, but refused to allow any GRU agents inside GPU. Trotsky and his generals disliked this arrangement, but they were overruled. Not until World War II did the GRU really come into its own, and afterwards it was again cut down in size and subordinated to the master agency. Dzerzhinsky was furious that Captain George Hill, a British secret agent, had advised Trotsky on the creation of the GRU, and gave orders for his assassination. However, Hill was tipped off in advance by friendly Russians and managed to escape.

The GPU, only slightly less powerful than the *Cheka*, came under the People's Commissariat of Internal Affairs (NKVD), but in practice it went its own way, unhindered by a higher authority. Indeed Dzerzhinsky not only became head of the NKVD as Commissar for Internal Affairs, but controlled the GPU and later became chairman of its successor, the Unified State Political Administration (OGPU), created in November 1923. The OGPU differed very little from the GPU, but it tidied up the administration and brought all sections of the GPU under a more efficient system of national control. Under Stalin rivalry between the two services, OGPU and GRU was actually encouraged, and the dictator himself played one off against the other.

In 1941 the political police section of the NKVD was made into a separate service known as the People's Committee for State Security (NKGB), and after World War II there were more changes (see *Beria, Lavrenti*, Part III and *Kruglov, Sergei*,

Part IV). By this time the Soviet Intelligence Services had established vast networks of agents all over the world as well as having infiltrated some of the highest ranks in the US Government, Treasury and civil service, the American OSS, the British MI5 and MI6. Within five years of the Bolshevik revolution it had even penetrated the British Foreign Office. Some of its greatest successes overseas were scored by the GRU rather than the NKVD or the NKGB. After Beria's death the political leaders again reorganized the whole set-up, and in 1954 created the KGB which assumed responsibility for internal security, the control of intelligence-gathering and operations abroad, and the guarding of the USSR's borders. It still takes precedence over the GRU.

Since its inception, the KGB has had five chiefs, the most influential of whom was probably Yuri Andropov (q.v. Part IV), during the years 1967-82. In a reverse of previous policy, he always promoted talent, looking for an ultimate successor; other chiefs had tended to demote promising executives in a misguided attempt to strengthen their own position. Andropov's two key men were Vitali Fedorchuk and Viktor Chebrikov (q.v. Part IV), both of whom eventually became heads of the KGB (see also *Serov, Ivan* Part IV). Apart from far-sightedness, his promotion of talented men may also have been due to Red Army taunts that the KGB were amateurs compared with the GRU in assessment of military intelligence. These taunts only spurred him on in making improvements, such as establishing additional KGB offices for electronic decoding.

The Organization of State Security, which includes the KGB, MGB and MVD, is impressive in its actual planning, though supervision of so many departments may well cause problems. At the peak of the structure there are four chief directorates. First there is the Headquarters elements, directing foreign operations and originally known as the Foreign Department (INO). Under this comes the Executive Action Department and the Executive Action Section, the latter referring to espionage missions involving assassinations. The Passport and Press Sections also come under this First Chief Directorate. The Second Chief Directorate covers internal security and counter-intelligence, as well as Department D (disinformation), the Secret Political Department and the strangely named Section for Extraordinary Matters. The Third Chief Directorate controls military counter-intelligence and the last Chief Directorate supervises the Border Guards. Altogether, including the lesser bodies such as the managerial and supply department, and the oddly titled Anti-Speculation Department, there are nine directorates.

In recent years a new force of the KGB has come very much to the fore – the *Spetsnaz*, short for *Spetznaznacheniya*, an élite military force rather like Britain's SAS, but under KGB control. It has been used effectively in Afghanistan and may, it is rumoured, be used in the Middle East and Third World crisis zones.

It is not easy to assess the total strength of the KGB and other Intelligence and Security Services of the USSR, as the army of informants, apart from 350,000 full-time officers, includes diplomats, journalists, Aeroflot pilots, members of international quangos and villagers living in remote corners of the country. However, one thing is certain: the KGB today is the largest secret service in the world, and larger than any other in history, probably not far short of two millions. Nicholas Daniloff, the American reporter accused of spying by the Russians in 1986, wrote in *US News and World Report* that 'the KGB now employs a nationwide staff of 90,000 officers supported by 150,000 technicians and clerical workers. It controls 250,000 border guards equipped with tanks, helicopters and armoured vehicles ... Abroad the KGB is reputed to employ 2500 agents – at least 500 in the USA. The KGB's annual budget is put at between $6 billion and $12 billion.' All indications are that the power and independence of the KGB is greater today than it was twenty-five years ago and it is now equipped with all the paraphernalia of modern espionage, surveillance machines, computerized data banks and retrieval systems.

Despite their power, it must be remembered that the KGB and the GRU have had far more defections from their ranks than any other secret service – many more than are reported in the media.

Further reading
A History of Russian Secret Service by Richard Deacon (Grafton Books, London 1987)
The KGB Today: The Hidden Land by John Barron (Reader's Digest Association 1983)

The New KGB by William R. Corson and Robert T. Crowley
(William Morrow, New York 1985)

SOUTH AFRICA

Virtually ostracized by both East and West, South Africa has many enemies and few friends. The Bureau of State Security (BOSS) was directed for many years by Afrikaners who were utterly ruthless in smearing their enemies. Among these was General Hendrik van den Bergh, who had been the closest confidante of former South African President Vorster. Then came the so-called 'Muldergate Scandal' which showed that van den Bergh was closely involved in the misuse of millions of pounds of State funds. The new President, P.W. Botha, decided to reorganize BOSS, rename it the National Intelligence Service and appoint a new chief in 1979 – Professor Neil Barnard, Dean of Bloemfontein University's Faculty of Political Science. It has been alleged that BOSS burgled the offices of anti-apartheid organizations in London and elsewhere, and made attempts to manufacture evidence against various Western politicians, notably Harold Wilson and Jeremy Thorpe. Wilson, when Prime Minister, frequently expressed his concern about this, but was unable to come up with any firm evidence. Gordon Winter, who claimed to have been an agent of BOSS, alleged that it employed sorters in London post offices to intercept 'communist, left-wing and Liberal Party letters to anti-apartheid organizations'. He also claimed that his BOSS 'handler' in London told him that the bank robbery charge against anti-apartheid activist, Peter Hain (of which he was found innocent), was 'a beautiful job, brilliantly carried out' by BOSS.

In recent years the NIS has paid more attention to collecting intelligence than to smear campaigns, and this has resulted in a number of successes, notably in counter-intelligence. Dr Renfrew Christie, an Oxford-trained scientist, was found to have used his status as a Cape Town University fellow to gain access to South Africa's nuclear secrets. He was convicted of conspiracy with the outlawed African National Congress (ANC) and officials of the Geneva-based International

University Educational Fund to supply the floor plan of the Koeberg nuclear power station.

The prize capture of NIS in recent years was undoubtedly Dieter Gerhardt (q.v. Part IV), a high-ranking South African naval officer, who together with his wife, was found guilty of high treason in 1983. Another prime achievement was the capture of Russian agent, Major Aleksei Kozlov at Jan Smuts airport in 1980. Kozlov had visited South Africa four times; when arrested he was travelling on a false Swedish passport, using the name of Suensson. Under interrogation Kozlov revealed details of various subversion plans, including aid for the ANC, sabotage targets in South Africa and the naming of a well-known white South African as one of ANC's leading operatives inside the Republic. He also disclosed information on various West German operatives in the Soviet interest. Kozlov was eventually exchanged for eight important West German spies, as well as South Africa's own Sapper Johan van der Mescht.

Around this time the South African government was trying to counter allegations that the NIS had been involved in an attempted coup on the government of the Seychelles by a group of mercenaries led by Colonel Michael Hoare. Nothing was ever proved, but it was conceded that one of Hoare's team, Martin Dolincheck, was a member of the NIS.

The NIS is certainly an improvement on BOSS, not least in having learned to handle the cases of suspected Soviet agents in a more sophisticated manner. They have learned much since the case of Yuri Loginov, a KGB 'illegal' arrested in 1967, who is alleged to have given information on Soviet networks in twenty-three countries, and is also suspected of contributing considerable disinformation.

SOUTH KOREA

When the Korean war ended and the country was divided into two separate nations, North and South, the government of the south with some assistance and advice from the Americans formed the South Korean Central Intelligence Agency. It has always been a tough and ruthless organization, as indeed it had to be in the face of opposition from the North and from the People's Republic of China. Both North Korea and China aimed at spying on South Korea and finding their own agents inside that country. To some extent the Chinese Communists were helped by the fact that all resident Chinese in South Korea carried Taiwanese passports and it was not difficult for them to visit Taiwan, Hong Kong and Japan, if they wished. There was also the fact that during the Korean War a number of Chinese in Korea were found guilty of spying for the Chinese Communists and were handed over to the Taiwanese who had them executed. The families of these people still live in South Korea, which is another reason why this country has always been a prime target for Chinese Intelligence.

South Korea's CIA scored one important success when they organized the arrest of Pak No-su (q.v. Part IV) soon after he returned from Cambridge University in 1969 and took up a post in the office of South Korea's President. He was accused of master-minding a spy-ring based at Cambridge and recruiting Korean intellectuals in Europe for the North Korean cause. Pak was rounded up with thirty-two others and most of the evidence in the case rested on 'confessions' obtained under torture. Pak himself was sentenced to death and executed two years later.

How close relationships are between the CIA services of the USA and South Korea is a matter of conjecture. The most recent indication of their collaboration was the shooting down of the Korean Airlines plane 007 by a Soviet fighter plane on 1 September 1983 in Russian airspace over Sakhalin Island. The plane was on its way to Seoul and all 269 people aboard were killed. The unanswered question has always been why the plane veered off its planned route and flew deep into Soviet airspace. The captain of the aircraft, Chun Byung-in, was one of KAL's ablest pilots and a former military air ace, who would certainly have noticed if anything was wrong with his navigational equipment. One widely favoured supposition is that it was a surveillance mission over Soviet territory by a civilian plane; another that it was being furtively used as a passive probe to switch on Soviet radars whose operations could then be monitored by the United States. Certainly at this time the United States had every reason to wish for detailed information on a vast new Soviet radar being built at Krasnoyarsk. If the CIA required a civilian aircraft to carry out such a probe, then its influence with the Korean CIA would point its planners in that direction. The Korean CIA had frequently granted favours to the American CIA in repayment for help given by the USA. Ernest Volkman, editor of the American journal, *Defence Science*, has stated that 'as a result of the KAL incident, United States intelligence received a bonanza, the likes of which they have never received in their lives before. Reason: because of the tragic incident it managed to turn on just about every single Soviet electromagnetic transmission over a period of about four hours ...'

Names of intelligence organizations can change rapidly, and the South Korean CIA is an example of this. It is sometimes known in the vernacular as KISS, but its full title is the Korean Intelligence and Security Service, linked to which are the National Security Planning Service and the Defence Security Organization.

SPAIN

Under General Franco's dictatorship Spain's Intelligence Service was mainly controlled by the naval and military authorities, rather than the police. Since the Civil War, its prime objective was to keep watch on Soviet infiltration and espionage. However, suspicions of Spanish cooperation with the Germans on matters of intelligence were fully proved when the body of the mythical 'Major Martin' was found near Huelva in south-west Spain in April 1943 (see *Man who never was*, Part III). The fisherman who found the body informed the authorities and eventually the body was given to the British vice-consul who arranged a burial with military honours. Shortly afterwards the Vice-consul was asked by London to make inquiries about 'papers of great importance' which were believed to be strapped to the wrist of the dead officer. It was two weeks, however, before the papers were handed over. In that time Spanish Intelligence had them photographed and passed copies to the Germans – exactly what the British had hoped for as the papers were deliberately full of inaccurate information.

The creation of Spain's modern Intelligence Service – *Centro*

Superior para la Información de la Defensa (CESID) – came about after the death of Franco and during Spain's return to democracy and proved to be extremely difficult. On one hand the socialists and others were highly suspicious of anything like a secret service, while the organizers of CESID inherited many intelligence operatives who were former Army officers and had served under Franco. Another stumbling block to creating an efficient and economic service was the fact that Franco's regime has employed eight intelligence sections, each being a tight little empire of its own. However, a brave decision was made to destroy a vast number of files on so-called 'political opponents of the regime', and CESID scored its first success in 1982 by discovering that a group of right-wing officers were planning a coup. This was promptly put down. In 1984 the Spanish weekly newspaper, *Tiempo*, was responsible for starting off a 'spy war' between the different intelligence sections by revealing that CESID was spying on Gregorio Peces-Barba, the president of the Spanish Parliament. As a result, a law was passed to bring the eight different sections under a single civilian director who would be responsible only to the Prime Minister. The eight sections included SIGC (the information service of the *Guardia*), the Ministry of the Interior's information service, SIPAN (concerning the National Police), and the intelligence services of the Army, Navy and Air Force and the Intelligence Division of the Joint Chiefs of Staff.

SWEDEN

Sweden's secret service is today known as the Information Bureau, a title which befits a neutral nation. In World War II the service was called the Combined Intelligence Bureau, of which Colonel Adlercreutz was the chief until October 1942. Adlercreutz was pro-German, as was Major Lindquist, the head of Security. Fortunately, during this period all foreign intelligence, including the Swedish interception service, was being handled by Colonel Bjoernstierna. The German cables and teleprinters between the High Command near Berlin and Norway passed through Denmark and then through Swedish waters to Norway. The Swedes were able to tap some of these lines. Colonel Bjoernstierna cooperated secretly with the British naval attaché in Stockholm, Captain Henry Denham, and proved an invaluable source of information to the British NID. This came about because a pro-German officer in the Swedish service was caught planting a microphone in Captain Denham's apartment. Both Denham and the British Ambassador agreed to overlook the matter, provided Bjoernstierna agreed to give undercover help. In fact, the Colonel was pro-British and needed little persuasion. During this period the Germans had two plans for attacking Sweden, including one from Norway, and Bjoernstierna fully understood this: indeed, Admiral Canaris passed a secret warning to Sweden that such plans had been considered. Despite this, the pro-German element in the Combined Intelligence Bureau remained on top and as a result of their collaboration with the Military Security Police, Bjoernstierna lost his job and was succeeded by Kommendor Landquist from Naval Operations.

The modern Information Bureau came under attack in 1973 when an East German magazine alleged that it was cooperating with the espionage services of Israel and the NATO countries. This was, of course, Soviet-inspired propaganda, but it made some mischief.

Further reading
See the papers of Captain Henry Denham, R.N., in the Archives Centre, Churchill College, Cambridge

SWITZERLAND

It should perhaps be stressed that, if Switzerland has an Intelligence and Security Service, it is primarily to support the policy of neutrality adopted by all Swiss governments, past and present. In other words the policies of such an organization would be to prevent Switzerland being linked with any other power or group of powers, externally or internally, and to ensure that Switzerland is not exploited by other powers as a territory for spying or sabotage operations. Generally speaking, this overall policy has been faithfully observed, so it was something of a shock when, in 1979, the Austrian police arrested a Swiss junior intelligence officer, Lieutenant Karl Schilling, for alleged spying on Austrian military exercises. There seemed to be absolutely no point to this operation by Schilling, and as Austria and Switzerland were both neutral countries, each was equally embarrassed. The Swiss officer was given a suspended sentence and returned to his native land, while Colonel Albert Bachmann, head of the Swiss Intelligence Service, was suspended from duty. Later a Swiss parliamentary inquiry committee criticized him for organizing a private intelligence service under cover of the official service, and he was dismissed from his post.

Most important of the Swiss intelligence organizations in the past has been the counter-espionage organization, *Espionage Abteilung*. This body had to cope with the problems created in World War II, later added to by the 'Cold War', as well as nationalist terrorism all around the globe and the tendency of several nations to use this neutral country as a safe base for organizing spy networks. In World War II Swiss military intelligence was in the hands of Lieutenant-Colonel Roger Masson (later Brigadier). Since 1937 he had organized a small outfit of ten people, divided into three bureaux, D, F and I, covering Germany, France and Italy respectively. Although staffing levels increased, even at the height of the war Masson never had more than 120 staff. He also set up a second unofficial intelligence organization based in a house in Lastanienbaum near Lucerne, headed by an anti-Nazi reserve officer, Captain Hans Hausamann. It was he who, with the approval of Masson, set up and privately funded the Bureau Ha, ostensibly a press-clippings agency. Masson also recruited Rudolf Roessler, a German publisher who moved to Switzerland after the Nazis came to power and started a firm named Vita Nova Verlag in Geneva. After the fall of France, when the Swiss were concerned about the possibility of a German invasion, Roessler's job was to assess military intelligence relating to Germany. He soon proved to be a highly competent analyst of such information and provided extremely accurate forecasts of Nazi strategy. What he did for the Swiss, however, he did in even greater detail for the Russians (see *Lucy Ring*, Part III), something which was aided and abetted by both the British and the Swiss. Masson had discreet contacts with the British SIS because at one time he had good reason to believe Hitler might attack Switzerland, and he posted a liaison officer, Captain Max Waibel, to Bureau Ha to monitor the activities of Nazi sympathizers in Switzerland.

Roessler, despite having twice been convicted of spying by Swiss courts, continued long after the war to deny that he had ever indulged in espionage for any power. In 1964 Marc Payot, the war-time chief cryptographer of the Swiss counter-espionage organization, stated that copies of information intercepted by the Swiss between various sources and the *Lucy* network, 'made it abundantly clear that there were Soviet-controlled sources of intelligence on the British side'. In the 1939-45 period Swiss counter-espionage had more trouble watching German spies in their own population than those of the Allies.

After World War II the Swiss were confronted with the problem of Arab-Israeli imbroglios, some of which actually involved Switzerland and Swiss firms. But an even bigger problem related to espionage operations conducted under cover of United Nations diplomacy from the various UN organizations in Geneva. Among many cases of this kind was that of the GRU colonel, Gregori Miagkov, posing as a railways expert at the International Labour Organization in Geneva. He left the country when the Swiss, armed with devastating proof of his espionage operations, pressurized the ILO to terminate his contract. The GRU has always taken a keen interest in railway systems, probably because the Red Army played a role in building many of Russia's own new railways.

Further reading
La Chasse aux Espions en Suisse by Colonel R. Jacquillard (Librairie Payot, Lausanne 1947)

SYRIA

For many years Military Intelligence was the supreme intelligence service in Syria. Ever since the *coup d'état* by Husni Zaim in 1949, the Army has dominated in the country. The development of the United Arab Republic, comprising Egypt and Syria, resulted in close intelligence cooperation between the two nations, as well as some joint clandestine action against

Lebanon, Iraq and Jordan. Ever since then the Syrian Secret Service has become much more politically-minded, indicated by Syria's relentless war against exiles, as well as the setting up of *fedayeen* groups to carry out sabotage and murder in Israel.

Syria's Intelligence Services employ agents in many parts of Europe and the Middle East, and in many instances they collaborate with terrorist organizations. Chief of all Syria's Intelligence and Security Services is Rifaat Assad, a brother of the President. He has uniformed military detachments at his disposal and has made Syria's espionage service dreaded in many neighbouring countries.

TAIWAN

When Chiang Kai-shek and his forces were finally defeated by the Chinese Communists in mainland China and they retreated to the island of Taiwan, they already had the nucleus of quite a useful intelligence and security service, which had been tested in World War II. The head of the Kuomintang Secret Service and Police was Tai Li (q.v. Part III). He was a member of Chiang's secret police in 1925 and he made a point of making friends with many foreigners. He took part in the campaign to arrest and eliminate Communists in and around Shanghai, and by so doing, rose to become head of Chiang's secret police.

Between 1937 and 1945 one of the major problems for the Kuomintang Secret Service was that it had to compete with three other Chinese secret services – those of the Communists, the Japanese puppet government in North China and the Wang Ching-wei so-called Nationalist Government in Outer Mongolia. Tai Li combated these other services by enrolling members of secret societies, such as the Triads. When the Americans entered the war, attempts at cooperation were made between Chiang's Secret Service and the American OSS and Military Intelligence. These were never very successful as neither side really trusted the other, and the Americans were divided between those who were pro-Chiang and those who were convinced that Chiang had no long-term future. Tai Li promised the utmost cooperation in launching a secret war on espionage behind the lines and guerrilla tactics against the Japanese, but nothing ever happened. His long-term aim was to ensure that neither Japan nor the USA won the war, but that each nation would eventually be persuaded to withdraw from China. In some instances he actively sabotaged American efforts against the Japanese, while making undercover deals with the enemy through his intermediaries.

Once Chiang Kai-shek had set up his regime in Taiwan, his intelligence system was tightened up considerably and internal security was largely controlled by the Investigation Bureau. A tight watch was kept for attempts by the Peking authorities to smuggle agents on to the island. Those attempts which succeeded were largely made by planting bogus defectors in Taiwan. Chiang's highly efficient but ruthless secret police were organized rather in Soviet-style by Chiang's son, Chiang Ching-kuo. Naturally, Chiang Kai-shek also maintained an intelligence unit in Hong Kong throughout this period, aimed at bartering information with double-agents and trying to establish indirect links with the People's Republic of China. The Taiwanese Intelligence Service also employed the Triads, but this source of information deteriorated rapidly as the Triads degenerated into gangsters who did little more than bring discredit to the Kuomintang forces. Nonetheless in 1949 the Nationalist General Koi Sui-heong organized some eighteen branches of the '14K' Triad in Hong Kong as a nucleus of secret agents and saboteurs. There was occasional cooperation with the CIA, but this was never very satisfactory from either side's viewpoint. In 1975 the Chinese Republic released 144 prisoners said to have been Chiang's spies, as an expression of 'leniency'. These agents were said to have been picked up by the Communists after landing secretly on the coast or dropped by parachute between 1962-65. Many of these prisoners were offered jobs in China and, having expressed support for the People's Republic, decided to stay there.

UNITED KINGDOM

The British Government's links with its Secret Service and other branches of intelligence today are largely through the Joint Intelligence Organization (JIO), which is situated inside the

Cabinet Office. The JIO's role is to coordinate all sources of intelligence from Current Intelligence Groups, said to be organized on a regional basis, theoretically logical, but practically rather muddled. It could be called a typical example of Parkinson's Law, in that the amount of work done is in inverse proportion to the number of people employed. This apparently harsh judgement was echoed by the Franks Committee after its examination of the organization's lamentable failure regarding the invasion of the Falkland Islands by Argentina.

Britain has always insisted on absolute secrecy in all its Intelligence operations, and until recently, this applied even to the appointment of heads of the Secret Service (MI6). The relationship between MI6 and the Foreign and Commonwealth Office has always been close, and there has usually been a liaison officer between the two services. MI6 (originally Military Intelligence, Department 6) is perhaps more accurately described by its other title of Secret Intelligence Service (SIS). Though Britain's secret service traditions date back to the reign of King Henry VII, the modern service was only established in 1911, and its purpose is to organize the collection of intelligence from overseas. Although some of its chiefs have been named, and the SIS has often been referred to in books and newspapers, it is astonishing that officials still pretend it does not exist. Since 1911 the SIS record has been rather erratic. In World War I it achieved some considerable successes – better known to the enemy than to the British people – and came to be regarded in Europe, and especially Russia, as much more powerful and efficient than it really was. Fortunately this legend lived on, even after the SIS had made a disastrous start in World War II when the networks in Europe were uncovered by the Nazis and some of its agents captured. Despite this, the Germans clung to the belief that the SIS was still a tremendous force. This belief was one of the main deterrents to a German invasion of Britain in 1940; some Nazi military leaders believed that news of Britain's unpreparedness was a deception put about by the SIS to lure them to destruction.

After the SIS had rebuilt its networks and ended the war a powerful force once again, the 1950s-80s brought a series of crushing blows, which revealed how it had been infiltrated by traitors and Soviet agents, not least of whom was 'Kim' Philby, a man who had been tipped as a future head of MI6. On the other hand, the SIS scored a major coup in recruiting Colonel Oleg Penkovsky (q.v. Part IV), its spy in Moscow whose information was of vital importance during events leading up to the Cuban crisis of 1960-2. Methods of recruitment have greatly improved in recent years, relying more on professionalism and less on the 'old boy network'. Attempts have been made by various politicians to have the SIS answerable to Parliamentary Select Committees, similar to the American set-up. So far, however, all prime ministers have flatly turned down any such suggestion.

A major criticism of British intelligence-gathering operations in recent years concerns the role played by the Foreign and Commonwealth Office. Sometimes there has been evidence of this ministry exercising too much influence in its own interests, which may not always be in the true interests of the SIS or the nation. Such abuses have been possible because the JIO has always had a senior civil servant from the Foreign Office as its chairman. Since the Franks Report on the handling of events leading up to the Falklands War revealed these abuses, Foreign Office wings have been clipped, and the chairman of the JIO is now chosen from the Cabinet Office by the Prime Minister.

Vitally important to Britain's intelligence-gathering organization is the Government's Communications Headquarters (GCHQ) at Cheltenham, which developed as a result of Britain breaking Germany's Enigma Code in World War II and exploiting it in the 'Ultra Operation' at Bletchley. GCHQ, established in 1952, intercepts communications from all over the world – diplomatic, military and occasionally commercial. It operates stations in other parts of the world and has close cooperation with the Americans, Australians and Canadians. GCHQ employs about 12,000 personnel, which must prompt the question, 'What are computers for'?

The UK's counter-intelligence organization is MI5, which was set up early in this century (see *Kell, Sir Vernon*, Part II). In World War I it worked closely with Scotland Yard, and later with the Special Branch. MI5 concentrates on collecting data about subversive characters and organizations; it does not have the power to make arrests. When arrests are necessary, the

Special Branch of the Police handles the case. MI5 was highly effective in rounding up enemy suspects on the outbreak of the World Wars, and it played an important role in World War II in helping to 'turn' enemy agents into relaying false information to their masters (see *Double Cross System*, Part III).

In pre-World War II days MI5 had one long-term chief, Sir Vernon Kell, who stayed in office for thirty-seven years, but since 1945 there have been frequent changes. Kell was succeeded by Sir David Petric, Sir Percy Sillitoe, Sir 'Dick' White and Sir Roger Hollis (q.v. Part IV) followed by Sir Martin Furnival Jones, a solicitor who served in security in Eisenhower's HQ in World War II. When Furnival Jones retired in 1972 his own nominee, Michael Hanley, became chief. Hanley had been a comparatively junior officer in MI5 in charge of 'Protective Security', and there was some criticism of his appointment on these grounds. But this was a period of 'musical chairs' in the intelligence establishment; a change was due at the top of MI6, and about this time Sir Dick White was replaced as Cabinet Coordinator by Sir Leonard Hooper, chief at GCHQ, who in turn was succeeded by Arthur Bonsall. After Hanley retired in 1979 the Prime Minister decided to seek a successor from outside the service, so the MI5 job went to Sir Howard Smith, a diplomat who had been Ambassador to Czechoslovakia, as well as having served in Moscow.

Like MI6, MI5 has suffered in recent years from revelations of infiltration by the Soviet Union, and from allegations that three or more of its leading executives had been betraying secrets to Russia. On top of all this came the spying scandals of Bettaney and Prime, and their subsequent trials which clearly showed that these two men should never have been allowed to enter MI5 or GCHQ on their personal records. The same failure in the vetting procedure applies also to such men as Anthony Blunt, Tom Driberg (later Lord Bradwell) and Brian Howard, all of whom were totally suspect. Scandals and rumours have plagued MI5 for many years. There was the recent allegation that the late Sir Roger Hollis was a Soviet agent, but a special inquiry cleared him – to the satisfaction of a majority, but the strong dissatisfaction of a minority. A further inquiry conducted by Sir Burke Trend, a former Secretary to the Cabinet, once again proved nothing. A similarly fruitless probe was made into

Graham Mitchell, the deputy director of MI5, again with no positive results. Afterwards there were allegations by politicians and some in the intelligence fraternity that a kind of lunatic right-wing group existed inside MI5, which tended to see Reds everywhere. The truth is that MI5 was infiltrated as long ago as the early 1920s, though no one will admit it now. As to the existence of a lunatic-right in MI5, one certainly existed in the days when Britain still had colonies. Some MI5 members encouraged dubious and bizarre ploys, including a madcap project in Kenya for creating a disease in the sacred baobab trees to make the Kikuyu tribe believe that the tree gods were against all people taking the Mau Mau oath. The Kikuyu people were far too intelligent to fall for this ludicrous plot.

While none of these incidents reflect well on MI5, the service has also been the victim of smear campaigns by left-wingers to detract attention from the fact that between 1960 and 1986 MI5 uncovered a number of pro-Soviet suspects inside the Labour and Liberal Parties. (No SDP members have been involved.)

Further reading
A History of the British Secret Service by Richard Deacon (Granada, 1980)
MI6: British Intelligence Operations, 1909-45 by Nigel West (Weidenfeld & Nicolson, 1983)
MI5: The Origin and History of the British Counter-Espionage Service by John Bulloch (Arthur Baker, London 1963)

UNITED STATES

In assessing the world's intelligence services it is always salutary to note which are the youngest and oldest. Sometimes assessments produce surprises, such as the remarkable success of Israel's Intelligence Service, established only twenty-five years ago. But a young intelligence service, especially if it belongs to a great power, can attract criticism simply because it takes time to build up the right kind of organization. This is particularly true of the USA which, as a result of isolation politics, relied for far too long upon inadequate military and naval intelligence, and the

Federal Bureau of Investigation (FBI). Only when the Japanese launched their attack on Pearl Harbour did the USA, at President Roosevelt's prompting, set up the Office of Strategic Services (OSS).

The OSS was always regarded as an amateur set-up, an unfair assessment because the Americans have always been quick to learn from their own mistakes. By the end of World War II the OSS was a force to be reckoned with and even aroused some jealousy in Britain's MI6 and other Allied secret services. There was no reason why the OSS should not have been maintained as a permanent intelligence service, but it was vetoed by President Truman, a Jekyll and Hyde character, despite all attempts to portray him as a normal, well-balanced American. The abolition of the OSS was an appalling blunder, partly the result of Truman listening to advice from J. Edgar Hoover, head of the FBI. It was soon obvious that something else would have to be put in its place, and so in 1947 the Central Intelligence Agency (CIA) was founded, on the grounds that 'the USA has carried on intelligence activities since the days of George Washington, but only since World War II has this work been systematized on a government-wide basis'. It was, of course, the 'Cold War' which largely led to the creation of the CIA, and it responded in kind to Russia's aggressive espionage. Sometimes its measures were excessive and led to anti-CIA propaganda in Western Europe, but it does seem that they may have had a mild deterrent effect on the Russians.

For the first twenty months of its existence the CIA was known as the C.I. Group and had three different directors: Admiral Souers, General Vandenberg and Admiral Roscoe Hillenkoetter (q.v. Part IV). In these early days the organization was under constant scrutiny by outsiders and there were many inquiries into alleged intelligence failures, with Admiral Hillenkoetter being called before a Congressional Committee to explain why the CIA had not warned about a revolution in Colombia.

General Walter Bedell Smith (q.v. Part IV) was called in as director in 1950. He cleared out the misfits in the service and introduced some military discipline, while at the same time bringing in Allen Dulles as his deputy. Dulles, with his wartime OSS experience, set out to make the CIA a highly respected and professional career and to encourage team spirit even to the point of encouraging inter-CIA marriages (see *Dulles, Allen Welsh*, Part IV). The organization grew rapidly, employing 15,000 employees at home and abroad, and gradually began to notch up a series of useful coups. They discovered the Anglo-French plan to launch an attack on Suez, and they made nonsense of British Foreign Office assessments when they rightly prophesied the Algiers coup which brought de Gaulle back to power. Since the Dulles era the CIA has carefully avoided sending native-born Americans into Russia as agents, but has succeeded in using emigré Russians to undertake such tasks. How many of these have proved their worth is another matter, but the USSR claims that twenty-three US agents were caught trying to penetrate the Soviet Union between 1951-61.

Inevitably, in any newly created intelligence service, there are disasters, and the CIA has had its fair share of these. There was the 'Bay of Pigs' fiasco when an attempted coup against Cuba failed, there were real doubts about the Agency's competence to handle some defectors from the Soviet bloc, as well as doubts about the genuineness of the defectors themselves, and finally, there was the purge of the CIA carried out under the directorship of Stansfield Turner (q.v. Part IV) after the Watergate scandal in the early 1970s. Many former CIA members believed that these sackings did more harm than good. However, over the past five years independent observers in the field of intelligence believe that the CIA has quietly and effectively progressed, and greatly improved its recruiting procedures. The CIA headquarters at Langley, Virginia covers a vast acreage and now has a staff not far short of 20,000. And despite criticism and adverse publicity from Senate and Congressional Committee probes, no one should underestimate the CIA in the long term. It has won the grudging respect of the KGB and at the same time managed to cooperate and exchange intelligence with some of its Western Allies.

Intelligence-gathering within the USA is covered by various agencies. The National Security Agency with headquarters in Fort Meade, Maryland, employs between 100,000 and 120,000 people, and is responsible for communications intelligence, thus matching Britain's GCHQ, with which it has links. Its track record in electronic espionage is second to none. Counter-espionage is still controlled by the FBI, the oldest of all the USA's intelligence agencies, having been founded in 1908 by President Theodore Roosevelt. It has a team of something approaching 15,000, including about 6500 full-time staff. Like the CIA, the FBI took many years to become really efficient, despite the results it achieved in the reign of that great self-publicizer, J. Edgar Hoover (q.v. Part IV). It was he who took the credit for clearing up the nests of Nazi saboteurs in World War II and the networks of the Soviet Union afterwards. Certainly the FBI as a whole deserved some credit, but it is doubtful how much of this can be attributed to Hoover. The FBI keeps well apart from the CIA, and it is the only agency which does not open up its files to the CIA. The CIA may obtain intelligence from the FBI upon request.

Army Intelligence passes a considerable amount of information to the CIA, as does the Office of Naval Intelligence (ONI), (q.v. Part II), and the Air Force's Intelligence not only assesses the air strength of other nations, but examines and analyses potential targets, as well as having its own counter-intelligence. Apart from this the State Department has its Bureau of Intelligence and Research which gleans information from embassies and consulates, though today much of this work is left to the CIA. The Atomic Energy Commission has its own intelligence division and, in this respect, is probably well in advance of most other powers. Over and above all these agencies is the National Security Council, similar in some way to Britain's Joint Intelligence Committee, which was set up in 1947. This Council brings together members of the government, the armed forces and the CIA. Comment on this body must be guarded because it is still in the process of evolution and its activities and purposes are frequently changing. This can be taken as an encouraging sign, indicating a body which is prepared to accept criticism and the need for change. In recent years it has been responsible for all major covert operations.

One final word is needed to correct misunderstandings in terminology. The United States Secret Service, unlike other secret services of the world, has nothing to do with the CIA or any similar body. It is, in fact, a tradition started after the Civil War to deal with forgery of currency, but for many years has simply been an organization to guard the President.

Further reading

Secret Service by R.V. Rowan with R.G. Deindorfer (Hawthorn Books, New York 1967)
The CIA and the Cult of Intelligence by Victor Marchetti and John D. Merks (Jonathan Cape, London 1974)
The Espionage establishment by David Wise and Thomas B. Ross (Random House, New York 1967)
The Craft of Intelligence by Allen Dulles (London, 1963)
The Real CIA by Lyman B. Kirkpatrick (London 1968)
The CIA and the U.S. Intelligence System by Scott D. Breckinridge (Westview Press, Colorado 1986)

WEST GERMANY

After the liquidation of the Nazi Intelligence and Security Services at the end of World War II, the formation of new services in West Germany started amidst dissension and aggravation. While the Americans wanted to see an efficient, aggressive counter-espionage service created, one which would keep close watch on Soviet subversion, many Europeans (the British and French among them), were anxious to ensure that it could never again develop into anything like the Nazi services. The Americans had already made much use of the ex-Nazi Military Intelligence chief General Gehlen (q.v. Part IV) and put him in control of a CIA-supported espionage unit, encouraging him to send agents into East Germany. Thus, unhappily, it came about that West Germany's two newly created Intelligence and Security Services were suspicious of each another, one fearing the effects of Nazi influences, the other suspecting the presence of Communist sympathizers. Gehlen became chief of the *Bundesnachrichtendienst* (BND) the West German Federal Intelligence Agency, largely on American support, while Dr Otto John, with strong British backing, was appointed chief of the *Bundesamt fur Verfassungsschutz* (BfV), the Office for the Protection of the Constitution, which was concerned with counter-espionage.

The BfV was formed in 1950 and came under the Ministry of the Interior. Like Britain's MI5 it had no powers of arrest. The BND was not formed until 1956, though Gehlen's unofficial

CIA-backed service had been functioning since 1953. The BfV suffered a serious blow in 1954 when Dr John disappeared and was later produced at a press conference in East Berlin. During this conference he made critical comments on some of the Western powers. Afterwards he escaped back to West Germany, alleging that he had been kidnapped and brainwashed. He was charged with treason in 1956, sentenced to four years' imprisonment, but released in 1958 (see *John, Dr Otto*, Part IV). It was after the John affair that Gehlen came into his own with the BND, but his attempts to infiltrate his own agents on a large scale into East Russia and the USSR mainly proved disastrous as his own organization was also infiltrated by the Russians. The truth is that both the BND and BfV have had appalling records throughout their history, suffering from both infiltration and defection. It must be admitted that the division of Germany into east and west has been partly responsible for this, as both nations share the same language, and before the creation of the Berlin Wall, passage from one zone to the other was subject only to occasional and ineffective controls. Unfortunately, it was West Germany rather than East, which suffered most from security lapses. Heinz Felfe (q.v. Part IV), a Soviet agent, installed himself on the Soviet desk in the Gehlen offices and it was not until 1961 that he was arrested. A year before this it was discovered that Alfred Frenzel, a member of the West German Parliament and a member of the Defence Committee, had been betraying military secrets to the Eastern bloc, and then in 1974 Gunther Guillaume, a key member of the staff of Federal Chancellor Willy Brandt, was arrested as a KGB agent and sentenced to thirteen years' imprisonment, thus precipitating the resignation of Brandt himself (see *Guillaume, Gunther*, Part IV).

The Guillaume affair was far from being the last espionage case in West Germany. In the mid-1980s the BfV suffered the defection of Hans Joachim Tiedge, a departmental head who had been in charge of counter-espionage operations against East Germany. Other defectors included Sonja Lueneburg, personal secretary of the West German Economics Minister, and Ursula Richter. Another secretary, Margarete Hoeke, was arrested after it was found that she had been in contact with East German agents. For years Hoeke had had access to highly classified documents, including some on defence matters (see *Tiedge, Hans Joachim*, Part IV).

Following the Tiedge affair the Chancellor announced that Heribert Hellenbroich, former head of the BfV and newly-appointed head of the BND was to take early retirement, having held the post for only one month. Hellenbroich's inadequate excuse for retaining Tiedge's services after the discovery of his drink problem was that 'removing him would have made him a greater risk'. In an attempt to improve security and screening in the BfV and BND Chancellor Kohl appointed Hans-Georg Wieck, a former envoy to Moscow and West Germany's Ambassador to NATO. Despite this it was estimated in 1986 that East Germany had about 8000 spies in West Germany, half of them East German agents and the rest West German informants to the East. Manipulating West Germans into love affairs with East Germans and staging road accidents by which they can frighten or threaten Westerners into working for them are ploys frequently used by East Germany to recruit spies in the West. It may seem astonishing that such obvious tricks can work, but in the case of a civil servant from the West who was recuperating in an East German hospital, he was visited by two agents who presented him with two accident reports, one falsely accusing him of drunken driving and the other stating that he was innocent. He was urged to give certain information if he wished to go free. On his return to West Germany, he reported what had happened. These and many other facts were revealed in June 1986 in a report issued from the BfV office, approved by the Minister of the Interior, Friederich Zimmerman.

YUGOSLAVIA

Yugoslavia's intelligence service today is conducted so discreetly that it is rarely, if ever, mentioned in the media. It seems to be largely concerned with its own internal problems, which are many, owing to the fact that the country is divided into six republics speaking a variety of languages and practising a number of religions, including Islam, Catholicism and Judaism. Although Yugoslavia's rift with Moscow had never been fully healed and its suspicion towards the Eastern bloc is reciprocated, the Belgrade government still regards itself as Marxist, and intelligence links with Moscow have never been totally severed.

During World War II, Tito, then a close ally of the USSR, was given more aid by British citizens acting as undercover agents of the Soviet Union than from any other country. The most prominent of these was the late James Klugmann, a member of the British Communist Party and a major on the SOE staff in Cairo, from where Balkan operations were directed. While the Yugoslav desk in London was originally staunchly pro-Mihailovich, leader of the Chetniks, SOE in Cairo was irrevocably committed to Tito through the efforts of Klugmann and others who shared his views. Yet after World War II, when Tito broke with Stalin, Klugmann suddenly changed his tune and denounced the Yugoslav leader in his book *From Trotsky to Tito*. This was when Yugoslavia was expelled from the Cominform. Not surprisingly, Yugoslavs have since been suspicous of any offers of British help concerning intelligence.

Despite maintaining a low profile, the Yugoslavs are remarkably astute in their counter-intelligence operations, demonstrated in October 1986 when Pjer Ivezaj, an American citizen of Albanian-Yugoslav descent, was jailed for seven years for 'hostile activity against the State', according to the official Tanjug news agency. It was alleged that Ivezaj belonged to the Detroit-based Albanian-American Student Organization which organized Albanian students and intellectuals to carry out hostile activity against Yugoslavia. He had been arrested while visiting relatives in Yugoslavia.

The astuteness of Yugoslavia's intelligence service was perhaps most clearly shown in 1986 when it supported the idea for holding the first Interpol congress in Belgrade, the only occasion when an Interpol conference had been held in a Communist state. Only two Eastern bloc countries – Rumania and Hungary – are members of the 138-nation international police organization based in Paris, and it was suggested that Belgrade was chosen partly to tempt other Eastern nations to join the fold. The twin evils plaguing the West, drugs and terrorism, were discussed at the conference, and it was agreed unanimously to fight terrorism as a criminal rather than a political offence.

An interesting survivor of the war years in Yugoslavia is Professor Stefan Dedijer of Lund University in Sweden where he has set up a special department called 'Social Intelligence', which has been nicknamed the 'Spy University'. Though born in Yugoslavia in 1911 and educated at Belgrade University, Dedijer is now a Swedish citizen. He has had an unusual career, having attended Princeton University, fought as an American paratrooper in the US 101 Airborne Division in World War II, and unashamedly admits that he worked at different times for the US, Yugoslav and Soviet intelligence services. After the war he was, for a time, an adviser to the Yugoslav Atomic Energy Commission. He became disenchanted with Marxism generally and emigrated to Sweden several years ago. 'Yugoslavia,' he says, 'is still blinded by the belief that democracy and deviation are capitalist luxuries, and the government in Belgrade was very slow to detect early on the extremely grave problems resulting in unemployment and the emigration of thousands of workers and intellectuals.' Not surprisingly his 'Spy University' has been misrepresented behind the Iron Curtain, being described as 'studies of the secret services' and allegedly having participants recruited from the 'circles of the notorious Anglo-American intelligence services'.

Further reading
Patriot or Traitor: the Case of General Mihailovich by David Martin; (Information sheets from Lund University Hoover Institution, 1980)

POSTSCRIPT

Although some countries have no secret service and intelligence organization, it is surprising how many do. For example, even the tiny state of Costa Rica, which has a population of fewer than two million, has a department called the Costa Rica Intelligence and Security Directorate. Sometimes the smaller the state, the more pretentious the name given to its police forces.) Even the Pacific archipelago of Vanuatu, formerly known as the New Hebrides, has its own intelligence service under Father Walter Lini, the Anglican priest who is Prime Minister. Father

Lini appears to take an interest in many distant countries, such as Cuba and Libya, both of whom he considers allies. At the time of writing he has stated that he intends to make a fishing agreement with the Soviet Union and to give Russian ships docking rights. Father Lini does not regard Libya as being involved in terrorism, but declares that both the USA and France are guilty of terrorist acts. In 1987 there was some consternation in both Australia and New Zealand when it was learned that a Libyan delegation had visited Vanuatu with the aim of extending its programme of terrorist and intelligence-gathering training for this area of the Pacific, including the Kanak Liberation movements from New Caledonia and Militants in Irian Jaya fighting against the Indonesian government.

Some European powers, notably Belgium, Holland and Norway, keep their intelligence-gathering and counter-espionage work to a minimum and for that reason they have not been individually included in Part I. However, their overall security systems are quietly efficient and they have had fewer espionage scandals than some of their neighbours. Since World War II Turkish Intelligence has given rather more assistance to NATO than some other member countries, not least in the use of facilities. It was from a remote military air base at Incirclik near Adana that Gary Powers, the U-2 pilot, was sent in the late 1950s. Here facilities were given for the US Ten/Ten Reconnaissance Detachment to make secret forays over Soviet territory. All Arab and Muslim states have their individual intelligence and security systems, often merely duplicating what their ethnic allies are doing. Those Arab territories which were previously under French rule usually have the better of such services and they have also copied the type of services which the French established. Morocco, for instance, has three services: Military Intelligence, the General Directorate for Research and Intelligence and the Directorate for Surveillance of the Territory, the last two being set up by King Hassan in 1973. There is little trust between the Arab states; in 1967 an Egyptian spy network was discovered to be operating inside the office of the Saudi Prime Minister and the King decided to deal personally with this matter. Jordan has a surveillance system called Jihaz al-Rasad (RASD), composed of two divisions – one for intelligence-gathering, mainly on Israel, and the other for counter-espionage.

PART II

c. 510 BC – AD 1918

AKASHI, GENERAL MOTOJIRO (d. 1919)

Akashi, who was also a baron, had been attached to Imperial GHQ in the Sino-Japanese War and towards the end of 1900 was sent to Europe as a roving attaché. He was briefed both by the War Office and the Black Dragon secret society, the latter ordering him to offer financial aid to Russian revolutionaries in exchange for information about the Russian Intelligence Services and the strength of their armed forces. It is believed that it was Akashi who lured Sidney Reilly (q.v.) into working for the Japanese. In this period the Black Dragon society proved to be an excellent source of intelligence for the Japanese War Office and the Navy. One of Akashi's other contacts was Konni Zilliacus, a Finnish revolutionary who later became a British socialist MP, but he also maintained close links with Muslims, even to the extent of establishing contacts between the Black Dragon and some Muslim secret societies. He became a favourite in the salons, as much because of his poems and paintings as his military reputation. Promoted to full General, he was on his way to take up the post of Governor-General of Formosa when he died.

AKBAR, JELIAL-UD-DIN MOHAMMED (1542-1605)

The greatest of all Mogul emperors, Akbar's empire at its greatest extended from Kashmir in the north to Ahmedabad in the south, and from Kabul in the west to Dacca in the east. Though he daringly changed his empire's policy from fanatical Mohammedanism to universal toleration, he also built up an apparently security-tight intelligence organization which impressed such foreign visitors as Britain's Sir John Hawkins. Akbar's organization not only had 4000 officers, but they controlled networks of spies all over the territory, recruiting chiefly from the untouchable caste.

ALEXANDER THE GREAT (356-323 BC)

Educated by Aristotle, Alexander the Great, King of Macedon, was one of the first rulers to make use of intelligence as a major weapon of government. He instigated a fairly simple method for passing secret messages, which involved all those sending and receiving such messages having identical scrolls and staffs. The scroll which contained the message was hidden in what seemed to be a straightforward report, but was wound spirally around the staff in such a way that the secret message could be deciphered from the characters which appeared in a straight line along the staff. Alexander also introduced postal censorship in an effort to assess the morale of his armies. Evidence suggests that this enabled him to weed out malcontents and put right various problems creating dissatisfaction. That he succeeded seems evident from his successes against the Persians, his capture of Egypt and penetration into India.

ANDRE, MAJOR JOHN (1751-1780)

Certainly one of the few, if not the only spy to be honoured by a memorial tablet in Westminster Abbey, John André, of the 54th Foot Regiment was a courageous British agent in the American War of Independence. A man of great integrity who had been immensely popular as Adjutant-General in New York, André was an army major born in London, where his father was a Swiss merchant. In 1780 when the American general, Benedict Arnold, made surrender overtures to the British, André was chosen to negotiate with him. He was provided with a pass describing him as a merchant named John Anderson, but when challenged by an American patrol he made the error of admitting that he was a British officer and offering them 100 guineas to let him go. He was arrested as a spy, tried by a military board and hanged at Tappan on 2 October 1780. So popular had he been that there was a widespread demand for his reprieve by Americans themselves, but the authorities turned down all such requests.

ASTON, MAJOR-GENERAL SIR GEORGE GREY (1861-1938)

Aston's first experience of secret service work was in South Africa during the Boer War, when he kept an eye on German activities over the whole area. He remained with Military Intelligence until 1913 when he was transferred to the Admiralty. Attached to the NID, he found that Naval Intelligence was constantly obstructed by civilians in the Admiralty. He wanted to introduce carrier pigeons for intelligence communication, wisely pointing out that 'pigeon post' (q.v. Part III) might well be effective if wireless links broke down, but he was overruled. Just before World War I broke out Sir George was called to join the Foreign Intelligence Committee of the Admiralty Secretariat and he then became the real director of secret service in the Middle East in that war. In his book, *Secret Service*, Aston described how he liquidated one of Turkey's ace spies. The Turk had been so successful in penetrating the secrets of Allenby's Expeditionary Force that he ensured the Turks had British plans in advance of almost every operation. Aston arranged for £30 in English banknotes to be put inside a letter addressed to the spy, implying that this was in payment for services to the British. The letter was intercepted by the Turks and on this evidence alone, the Turco-German command had their ace spy shot on the grounds that he was a double-agent.

AUCKLAND, LORD (WILLIAM EDEN) (1784-1849)

William Eden entered the House of Commons as member for Woodstock, joining Lord North's party, and he became a devoted follower of Pitt who sent him as minister-plenipotentiary to France where, in 1786, he negotiated a commercial treaty. He also served as Ambassador in Spain and Holland, and held the post of Postmaster-General (1798-1801), but it was as a reorganizer of the British Secret Service that he revealed his best talents. An able administrator, he acquired more detailed information on America's relations in foreign capitals than Washington himself received. It was no fault of Eden's that Britain failed to regain her colonies. His vast collection of papers, which in 1889 the British Government released to F.B. Stevens, an American scholar in London, testify eloquently to the range of his espionage system. Research into these papers shows that many men who had hitherto been held up as American patriots were actually agents of the British Secret Service (see *Franklin, Benjamin*, Part II).

AZEFF, YEVNO (1869-1918)

The son of a poor Jewish tailor, Azeff was born in Lyskovo, USSR. He tried various jobs, being in turn a clerk, a commercial traveller and a reporter on a local paper. At the same time he became acquainted with a number of young revolutionaries and married a young woman devoted to the cause. When threatened with arrest for distributing revolutionary propaganda in 1892, he absconded with money he owed to his firm and escaped to Karlsruhe in Germany where he entered the Polytechnic Institute. Here he joined the Russian Social Democratic Group. Then it dawned on him that he could obtain both money and safety by betraying the group to the *Ochrana* (Russian secret police). Azeff had become what he was to remain throughout his life – an ace conman who used espionage for his own needs.

He was taken on as an *Ochrana* agent from 1893. He travelled around Germany and Switzerland, meeting all manner of revolutionaries. In 1899, on the strength of his reports, his salary was raised to 100 roubles a month and he returned to Russia. Through his information the *Ochrana* were able to track down various revolutionaries and arrest them. Then, just to prove what a master of conmanship he was, when all the leaders of one terrorist group were arrested, Azeff got himself elected leader of their whole organization. By the turn of the century Azeff was earning 500 roubles a month from the *Ochrana*, possibly the highest rate of pay for any of their agents. He informed the police of a special squad of revolutionaries known as the 'Battle Organization', whose aim was the assassination of top Russian statesmen. This did not stop some of the assassinations being carried out, and about this time Azeff started to pass back to the revolutionaries information he gained from his police contacts. In a tangled web of his own weaving this adroit police agent operated with cunning, skill and astute judgement. For example, he revealed to the *Ochrana* the plans hatched by Gershuni, head of the 'Battle Organization', for killing Plehve, the Minister of the Interior, and Zubatov, head of the Moscow branch of the Ochrana, but he kept silent on the target for the next killing – Obolensky, Governor of Kharkov. His tactics were to safeguard all his supporters within the revolutionary movement, but to eliminate his enemies and those suspicious of him by giving them away to the police. Later the Petersburg Social Revolutionary Committee came completely under Azeff's direction. He also formed several new branches of the movement, quite often manning them with *Ochrana* agents.

When Gershuni was arrested Azeff acquired supreme command of the revolutionary group and directed tactics. He had large sums of money under his control. When a fanatical woman terrorist founded her own group of assassins to kill Plehve, Azeff revealed her plot to the *Ochrana*, but when Plehve was killed by a bomb in 1904 the *Ochrana* became suspicious because they had had no tip-off from Azeff. Ultimately Azeff was regarded with suspicion both by the *Ochrana* and the revolutionaries, as some of the latter who had infiltrated the *Ochrana* reported back that he was systematically betraying the organization. During this period Azeff was earning something like 16,000 roubles a year from the secret police. After this he temporarily retired to the Italian Riviera to live a life of ease and luxury.

To some extent Azeff's position was impregnable because unlike most double-agents, he had allowed each side to know something of his dealings with the other. Just how security-minded Azeff was may be gathered from the fact that his wife, a fanatical, idealistic revolutionary would almost certainly have denounced her husband if she had had any inkling of his role with the *Ochrana*, but she never guessed. In a last attempt to convince the revolutionaries that he was on their side, he even made plans to assassinate the Tsar, but the attempt never came off and from then on Azeff was doomed. The revolutionaries sent a delegation to cross-examine him in Paris, but he disappeared to Germany with his mistress. A number of heads rolled in the *Ochrana* and the 'Azeff Affair' was something which that organization never recovered from. Azeff kept on the move, changing his name to Alexander Neumayer, but the German secret police discovered his true identity and arrested him. In 1917 he was released from prison, and he died the following year.

Further reading
Take Nine Spies by Fitzroy Macleen (Weidenfeld & Nicolson, London 1978)
Azeff: The Spy, Russian Terrorist and Police Stool by Boris Nicolaievsky (Doubleday, Doran & Co., New York 1934)

BACKHOUSE, SIR EDMUND (1873-1944)

Though coming from a Quaker family and background, Backhouse eschewed most of the virtues of that sect, having gone to Winchester and Oxford, and indulging in quite riotous and extravagant living at the university. In 1895 he was declared bankrupt, after which he went to China. His early days in Peking remain rather a mystery; it was the period of the Boxer Rebellion, recurring crises at the court of the Dowager Empress and the siege of the legations against the Boxers. Gradually, Backhouse established himself as an agent in Peking to railway and ship builders, as the author of a pornographic novelette, and ultimately as a British secret agent. His first task as such was apparently an undercover arms deal of the type which, in the early part of this century, eventually led to an all-round arms race and World War I. It resulted in Backhouse negotiating with Chinese officials, giving orders to Chinese generals, passing information to the British Legation, and culminated in a report to London which stated that there was 'an arrangement here with Backhouse, with the secret connivance of the Chinese government, to dispose of such arms under control of himself and his friends in other provinces as are available for sale'. These undercover deals multiplied once World War I began. Backhouse seems to have ingratiated himself with all manner of Chinese officials right up to the Empress herself, and he even claimed to have had a love affair with her.

Further reading
Hermit of Peking by Hugh Trevor-Roper (1976)

BADEN-POWELL, LIEUT.-GENERAL LORD ROBERT STEPHENSON (1857-1941)

Though better known as founder of the Boy Scout movement, Baden-Powell was an active spy on a number of occasions. Perhaps it was because of this connection that during World War II, Himmler, head of the Gestapo in Nazi Germany, seriously believed that the Boy Scouts were a branch of British Secret Service! Baden-Powell was always an embarrassingly eccentric officer with a penchant for dressing up, playing charades and indulging in disguises and practical jokes. However, his eccentricities bore fruit in the field of intelligence.

Once when he had been asked to obtain details of the guns in the Dalmatian fortress of Cattara, Baden-Powell went there as an entomologist, taking pains to learn entomology and how to handle a butterfly net before he set out. He was quite a skilled artist and prior to his mission he made coloured sketches of butterflies he would be likely to encounter. Into the wings of those sketched butterflies he drew outlines of the fortifications and details of the armaments. On another occasion he posed as a drunk, soaking his clothes in brandy and staggering off in the direction of a secret German military installation. He was swiftly arrested, but believing him to be hopelessly drunk and incapable of finding out any secrets, the German sentries let him go.

In South Africa during the Boer War he was given a solitary reconnaissance mission into the Drakensburg Mountains and he succeeded in making friends with a number of Boer farmers. In the defence of Mafeking, Baden-Powell recruited Zulus for scouting activities and trained them in the use of disguise. With typical modesty he gave most of the credit for this to a Zulu assistant named Jan Grootboom. He was convinced throughout this war that Britain was fighting the Germans as well as the Boers, but he failed to convince the Secret Service of this. Throughout his career he indulged in espionage, often while on leave, in Europe, Algeria, Tunisia, deep into the heart of the Sahara and in Turkey.

Further reading
Baden-Powell: the Two Lives of a Hero by William Hillcourt (Heinemann, London 1964)

BANCROFT, DR EDWARD (1744-1821)

Inside the American Embassy in Paris during the reign of King George III was a cell of British Intelligence organized by Edward Bancroft and aided by Benjamin Franklin, who was then in charge. Both men were scientists of distinction, and great friends to boot. Bancroft passed all the information he obtained from Franklin and others to the British who, as a result, learned not only all the American secrets, but many items of French intelligence as well. During the War of Independence Bancroft supplied Lord Wentworth at the British Foreign Office with more detailed intelligence than ever reached the American President, George Washington. But Bancroft's error was to speculate in securities connected with the American colonies which, when the King heard of it, caused him to think Bancroft was a double-agent and dismiss him. However, Lord Wentworth arranged for him to have a pension for his services. Franklin refused to admit that Bancroft was a British agent when the American agent, Arthur Lee, produced evidence of his espionage. He denounced Lee and insisted that Bancroft's visits to London produced worthwhile intelligence for America. Yet all Bancroft brought back on these trips was false information provided by the British.

Further reading
The Published Letters of King George III (Revised edition, London 1932)

BEACH, THOMAS (1840-1894)

Born in Colchester, Thomas Beach enlisted in the American cavalry as a private soldier and finished his military career as a major. In 1865 he came across a strange-looking twenty-dollar bill with the words 'Irish Republic' stamped across it. He discovered that this was a Fenian method of raising funds. (The Fenians was the name then given to the Irish Republican Brotherhood, founded in the USA by John O'Mahony in 1858.) The counterfeit money was sold to gullible Irish immigrants who believed in the possibility of an Irish republic. Beach wrote home to his father about this, having amassed quite a bit of information on the Fenians, and his father passed it on to his MP.

This was how Beach came to the attention of the British Secret Service and he was asked to supply further details. In 1866 he accurately forecast an invasion of Canada by the Fenians. The attempt was an utter failure, but when Beach returned to England the following year it was agreed he should become a paid agent of the British government. He returned to the USA and offered his services to the Fenians under the name of Major Henri le Caron and immediately organized a Fenian camp in Lockhart, Illinois, where as commandant he received all official reports and documents issued by the Fenian hierarchy. Later he was appointed Military Organizer of the Irish Republican Army at a salary of $60 a month with $7 a day expenses, and eventually he was promoted to the rank of Inspector-General of the revolutionary forces. As a result of the intelligence he gleaned, the Fenian organization was largely disrupted by 1870, but not before a second invasion of Canada was planned. However, this invasion also fizzled out ignominiously. Still posing as le Caron, Beach reported a Fenian project to build a submarine torpedo boat which was intended to destroy the Royal Navy. As the British Navy had not yet considered the idea of a submarine, it could have had a devastating effect. Beach's report on the plan was passed to the British Admiralty, but it was not until many years later – 1901 – that Britain acquired its first submarine and then it was largely due to Beach's information.

When he returned to Britain in the 1880s, Beach was asked to gain the confidence of Charles Stewart Parnell, the leader of the Irish Party in the House of Commons. In this case, Beach found himself completely out of his depth and merely provided ammunition for those who wished to see Parnell destroyed.

Further reading
Twenty-five Years in the Secret Service by Henri le Caron (Heinemann, London 1892)

BEHN, APHRA (1640-1689)

Born at Wye at Kent, and married to a London merchant of Dutch extraction, Aphra Behn was forced to support herself after her husband's death. This she did not only by the pen, but also by her wits and enterprise as a British secret agent. Apart from writing plays and books, of which *Oroonoko, or The Royal Slave* is probably the best known today, she was sent to

Antwerp to spy on the Dutch. Her coded correspondence bears adequate testimony to her ability, though until recent years there was a tendency to belittle her achievements as a spy. This may well have been due to an attempt to cover up the shameful episode of 1667, when the Dutch fleet sailed up the Thames, anchored in the Medway and burnt some of Britain's leading warships. Mrs Aphra Behn had reported Admiral de Ruyter's plot to launch his fire-ships against the British fleet, but London declined to take her warnings seriously. She was the first British female spy of any note.

BESTUCHEV, ALEXEI

As Russian Chancellor in the reign of the Tsarina Elizabeth, Bestuchev became a supreme spymaster. Espionage by barter was the custom of the day and he was passing information to the English Minister, Sir Charles Hanbury-Williams, who was also a close friend of Grand Duchess Catherine. Sir Charles, who knew that bribery was essential to gain allies, offered Bestuchev £10,000 if he could bring about an agreement between England and Russia. Bestuchev had his spies everywhere and through his 'Black Cabinet' organized the interception of diplomatic dispatches, especially those of the French. Under Bestuchev the Russians even found the secret of deciphering dispatches, having employed three Germans, known as cryptologists, in the Muscovite Post Office. The contents of these he passed on to the Tsarina, and so paved the way to an alliance with England and Austria against Prussia. But the Chancellor, with his personal secret service, was up against the head of the official Russian Imperial Secret Service under Alexander Shuvaloff, a favourite of the Tsarina. Schuvaloff was as pro-French as Bestuchev was pro-English. Despite this, both Bestuchev and the English Ambassador failed to get their way, when news came through from London that England and Prussia had signed an alliance. The Tsarina backed Shuvaloff against Bestuchev and demanded the recall of Hanbury-Williams.

The correspondence between the Grand Duchess Catherine and Hanbury-Williams reveals how the future Tsarina felt the need for her own secret intelligence. It is clear that not only was she pro-English, but that she honestly believed the information she passed to him would ultimately benefit Russia as well as England. Whether they were ever actually lovers is open to question, but the dream of an Anglo-Russian alliance was in ruins when in 1759 Sir Charles died.

Further reading
The Life of Sir Charles Hanbury-Williams by the Earl of Ilchester and Mrs Langford-Brooke (Thornton Butterworth, London 1929)
Correspondence of Catherine the Great when Grand Duchess with Sir Charles Hanbury-Williams by the Earl of Ilchester and Mrs Langford-Brooke 1928)

BLACKWELL, JOSEPH ANDREW

Papers and letters, throwing light on the life and espionage methods of this remarkable Victorian spy, were exhibited at the Gladstone Pottery Museum in Longton, Staffordshire, in 1982. Born into a wealthy pottery family, Blackwell was president of the Society of Amateur Musicians and a linguist with a command of twenty languages. The year of his recruitment as a spy remains unknown, but by 1847, when Lord Palmerston was at the Foreign Office, he was writing to a friend, saying: 'I have managed to get into the good graces of Lord Palmerston ... and I trust have now much better prospects before me than scribbling books ... I shall set off on the 15th for Hungary on the service of Her Majesty's Government with the same salary as before (two guineas a day and travelling expenses).' His dispatches from the crumbling Austro-Hungarian empire, where he wormed his way into the confidence of the Hungarian rebels, were apparently invaluable. The historian Charles Sproxton, writing in 1919, stated that Blackwell 'was a far more intelligent observer and acute judge of events and men than Lord Ponsonby' (then the British ambassador in Vienna).

BLONDEL LE NESLE

A troubadour and native of Nesle in Picardy, Blondel was a friend and fellow-minstrel of Richard I ('Coeur de Lion'), King of England. When Richard was captured by Leopold, Duke of Austria, while returning from the Holy Land, the exact whereabouts of his prison was not known. Blondel was given the mission of travelling across Germany and Austria as a troubadour with the aim of finding just where the King was imprisoned. Blondel's ploy was to sing one of the songs Richard had composed outside various jails and dungeons in the hope that the King would hear him and reply with a verse from the song. Eventually Blondel's song was recognized by Richard from his place of incarceration at Dürrenstein and he answered Blondel with a verse. Blondel swiftly returned to England and arranged for the payment of the ransom which eventually set the King free.

BOYD, BELLE (MRS BELLE HARDINGE) (1844-1901)

This pert, pretty girl in her crinolines and lace was only seventeen when invading Federal soldiers in the American Civil War forced their way into her home and insulted her mother. Belle was so enraged that she took a pistol and shot one of the Federal sergeants, killing him. On that occasion her sex and youthfulness saved her from punishment. From that day onwards, however, Belle spied for the Rebels. She collected information, ventured far afield into the enemy lines and beyond, and on several occasions brought back intelligence of great value. She used her charm and femininity to devastating effect, not only in collecting information, but in bewitching her enemies. Even when she was captured, Abraham Lincoln himself intervened to save her from the death penalty.

'The most famous woman concerned with official secret activities in the Civil War' is how Belle's biographer, Joseph Hergesheimer, described her. Belle Boyd was unquestionably lucky. Making little effort to disguise herself on her forays behind the enemy lines, she often came under fire and seems to have relied solely on her persuasive charms. In captivity she used the same tactics with her warders, though not always quite so successfully. Eventually she was exchanged for another prisoner, travelled the world, married and later gave lectures on her experiences as a spy. She will always be remembered as Belle Boyd, but the man who married her, resigning his commission to do so was a Federal naval officer, Sam Wylde Hardinge.

Further reading
Belle Boyd or Camp and Prison (2 volumes) by Joseph Hergesheimer (Saunders, Otley & Co., London 1865)

BURTON, SIR RICHARD (1821-1890)

The superhuman qualities and gratuitous efforts of some great Victorian eccentrics virtually sustained the largely amateur British Secret Service of that era. Of these, perhaps none was more typical than Burton. His biographer, Byron Farwell, said Burton was 'an adventurer in the purest sense of the word', and in the course of his travels in Africa, Asia and the Middle East he unearthed much that was of value to intelligence-gatherers. Certainly when the British captured Sind his ability to provide brilliantly detailed intelligence reports was soon demonstrated to Sir Charles Napier, the Commander-in-chief. As a young subaltern, Burton disguised himself as a native and speaking the local language, opened three small shops in Karachi, selling cloth and tobacco for a few rupees and a mass of information. Whether his report on pederasty in Karachi, which he was asked to make by Sir Charles Napier, was a cover for rather more practical intelligence one does not know. Staining himself with henna and posing as Mirza Abdullah of Bushire, Burton disappeared into the male brothels of Karachi night after night. He was so skilful at disguising himself as an Indian that he often passed his commanding officer without being recognized.

Further reading
A Biography of Sir Richard Francis Burton by Byron Farwell
(Longman, London 1963)

CABINET NOIR

The *Cabinet Noir* was the creation of Cardinal Richelieu (q.v.)
when he was made a minister to King Louis XIII in 1624. Its
purpose was to intercept and analyse correspondence and it
became the *Haute Police*, which was the service concerned with
snuffing out plots. It soon established extensive spy networks in
all quarters of Paris. The fear then was of political plots in high
places rather than revolutionary sentiments among the masses.
An unusual feature of the *Cabinet Noir* was its paternalistic
attitude. Much secret police work under the *ancien régime* was
for the purpose of suppressing 'private disorder' and to prevent
the occurrence of scandals in the aristocratic families and at
court. It was this mixture of intelligence work and paternalism
which contributed to Fouché's views on the proper role of the
police.

CHARLES II, KING OF ENGLAND (1630-1685)

It may seem questionable to include a King of England as a spy
chief, yet Charles II undoubtedly was. Probably the most
worldly and intelligent monarch ever to sit on the throne of
England, Charles's long period in exile had made him realize
that few men were to be trusted, least of all his own supporters.
So he decided to keep a wary eye on all sources of intelligence,
checking and double-checking reports he received from one
quarter with those he got from another. After the Restoration
the Secret Service ceased to be centralized: it was split up into
various independent entities, being divided between the King
himself (the real chief), Secretary Morrice and Lord Arlington.
Samuel Pepys in his diaries noted a dispute in the House of
Commons about 'the King's Intelligence', adding that 'Secretary

Morrice declared that "he was allowed but £700 a year for intelligence, whereas in Cromwell's time, he [Cromwell] did allow £70,000 a year for it" '. Pepys also referred to complaints that the King 'paid too dear for my Lord Arlington's [intelligence] in giving £10,000 and a barony for it'. Charles was, of course, short of funds, so he combined business with pleasure by spending lavishly on his mistresses and frequently using them as spies, especially at the court of the French King. Some Secret Service funds found their way into the hands of the beautiful Louise de Kéroualle, who was also a double-agent. Charles's other contribution to the Secret Service was a new cipher which bore his name. This was the same cipher as he had used when in exile in the Netherlands.

Further reading
See the transcription from the tachygraphical manuscript in the Pepysian Library in Magdalene College, Cambridge, by the Rev. Mynors Bright

CHILDERS, ERSKINE (1870-1922)

Although more a propagandist than a spy, Childers was one of the few authors whose spy fiction led to a positive change in policy by the Royal Navy. His book, *The Riddle of the Sands*, was published in 1903, and was a lively narrative of yachting and espionage off the north-west coast of Germany. This was fiction based on fact, written with the purpose of arousing public support for building a stronger navy, and motivated by Childers' intense love of England and Ireland. Its factual basis was the result of Childers' own yachting experiences in the *Vixen* off the coasts of Germany, Holland and elsewhere. The story concerns two young Englishmen making a trip to the Frisian Islands and discovering the Germans rehearsing plans for an invasion of Britain.

After publication of Childers' novel, Britain's Naval Intelligence Division discovered that existing Admiralty charts of this area of the German coast were out of date and that the only accurate data about the Frisian Islands was to be obtained in Childers' book. (To achieve this, Childers had simply 'married' German and British charts, something the NID had failed to do.) As a result two officers, Lieutenant Brandon and Captain Trench, were sent out to do some spying around these coasts to put the records straight. Unluckily they were detected and arrested by the Germans, finally being sentenced to a term of imprisonment in Germany. They were released in May 1913, being pardoned by the Kaiser on the occasion of King George V's visit to Germany.

Childers served in the Royal Navy in World War I and was awarded the DSC. Afterwards he devoted his time to the fight for Irish independence. In 1919 he settled in Dublin and became the principal secretary of the delegation which negotiated an Irish Treaty with the British Government. Childers vehemently opposed both Arthur Griffiths and Michael Collins who favoured accepting the Treaty, on the grounds that it did not provide for complete independence. Prophetically, he maintained that to separate Ulster would only prolong bloodshed 'not just for a few years, but for a dozen or more generations to come'.

Brandon and Trench, who had undertaken their spy mission on orders from Captain Bethell, then head of the NID, were disgracefully treated by naval authorities after their release from prison. The Admiralty denied the official nature of their mission and declined to give them any compensation on the grounds that they were taking a pleasure trip and whatever happened to them was their own fault. It was a squalid story of cheese-paring indifference; the two men suffered severe financial hardship, as the expenses of their trial amounted to £380 each.

COLLEGE OF GOSTS

In seventeenth-century Russia foreigners were adept at penetrating Russian secrets, despite the existence of the Secret Bureau which was supposed to watch them. J.P. Kilburger, the historian of the period, wrote that all trade was in the hands of the Dutch and the Germans and that foreigners had actually gained membership of the College of Gosts, comprising merchants to whom special privileges were extended, enabling them to become unofficial agents of the Tsar. The English at this time were exceptionally well informed about what was going on inside Russia.

CONSIGLIO DEI DIECE

The *Consiglio Dei Dieci* (Council of the Tens) played a very significant role during the early Renaissance period as a state security and intelligence body of the Venetian Republic. The Council was formed in 1310 when a political conspiracy, under the leadership of the Doge, Marino Falieri, was uncovered not by the secret police, but by one of the conspirators who acted as informer because one of his best friends was involved. The Doge wanted to overthrow the constitutional order of the Venetian Republic, and for this attempt he paid with his life. Although intended for temporary functioning, the Council of Tens became a permanent fixture. As a remarkably efficient combination of secret police, political and military spies and a powerful trade and commercial intelligence-gathering organization from 1355 until 1454, it had nearly unlimited power as a security, judicial and intelligence organ of the Venetian Republic.

Members of the Council of the Tens covered their faces with masks when they attended official proceedings. When they were required to identify themselves, they opened their cloaks to show the lining into which the insignia CDX was woven by a special process. The so-called 'black members' wore black cloaks and masks while attending the meetings of the State Inquisition, while the 'red members', elected from the Council of the Doge, wore red cloaks and masks. In 1454 the Council represented itself with two 'black' members in the permanently established State Inquisition of the Venetian Republic. Agents of the Council were mostly priests and Jews who, by their professions, were allowed entry to all manner of places. It is recorded that Venetian counter-intelligence agents successfully thwarted the 'industrial spies of Genoa' in their attempt to acquire the manufacturing secrets of the Venetian cannon-makers.

CUMMING, CAPTAIN SIR MANSFIELD (1859-1923)

Originally known as Commander Mansfield Smith-Cumming, this was the man who became the first 'C', or head of the British Secret Service. A fifty-year-old naval officer when appointed to this office, he later dropped the name Smith and became simply Mansfield Cumming. It was he who insisted upon being known as 'C' both inside and out of the office. So effectively did he ensure the anonymity of his organization that many of his greatest successes have never been recorded. In a car accident in France in 1914 his son was killed and he himself lost a leg. When interviewing people, he drew attention to his wooden leg by tapping it with a paper knife, or striking matches on it before lighting his pipe. He also terrified female typists when he worked in the War Office by speeding down the corridors at an alarming speed with his wooden leg placed on a child's scooter, propelling it along with his good leg. It is surprising that his quixotic behaviour did not lead to his cover being broken.

Mansfield Cumming was a resourceful and inspiring leader, ruthless in many ways, but rather liking his agents to be philanderers, especially when this 'furthered the cause'. He was fearless to the point of calmly ordering an assassination, even if it meant killing one of his own agents. After World War I he had to fight hard to prevent drastic cuts in expenditure on the Secret Service. Despite his efforts he lost Secret Service stations in Madrid, Lisbon, Zurich and Luxembourg, while offices in Rome and at The Hague also suffered from cuts.

DEE, JOHN (1527-1608)

In the view of many of his contemporaries Dee was a charlatan and dabbler in black magic, yet his abundant output of erudite works reveal him as one of the most remarkable of Elizabethan scholars. A Fellow of Trinity College, Cambridge, he became an authority on mathematics, navigation, astronomy and optics, as well as being Astrologer Royal to Queen Elizabeth I. He spent many years travelling all over Europe, and in one sense can be said to have been the first Englishman to indulge in industrial espionage, for he passed back to England all the information he learned from a variety of clever people, including Mercator, the Flemish cartographer. To what extent he indulged in intelligence work is still something of a mystery, and it is uncertain whether his dabbling in the occult was a cover for espionage activities.

Often he was away for months on secret missions, sometimes for the Queen, more often for Sir William Cecil (Lord Burghley) and Sir Francis Walsingham, who was in charge of Elizabeth's intelligence system. His *Monas Hieroglyphica*, upon which he worked for seven years, dealt with the relation of numbers to natural magic and used a code and symbols which could only be understood by Dee himself and those he had initiated into the secrets of translation. Yet Cecil declared it to be 'of the utmost value for the security of the realm'. One of Dee's most valuable reports to Walsingham was a warning that the Spaniards knew England was committed to building new and bigger ships, and that they intended to check this plan by attacking timber supplies. Dee's message, conveyed in the form of a conversation with an angel named Madimi, was that a small party of Frenchmen, acting as agents of Spain, intended to visit the Forest of Dean and bribe foresters to burn down the trees. The warning proved to be accurate and it enabled the Verderers to catch the agents who had claimed squatters' rights in the forest and were planning a series of simultaneous fires in key points of the area (see *Astrology and Espionage*, Part III).

Further reading
John Dee: Scientist, Geographer, Astrologer and Secret Agent to Elizabeth I by Richard Deacon (Muller, London 1968)

DEFOE, DANIEL (1659-1731)

Son of a London butcher and author of *Robinson Crusoe* and *Moll Flanders*, Defoe was a key man in the British Secret Service in the early part of the eighteenth century. He was an unlikely choice for such a role. Rebel, revolutionary pamphleteer, twice imprisoned, pilloried, and convicted of seditious libel, he nevertheless admitted that he had been employed by Queen Anne 'in several honourable, though secret, services'. It was not an empty boast. He was highly regarded by Robert Harley, Earl of Oxford, who saw in Defoe a trained and meticulous observer who could put into coherent form and with a wealth of detail, all he saw and heard. Harley obtained Defoe's release from prison and the Harley Papers make it abundantly clear that Defoe worked as a secret agent under both Harley and Lord Godolphin. Even more remarkably Lord Godolphin, when forced out of office by Queen Anne in 1710, recommended Defoe to be his successor. One of his chief talents, as far as espionage was concerned, seems to have been an ability to discover the hiding places of Jacobites, sometimes even managing to stay in their homes and monitor their conversations.

Emboldened by his success, Defoe once wrote to Harley urging the creation of a new secret service for England, by which the Queen's Ministers could be provided with intelligence from all parts of the kingdom. But it was under George I that Defoe scored his major achievements in this field. He was sent on a tour of the country as the principal secret agent, organizing other spies as he went along, travelling incognito, sometimes as 'Alexander Goldsmith' and at others as 'Claude Guilot'. He posed as a writer during his travels and his book, *Tour Through England and Wales*, was a lucrative sideline to his espionage. He seems to have revelled in intrigue for its own sake.

Further reading
Defoe by James Sutherland (Methuen, London 1937)
The Life of Daniel Defoe by Thomas Wright (Cassell, London 1894)
The Incredible Defoe by W. Freeman (Herbert Jenkins, London 1930)

D'EON DE BEAUMONT, THE CHEVALIER CHARLES GENEVIEVE (1728-1810)

Born at Tonnere in France, the young Chevalier's mother insisted that he wear female attire until his early teens. Being slight of build, with delicate features and a pretty face, he was quite easily able to masquerade as a woman, which he often did. However, d'Eon was no mincing queen; he had proved himself an accomplished swordsman and been elected *grand prevôt* of the *Salle d'Armes* as a result. He was admitted to the French bar and soon came to the attention of King Louis XV who chose him for a remarkable mission – nothing less than going to the court of the Tsarina Elizabeth in Russia, disguised as a woman named Mlle Lia de Beaumont. His orders were to detach the Russians from adopting a pro-English policy and to win them as allies. He took with him a copy of Montesquieu's *L'Esprit des Lois*, in the binding of which was hidden a letter from King Louis XV to the Tsarina. The latter promptly made Lia her maid of honour and soon the French spy became something of a legend at court and a number of painters begged permission to paint 'her'.

Gradually the Chevalier managed to change the Tsarina's attitude toward the French, and even persuaded her not to sign a treaty with England. Eventually he revealed his true identity to the Tsarina, and she not only forgave the subterfuge, but is said to have offered him a post at court and in her government. D'Eon declined this offer and returned to France. Louis XV gave him a permanent post and a salary of 3000 livres a year. He was sent on various spying missions, sometimes in the guise of a woman. His one fatal error was to fall foul of Mme de Pompadour, the King's mistress, and after he was sent to London officially as secretary to the French Ambassador, but chiefly as a spy, she conspired against him. While in England he made a study of the Home Counties to work out the best routes for a French army to take when it invaded the country. His enemies in France arranged for him to be recalled peremptorily ordering him to put on 'women's garments' once again. It was more than a snub: it was a calculated insult. France's loss became Britain's gain, as d'Eon's request for sanctuary in London was granted. Even then he was never very safe as the French made various efforts to discredit and even poison him. However, he made friends in England, survived many ordeals and died there at the age of eighty-two.

Further reading
The Hell-Fire Club by Donald McCormick (Jarrolds, London 1958)

DUKES, SIR PAUL (1889-1967)

Paul Dukes was head of the British intelligence network in Russia immediately after the revolution when the network needed rebuilding. Prior to the war he had studied music at the Moscow Conservatory and in consequence had become a fluent Russian speaker with a talent for mixing with all classes of society. During the early part of World War I he had been attached to the Marinsky Theatre. In 1915 he was made a member of the Anglo-Russian Commission and carried the passport of a King's Messenger, charged with a roving assignment to investigate what was going on in the revolutionary underworld.

Later as Agent ST 25, using a number of disguises, he spent nearly ten months collecting intelligence. In 1919 he obtained a Russian passport which showed him to be an agent of the *Cheka*. He frequently changed both his name and his residence, sending out reports as often as he could. With an ex-Russian officer, Kolya Orlov, he organized raids on the Communists' store of stolen wealth. Sometimes he had to bury his reports in cemeteries and parks until it was safe to send them off. At this time the British Secret Service was using a coastal motor-boat, manned by naval personnel, to make contact with agents such as Dukes. The variety of disguises he used says much for his versatility; he posed as an epileptic, a bearded proletarian, an ailing intellectual and even Comrade Piotrovsky, committee member of the Communist Party. In September 1919 he returned to London where he was knighted for his services.

In 1939, before war was declared, Dukes had yet another spectacular adventure in the sphere of espionage. He was sent to Germany, ostensibly on behalf of a group of London industrialists, but actually to ascertain the truth about the disappearance of a wealthy Czech business man on his way from Prague to Switzerland. Alfred Obry had fallen foul of the Nazis during the German occupation of Czechoslovakia. The Nazis coveted the huge enterprises he controlled and wanted to force him to sign them away. It was known that he had bought himself a false passport and was planning to escape. Dukes, always a meticulous agent, read through all the local papers and noticed a report about a man named Friedrich Schweiger, a tailor from Prague, whose body had been found mutilated on the railway line. Suspecting that the corpse could be that of Obry, he demanded the exhumation of the body. The Germans eventually met his demand and the corpse did indeed prove to be that of Obry.

Further reading
The Story of ST 25 by Paul Dukes (1938)

FOUCHÉ, JOSEPH, DUKE OF OTRANTO (1754-1820)

Born at Nantes, Fouché was originally destined for the Church. He joined the Oratorian Order in 1779, but resolutely declined to take the vows of the Order or to be ordained. Then in 1792 he abandoned his clerical dress and was elected to the National Convention. Thereafter he switched from being a conservative to a radical politician, and in doing so he acquired great powers, not only as Minister of Police, but as a spymaster extraordinary who created a nation-wide network of agents. Napoleon dismissed him from office in 1802 on the grounds that Fouché had become too powerful and had exceeded his rights. He was a Jacobin who had used the Revolution to ensure his own future, and in doing so had made himself one of the richest men in France. Balzac said of him that he was a 'remarkable genius who inspired in Napoleon something closely akin to terror ... an obscure member of the National Convention, one of the most exceptional men of his day and one of the most misconstrued, he was moulded in the storms that were then raging'.

In 1804 Napoleon reinstated Fouché, realizing that the security of the realm called for someone with Fouché's peculiar qualities. Fouché's aim then became to maintain himself not merely as the sole arbiter of the French Secret Service, but to make that service so efficient and indispensable that he would become indispensable. Napoleon became a hero of the Irish revolutionaries of that era and Fouché was not slow in recruiting them to his own ranks. His police service, while showing great foresight in carrying France through periods of intense internal struggles, also extended its tentacles to other countries. His downfall came about when he decided by shrewd analysis of his intelligence that no good purpose could be served in continuing any hostilities with Britain. To aim for peace and understanding with that country he used secret intermediaries in other countries, including Holland. Napoleon was furious, even though his Empress and others pleaded Fouché's cause. He regarded Fouché as being almost a British agent, and dismissed him from office. But before he left his ministry Fouché removed a vast number of documents and the names and addresses of many agents. As a result he was banished and died in exile in Trieste.

Further reading
Etude sur Fouché by Martel (1873-9)
Memoires de Fouché 1824, English translation, new edition, 1892)

FRANKLIN, BENJAMIN (1706-1790)

The idea of the Presbyterian moralist, Benjamin Franklin, being a secret agent of any kind, let alone a British agent, is one which many historians still steadfastly refute. Yet research of existing papers and dispatches shows that in an attempt to cover his tracks as a British agent Franklin sometimes signed himself as Jackson, Johnson, Nicholson and Watson, and that during the time he was American Ambassador to France, the British Secret Service referred to him as 'Agent Number Seventy-Two'. Yet this was the man who not only helped to frame the American Declaration of Independence from the British, but who had denounced the corruption of the British ruling class and said that any attempt at closer union between the colonies and the United Kingdom would be 'coupling the living and the dead'.

Considering his prejudices, it comes as a surprise that Franklin was a member of the bizarre secret society known as the Hell-Fire Club, which met in caves beneath the hill upon which was built West Wycombe Church in Buckinghamshire. The male members of the club were known as 'monks' and wore habits of various colours; the females were called 'nuns' and wore white habits and masks to protect their anonymity. The founder of the club was Sir Francis Dashwood (later Lord Despencer, and Chancellor of the Exchequer), and among its members were John Wilkes, Lord Sandwich and Lord Bute, the Prime Minister. Franklin was known as 'Brother Benjamin of Cookham', and his name appears in the society's wine books. From his headquarters in Passy, Franklin wrote to statesmen, diplomats and business partners in England. Many of those who worked in Franklin's offices and house in Passy were active members of the British Secret Service. Arthur Lee, one time American representative in London, caustically commented that no precautions were taken in Franklin's Paris Embassy to guard secrets. Inside this Embassy was a cell of British Intelligence organized by Edward Bancroft, Franklin's friend and chief assistant, who passed all the information he obtained from his master straight to London. Not only did Whitehall learn all the American secrets, but many items of French intelligence as well, for the French trusted Franklin and gave him a great deal of information.

What these leakages ensured, and what Franklin's undercover dealings with the British underlined, was that his standing with London remained high and that, in the event of the Colonies failing to win the war, his influence with the British would be considerable. Among the papers of John Norris of Hughenden

Manor, there is this enigmatic comment: '3rd June 1778. Did this day Heliograph Intelligence from Dr Franklin in Paris to Wycombe.' Norris had built a 100-foot tower on a hill at Camberley in Surrey, from the top of which he used to signal and place bets by heliograph with Lord Despencer at West Wycombe. Other agents of the British at this time were Paul Wentworth, American-born and a former agent for New Hampshire, and Silas Deane of Connecticut, a close friend of Franklin. Copies of most of Franklin's reports sent from Passy to America during the War of Independence are today in the British archives and many of these must have been sent to London by Bancroft, under the code-name of Edward Edwards, with the knowledge of Franklin.

In 1777 the Honourable William Eden (see *Auckland, Lord*, Part II), who had directed the British Secret Service, authorized Paul Wentworth to pass on to Franklin the news that, without prejudice to past events, any American who could establish an accord between Britain and the Colonies could expect as his right any reward he desired. Though he would not commit himself irrevocably to the British cause, Franklin continued to aid London with information. On 11 July 1782 Richard Oswald was writing from Paris to Lord Shelburne in London, saying, '... I really believe the Doctor [Franklin] sincerely wishes for a speedy settlement and that after the loss of dependence we may lose no more, but on the contrary that a cordial reconciliation may take place over all that country. I was pleased at his shewing me a State of the Aids they had received from France, as it looked as if it was the only foundation of the ties France had over them ... which the Doctor owned in so many words.' In another memorandum he referred to a tip-off from Franklin 'of an alliance with Spain. This information ... communicated, also, and most likely, with the same good intentions as on former occasions'.

It should be remembered that Franklin's mission to France was to win that nation as an ally against Britain. Yet in the early years in Paris he expressed doubts about the wisdom of this policy. John Vardill, a loyalist clergyman who was a British spy in London, revealed in correspondence with Joseph Hynson that Franklin passed on to London information about sailing dates, shipments and supplies to America and details of cargoes. (The letters are in the British Library in London.) This act caused great losses to American ships and cargoes. Franklin's aim seems to have been to have a friend in every camp – an aim that paid off. At the time of the peace negotiations, John Quincy Adams, who eventually became second President of the USA, seems to have been convinced Franklin was playing a double-game with the British. Adams saw in these negotiations that 'Franklin's cunning will be to divide us; to this end he will provoke, he will insinuate, he will intrigue, he will manoeuvre'.

Further reading
'*The Origin of the Franklin-Lee Imbroglio*' (North Carolina Historical Review XV, 1938)
The Papers of Benjamin Franklin (11 volumes) ed. Leonard W. Labaree, 1959-69
Franklin Papers (APSL XIX, 22) papers in the Public Record Office, London; Correspondence of John Vardill to Joseph Hynson (British Museum, Add Mss 1505, f.3)

FUKUSHIMA, MAJOR-GENERAL BARON (1858-1919)

Born at Matsumoto in Shinano province to a *samurai* family, Fukushima started life as a drummer-boy, then studied at Tokyo University and spent a year in the Japanese Judicial Department. His quick mind and nimble wit caused him to be transferred to the General Staff in 1875. The following year he visited the United States and, on his return home, he was commissioned as a lieutenant in the Army. During the next few years he travelled extensively in Mongolia, India and China where he was military attaché from 1882-84. In 1887 he was pomoted to the rank of major and appointed military attaché in Berlin, where he was immensely popular. One day he happened to mention to some German officers that his own horse was capable of taking him all the way from Berlin to Vladivostock. They laughed and said it was impossible and challenged him to carry out this exploit which would cover all of 9000 miles. They never expected him to accept the challenge but he did, obtaining permission from his superiors to do so. In 1892 this gallant Japanese officer set off on his journey across two continents, but it now seems that Fukushima indulged in this escapade to obtain intelligence on Russia.

When General Sir Ian Hamilton led the British military mission attached to the First Japanese Army, Fukushima was a major-general and Hamilton regarded him as 'a very able director of intelligence and obtainer of information' when they first met in 1904. In the period leading up to the Russo-Japanese War Fukushima extended intelligence-gathering to Manchuria, Korea and Mongolia and regarded the Japanese prostitute as a vital asset in all this. He even composed a poem entitled 'From Fallen Petal to Rising Star' in which he told how a prostitute became a noble patriot. He was so highly regarded after the Russo-Japanese War that in 1912 he was given a rank equivalent to that of a Governor-General in the Kwantung province of China.

GAPON, FATHER G.A.

The priest Gapon was recruited into the Russian Secret Service by Manassyevitch-Manuiloff, one of the astutest of all Tsarist intelligence chiefs. It was Gapon who, crucifix in hand, had led the crowds to the Winter Palace on 'Bloody Sunday' in 1905. He escaped the soldiers' bullets that day and became a popular hero for a while. However, adulation went to his head and, after joining the Social Democrats, he broke with them because they would not make him their leader. Meanwhile the man who had been revered as a priest on the side of the people descended to the depths of debauchery, whiling away his nights in disreputable clubs and drinking with prostitutes. It was then that he was persuaded to work for the *Ochrana*. Ratchkovsky, head of the *Ochrana* and an astute psychologist, even hinted to Gapon that he might become his successor. But Gapon became greedy; he demanded too much, and though his demands were met, doubts were expressed about him. Eventually underground revolutionaries learned of Gapon's treachery and they lured him to a lonely villa outside St Petersburg where they hanged him with a clothes rope on a rafter.

GENGHIS KHAN (1162-1227)

When Genghis Khan launched his invasion of Russia, he was an obscure Mongol chieftain living with his tribesmen among his flocks and herds, but he organized a system of intelligence to discover the weak points of each of his opponents in succession. The methods adopted were to send out scouts to tribes not yet conquered and to pose as deserters from the ranks of Genghis Khan, laying false trails of information. These scouts would return in due course, having obtained detailed intelligence about the terrain they visited and the state of its defences. Subutai, the most formidable of Genghis Khan's generals, was one of the first to claim that wars were won on the strength of espionage. In order to obtain intelligence swiftly, Khan used a relay system of fast riders who could return detailed news within twenty-four to thirty-six hours. It was from their Mongol conquerors that Russia first learned the arts of infiltration.

Further reading
The Mongols: A History by Jeremiah Curtin (Little, Brown & Co., Boston 1908)

GEORGI, JOSEF (1879-1953)

Born Josef Vissarionovich Dzhugashvili, Josef Georgi eventually became the Soviet dictator, Josef Stalin. As a young man he worked as a double-agent for the *Ochrana* (the Tsar's secret service) and the Bolshevik underground intelligence. It is known for certain that he was in Switzerland in 1909, operating for the *Ochrana*. It is also known that a person named Georgi attended a revolutionary congress held in London in 1907. In 1910 he frequented the Continental Café in Little Newport Street, in the Soho area of London. This was only a short walk from the Communist Club in Charlotte Street where Georgi was a regular visitor. It was alleged at the time that he was leader of a group who were keeping a watch on the mystery figure of the Siege of Sidney Street, later known as 'Peter the Painter'.

GERSON, CAPTAIN VASSILY VASSILIJEVICH

In World War I, when the Russians were lacking intelligence on Austrian Army moves, Gerson carved himself a place in espionage history by volunteering to go to a medical unit at the front in Galicia, disguised as a nun. For five months he learned a great deal of valuable information from Austrians passing through the unit and sent it back to Russia. The Austrians began to suspect a leakage of intelligence and sent an officer into the medical unit to make inquiries. He was told that the most beloved and hard-working nun in the camp was Sister St Innocent. Despite protests from the Mother Superior, he ordered the sister to strip and thus discovered Captain Gerson of the Russian Imperial Army. Gerson was executed as a spy.

GOLTZ, HORST VON DER

In November 1914 the Germans sent to Britain a replacement for the unfortunate spy, Carl Hans Lody, who had been caught. Von der Goltz was given an American passport in the name of Bridgman Taylor. He immediately presented himself at the British Foreign Office and offered to supply information about projected German air raids, the source from which the German naval vessel *Emden* obtained her information about British ships she raided on the high seas, and how Germany got her coal supplies. The Foreign Office sent Goltz to Sir Basil Thomson, head of the Special Branch, who was unimpressed and found him 'thoroughly unconvincing'. At the end of intensive interrogation von der Goltz confessed to Thomson that he had left valuable papers in a safe deposit box in Holland. Three days later British Intelligence got hold of the papers and found they were of no importance. Convinced he was a spy, but with insufficient evidence to convict, Thomson had von der Goltz charged with failing to register with the police and he was sentenced to six months' imprisonment and recommended for deportation. Eventually Thomson acquired sufficient evidence to tackle von der Goltz once again, and this time he got a complete confession that the suspected spy was a German who had been a mercenary in the Mexican Army and had later been employed by the Germans in dynamite operations in the USA.

GRANT OF BLAIRFINDY, COLONEL

The exact identity of this member of the Grant of Blairfindy family remains something of a mystery, maybe because he was disowned by his relatives. However, it would seem that he was also known as Baron Grant and that he was a nephew of Alexander Grant (1723-91) who went to France from Scotland and married the Countess de Ancelet. In 1767 Lord Chatham organized the theft of French military plans for an invasion of England. The French had made a very detailed survey of the English south coast and had been assisted in doing so by Colonel Grant, who had become a secret agent of France. He had revealed to the French the exact number of landing places which would be available to their troops. Once they had landed the French forces were to rendezvous inland and march in two columns on London. In the estimate of this over-optimistic agent '4000 French grenadiers could beat all the militia of England'. The reports of the French spies and surveyors of the English coasts are now in the Public Record Office in London.

GRANT, LIEUTENANT-COLONEL COLQUHOUN (1780-1829)

During the Pensinsular War the Duke of Wellington insisted on giving a high priority to intelligence-gathering, claiming afterwards with considerable truth that 'I knew everything the enemy was doing and planning to do'. Much of his intelligence was obtained cheaply, a great deal of it at no cost at all, for the Spanish peasants, who loathed the French, voluntarily brought in information, sometimes even intercepting French dispatches. Help was also obtained from the priests. Wellington's most trusted intelligence officer in the Peninsula was Major Colquhoun Grant, who had a network of spies which even included some town mayors. When captured by the French near Sabugal in 1812 and threatened with death, Grant remained cool and resourceful, even managing to smuggle out items of intelligence when he was in confinement. Later, when sent to France under escort, he escaped, secured an American passport and sent Wellington reports on Napoleon's plan for his Russian campaign. Eventually he escaped to England in a fishing boat. Wellington was so impressed with his services that he made him a colonel and gave him the task of heading his whole Intelligence Service. However, after the fall of Napoleon, when cuts were made in British military spending, Grant was one of those relegated to half-pay.

Further reading
The First Respectable Spy (Colquhoun Grant) by Jock Haswell (London 1969)

GRAVES, DR ARMGAARD KARL

As far as both the British and the Germans are concerned, Dr Graves must go down as one of the most disasatrously useless spies in history. He boasted that he knew how to find his way around the port and harbour areas of Scotland, but the amateurish fashion in which he set about spying in Edinburgh, posing as a Dutchman, soon aroused attention. He was arrested and in his room were found a code from Amsterdam, photographs of the naval base at Rosyth and specially drawn maps. Graves was sentenced to eighteen months' imprisonment in 1912, but within four months he was released on special instructions from Sir Vernon Kell (q.v.) chief of MI5, and given a free passage to the USA. This was one of Kell's few gambles which did not come off. He had learned that Graves' boss, Gustav Steinhauer (q.v.), did not put too much trust in his employee and had, in fact, decided to liquidate him. While in prison, however, Graves had sought interviews with officers of MI5, claiming that if he was set free he would be prepared to work as a double-agent. All he asked for was a free passage and some cash. His suggestion was acted upon, but Graves never had any intention of working for the British and sent them no reports from America. Instead he spent his time writing a book entitled *The Secrets of the German War Office.* It was published just before war broke out in 1914 and had quite considerable sales. Unfortunately for Kell, newspaper inquiries about Graves in 1913 raised the question as to when he was due to leave prison. There was a question in the House of Commons and the Home Secretary had to parry it with a deliberate piece of disinformation – that Graves had been moved from his cell because he was in a poor state of health.

HALL, ADMIRAL SIR REGINALD (1870-1943)

It was Admiral Hall, far more than any other British Intelligence chief, who struck terror into the hearts of the Germans and alarmed intelligence services around the world. The legend of 'Blinker' Hall lived on long after he had ceased work and even after his death, for he was one of the most formidable, devious and ruthless intelligence chiefs ever. The son of Captain William Hall, first head of the Naval Intelligence Division of the Royal Navy, 'Blinker' Hall became head of the NID in November 1914. He was able to reap results from the deciphering system set up by his predecessor, Captain (later Admiral Sir Henry) Oliver. Hall built up a team of civilians to help with deciphering, including Thomas Inskip (later to be Lord Chancellor), A.J. Alan, the short-story writer, and Sir Philip Wilbraham, a Fellow of All Souls. At the same time he set up the Code and Cipher School, which proved invaluable in coping with the long backlog of undeciphered messages.

The phrase NID was hardly used by those in the know – it was always 'Room 40' or '40 OB', the OB referring to the Old Building of the Admiralty. Hall had a genius for talent-spotting among civilians, so there was an incongruous assortment of individuals in the NID during his time – academics, a director of the Bank of England, a famous music critic, a well-known actor, a publisher, an art expert, a world-famous dress designer and a Roman Catholic priest. Whenever a German vessel sank in relatively shallow waters, Hall insisted that dredging should be carried out to see if any signal- or code-books could be located. Von Rintelen, the ace German spy eventually caught by the British, was astonished to find that Admiral Hall had full knowledge of all the various routes the Germans used for sending telegrams to America: 'There were five such routes, but none of them in the end was secret, and they all led to Admiral Hall,' declared von Rintelen (q.v.).

'Hall is one genius that the war has developed,' wrote Dr Page, the US Ambassador in London, to President Wilson. 'Neither in fiction nor in fact can you find any such man to match him ... All other secret service men are amateurs by comparison.' Often Hall was better informed than the British Foreign Office or the Secret Service. Had he got his way earlier in the war when he received information from a Turkish agent that the Muslim faithful were praying for the arrival of the British, his plan for paying £500,000 for the surrender of the Dardanelles might have succeeded and the war been shortened. But neither the Admiralty nor the War Cabinet cooperated.

Hall's supreme success, and the one move which brought the United States into the war, was his handling of the Zimmermann telegram affair. Partly as a result of the work of one of his agents, Alexander Szek (q.v.) and a Dutchman named Kraft whom he sent to Mexico City, plus two NID cryptographers, Nigel de Grey and the Reverend William Montgomery, Hall intercepted a message from Arthur Zimmermann, the German Foreign Minister, to his Ambassador in Washington, indicating that the Germans proposed to introduce unrestricted submarine warfare. The message claimed that they would try to keep America neutral, adding 'if we should succeed in doing so, we propose an alliance with Mexico'. The rest of the message suggested that, if necessary, Germany and Mexico would make war together and enable Mexico to reconquer lost territories in Texas, New Mexico and Arizona. Hall showed the telegram to Balfour, the British Foreign Secretary, who wisely decided to take no action himself, but to give Hall a free hand. The

Americans were eventually convinced of the genuineness of the message by Hall's explanation of how it had been deciphered. He was never given the honours he so richly deserved after the war. In 1919 he was elected Conservative Member of Parliament for the Liverpool constituency of West Derby, a seat he lost four years later.

Further reading
The Eyes of the Navy by Admiral Sir William James (Methuen, London 1955)

HENDERSON, LIEUTENANT-GENERAL SIR DAVID (1862-1921)

In the Boer War Colonel David Henderson helped to create a Field Intelligence Department in which new techniques for acquiring intelligence were evolved: pigeons for swift communication, balloons for observation, and the development of signals intelligence by sending signalmen to read Boer heliographs. Though this department was disbanded when war ended, Henderson produced a military intelligence manual in 1904 (see below). He urged that a permanent Intelligence Department should be set up, ready to operate in the event of war. Nothing was done officially, but a Captain Macdonagh (later General Macdonagh) started to compile a list of suitable men to staff an Intelligence Corps if war broke out. Henderson played a notable role in paving the way for the creation of an Intelligence Corps in the British Army.

Further reading
Field Intelligence, Its Principles and Practice by David Henderson (London 1904)

KALEDIN, COLONEL VIKTOR

Serving as a member of the Russian Military Intelligence in World War I, Kaledin was known as Agent K 14 of the Seventh Section of the General Staff, but he was also a double-agent. His own blunt statement on the role he filled was: 'I became part and parcel of two select corps known as the *Kontrrazviedka Generalnago Schtaba* (Russian) and the *Nachrichtendienst* (German) with two secret ciphers.' He was a cool, dispassionate operator who worked for financial gain. While nominally serving the Russians, he was selling secrets to Austro-Hungary and Germany. In addition he set up a secret section of the German spy network at various addresses around St Petersburg from which intelligence was passed back to Germany through Heinrich Schtaub, a German parachute spy who landed several times behind the enemy lines. Kaledin survived to tell his own story much later. His treachery was one of the reasons for Dzerzhinsky's ruthless purges of the Intelligence Services after the revolution.

KAMARILLA, THE

During the Habsburg empire in the eighteenth and nineteenth centuries Austria established the *Kamarilla* as a national security council with a network of spies. The Emperor Joseph II (1741-90) brought to Vienna ideas he had adopted from those of Frederick II of Prussia. He moulded these Prussian ideas into the new agency along with other techniques borrowed from the espionage networks of the city states of Venice and Florence.

Only top level political and military administrators of the Habsburg empire were appointed as members of the *Kamarilla*. They alone had access to the highly classified secret intelligence summaries which had been prepared either by the supreme chancellors of state, or by the police minister. Joseph II developed a complex but all-pervasive police system to observe the calibre and work of his officials through his Minister of the

Interior, who was also a member of the *Kamarilla*. He had direct access to the Emperor. It was not, of course, the first occasion that a government in the eighteenth century had set up a secret police network, but the Emperor's new system was the first of the modern age in its penetration of all classes of the community.

The *Kamarilla* was primarily created to exercise surveillance of the armed forces and bureaucrats, rather than to monitor court intrigue or revolutionaries. This organization reached its peak of efficiency when Chancellor Metternich was in power and lasted until the 1860s when the repression of Hungary by the Austrians became less severe.

The executive body of the *Kamarilla*'s secret intelligence-gathering was the '*Haute Police*', the political section of the Police Ministry. Numerous secret protocols of the meetings of the *Kamarilla* kept in the Vienna archives reveal the importance of the spy networks and show how Joseph II introduced the collection of public opinion intelligence. Most of these reports came from the Hungarian, Italian and Polish provinces of the empire. Count Sedlnitzky was an enthusiastic, diligent and talented collector/analyst of such reports during the era of reforms which preceded the stormy years of 1848-49, while Chancellor Metternich had himself organized his own notorious network of spies who penetrated the postal services for the illegal opening of private mail. The recruitment of postal spies had been achieved mainly by bribing the higher officials working in the offices of the Imperial and Royal Post Office. By this means the Chancellor was quickly informed on latent or manifest dangers which threatened the security of the Habsburg empire.

By the middle of the nineteenth century Vienna had become an espionage capital of the world. Not only was there an Austrian network which included people from all classes – politicians, servants, coach drivers, porters – but the French and the Russians maintained their own espionage services inside Austria.

KELL, MAJOR-GENERAL SIR VERNON (1873-1942)

His mother being the daughter of a Polish count, Vernon Kell grew up with a wide circle of friends throughout Europe, and as a boy learned to speak French, German, Italian and Polish. He made full use of his linguistic talents in the Army when, as a captain in the South Staffordshire regiment, he studied Russian in Russia and Chinese in China, passing his examinations as an interpreter in each language. He saw service in the Boxer Rebellion in China and had been Intelligence Officer on General Lorne Campbell's staff in Tientsin. Ill-health interrupted his military career and, four years after being made a staff captain in the German section of the War Office in 1902, he was retired from the Army, but given the job of organizing from scratch MO5, which later became MI5. A lesser man than Kell might have lost heart in the first six months of this job. He was told to keep expenses down and, when he asked for a clerk, there were immediate protests. Eventually he was given one assistant and gradually he produced a mass of impressive reports which showed that Britain urgently needed a strong counter-espionage unit.

Kell's greatest initial success was in winning the cooperation of the police and working effectively with Scotland Yard. He frequently travelled to distant parts of the country to make personal investigations. Quickly he discovered that the biggest obstacle to spy-catching was the outdated Official Secrets Act. He pointed out to the War Office that in case after case Germans had been found gathering information about ships, factories and harbours, but that nothing could be done to check this because in law the spies were committing no offence. Vigorously he pressed for changes in the law, which ultimately were made. He also applied to the Home Secretary for permission to intercept the mail of suspected German spies, and it was as a result of this that a barber known as Karl Gustav Ernst living in the Caledonian road was discovered to be acting as a 'post office' for the German espionage machine.

Gradually Kell won his battle to expand MI5, and he began to chalk up some successes. The barber was trapped and caught and in 1911 an officer of the German Hussars was arrested at Plymouth. By the eve of World War I he had found an extensive German spy network in Britain and his staff had been increased to include four officers, one barrister, two investigators and seven clerks. MI5's offices were transferred to the basement of the Little Theatre in John Street, off the Strand. As a result of the hard work put in by this small unit, when war was declared in 1914, twenty-two German spies were rounded up in Britain and arrested within a single day. This meant that for the best part of a year Germany had no effective spy service in Britain. The following year a further seven spies were caught and from then on MI5's future was guaranteed. From 1906 to 1939 Kell remained in charge of the organization, a service record unsurpassed in modern times.

The troubles in Ireland occupied Kell's time in the years immediately after the war. Later the threat of subversion from Soviet sources became the major problem. By the time World War II began, Kell had achieved the rank of Major-General and supervised a staff of nearly 6000. He had not only infiltrated the Communist and Fascist ranks in Britain, but had most effectively penetrated the organization which was handling recruitment for the Spanish Republican Army. The result was that when war broke out again, some 6000 people were rounded up and interned as suspects, though only thirty-five of these were Britons. Early in 1940 Kell was forced to resign owing to ill-health, having carried on indomitably for many years, despite suffering which would have defeated a lesser man.

Further reading
MI5 by John Bulloch (London 1963)

LINCOLN, IGNATZ TIMOTHEUS TREBITSCH (1879-1943)

Born of devout Jewish parents in Hungary, Lincoln's father wanted him to become a rabbi and he was sent to a Jewish seminary in Hamburg. Irked by the fact that students were not allowed to have female companions, he defied the ban and, as a result, broke with his family. He made a trip to England, abandoned his Jewish faith and became an Anglican. Returning to Hamburg, he was received into the Lutheran faith as a trainee for the ministry. Then he went to Canada where he married a girl of German origin and made a name for himself as a preacher. In 1902 his mission was taken over by the Anglican Church and Lincoln was consecrated a deacon by the Bishop of Montreal. Shortly afterwards he sailed for England and in 1902 became a curate at Appledore in Kent. It seems likely that Trebitsch, as he then was, had already become involved in espionage and that religion was merely his cover. His next step was to change his name by deed poll to Trebitsch Lincoln. He then gave up his curacy and obtained a post from Seebohm Rowntree, the cocoa manufacturer and philanthropist, as a research specialist in Europe.

Once he obtained naturalization as a British subject, Lincoln was adopted as Liberal candidate for Darlington in 1909, preaching a fiery left-wing radicalism. Yet as a so-called adviser on oilfields during this period who seemed to be on the verge of success, he speculated and found himself in dire financial straits. At the next general election he could not afford to defend his seat and shortly afterwards he was made bankrupt. Two weeks after World War I broke out he applied for a post as censor of Hungarian and Rumanian mails and was given the job. He was dismissed after only a few months, the official reason being that he wrote indecent comments in the margins of letters addressed to women. However, it was suspected that he might be adding code messages of his own to the letters. Unabashed by his dismissal, Lincoln offered his services to the Naval Intelligence Division. When Admiral Hall, chief of the NID, interviewed him, he produced a fantastic scheme for tempting the German Fleet into the North Sea, which, he claimed, could be implemented if he crossed to Holland and offered his services to the Germans in Rotterdam. Hall declined the offer, but Lincoln went to Rotterdam just the same. He visited Gneist, the German Consul, who was known to be an espionage agent, then returned to London and again called on the NID. This time Hall, convinced that Lincoln's offer of help masked an attempt to lure the British Fleet into a trap, called his bluff, told him he was not wanted in this country and that, if he wished to avoid internment, he had better leave on the next ship. Lincoln went to the USA, contacted the German Consulate in New York and for a while was employed writing anti-British articles in the American newspapers, possibly doing more harm this way than by spying, as he played upon the fact that he had been a British MP. Eventually the British asked for his extradition for forgery and other frauds. He was shipped back to the UK in 1916 and sentenced to three years' imprisonment.

After leaving prison Lincoln went to Hungary, the land of his parents, but found the Bela Kun Communist rule uncongenial and promptly moved to Germany. There he offered his services to Count von Bernstorff, and was involved in the notorious Kapp conspiracy which aimed at staging a counter-revolution in Germany, planning to overthrow the conditions of the Versailles Treaty and to use right-wing forces on the one hand and to make a deal with Russia on the other. But the attempted *putsch* ended in ignominy. After this, Lincoln went out to the Far East and made contact with the Chinese Government, claiming to be a Buddhist. From then on he went underground, using the name of Chao Kung, and in return for promises of protection he joined the staff of the pro-British war-lord, Wu Pei-fu, to spy on him for the Chinese government. There are some hints that he was also spying for the Germans in China. Wherever he went there were doubts: was he pro-German, or pro-Bolshevik, or was he now just anti-Westerners? Later he became a Buddhist priest, calling himself Abbot Chao Kung, and it was under this name that he tried to re-enter Britain in 1926, when his eldest son was sentenced to death for murder. He was refused entry.

The following year he was travelling around Europe negotiating a secret £4 million loan to buy munitions for the Chinese government. Soon afterwards the Chinese experienced his treachery when it was learned that he had not only misused their funds, but entered into relations with the Japanese. He was ordered out of Peking in 1927. He ended up with no nationality and wandered from one country to another. The last reports of him were that he was broadcasting Axis propaganda from Tibet in the early years of World War II. In 1943 a Japanese news agency reported his death in Shanghai. But the 'Lincoln Legend' did not easily disappear. In May 1947 Reuter reports appeared in the British press claiming that 'Trebitsch Lincoln is still alive'. It seems that a local journalist in Ceylon had received a letter from Lincoln, bearing a Darjeeling-Bengal postmark. Nothing further was ever heard of him.

LODY, LIEUTENANT CARL HANS (1871-1916)

A German Naval Reserve officer, Lody went to America and married a girl in New York. He knew Britain well, having been a tourist guide for the Hamburg-American shipping line. Just before World War I broke out he had gone to Hamburg on a holiday, and here he was persuaded to become a spy by Colonel Nicolai, head of the German Secret Service. As he had an American accent he was sent to Edinburgh in September 1914 carrying a forged US passport in the name of Charles A. Inglis. Lody was a disastrous choice as an agent, for he bungled everything. When he landed in Scotland he immediately compromised himself by sending a telegram to his contact in Sweden saying, 'Hope we beat these damned Germans soon'. An alert and intelligent postmaster thought it was strange for a neutral to waste money on sending such a cable to another neutral. He alerted the security forces and thereafter Lody's correspondence was watched.

Lody is perhaps best remembered for the rumour he started that a Russian army had landed in Scotland en route to the Western front. The only detail which he omitted, and which later went down in history as one of the great jokes of the war, was that the Russians had landed 'with snow on their boots'. The story of the Russians arriving in Britain was supposed to have originated in a query which a porter made to some Scottish soldiers when their train halted in a small English station. The porter wanted to know where they came from. The soldiers replied 'Ross-shire' and the porter, mistaking their broad accents, though they said Russia. Lody is said to have passed this story on to his contact in Sweden with the result that the Germans failed to win the decisive battle of the Marne in September 1914 because two divisions were withheld to counter

119

the Russian threat to the Channel coast. Lody was shadowed from Edinburgh to London and on to other key cities. MI5 finally tracked him down in Ireland, and he was arrested tried and sentenced to death, being shot at the Tower of London in 1916.

McKENNA, MARTHE (1893-1969)

Here is an example of a spy who turned to writing spy fiction. Born Marthe Cnockaert in Roulers in Belgium, she became a spy for the British when the German armies overran her country in World War I. While working as a nurse at the German military hospital in Roulers, she enticed secrets out of senior German officers, managing to preserve her virtue, 'though often precariously,' she later declared in her book *I Was a Spy*. Relating how churches were rendezvous places for spies in Flanders, she wrote 'no celebration of divine service took place without a Secret Service agent being present'. Eventually she was caught, court-martialled and sentenced to death, but she was rescued by the declaration of armistice while she was in prison. Field-Marshal Earl Haig mentioned her in a dispatch for 'gallant and distinguished services in the field', and Sir Winston Churchill wrote a foreword to *I Was a Spy*. She married a young British officer, Jock McKenna, and wrote several spy novels over a period of twenty years.

Further reading
I Was A Spy, Marthe McKenna (Jarrolds, London, 1953)

MARLOWE, CHRISTOPHER (1564-1593?)

Better known as a poet and playwright, Marlowe began his spying career as a young student from Cambridge. From 1580 onwards Sir Francis Walsingham, as head of the British Secret Service, recruited a number of promising young men from Cambridge, some of them on the advice of John Dee, astrologer to Queen Elizabeth I. There is proof of this from enemy sources, supplied by Father Robert Parsons, a Jesuit agent, who in his reports to the Jesuit headquarters in Rome states, 'at Cambridge I have at length insinuated a certain priest into the very university under the guise of a scholar or a gentleman commoner and have procured from him help from a place not far from town. Within a few months he has sent over to Rheims seven very fit youths.' Here espionage and enemy counter-espionage were inextricably interwoven.

It was some time in 1587 that Marlowe was most active as a secret agent. It seems that he served his country by pretending to be a Catholic sympathizer and was probably one of the 'seven fit youths' who were lured to Rheims by Father Parsons. While there he enjoyed the hospitality of the Duc de Guise, leader of orthodox Catholicism and ally of Philip of Spain. But it is equally clear that he went abroad with the connivance of the English authorities to spy upon Catholic conspirators by posing as one of their allies.

Suddenly, however, Marlowe found himself in serious trouble – why is still not absolutely clear – and he was arrested on 20 May 1593 at the house of Thomas Walsingham, a cousin of Sir Francis. Though released on bail, it looked as though he might have to answer charges which could result in his being sent to the Tower. Ten days later it was alleged that his body had been found after a drunken brawl at a Deptford tavern. Nevertheless some historians have suggested that this was a faked murder and that it had been staged to enable Marlowe to escape to the Continent under a new identity. Some have pursued this theory even further, suggesting that Marlowe wrote all the poems and plays generally attributed to Shakespeare. Certainly it is true that Shakespeare's first publication, *Venus and Adonis*, was dated the first September after Marlowe's supposed death. Though this theory has never been substantiated, there is considerable doubt as to whether Marlowe was killed accidentally in a tavern brawl, or deliberately murdered. Frizer, Marlowe's alleged killer, was given a free pardon and nobody has ever explained satisfactorily what Robert Poley, a known spy in the Secret Service, was doing in an upstairs room at the

Deptford tavern at the time. Poley had been a steward to Lady Sidney, Walsingham's daughter, and was a key figure in the espionage network.

Further reading
Christopher Marlowe by Philip Henderson (Longmans, London 1952)
Christopher Marlowe – A Biography by Dr A.L. Rowse (Macmillan, London 1964)
Shakespeare: Thy Name is Marlowe by David Rhys Williams, Philosophical Library, New York, 1966.

MARVIN, CHARLES

Though this temporary clerk at the British Foreign Office was not a spy, his name deserves a place in history, if only because his actions led to the introduction of Britain's first Official Secrets Act. *The Globe*, a London evening newspaper founded in 1803, was at one time published by a Tory syndicate and supported Disraeli. Later it became an implacable enemy of 'Little Englandism' and caused a sensation in 1878 by publishing the text of the Salisbury-Schuvaloff Anglo-Russian Treaty. Marvin had borrowed a copy of this secret treaty and passed details to *The Globe*. An astonished government was amazed to learn that Marvin could not be prosecuted since the government document had been borrowed rather than stolen, and thus in British law Marvin had committed no crime. It was not until 1889 that the first Official Secrets Act was passed by Parliament; it has since been twice amended.

MASON, A.E.W. (1865-1948)

Alfred Edward Woodley Mason attended Dulwich College and Trinity, Oxford, before embarking on a career as an actor. For some years he toured the provinces, and then took up writing. Substantial earnings from his books, most notably *The Four Feathers*, enabled him to satisfy his zest for travel, and he explored the interior of Morocco at a time when this was still rather dangerous, sailed in quest of small, uninhabited islands in the Mediterranean, and did much Alpine climbing. In addition, he was also a Liberal MP for Coventry from 1906-10. From 1914-18 he served in the Royal Marines, reaching the rank of major, but his principal war work was as a secret agent of the NID. Admiral Hall, chief of the NID, called him 'my star turn', and Admiral Sir William James commented that, although Mason 'used his experiences for several of his novels, the true story of his adventures in Spain, Morocco and Mexico was still unpublished when he died thirty years later. It would have been a prince of thrillers.'

Mason sailed a yacht around the Spanish and Moroccan ports during World War I, obtaining much useful information about German ships and submarines which made use of Spanish facilities by surreptitiously re-fuelling in their ports. In 1915 he went to Morocco to report on the best methods of preventing a revolt among the tribes engineered by the Germans. Admiral James stated that Mason 'sent in a long report of what he found … and recommended that the best way to destroy the German influence was to discover and cut off the channel by which their money was flowing into Morocco. This he proceeded to do himself'.

Perhaps Mason's most important Secret Service mission was one about which few details are available. His biographer, Roger Lancelyn Green, says that it is referred to in Mason's notes as 'Anthrax through Spain'. A report had reached the British SIS that the Germans were aiming to spread an anthrax epidemic on the Western Front among the Allies. Two methods were to be used: first, to inject anthrax germs into mules and, secondly, to infect shaving-brushes which were to be imported for the French Army via Spain and South America. Mason managed to intercept a cargo of shaving-brushes, but there is no information as to what happened to the mules.

In Mexico later in the war Mason emulated Sir Robert Baden-Powell's ruse of posing as a lepidopterist when spying. (It was speculated that Sir Robert originally borrowed this idea from Conan Doyle's villain, Stapleton, in *The Hound of the Baskervilles*. There is no evidence to support this, but Mason afterwards admitted that *he* had got the idea from this book.) Using this disguise, Mason discovered that German wireless officers from the ships interned in the harbour at Vera Cruz were using the wireless station at Ixtapalapa every night. Mason's staff at that time consisted of 'three Mexicans of worth; the first had been a prominent officer of President Madero's private police, the second had been chief of President Huerta's police, and the third was a young fellow with a great charm of manner who held one of the highest positions as a burglar in Mexico'. With the help of this trio he managed to put the wireless station out of action.

Yet, despite these achievements, Mason's activities have never received their full due. His influence in British Secret Service even after World War I was still considerable. It is said that he was entirely responsible for recruiting the head of a powerful smuggling ring operating in Southern Spain. This was Juan March (q.v.) who lived in Majorca and became a millionaire and one of the most influential men in Spain.

MATA HARI (1876-1917)

Of all spies in history, the name of Mata Hari is probably the best known. Born Gertrud Margarete Zelle in Leeuwarden in Holland where her father kept a hat shop, she displayed her liking for an adventurous life when at the age of seventeen she answered a 'lonely hearts' advertisement placed by John MacLeod, thirty-eight-year-old officer from the Dutch East Indies. After their marriage, she returned with him to Java where she became fascinated by Javanese dancing. However, the marriage was unhappy and in 1902 they divorced and Margarete returned to Holland. The alimony her ex-husband was supposed to pay her never materialized and she was penniless. In 1904 she went to Paris where initially she found work in a circus, later becoming an exotic oriental dancer known as Mata Hari. Soon she was in great demand socially and became a courtesan, cultivating men of good class and position in society.

When World War I broke out she was in Berlin where she had made a friend of the chief of police and was consequently engaged as an agent of the German Secret Service. She does not seem to have felt any positive commitment to that side. Despite a liaison with a German intelligence officer in Madrid, she also dallied with the French Secret Service while having a love affair with a Captain Ladoux. However, none of these people really trusted her. She was, in fact, a most incompetent spy and had she heeded the stern warning of Sir Basil Thomson (q.v.) head of the Special Branch at Scotland Yard, she might have saved her life. Her relationships with German agents were reported to Naval Intelligence in London, and when the ship in which she was returning to Holland put in at Falmouth early in 1916, she was removed from it and interrogated. Eventually she was arrested by the French in 1917, charged with espionage and shot by a firing squad on 15 October. Yet the truth was that she had never given the Germans intelligence of any real value. Her sentence of death was totally unexpected and was based more on the need to boost French morale than from any sense of justice. (See *Mata Hari's Daughter*, Part III.)

Further reading
Take Nine Spies by Fitzroy Maclean (London 1978)
Mata Hari, Courtesan and Spy by Thomas Coulson (London 1930)

MAUGHAM, WILLIAM SOMERSET (1874-1965)

Novelist, short-story writer, playwright and man of medicine, Maugham was born in the British Embassy in Paris and, as he himself said, the accident of birth 'enabled me to learn French and English simultaneously ... instilled into me two modes of life'. For seven years he studied medicine, but then decided to become a professional writer. During World War I Maugham joined the Red Cross in France as a dresser, ambulance driver and interpreter. Later he joined the SIS and spent a year in Geneva as a secret agent. In 1917 he was sent to Russia with the task of supporting the Provisional Government against the Bolsheviks, who were then planning to make a separate peace with Germany. In his book, *The Summing Up*, he claimed that the Russian revolution might have been prevented if he had arrived six months earlier.

There is ample evidence in the private papers of Sir William Wiseman (q.v.) in the E.M. House Collection at Yale University Library, that Maugham played a considerable role in espionage in Russia in 1917. He kept letters and lengthy reports from Maugham in which he named the chief German agent in Russia, analysed the political situation and made various suggestions. Among these was an outline plan for 'a Propaganda and Secret Service organization in Russia to combat German influence'. There is also a receipt from Maugham for $21,000. An interesting revelation in Wiseman's papers is that Maugham's cover name was 'Somerville'. Later he used this as a character's code-name in his novel, *Ashenden: or The British Agent*, published in 1928.

NICOLAI, COLONEL WALTHER

After World War I, in which he had been General Staff Officer in charge of the German Secret Service, Nicolai confessed that 'it only gradually dawned on the General Staff how defective the Intelligence Service of the Government actually was ... a very different picture from that which was presented by the Intelligence Service under Bismarck'. Nevertheless, the *Nachrichtendienst*, which he steadily built up, became a formidable instrument in that war. He had a high regard for female agents and stated that 'it was an unusually well-educated woman who knew best how to deal with the agents, even the most difficult and crafty of them'. Nicolai also complained frequently about the poor funding of his intelligence work, comparing it unfavourably with what the Russians were spending. It is clear that German Intelligence had an uphill task throughout this war in competing with its adversaries.

Further reading
The German Secret Service by Colonel Walther Nicolai (translated by George Fenwick)

NINJA, THE

The *Ninja* were a highly skilled team, 'masters of invisibility and deception', who operated as military espionage agents in the feudal era of Japan. The word *Ninja* derives from the word *ninjitsu*, which is defined as the 'art of making oneself invisible'. A *Ninja* was reputed to be able to walk on water, to appear and disappear at will and to obtain intelligence while 'invisible'. It all sounds rather like a combination of James Bond and Batman, but in the twelfth century the *Ninja* were members of the noble or *samurai* class, specially trained to go on spying missions for the Shogunate, and sometimes used by the war lords. The *Ninja* tradition was carried on by families and training started as early as five or six years. Apprentices were taught to walk tightropes, to hang on to the branches of trees for long periods, to swim underwater and to use mechanical flying devices, as well as all manner of tricks and disguises to render themselves invisible.

Further reading
Ninjitsu: the Art of Invisibility by Donn Praeger (Lotus Press, Tokyo 1977)
The Ninja and their Secret Fighting Art by Stephen K. Hayes (Chas E. Tuttle, Tokyo 1981)

OCHRANA, THE

What began as the Russian Secret Police system of Alexander II's reign eventually became the *Ochrana*, the Tsarist Secret Service – a comprehensive, coordinated espionage and counter-espionage organization. Its main fault was extravagance, spending vast sums of money and employing large numbers of agents, many of them mediocre. It obtained results, but often at a disproportionate cost. By the end of the nineteenth century as many as 100,000 people all over Russia had at some time or other been members of the *Ochrana*. Branches were set up in all cities and large communities and it was not long before the *Ochrana* was infiltrated by various secret revolutionary groups.

Lyov Tolstoy has recorded the absurdities of much of the *Ochrana*'s information-gathering. Describing how he was shadowed while visiting St Petersburg in 1897, Tolstoy said he was never left alone by the *Ochrana* the whole time he was in the city. This is confirmed in the *Ochrana* records in which he was listed not as the celebrated writer, but as 'Lieutenant Lyov Nickolaievich, retired'. Other details on his file card included the colour of his hair, his clothes, what type of tobacco he purchased, what he had for lunch, how long he stayed at table, how much his meal cost, where he walked and to whom he raised his hat. Yet in this period, Tolstoy was one of the best known figures in Russia and certainly not indulging in subversive activities. The *Ochrana* was ruthlessly liquidated when the Bolsheviks seized power in 1917-18 and scores of its chief agents were executed summarily.

Further reading
The Ochrana by Aleksy T. Vassilyev (Lippincott, Philadelphia 1930)

OFFICE OF NAVAL INTELLIGENCE

In March 1882 a General Order, signed by William H. Hunt as Secretary of the US Navy, stated: 'An "Office of Intelligence" [ONI] is hereby established in the Bureau of Navigation for the purpose of collecting and recording such naval information as may be useful to the Department in time of war, as well as in peace.' The ONI was the first real Government intelligence agency to function in Washington and it had a five years' start on the British, whose Naval Intelligence Division (NID) was not created until 1887. Its first chief was Lieutenant Theodorus Mason, and the ONI proved its value when the Spanish-American War broke out in 1898. Altogether some 600 people inside the USA were denounced as spies during this war, and most of the intelligence concerning them came from naval sources. A Texan of Spanish descent and a graduate of the military academy, West Point, was employed as an agent by the

ONI and sent to Madrid where he adopted the name of Fernandez del Campo, posing as a wealthy Mexican of Spanish sympathies. The Texan learned details of a 'punitive fleet' which the Spaniards were to send to the Philippines to destroy an American cruiser squadron. The agent speedily left Spain for Tangier and here passed on his information to the ONI. It was to the credit of the ONI that the identity of the agent was kept a secret throughout a long and hazardous operation. Yet even as late as 1913 the ONI was still a very small office, having eight officers and as many clerks, and only seven naval attachés with two assistants covering eleven capitals.

Further reading
The First Sixty Years of the Office of Naval Intelligence by J.R. Green (American University Library, Washington D.C.]

OPRICHNIKI, THE

The forerunners of the *Ochrana* and the *Cheka* were the *Oprichniki*, or Secret Police, established by the Tsar Ivan IV, more usually known as Ivan 'the Terrible'. He was an absolute and ruthless despot who regarded the princes and land-owning aristocracy known as the *boyars* as his enemies. To destroy their influence and acquire their estates he created the *Oprichniki*, an innocent-sounding name taken from the title given to estates, which in former times had been allotted to widowed princesses. Ivan used the *Oprichniki* to carry out his policy of *Oprichnina* which involved spying on the *boyars* and winning over the commercial classes to the Tsar's side so that he could control the nation's trade. As a result, many *boyars* were listed as traitors and either executed or banished for life to Kazan, and their property confiscated. Eventually the obsessively suspicious Tsar began to find serious fault with the *Oprichniki*, accusing some of them with treachery. In due course the whole organization was disbanded and the *Oprichniki* dispossessed of their estates.

OTTOMAN EMPIRE AND TURKEY

The espionage services of the central and regional Ottoman rulers and their military commanders were superior to those of their Christian contemporaries in South-East and Central Europe. According to military scholars, this superiority manifested itself in successful campaigns which surprised ill-prepared enemies, in the administration of occupied territories and in the management of diplomatic relations with those countries which were not occupied by the Turks.

Between the late fourteenth and early seventeenth centuries the spy services of the Ottoman Empire were based largely in Constantinople with direct links to the Sultans. Teams of court spy-masters to the Sultans included not only Turks, but foreigners (including religious converts to the Muslim faith), who offered their services for good salaries or privileges. The various ethnic groups living in those parts of South-East and Central Europe which were occupied by the Turks for centuries played an important part in the organization of these extensive spy networks. For example, the court of Vienna was penetrated by the Turkish secret service over a long period. Much emphasis was placed upon what the Turks called 'intelligence on the sentiments and frame of mind' of the Christian armies, and they also spread 'disinformation', as well as using double spies. Merchants, traders, herdsmen and farmers were recruited as 'irregular spies' who provided their services solely for favours or small financial returns. To be multilingual, educated and intelligent were basic requirements for becoming an 'irregular' or professional spy working for the Ottoman in this period. A spy-master was known as a *Kapudshik*, and a *Chauss* was the old Turkish term for the spy-master employed in the regional residence of the Sultans' administrator of occupied lands.

In the latter part of the nineteenth century, the interrogators of the Turkish Secret Service became notorious for brutality and torture. This was largely due to an organized Macedonian revolt against Turkish occupation and control which led to the creation of the International Macedonian Revolutionary Organization

(IMRO). Later, in the Balkan Wars of 1912-13, the Turks became one of the earliest powers to use 'air-spies', engaging Lieutenant Bert Hall, an American pioneer in the field of aviation. The Turks paid him $100 a day in gold solely to obtain intelligence from the air. Later he worked for Turkey's enemy, Bulgaria. When the Bulgars ceased paying him, he decided to quit and was immediately arrested as an enemy spy.

In World War I Turkish intelligence was often better than that of the Allies. For example, according to US Ambassador Henry Morgenthau, the Allies found out too late in the day that the Turkish Government was so convinced that the Anglo-French Mediterranean Fleet under Admiral de Roebeck would capture Constantinople that they made plans to evacuate to Asia Minor. Meanwhile Turkey was saved because de Roebeck's fleet steamed away from the area, as intelligence had not informed them how weak the shore defences really were.

Further reading
The German Secret Service by Colonel Walther Nicolai

PINKERTON, ALLAN (1819-1884)

Born in Glasgow, Allan Pinkerton became a Chartist for a brief period before going to the USA and settling in Chicago where he founded Pinkerton's National Detective Agency in 1850. Samuel M. Felton of the Philadelphia, Wilmington & Baltimore Railroad, asked Pinkerton to bring a number of his operatives to act as the company's private counter-spies against secessionist plotters in Maryland who threatened to sabotage the railroads. Pinkerton not only carried out this assignment successfully, but thwarted a plot by the secessionists to assassinate newly-elected President Abraham Lincoln. As a direct result of this Pinkerton was asked to organize the secret service division of the national army in Virginia in 1861, or what became known as the Federal Secret Service. But while Pinkerton was an excellent detective, he had little if any competence in assessing, or even acquiring, military intelligence. Partly as a result of this, one of his chief agents, Timothy Webster, was caught and hanged by the Confederates. When the Civil War ended Pinkerton's time was devoted to tackling both the Molly Maguires (criminals masquerading as champions of the underdog), and the Ku Klux Klan.

Further reading
The Molly Maguires and the Detectives by Allan Pinkerton
Thirty Years a Detective by Allan Pinkerton
Spy of the Rebellion by Allan Pinkerton (New York, 1883)

REDL, COLONEL ALFRED VICTOR (1864-1913)

One of fourteen children of a poor railway official in Austria, Redl went to the Lemberg Cadet School at the age of fourteen and from there graduated to the Imperial Austrian Army. He worked his way up the military ladder, compensating for what he lacked in birth and wealth by having an astute mind, a command of several languages and a talent for organization. In 1900 he was appointed head of the *Kundschafts Stelle*, the Austrian espionage and counter-espionage organization which came directly under the orders of the head of the Austrian Secret Service, General Baron von Giesl. Russian spies of the External Agency had been briefed to ascertain the weaknesses of key figures in foreign intelligence services. One of these reported back to St Petersburg that Colonel Redl had a secret passion for boys. Armed with this knowledge, the Russians set out ruthlessly to blackmail him, warned him that they had abundant evidence of his homosexuality and threatened to expose him unless he agreed to work for them. There were, of course, attractive inducements, such as the provision of boys and cash.

St Petersburg's prime interest was in obtaining a full list of every Austrian spy in Russia and complete details of the Austro-Hungarian military code. Redl not only provided the answers, but for good measure gave the Russians details of

Austria's war plans in the event of an attack on Russia. For the last seven years of his service Redl divided his time equally in spying for Russia and Austria. In due course he was appointed Chief of Staff of the 8th Army Corps in Prague. It was not until 1912 that Redl began to arouse suspicion. Then in March 1913 came a surprise clue to his treason. The Austrian secret censors opened two envelopes posted from East Prussia, close to the Russian border, and addressed to 'Opera Ball, Post Restante 13, GPO, Vienna'. They contained banknotes totalling 14,000 Austrian kronen. The letters were resealed and the Austrian Secret Police waited to see who would collect them. It turned out to be Redl. Further investigation revealed the alarming extent of his treachery. While determined to punish him, the authorities were equally determined to keep his treachery a secret. Four senior officers were sent to call on him, to kill him if necessary, but preferably to induce him to kill himself. He was given a revolver and left alone. The master-spy then shot himself in front of a mirror, leaving a note which stated, 'Levity and passion have destroyed me. Pray for me. I pay with my life for my sins.'

The extent of Redl's treason was appalling. His information proved its true value to the Russians when war broke out and they defeated Austria in Galicia in the early part of the war. The Russians had full details of the entire Austrian railway system, their forts and installations, while the military code Redl had provided enabled them to tap all military radio secrets until the code was changed in November 1914. In addition Redl had denounced every Austro-Hungarian spy inside Russia and handed over full details of 'Plan 3', the detailed scheme for action in the event of war against Serbia, to which years of planning had been devoted.

Further reading
The Story of Colonel Redl by George Fenwick FRGS, London; *Take Nine Spies* by Fitzroy Maclean, Weidenfeld & Nicolson, London, 1978.

REILLY, SIDNEY (1874-?)

Born in southern Russia, not far from Odessa, Reilly's original name was Sigmund Georgievich Rosenblum. His mother was Russian of Polish descent and his father apparently a colonel in the Russian Army, with connections at the court of the Tsar. At the age of nineteen he discovered that he was not his father's son at all, but the product of an illicit union between his mother and a Jewish doctor from Vienna. It is not surprising, therefore, that Reilly told different stories about his origins, even to people who thought they knew him well. Many years later, when having his passport endorsed while working for the British, he was asked, 'How comes it, Mr Reilly, that you yourself admitted several times you were born in Odessa?' 'There was a war and I came over to fight for England,' replied Reilly. 'I had to have a British passport and therefore a British birthplace, and you see, from Odessa, it's a long, long way to Tipperary!'

After discovering his true identity Reilly left his family and stowed away on a British ship bound for South America. There followed a variety of jobs as docker, road-mender and plantation worker, but finally he became cook to a British expeditionary party in Brazil, led by Major Fothergill of the British Secret Service. From about 1896 onwards, he was firmly involved in international espionage. At first he was no more than a freelance agent for the British, but shortly before the Russo-Japanese War he turned up in the Far East as a double-agent serving both the British and the Japanese. Suddenly he went off to China and lived in a lamasery for several months, allegedly becoming a Buddhist. Then he returned to Russia and, while still working for the British, is alleged to have started spying for the Tsarist regime. He was certainly being well paid as in 1906 he had a lavish apartment in St Petersburg, a splendid art collection and was a member of the most exclusive club in the city. At this time, of course, Britain and Russia were allies so that this did not mean that he was double-crossing the British. But he had almost certainly double-crossed the Japanese to whom he had previously sold information about Russia.

Reilly frequently acted on his own initiative. For example, when working as a welder in Krupp's arms factory in Germany before World War I, he not only stole plans of the factory, but killed two watchmen in making his getaway. Then he got the job as sole agent in Russia for a firm of German naval ship-builders. By this means he managed to see and copy all blueprints and specifications of the latest German naval construction. These he passed back to Britain. Reilly also had the impudence to point out to the British Secret Service that by taking commissions from the Germans he was patriotically saving the British the cost of paying him a proper salary! At the beginning of World War I he was in the Far East again. Then he went to the USA and bought arms supplies for the Russians. There are grounds for believing that at this time he may have been helping American Intelligence as well, but in 1917 he arrived back in Britain, joined the Royal Flying Corps and was parachuted behind German lines on a number of occasions. Once, disguised as a German, he spent three weeks inside Germany, gathering information about the next planned thrust against the Allies. For all these missions he was decorated with the Military Cross.

However, Reilly's greatest and most daring feats took place after the war during the Bolshevik revolution, when a number of Allied governments were anxious to see an end to the Communist regime in Russia. Partly as a secret agent, but even more dangerously, as an unofficial envoy of the British Government. Reilly was sent to Russia in April 1918. This was a risky business in two ways: it made the Bolsheviks aware of his presence in Russia and it gave Reilly the chance to play his own game as a policy-maker. In retrospect it was a classic blunder, for espionage and politics do not mix. Reilly was forced to go underground. Disguising himself as a Turkish merchant, he began to plot a coup with counter-revolutionaries. He raised funds and began to form his own shadow cabinet, while working out a scheme for having all the Red leaders arrested at a meeting which was to be held in August 1918. If the plot had succeeded, Sidney Reilly might have changed the whole course of history. But all was ruined when a woman tried to assassinate Lenin and the Bolsheviks ordered the arrest of all suspects, uncovering Reilly's plot in the process.

During the next few years Reilly made frequent trips in and out of Russia, sometimes even carrying a pass showing him to be a member of the *Cheka*, the Russian secret police. Then in the 1920s there emerged a strange secret organization known as 'The Trust' (q.v. Part III), apparently backed by anti-Bolshevik Russians living in exile in the USA and Finland, and supposedly supported inside Russia by counter-revolutionaries. Reilly told the British Secret Service that he believed in the authenticity of

'The Trust' and suggested he should make one more trip to Russia. In September 1925 he undertook this last, fatal mission. News came through that he had been shot while trying to cross the border from Finland. After that there was a long silence. Various reports came back to London from individuals who claimed either to have seen Reilly alive, or to have heard he was in prison.

Finally, 'The Trust' was revealed as a bogus organization, which claimed to support counter-revolutionaries, but was actually controlled by the Soviet Secret Service. It is hard to see how so shrewd and experienced a character as Reilly could have been deceived by this. Perhaps he realized the dangers, but thought he could pretend to join the Bolsheviks and then double-cross them in the long run. In June 1966 the journal, *Nedelya*, gave a Russian version of the fate of Sidney Reilly. They admit that he was lured back into Russia by 'The Trust', but claim that he was captured and held in custody, rather than shot at the border. The article stated that on 13 October 1925 Reilly wrote to Dzerzhinsky, head of the *Cheka*, saying he was ready to cooperate and give full information on the British and American Intelligence Services. According to *Nedelya*, Reilly was executed on 5 November 1925. Other reports suggest he was still alive in 1927.

Further reading
Ace of Spies by Robin Bruce Lockhart (Stein & Day, New York 1968)
Memoirs of a British Agent by Sir Robert Bruce Lockhart (New York and London 1933)
Reilly the First Man, (Penguin Books, 1987)

RICHELIEU, CARDINAL ARMAND JEAN DUPLESSIS, DUKE OF (1585-1642)

Born in Paris, Richelieu was consecrated as a bishop of Lucon at the astonishingly early age of twenty-two. Nine years later he was appointed a Minister of State by the Queen-Mother of

France, Marie de Medici, but was driven from office shortly after on the assassination of Concini. In 1622, however, he was made a cardinal and in 1624 he was recalled to State office by King Louis XIII. From that time until his death he virtually ruled France, and was the mastermind of the nation's intelligence service, creating the all-important *Cabinet Noir* (q.v.). His chief adviser and mentor was Father Joseph du Tremblay, who was in effect the director of his secret service.

It could truly be said that Richelieu was a statesman first and a man of the Church second, for he made his judgements almost entirely upon expediency and political nous. Many of his agents were English, for he personally assessed them as being 'fearless, reliable and without bias'. It was Richelieu who ordered the kidnapping of an English agent, Montague, and as a result was able to thwart the schemes of George Villiers, Duke of Buckingham, who had become entranced by the French Queen, as well as implicating himself in the affairs of France. Richelieu used the intelligence he collected for formulating political policies. His secret service gave the monarchy despotic power and his network of spies aimed at snuffing out trouble as early as possible. He also stirred up Gustavus Adolphus to support the Protestant cause in Germany in the Thirty Years War and enabled himself to seize Alsace. He aimed to weaken the power of Spain by encouraging a rebellion in Portugal and another rising in Catalonia.

RINTELEN, CAPTAIN FRANZ VON KLEIST (d. 1949)

An officer of the German Naval Reserve, Rintelen was sent to the USA in World War I with the aim of organizing sabotage, including fomenting strikes, holding up ships and planting bombs aboard them. He spoke perfect English and had already had some experience in naval intelligence, including the dispatch of funds by circuitous routes to German warships in foreign waters. Rintelen's sabotage succeeded remarkably well. Ship fires he started caused heat and water damage to ammunition cargo, making the American shells unreliable in combat and giving them a bad reputation among Allied troops. Rintelen eventually developed other devices, such as the rudder bomb, by which he aimed to destroy ships' steering gear.

American Naval Intelligence took a long time to recognize that sabotage was being planned around its own dockyards and the nation's ports. The ONI was unable to cope with the necessary investigation, so the Navy Department asked the Burns Detective Agency to investigate the theft of plans from the US battleship, *Pennsylvania*. In the end it was British Naval Intelligence which spearheaded the effort to break up the sabotage ring in the USA. Von Rintelen declared that 'my most fanatical helpers were the Irish. They swarmed about the various ports with detonators in their pockets and lost no opportunity of having a smack at an English ship ... they had been told I was connected with Irish Home Rule organizations. I soon had to refrain from employing them, for in their blind hatred of England they had begun to use their bombs in a way we had not intended.'

Admiral Hall, of the NID, ordered the British naval attaché in Washington, Commodore Guy Gaunt, to organize a counter-espionage effort against von Rintelen. Gaunt, a rogue sea-dog in the Elizabethan tradition, had no inhibitions about this assignment. He recruited some Czech agents hostile to the Central Powers and managed to get them jobs inside the Austrian Consulate-General in New York. As a result he secured copies of documents being sent to Berlin and Vienna. Harried by Gaunt's agents and frustrated by hostile colleagues in his own Embassy, Rintelen was ordered to return to Germany. The message telling him to do so was intercepted by the British NID. Rintelen returned in a Holland-America Line ship, posing as E.V. Gache, a Swiss national. He was eventually arrested at Ramsgate and interviewed by Admiral Hall. He was then briefly interned at Donnington Hall before escaping, but was recaptured at Leicester. Hall and Rintelen became great friends, each admiring the other's talents. This friendship continued after World War I and Hall believed that his prestige and sponsorship could clinch Rintelen's application for British nationality. (The German espionage ace did not like life in Germany and despised the Nazis.) But despite Hall's backing (viewed with vigorous disapproval by the Secret Service),

Rintelen's application was turned down and in 1940 he was interned on the Isle of Man. He was practically penniless when released from internment, and he was later found dead in a tube train in London in 1949.

Further reading
The Dark Invader by Franz von Rintelen (London 1933)

ROBERTSON, JAMES

There is little doubt that James Robertson was one of the Duke of Wellington's ablest agents during the Peninsular War, when Wellington was able to boast proudly, 'I knew everything the enemy was doing and planning to do.' Robertson was known as 'Brother James', having spent most of his life in the Scottish Benedictine monastery in Regensburg. He also spoke German fluently. He was recommended by Wellesley (the Duke of Wellington) for secret service in Germany, but actually worked for the Foreign Office, his mission being to visit North Germany and find out what had happened to some 15,000 Spanish troops believed to be stranded in Denmark. The story of how they came to be in Denmark was yet another example of Napoleon's wiles. Before Bonaparte launched his attack on Spain he had cunningly persuaded the Spaniards to dispatch some of their best troops to Denmark, claiming that it was threatened by Britain. Now the Spanish forces, under the Marquis de la Romana, were trapped somewhere in Denmark. The British aim was to enable them to escape by sea.

Robertson went first of all to Heligoland, where the British Secret Service had already set up a listening post and centre for gathering intelligence. From here he was smuggled in a small craft up the mouth of the River Weser into Germany. Assuming the identity of Adam Rohrauer, Robertson learned that the Spanish forces had been split up into small groups to render them ineffective and that they were virtually marooned on various small islands off the Danish coast. Crossing to the island of Funen, Robertson found La Romana, head of the Spanish forces, and passed on the British Government's promise of help. The Foreign Office were highly doubtful about the wisdom of employing a supposedly unworldly monk, but Robertson's resourcefulness carried him through. After many adventures he was able to inform the British Admiral Keates at Heligoland that the Spanish troops could leave within a few days. Some 9000 of the 15,000 troops boarded British ships and were taken back to Spain to play their part in the Duke of Wellington's campaign.

ROMAN REPUBLIC AND EMPIRE

Literary works of Roman military authors, Cato Censorius, Cornelius Celsus, Frontinus, Flavius Vegetius and Julius Caesar, all testify to the fact that there was a systematic use of intelligence and espionage in the ancient Roman Republic and the Empire. Caesar's *Commentarii de bello Gallico* particularly reveals that a well-organized spy network existed in his time, although it did not succeed in preventing his assassination.

While spies were used for safeguarding the lives of the emperors and leading figures, the Romans also had 'double spies', who posed as allies of the enemy, and long-term resident spies in distant territories. The function of a 'political police' with its domestic network of informers and spies began to evolve during the rule of Caesar Augustus. Communications were made secure by the introduction of primitive ciphers. *Exploratores* was the Latin name for the Roman military detachment formed to collect and deliver accurate and timely intelligence on the strength, movements and intentions of an enemy. According to the Roman military author Hyginius, 200 *exploratores* under the command of a *praefecti* or *praeposti* were deployed to those Roman garrisons which were placed in the strategically important and security-sensitive stations of the border areas.

Speculatores performed tasks similar to those of modern spies. They were initially recruited from public and private slaves, and later on from a pool of Roman citizens and warrant officers serving in the legions. During the period of the Caesars, ten *speculatores* were attached to the command staff of each legion as secret intelligence service operators. The *schola speculaturum* was the social club of the *speculatores* where they met to exchange information on their espionage experiences. There were, however, no spy schools, as we understand them today. Julius Caesar employed a personal cipher based on a simple transposition of the alphabet.

SCHRAGMULLER, DR ELSBETH

This remarkable woman, also known as 'Tiger Eyes', was one of the very few spy-mistresses of World War I. In 1913 she had taken her doctorate in philosophy at Freiburg University and, being an ardent patriot with a desire to do something special for her country, she persuaded Colonel Nicolai (q.v.) to give her a post in the *Nachrichtendienst*. After a while he put her in charge of a school for spies in Antwerp where she ruled her pupils with an almost sadistic severity, insisting on their being known only by numbers, wearing masks all the time and on occasions being locked in their rooms. No doubt this gave rise to her nickname. Being a somewhat humourless and unimaginative martinet, she thought that to turn out an efficient spy was simply a matter of training. Two of her pupils, Jenssen and Roos, who were sent to England, were caught and shot. Yet she received high praise from Colonel Nicolai and others.

SILBER, JULES CRAWFORD

One of the very few spies who escaped MI5's vigilance during World War I was this non-professional spy who was painstaking, sober and likeable. Silber, a German national, had spent a great deal of his life in South Africa and Canada, even working for Britain against the Boers. When war broke out in 1914 Silber, who spoke perfect English, offered his services to Britain from Canada. He was accepted and given a job in the postal censorship service, the perfect cover for a spy. He was fond of the British and always felt rather guilty about his work against them. As a censor he was in a position to pass his own outgoing intelligence messages in whatever guise was necessary. He took the precaution (in order to get the right postmark), of sending himself letters from various points in London, using a window envelope. He would open the envelope, insert a new letter with a different address then re-seal it and stamp it with the censor's mark. In this way Silber was able to give German Naval Intelligence the first warning about the use of Q-ships.

He showed initiative of the highest quality for an amateur spy. One day he opened a letter in which a woman had written to say how glad she was to have her brother, a naval officer, stationed in a port near her home. He was, she said, working on some hush-hush project for the Navy about arming merchant ships. This was, in fact, the Q-ship plan. Making an excuse to be away from his duties for a day or two, Silber travelled to see the woman and, posing as a British security officer, warned her that what she had written was a dangerous breach of security regulations. It was also dangerous for her brother who risked being prosecuted and his whole career ruined. If she told him all her brother had written or told her about the Q-ships, then he would consider whether prosecution might be waived. His gamble worked.

Silber was later transferred to Liverpool. He proved himself an invaluable informant and survived the war until the Armistice. He was extremely popular with his colleagues in the censorship department and they gave him a farewell party when he left the service on 27 June 1919, being given a certificate which described him as 'a very able man, a good linguist, thorough and competent and of exemplary conduct'.

Further reading
Invisible Weapons by Jules Crawford Silber

STAFFORD, SIR EDWARD (1552?-1605)

Probably Britain's first important double-agent, Sir Edward Stafford was a relative of Queen Elizabeth I and was appointed Ambassador to France in 1583. He was mistrusted by Sir

Francis Walsingham (q.v.), the Secret Service chief, from the beginning, though in the end was given every benefit of the doubt. The Spaniards were quick to notice that he was short of cash and put him on their pay-roll as a spy. That he provided them with intelligence is clearly proved, although he may have convinced Walsingham that what he obtained from the Spaniards was far more important. Walsingham almost certainly concealed some of Stafford's reports from the Queen, and he sent an agent called Rogers to keep a watch on Stafford in Paris. The reports were damning, but Walsingham believed that if Stafford possessed the confidence of the enemy then they would believe any information which Stafford passed on to them. What could suit Walsingham's purpose better than to feed Stafford with false reports to bewilder the French and Spaniards?

Stafford kept the Spanish King informed of the movements of English ships, but he was never brought to trial and returned to England with his reputation intact. One cannot say for certain that he was an absolute traitor any more than one can say Walsingham was seriously negligent in not having him impeached. If Walsingham was really playing a subtle game, it certainly paid off, for while Stafford told the Spaniards of England's preparations against the Armada, he also reported to Walsingham about the Spanish fleet: 'The Spanish party here [in Paris] brag that within three months Her Majesty will be assailed in her own realm, and that a great army is preparing for it,' he wrote in July 1586.

STALIN, JOSEF (see *Georgi Josef*)

STEINHAUER, GUSTAV

Steinhauer's description of himself in later life as 'the Kaiser's Master Spy' must be dismissed as a gross exaggeration of his talents. If any man could be held responsible for Germany's disastrous attempts to infiltrate Britain with spies in World War

I, Steinhauer was the culprit. His early 'spy' experience was as a private detective with the celebrated Pinkerton Agency in the USA. He started his service with the Germans as an agent of the Political Police under von Tausch, but he had little grasp of military and naval espionage, and his big mistake was to send so many spies into Britain in the early part of the twentieth century. That he succeeded at all was due to the laxity of the British authorities and their pig-headed refusal to take seriously allegations of German espionage on their own territory. But the inefficiency and indifference of the British made the spies careless, and then Steinhauer himself started paying visits to the UK. He visited his agents in such places as Walthamstow, Exeter, Hull and Edinburgh, and slowly the newly-created British counter-espionage service closed in on him and his agents. Just before war broke out in 1914 there were twenty-six German spies in Britain. Soon MI5 had all of them noted and listed, even learning that Steinhauer's real name was Reimers. When war came they were swiftly rounded up. Perhaps the most remarkable story about Steinhauer is that it was not until July 1914, within a month of the outbreak of war, that he realized the Germans had no adequate intelligence on Britain's most northerly naval bases. So, posing as a fisherman, he went to Scapa Flow and, fishing with a knotted line, took soundings of the naval anchorage, and realized that the largest of British battleships could anchor there.

STIEBER, WILHELM (1818-82)

In many ways the Prussian spy, Wilhelm Stieber, revolutionized the whole system of espionage in the nineteenth century. He began his career in the legal profession, specializing in criminal cases, and through his close association with the police turned to espionage. In 1848 when Europe was in the grip of political agitation with foment in France and Karl Marx's brand of socialism in Germany, Stieber came into his own. He introduced to Prussia the technique of *agent provocateur*, using it to uncover and entrap Radicals and working-class supporters of socialism. The story is told how he influenced Friedrich Wilhelm of Prussia by posing as a rabble-rouser in a mob that confronted the King and then managing to get close enough to the monarch to whisper to him that all was well and that he was protecting the King by infiltrating the mob. Whatever the truth of this story, Stieber was soon to become the chief spy-master of Prussia. But this role lasted only as long as Friedrich was on the throne. When Friedrich was pronounced insane and succeeded by Wilhelm I, Stieber was given short shrift. From 1858 until 1863 he was out of work and out of favour. His career seemed to be in ruins.

In 1851, in his capacity as head of the Prussian espionage service, Stieber went to London to investigate the activities of Prussian Radicals, including Karl Marx. He and his investigations were not welcomed by British officialdom. However, Stieber conducted his enquiries and noticed that a number of Russian revolutionaries active in London were unobserved by the authorities. Seven years later Stieber recalled this discovery and consulted the dossiers he had compiled.

He also remembered that he had once done the Russians a good turn by hushing up a scandal involving the wife of a Russian attaché in Berlin. So off he went to St Petersburg to remind the authorities there of his past assistance to a Russian envoy and to give them his dossiers on Russian revolutionaries in London. Though the tactics of *agents provocateurs* were second nature to the Russians, Stieber was able to prove that they could be even more usefully employed outside Russia. Despite their suspicion of foreigners, the Russians were impressed by Stieber's dossiers and, guardedly, asked for his help in reorganizing their secret service. Stieber could hardly have arrived at St Petersburg at a more opportune moment. The Special Corps of the Gendarmerie had been dissolved, the Third Section was in the process of being absorbed into the control of the Ministry of the Interior, and the Tsar was anxious to re-cast the whole Secret Service.

Stieber was not trusted sufficiently to play a part in the formation of the Department of State Protection; nor did he stay long in Russia. His assignment was to advise on and help organize an external spy system which would enable the Russians to track down expatriate revolutionaries, Radicals, criminals and forgers. Stieber remained loyal to Prussia and only passed information to the Russians concerning their own nationals abroad. At the same time he accumulated a good deal of valuable information on Russia which he eventually passed on to Bismarck. His successful work for the Russians impressed the Tsar and ultimately Stieber became the supreme spymaster in Europe under Bismarck. He not only controlled Prussian espionage, but actually went on missions himself. It was said of him that when he went to Austria he took with him a collection of cheap religious statuettes and obscene pictures in order to be prepared for all eventualities.

In 1866 came the Prussian conquest of Austria, a short, sharp campaign more or less determined by Stieber's intelligence. Much later Stieber and a few of his lieutenants spent eighteen months in France, spying, recording, reporting and recruiting – placing spies (including many women) in high places. This gave Prussia and Germany a devastating intelligence lead over the rest of Europe.

SUN TZU (*c.* 510 BC)

To assert with confidence who first started a formal system of espionage would be rash indeed, as the most primitive people have indulged in the craft of spying. But Sun Tzu, the reputed author of *Ping Fa* (*The Principles of War*), which is believed to have been in circulation as early as 510 BC, is certainly a candidate for this honour. This book is the earliest known text-book on espionage and war generally, and on the organization of a secret service particularly. What is even more remarkable is that it is still regarded as a seminal work on the subject and respected even by Mao Tse-tung. *Ping Fa* has been compulsory reading for Chinese generals down the centuries, but it was being studied by the Japanese Army from the late nineteenth century up to the time of Pearl Harbour. An English translation was published during World War II mainly because it was known that the Japanese were basing their tactics on the book.

Sun Tzu was a native of Ch'i state at the mouth of the Yellow River, but he spent most of his life in the service of the neighbouring state of Wu. *Ping Fa* brought him to the attention of Ho Lu, who was King of the state from 514-496 BC, and Sun Tzu was appointed general of all Ho Lu's troops. Sun Tzu defeated the Ch'u state in the west and forced his way into Ying, the capital, while in the north he 'put fear into the states of Ch'i and Chin and spread his face among the feudal princes'. Sun Tzu believed that to wage war economically and to defend the state against others there should be a permanent espionage service spying on both neighbours and enemies. He even defined the various types of spy who should be employed – local spies, internal spies, converted spies and 'condemned spies'. The purpose of the latter was to give false information to the enemy, but their role is defined more accurately by Tu Yu: 'We ostentatiously do things calculated to deceive our own spies, who must be led to believe that they have been unwittingly disclosed. Then, when these spies are captured in the enemy's lines, they will make an entirely false report and the enemy will take measures accordingly, only to find that we do something quite different. The spies will thereupon be put to death.'

Sun Tzu urged that the superior spy be honoured above all others and that he should have 'access to his leader at all times'. He claimed that the enemy's spies must be sought out and 'tempted with bribes, led away and comfortably housed': in this way they would become 'converted spies'. He believed that information brought by the converted spy made it possible to acquire and employ local and inward spies: 'We must tempt the converted spy into our service because it is he who knows which of the local inhabitants are greedy of gain and which of the officials are open to corruption. It is owing to his information again, that we can cause the condemned spy to carry false tidings to the enemy.'

Further reading
The Principles of War by Sun Tzu (Royal Air Force, Colombo 1943)
Sun Tzu on the Art of War by Luzac, (London 1910)
Les Treizes Articles de Sun-tse translated by Fr Joseph Amiot (Paris 1782)

SZEK, ALEXANDER (1894-1917)

Despite the fact that his father was an Austro-Hungarian, Szek was a British subject, being born of an English mother in Sydenham, South London. At an early age Szek became one of the first students of wireless telegraphy. When World War I broke out he was in Brussels and, as wireless operators were scarce, it was not long before the Germans decided to employ him. However, Szek was secretly pro-British and had conveniently acquired dual nationality, so it was not long before he was recruited by Captain Trench of the Royal Marines, who had long been an agent of the NID. Through a combined operation of Britain's NID and the SIS, Szek was asked to obtained a German cipher book. His success in doing so led Britain to one of the greatest espionage triumphs of the war – the interception of the notorious Zimmermann telegram sent by the German Foreign Minister for his ambassador in Washington. It contained the threat of unrestricted submarine warfare, and suggested that a German-Mexican alliance would guarantee German help in returning the US territories of New Mexico, some of Texas and Arizona, to the Mexicans. It was this telegram that led to America entering the war.

When the Germans began to investigate a possible leakage from their Brussels radio station, Szek tipped off the British. Shortly afterwards, Szek left his job and disappeared. According to an SIS source, there was a dispute between the SIS and the NID as to whether Szek should be removed to safety to avoid possible questioning by the Germans, or merely caused to 'disappear', that euphemism which secret services use for wiping out one of their own agents. The truth was revealed in 1981 by Captain Stephen Roskill, the naval historian, in a footnote to his biography of Admiral of the Fleet Earl Beatty. According to Roskill, a hit-man was paid £1000 to kill Szek on the orders of British Naval Intelligence. The order was given to prevent the Germans from discovering that their ciphers had been handed over to the British. Captain Roskill named Admiral of the Fleet Sir Henry Oliver, Chief of War Staff, as the source of this story.

THOMSON, SIR BASIL HOME (1861-1939)

'If the Pharaoh Memptah had been given an efficient intelligence service, there would have been no exodus,' drily remarked Sir Basil Thomson, who was the creator of Britain's Special Branch at Scotland Yard. The son of an Archbishop of York, educated at Eton and Oxford, Thomson started his career as a farming pupil in Canada. After a year he returned to the UK and was nominated for a cadetship in the Colonial Service in the newly acquired colony of Fiji. He had a natural gift for learning languages and was made a magistrate at the end of three months, insteading of having to wait two years like his fellow cadets. At the age of twenty-eight he was made Prime Minister to the King of Tonga. Abruptly summoned home to undertake a most unusual job – the education of the sons of the King of Siam – Thomson qualified as a barrister and was employed by the Home Office, first as a deputy governor in the prison service and then as Governor of Dartmoor Prison. While working under the Home Office he paid particular attention to the anarchist movement in the East End of London, which proved invaluable when he was appointed first head of the Special Branch in 1913.

Though Thomson worked with MI5 both before and after the outbreak of World War II, he also built up his own spy service and even recruited foreign agents. Extremely ambitious, Thomson teamed up with Admiral Hall (q.v.), head of the NID, who sat in on interrogations of all naval prisoners he caught. Thomson was contemptuous of the calibre of German spies, claiming that they were untrained for gathering information of any practical value. He was himself one of the most formidable interrogators of his day. After the war he was concerned with Bolshevik activities in Britain, having held office as Security Officer to the British delegation in Paris for the peace talks. Documents which came into his possession revealed that the Communist International expected revolution in Britain within six months. 'February 1919,' he wrote, 'was the high-water mark of revolutionary danger in Great Britain. Many of the soldiers were impatient at the delay in demobilization. Russia had shown how apparently easy it was for a determined minority to seize the reins of power.'

Thomson was also concerned with the threat of trouble inside the police force. He had little support from the Prime Minister, Lloyd George, in dealing with these matters, and whether he went over his head and raised the matter of disaffection with King George V is a matter of conjecture, but he was summoned to Buckingham Palace for talks. It is believed that it was on Thomson's advice that the King intervened and persuaded Lloyd George to increase soldiers' pay after 3000 troops in London had marched on Whitehall. Not long afterwards Thomson was forced to resign by the Home Secretary. It was an unhappy end to a successful career. In December 1925 he and a young woman named Thelma de Lava were arrested in Hyde Park and summonsed for committing an act in violation of public decency. Thomson pleaded 'not guilty' and said he was carrying out investigations in Hyde Park into reports of soliciting by women with a view to writing articles on this subject. (It was perfectly true that since retirement he had written books and articles on various subjects connected with crime.) Yet he was found guilty and fined £5. There was always a strong suspicion that Thomson was framed.

Further reading
The Scene Changes by Sir Basil Thomson (Gollancz, London 1939)
'*Scotland Yard from within*' by Sir Basil Thomson (*The Times*, 2 December 1921)

THURLOE, JOHN (1616-1668)

Just as Elizabeth I found in Walsingham the intelligence genius which the hour demanded, so did Oliver Cromwell in the person of John Thurloe, a secret service chief who must rank as one of the greatest in English history. A quietly spoken Essex lawyer, Thurloe achieved authority without publicity or fuss, and reorganized intelligence-gathering both inside and outside the country. To be fair, he was given twenty times as much money for his work as Elizabeth gave Walsingham, who often paid for intelligence out of his own pocket. This money enabled him to make the English Secret Service the most efficient in Europe in the space of a few years. It was built up in Thurloe's capacity as Postmaster-General, when he intercepted a vast amount of correspondence, mostly that of Royalists. Soon he set up agents in every court and developed an extensive network of spies at home.

As his Secret Service grew, so Thurloe extended his powers, becoming at one time Secretary of State, Home Secretary, Chief of Police, head of the Secret Service, Foreign Secretary, War Secretary and Councillor of States. In this way Thurloe was able to snuff out almost any plots against the regime. Cardinal Mazarin, himself an adept in the organization of intelligence, frequently confessed himself baffled that French Cabinet secrets inevitably leaked out to Thurloe within a few days. Nor was this an isolated view of the efficiency of the Service. Sagredo, the Venetian Ambassador in London, wrote to the Council of Tens that 'there is no government on earth which divulges its affairs less than England, or is more punctually informed of those of the others'.

Copies of many of the letters Thurloe was sent by his agents still exist. His own instructions to his agents showed that he realized the value of paying for information. To his agent in Leghorn he wrote, 'These people cannot be gained, but by money, but for money they will do anything ... Such intelligence must be procured from a Monsignor, a secretary or a Cardinal ... I should say £1000 a year were well spent ...' Thurloe's ability to divorce his job from his Puritan prejudices stood him in good stead. He was one of the first to appreciate the value of Jews as secret agents and to use their talents in England's favour. Not only did he encourage the migration of Jews to England, but he also obtained the services of the continental correspondents of a Jewish merchant, Antonio Carvajal, and he received valuable American intelligence from his Jewish agents in the West Indies. It was a Jewish agent's information to Thurloe which enabled Admiral Blake to capture the Spanish Plate Fleet at Tenerife.

Thurloe survived Cromwell and his son, Richard, who retained his services. In the end, however, just as Thurloe's men had infiltrated the Royalist ranks, so the latter began to infiltrate the Secret Service. Thurloe survived the restoration of the monarchy, but died in 1668.

Further reading
A History of Diplomacy in the International Development of Europe by D.J. Hill
Secret Diplomacy by H.W. Thomson and S.E. Padover (Jarrolds, London 1937)

VAN LEW, ELIZABETH (1818-1900)

Born in 1818, Elizabeth van Lew was a Southerner who supported the North in the American Civil War. She had long since favoured the abolition of slavery, setting an example by giving freedom to her own family slaves. She lived in Richmond, Virginia, and though some Southerners suspected her lukewarm feelings about the war, few thought that a member of a leading aristocratic family would oppose the cause of the South. Miss van Lew did secretly oppose the war and acted as one of the most effective spies for the North, putting her life and her mother's at risk in doing so. What is more, she spent large sums of her own money to support the cause and built up a network of informants. Her controller was General George H. Sharpe, chief of the Federal Bureau of Military Information, and with his cooperation, she established five secret communications centres between her home and his headquarters. Thus most of the intelligence obtained by the North's army came from her own networks.

In her home was a cunning secret room in which she hid other spies and escaped prisoners-of-war, and even the celebrated Colonel Paul Revere. Yet by neighbours and others in Richmond she was merely regarded as 'loonie Betty', an eccentric to be tolerated. At the end of the war she made a claim for $15,000 which she had spent in developing her spy network, but though General Grant agreed the amount, she never received anything at all. When Grant was President she was made postmistress of Richmond, but later she was demoted to being a mere clerk. She spent her last years in poverty, ostracized by Richmond society because of her wartime espionage, though her Negro servants stayed with her to the end. Her sole income was a pension paid to her by friends and relatives of Paul Revere.

WALSINGHAM, SIR FRANCIS (*c.* 1530-1590)

Walsingham was the first man to create anything resembling an adequate national Secret Service for England. As an assistant to Cecil, the Secretary of State, he had initially been largely concerned with counter-espionage and was always searching for potential enemies on English soil. He arranged with the Lord Mayor of London to have weekly reports on all foreigners who stayed in the city. In 1570 Walsingham was appointed Ambassador to France and it was during this period that he began to build up an Intelligence Service overseas as well as at home. But his Queen was parsimonious in supplying funds for such work, and throughout his life Walsingham was often forced to spend his own money in developing the Service. In 1573 he returned to England and became a member of the Privy Council, as well as Principal Secretary. His duties were set out in some detail and included this important dictum: 'To have care to the intelligence abroad.'

That England had a useful Secret Service at all at this time was due almost entirely to Walsingham's patriotism and enthusiasm. Officially, England spent far less on intelligence-gathering than any other major power in Europe, leading Walsingham to subsidize it and eventually bankrupt himself. It was one of Walsingham's rules that even an English Ambassador overseas must be regarded with suspicion and mistrust until he had proved his integrity. The case of Sir Edward Stafford (q.v.), the first concrete example of a double-agent in British history, revealed something of these temptations. When Stafford was made Ambassador in Paris, the Spaniards were quick to notice he was short of money and put him on their pay-roll.

It took many years before Walsingham was able to build up an effective network overseas. By 1587 he was convinced that Spain was amassing a vast Armada of ships for an attack on England. In the spring he drew up his 'Plot for Intelligence out of Spain', which is still preserved in the State Paper Office. This included the following plans: to obtain some correspondence with the French Ambassador in Spain; to have agents at Nantes, Rouen, Le Havre and Dieppe; to set up an intelligence post in Cracow for receiving reports on Spanish matters coming from the Vatican; to nominate persons to travel along the Spanish coasts and report what preparations were being made; to obtain intelligence from the Court of Spain and from Genoa; to arrange intelligence at Brussels, Leyden and in Denmark.

Gradually this 'Plot for Intelligence' produced results. It was one of Walsingham's maxims that 'if there were no knaves, honest men should hardly come by the truth of any enterprise against them'. Acting on this assumption, Walsingham was daring enough to use rogues and even improbable allies. Two of his most active agents were two young English Catholics, the Standen brothers, who were notorious for their reckless behaviour and constituted something of a security risk. In fact – and this is a tribute to Walsingham's judgement – they were brilliantly successful. Their Catholicism was not the fanatical kind and in no sense checked them from spying on Spain. Walsingham went far beyond being simply a receiver and coordinator of intelligence. On the strength of what he learned he deliberately played for time – a tactic which has always been a vital factor in British Intelligence – and schemed to delay the Armada preparations. Through his influence, bankers in Genoa were persuaded to delay loans to Philip of Spain so that Spanish war funds were effectively controlled by the British Secret Service. If England defeated the Spaniards' attempt to invade, then the credit should largely go to Walsingham. When he died in 1590, a Spanish agent wrote to King Philip of Spain to give him the news: 'Secretary Walsingham has just expired, at which there is much sorrow.' 'There, yes!' wrote the Spanish monarch in a marginal comment on the letter, 'but it is good news here.'

Further reading
Mr Secretary Walsingham and the Policy of Queen Elizabeth (3

volumes) by Conyers Reed (Oxford University Press 1925)
Harleian MSS (British Museum, 6991 no.39; 286, f.122; 6994m
f.76)

WISEMAN, SIR WILLIAM GEORGE EDEN (1885-1962)

Educated at Winchester and Cambridge, Wiseman was officially
appointed as head of the British Purchasing Mission to the USA
in World War I, but in effect he was in control of all Britain's
Secret Service agents in that country, while keeping a close
watch on all German activities from his office in New York. It
was he who persuaded Sidney Reilly (q.v.) to take a more active
part in the war by joining the Royal Canadian Flying Corps,
even though this was simply to be a cover for Secret Service
work. Still alive at the outset of World War II, Wiseman not
only gave his successor, Sir William Stephenson, a great deal of
help, but even indulged in a little espionage himself. The latter
included talks with the Princess Stephanie Hohenlohe-
Waldenberg-Schillingsfurst and Captain Fritz Weidemann, then
Consul-General in San Francisco, on the possibility of a coup of
monarchists and Army officers against the Hitler regime.
Wiseman also gave much sound advice on coordinating
intelligence matters with the Americans.

WOTTON, SIR HENRY (1568-1639)

'An ambassador is an honest man sent to lie abroad for the good
of his own country' was Sir Henry Wotton's comment on his
career. Courtier, diplomat and poet, he achieved as much
success in literature as in diplomacy. It was in 1602 when he
went to Venice that he undertook his first mission in espionage.
Disguised and using the name of Octavio Baldi, he was sent by
the Duke of Tuscany to warn James VI of Scotland of a plot
against him. Wotton was yet another ambassador who built up

his country's secret service more or less single-handed. He was also adept at supplementing his own Secret Service funds by selling confidential information to other friendly countries. He gave the Venetian government intelligence about the Jesuits' activities at the same time that he passed it on to James I. He robbed the posts and stole the Jesuits' correspondence, making a study of the seals used by the Jesuits on their mails and the methods they used for communications.

Further reading
Life and Letters of Sir Henry Wotton by L.P. Smith (Oxford University Press, 1907)

YELLOW BOX

When Catherine the Great died in 1796 she was succeeded by her son, Paul. He had been kept in relative obscurity from childhood and, as a result, showed his resentment by reversing his mother's policies. Tsar Paul retained Catherine's secret service, or the Secret Expedition, as it was known, and also conceived a novel idea for boosting its sources of information. It was a typically Russian inspiration and was perhaps one of the sanest he ever had. The tragedy was that Paul was not the man to take advantage of it. His idea was that anyone in the realm, *boyar*, merchant, police informant, peasant or returned exile, should have the opportunity of providing him with secret intelligence, anonymously if necessary. So outside the Winter Palace he had placed the Yellow Box into which any of his subjects could place communications containing intelligence, complaints or allegations of treachery. A Tsar who wanted to know what the people thought and felt and to learn what they observed might have gleaned a lot from the Yellow Box, but Paul reacted bizarrely to these reports. For example, on hearing that an officer wore his hat at the wrong angle, he had him sent off to Siberia!

PART III

1919–1945

ABWEHR, THE

This organization was created after World War I as a small intelligence section of the German Ministry of Defence when Germany was observing the Versailles Treaty of arms limitation. Its first chief was Colonel Gempp who was succeeded in 1933 by Captain Patzig. Within a year the Nazis came to power and it was immediately planned to expand the *Abwehr*. In 1934 Admiral Canaris (q.v. Part III) was appointed head of the service and he set up his headquarters at Tirpitsufer in Berlin. Canaris formed the *Abwehr* into four divisions – the Central Division, responsible for administration, was under Colonel Oster; the other three divisions were for espionage, contacts with discontented minority groups in other countries, under Lieutenant-Colonel Lahousen, and counter-espionage. The *Abwehr* was a relatively civilized service and intelligently directed by Canaris, who was almost a twentieth-century Metternich, but it soon ran into opposition from the more rigidly Nazi-controlled rival intelligence services.

ALLEY, MAJOR STEPHEN

After the Russian revolution in 1917, when the British Ambassador was evacuated, Major Alley was a senior intelligence officer working with MI6 inside Russia. He was an old friend of Sidney Reilly (q.v. Part II), whom he helped out of trouble on a number of occasions. In appearance he was a figure of splendid old-world courtesy, yet he had been involved in some hair-raising adventures with the Bolsheviks. His colleagues were surprised when some time after the Bolsheviks had gained total power he was withdrawn from the USSR. Asked the reason for this many years later, Alley told a close personal friend: 'I didn't always obey orders. Once I was asked to rub out Stalin. Never did like the chap much, but he regarded me as a friend, and the idea of walking into his office and killing him offended me. In any case I wasn't satisfied with the arrangements for getting me out afterwards.' For a while after his retirement Alley ran a business in Paris and then settled down in Berkshire.

AMTORG TRADING ASSOCIATION

Soviet Intelligence set up the Amtorg Trading Association in New York in 1924, financing it by the sale of Romanoff jewels smuggled into America by merchant seamen in the pay of Ernst Wollweber's seamen's union. The agency, posing as a legitimate trading association, was manned by Soviet spies and its prime job was to recruit agents in the USA. George Besdovsky, a former Russian agent, has stated that his immediate boss was a GRU officer named Filin who held a Polish passport and ran a herb-importing business as cover. 'Representatives of the Soviet War Department came to the USA with lists of products necessary for the military organization of the Soviet Union. They gave Filin instructions and brought back to Moscow the information obtained by him and his agents.'

As it was not until 1933 that the USA gave diplomatic recognition to the USSR, Amtorg was a vital organization for the Russians. It was, however, mainly the NKVD who operated Amtorg. A great deal of the espionage was purely commercial and industrial, but even then the Soviets were concentrating on scientific intelligence. After World War II Amtorg was used to obtain atomic instruments for Russia and, as a result of FBI watchfulness, a shipment of these was removed from the steamship *Murmansk* in New York harbour in 1948. A further shipment was seized in New Jersey the following year.

ARCOS

The All Russian Cooperative Society, like Amtorg, was a cover for espionage. In the 1920s the Russian Trade Delegation, with a staff of more than 300, set up offices under the name of Arcos in Moorgate, London. Some time later a British technician serving with the RAF was arrested and charged with the theft of top-secret documents, and it was discovered that they had been transmitted to Arcos. On 12 May 1927 Arcos offices were raided by members of the Special Branch of the Metropolitan Police. In the basement they found Russian officials burning papers, but they gathered enough evidence to prove that espionage was being conducted from these offices, which were closed down forthwith and the trade delegation ordered back to Russia.

ASTROLOGY AND ESPIONAGE

The use of astrology in the espionage business is common today as it was centuries ago. Confucius tells us how oracular devices were consulted for advice on war and diplomacy. These were based on Chinese astrology which some still claim is more accurate than Western systems. In Elizabethan times the Queen's astrologer, John Dee (q.v. Part II), was an English agent in continental Europe. His astrological calculations warned of violent and abnormal storms in 1588 and that these should be taken into account when preparing to resist invasion. Not only did his warnings help the English to plan for the arrival of the Spanish Armada, but in Europe Dee helped to spread despondency by giving these same warnings to Emperor Rudolf of Bohemia, knowing he would pass this on to the Papal Nuncio, who in turn would give the news to Spain. Spanish recruiting was hindered by these prophecies and there were even desertions from the Spanish Fleet.

William Lilly, the professional astrologer of the seventeenth century, was used both by Cromwellian and Royalist

161

intelligence services. Astrology was exploited by Lilly for what we now call psychological warfare. During the Napoleonic Wars, Bonaparte himself insisted on consulting his generals' horoscopes before he promoted them. In World War I Aleister Crowley ingratiated himself with an Hermetic sect in order to reveal to the Americans that its head was a highly dangerous German agent. In World War II it was well known in British Intelligence that many leading Nazis were interested in the occult and especially in astrology. Crowley did some work for MI5, but his project for dropping occult information by leaflet on the enemy was rejected by the authorities. But the Hungarian astrologer, Louis de Wohl, was made a captain in the British Army largely because he claimed intimate knowledge of the working of one of Hitler's astrologers. 'I had learned the technique of Karl Krafft, Hitler's favourite astrologer,' said de Wohl afterwards, 'and I knew what his advice to Hitler would be long before he was summoned by the Führer.'

To counter some of Dr Goebbels' astrological propaganda, the British Secret Service subsidized a number of astrologers in foreign countries to put out horoscopes more favourable to British prospects than to Hitler's. The full story of how Rudolf Hess was lured into making his lone flight to Britain on 10 May 1941 is unknown, but is believed to be as a result of astrological advice planted on him by British agents (see *Fleming, Ian Lancaster*, Part III). The German High Command got wind of this and organized the *Aktion Hess*, a widescale operation which entailed the arrest of hundreds of people, including many astrologers. It was discovered that in March 1941 Hess had asked Frau Marian Nagengast, a Munich astrologer, what would be a propitious day for a trip overseas in the near future. She recommended 10 May and was duly paid for her advice.

Before the Israelis launched their raid on Entebbe in July 1976, to rescue more than 100 hostages detained by Uganda's Idi Amin, their secret service, Mossad, supplied astrological data. Close attention was paid to the constantly monitored Israel 'foundation chart' which had been kept up to date since the creation of the state in 1948. Experience had shown previously that it had been astonishingly accurate about both the Six-Day War and the Yom Kippur War. Similar studies of national horoscopes have been conducted in Russia, Bulgaria,

Poland, Japan and the USA in recent years by special Intelligence Research groups. It is estimated that the Russians spend about ten times more than the Americans on psychic research, including some astrology (see *PSI Espionage*, Part V).

Further reading
John Dee by Richard Deacon (Muller, London 1968)
A History of the British Secret Service by Richard Deacon (Muller, London 1969)
Urania's Children by Ellic Howe (Kimber, London 1967)
William Lilly's History of his Life and Times (London, 1715)

BERIA, LAVRENTI PAVLOVICH (1898-1953)

A prematurely balding young man, who had made his name as an organizer of Communist cells among the oil workers of Baku, Beria was a crony of Stalin's, which led to his enrolment in the NKVD. This was at a time when Stalin was seriously concerned at the apparent failure of Soviet espionage under the Comintern. One of Beria's first missions was in Paris where he was entrusted with linking up the French network of the NKVD (code-named 'Neighbours') with the British network after the Russians (rightly, as it turned out), believed that the London cover organization, Arcos (q.v.), was under suspicion by MI5. Later Beria was used as the chief organizer of distributing forged dollar bills through small banks in Germany.

Beria succeeded Yezhov, and it was said of him that as long as Stalin lived, he would be safe – a high tribute bearing in mind the fate of some of the earlier Secret Service chiefs. Like Stalin, Beria was a Georgian, born in Tiflis and the son of a civil servant, though belonging to a peasant family. Educated in a teachers' training college, he had served in the Tsar's army in World War I, despite poor eyesight. He had, however, played down his army service and conjured up a picture, albeit fictitious, of an earlier career devoted to active revolutionary zeal. At the age of twenty-three he had already seen successful service as a secret agent in Prague, and as he was a good mixer in all classes of society, he used many aliases abroad and was particularly successful in gaining the confidence of some exiled White Russians in whose restaurants and nightclubs he posed as a moderate socialist intellectual opposed to the Soviet regime. This enabled him to keep tabs on the White Russians and also to track down the movements of Trotsky in exile.

Beria could read Stalin's mind more accurately than anyone else. He took over the dreaded Index of counter-intelligence originally planned by Trilisser (q.v.), added to it, amended it and used it much more effectively for such things as blackmail, recruitment and elimination. Under Beria's regime it is estimated that more than 30,000 members of the Red Army and Naval forces, and more than 500 members of the Secret Services were executed. He brought the NKVD under much tighter control, creating hundreds of new agents to take the places of defectors and those liquidated. As a realist, he was convinced that war was coming to Europe and advised Stalin that there should be a quiet cultural revolution which would revive a spirit of nationalism and patriotism in Russia and play upon the people's fondness for military heroes of the past. This led to a spate of films glorifying previous Russian rulers, such as Ivan the Terrible and Peter the Great.

It was Beria who decreed that the Soviet network in Germany, largely broken up in the 1930s, but which had once been so strong, should be rebuilt from Switzerland, Holland and Belgium. It was a wise move which paid many dividends during World War II. It is worth noting that during his long reign as head of secret service in Russia, Beria was chief of the NKVD until 1945, when he took over the chairmanship of the Ministry of Internal Affairs (MVD) as well, and that in effect he was supremo of all the intelligence services immediately after the war. It was Beria who directed and controlled attempts to establish a Czech Communist government after the war and who planned the death of Jan Masaryk, the Czech Foreign Minister, who had aimed to keep Czechoslovakia neutral and to maintain close ties with the West. In 1948 Masaryk's body was found sprawled in the courtyard of the Czernin Palace in Prague.

Beria's one major mistake was his failure to make friends with the Army, which deeply resented the part he played in the purge of the generals in the late 1930s. When Stalin died the Army lined up with Malenkov, Stalin's successor, and this ensured the downfall of Beria. Unaware of the moves going on behind his back, Beria made two mistakes. First, he failed to act quickly enough, then he underestimated Malenkov's influence with the Army. Immediately after Stalin's death the MGB was absorbed into the MVD and Beria personally took full charge of the MVD from Sergei Kruglov (q.v. Part IV), something which counted in Kruglov's favour later. Shortly after this Beria was arrested and executed along with various other Secret Service heads of department.

BLACK CHAMBER, THE AMERICAN

For many years it was an American tradition that espionage in peacetime was immoral, so until World War II and afterwards the USA had no formal espionage service or national secret service. In World War I Section Eight of Military Intelligence in the USA, known as the 'Black Chamber', had been created under Major Herbert Yardley, a brilliant cryptologist. This was continued furtively after the war, allowing Yardley to decipher messages from the Japanese Government to their delegates at the Washington Naval Conference of 1922. This information was used to help impose a five/five/three ration of naval power on the Japanese. When this espionage was discovered (it led to the Japanese denouncement of the current naval treaties), Secretary of State Henry L. Stimson closed the 'Black Chamber' in 1929, commenting that 'Gentlemen do not read each other's mail'.

Further reading
The American Black Chamber by Herbert O. Yardley (Bobbs Merrill, Indianapolis 1931)

BOXSHALL, LIEUTENANT-COLONEL EDWARD G. (1897-1984)

Boxhall spent longer in Britain's Secret Service than probably any other man in history and was still being consulted on some of its affairs right up to the time of his death. He graduated from Military Intelligence in World War I to MI6 immediately afterwards, and having become acquainted with Sir Basil Zaharoff, the arms magnate, he became his personal representative and also official agent for the Vickers arms firm in Bucharest. This was his cover as head of station in the Romanian capital where he remained for some twenty years, having married the daughter of Prince Barbo Dimitrie Stirbey, a Romanian statesman whose real name was Bibescu and who had been Minister of the Interior.

BURGESS, GUY FRANCIS DE MONCY (1911-1964)

In many ways Guy Burgess was the most improbable spy of all time. Frequently drunk, compulsively homosexual, outrageous in his social behaviour, often failing to pay bills, he nonetheless remained within the British Establishment network for many years. The truth is that Burgess had a first-class brain and the gift of making friends in high places all around the world. Originally intended as a candidate for a naval career, he was educated at Dartmouth, but finished off his education at Eton and Cambridge, supposedly because of bad eyesight. Like his friend, Anthony Blunt (q.v. Part IV), he was a member of the exclusive Cambridge secret society, the Apostles, and was recruited to work for the Soviet cause in the 1930s after a visit to Moscow. For a long time he concealed his activities by advertising the fact that he had fascist friends and was a member of the Anglo-German Fellowship. In fact, such connections brought him into contact with Baron Wolfgang Adler zu Puttlitz, a secret Communist sympathizer inside the German Diplomatic Service in London, and with the Baroness Moura Budberg, a former secretary of Maxim Gorky.

When World War II broke, Burgess was working in the BBC, but managed to create a liaison with the Foreign Office. 'He helped ... to remove the anti-Russian bias from Poles whom we were training for sabotage,' wrote Cyril Connolly, 'and in 1942 he attempted a mission to Moscow which got no further than Washington.' Like Blunt, Burgess used homosexual blackmail to win and retain agents, and in 1941 in order to keep Donald Maclean (q.v. Part IV) firmly on the Soviet side, he got him drunk and photographed him in the nude in another man's arms. In 1944 he was taken on by the Foreign Office, becoming a personal assistant to Hector McNeil, the Minister of State, and in 1950 was appointed to the British Embassy in Washington. On his return to London it became clear to him that the counter-espionage net was tightening on both Maclean and Philby, and there is little doubt that he was instructed to force Maclean's disappearance from the UK and accompany him to Moscow. He spent his last years rather unhappily in the USSR where he died of a heart attack.

Further reading
Guy Burgess: A Portrait with Background by Tom Driberg (London 1956)

CAHAN, SAMUEL BORISOVICH

While holding diplomatic rank in the Soviet Embassy in London, in the 1930s, Cahan was a regional director of Soviet Intelligence with the authority to seek new agents among British subjects. His instructions were to concentrate on talent in the universities and to win them over to Russia. It was Cahan who personally controlled Maclean, Philby and Burgess among other recruits from both Oxford and Cambridge universities. He not only recruited these men, but also trained and advised them on what careers to pursue, as well as receiving their reports. Afterwards some of his work was switched to Paris for security reasons, being taken on by Igor Khopliakin, another Soviet recruiter of talent.

CANARIS, ADMIRAL WILHELM (1883-1945)

Even when he was an officer serving in U-boats with the German Navy in World War I, Canaris was given the nickname of 'Kieker' (peeper) because of his intense curiosity. Rumours dogged him all his life – stories of espionage, even while still in the Navy, of his role in liquidating German revolutionaries afterwards, and then his climb up the ladder in the service of German Intelligence. Here at 74-76 Tirpitzufer in Berlin Admiral Canaris became chief of the *Abwehr* (q.v.) in 1935, and soon legend was proclaiming him as the supreme intelligence chief in the whole world.

He was known to be an instinctive and forthright opponent of Bolshevism, seeing it as the ultimate threat to Germany, and he sometimes shuddered at the manner in which his World War I predecessor, Colonel Nicolai, had actually subsidized some Bolsheviks as a means of destroying Tsarist Russia's war effort. Canaris was much more at home with Latin and Mediterranean peoples than with Teutons and for this reason he set out to acquire friends and agents in such countries as Spain and Greece. Juan March, former head of a smuggling ring who had been won over to the side of British Intelligence in World War I, and later firmly on the side of Franco, wrote to a British Naval Intelligence friend in Madrid in 1935 that Canaris 'does not love, nor trust his new masters ... he is horrified that Germany may once again perpetrate a world war'. From this time onwards and throughout World War II the hierarchy of the British Secret Service was deeply split on the question of whether an understanding with Canaris was desirable, not least because he was known to profess a love of Britain to intimates and a great admiration for its Navy. His record as a spy during World War I was considerable. In between serving in submarines and cruisers, he organized the sabotage of French installations in Morocco; landing in New York from a neutral ship in 1916 under the name of Moses Meyerbeer he carried bombs in his violin case and planted them in US arms factories; he then escaped back across the Atlantic with a Chilean passport under the name of Mr Reed-Rosas.

Even before World War II Canaris had hinted to a few intimates, such as Fabian von Schlabrendorff, a young Conservative Prussian, that he might work clandestinely with the British Secret Service against Hitler. Later in World War II there is no doubt that Canaris's cautious feelers to the SIS were snuffed out by some SIS personnel, 'Kim' Philby included. Certainly it seems that he did his utmost to stave off moves that led to World War II, and that afterwards he passed warnings and information to the British Secret Service unit in Switzerland through the intermediary of Madame Szymanska, a close Polish friend of Canaris. At one time there had been a plan for a British Secret Service kidnapping of Canaris on one of his visits to Algeciras. It was so close to Gibraltar that the Admiral could have been smuggled out by a fast speedboat within minutes, but the operation was cancelled on instructions from London, the view being that Canaris was much more useful to the Allies if he remained in his post. Certainly, up to the last year of the war, some on the Allied side believed that Canaris was vital to their cause – one man who could help to shorten the war, see Hitler overthrown and check the advance of Communism across Eastern Europe. But it was not to be. On 12 February 1944 Hitler ordered the *Abwehr* to be absorbed into the *Sicherheitsdienst*, the rival secret service, and a week later Canaris was dismissed, ostensibly a punishment for the defection of an *Abwehr* agent, Dr Erich Vermehrer. In July 1944 Canaris was arrested and imprisoned in a concentration camp at Flossenburg, and after being tried for treachery was hanged in April 1945.

Further reading
Canaris by Karl Heinz Abshagen (Union Verlag, Stuttgart)
Chief of Intelligence by Ian Colvin (Gollancz, London 1951)
MI6 by Nigel West, (1983)

'CICERO' (BAZNA, ELYEZA) (1905-1971)

'Cicero' was the code-name used for a German spy who was working as valet to the British Ambassador in Ankara during World War II. Under his real name of Elyeza Bazna he had approached the Germans in Ankara in October 1943. He told them he was a thirty-eight-year-old son of a Muslim religious teacher who had been born at Pristina in Yugoslavia. His family had moved to Turkey and he had been a servant at the Yugoslav Embassy, then with the American military attaché and later with the British Embassy. 'Now that I am valet to the Ambassador, I can offer you top-secret information from his safe,' was his plea, making it clear that he expected large sums of money for his services. Just how lax British security must have been even in wartime Ankara may be judged from the fact that Bazna had at one time been employed by a German diplomat, yet he managed to acquire copies of the keys of the Ambassador's private safe and to photograph the contents of this and a private dispatch box. He also discovered that, whereas all official papers were subject to stringent security regulations, far more important and interesting papers were often left in the black leather box by the Ambassador's bedside.

The situation was saved for Britain when Cornelia Kapp, who was secretary to 'Cicero's' controller, Ludwig Moyzisch, defected to the Allies through a love affair with an American OSS officer, Ewart Seager. She provided some clues which pointed in the direction of 'Cicero'. Bazna quickly realized that trouble lay ahead and he resigned his post, disappearing with some £200,000 in forged notes. The SIS report on this affair was that Bazna had 'succeeded in photographing a number of highly secret documents ... and selling them to the Germans. He would not have been able to do so if the Ambassador had conformed to the regulations'. As for Bazna, he soon found out that of the £200,000 he had been paid only about a tenth of this was in genuine notes. However, he married a wife twenty years younger than himself, had four children by her and died in 1971.

Further reading
Operation 'Cicero' by L.C. Moyzisch (Coward-McCann, New York, 1981)

'CYNTHIA' (AMY ELIZABETH BROUSSE) (1910-1963)

'Cynthia' became as legendary a figure of World War II as Mata Hari did in World War I, except that she was considerably more professional. She was born Amy Elizabeth Thorpe in Minneapolis and at the age of twenty married Arthur Pack, a secretary on the commercial side at the British Embassy in Washington, who was nearly twice her age. She sought consolation during what proved to be an unhappy marriage with a series of lovers in Chile, Spain and Poland. During the Spanish Civil War she helped a number of Franco supporters to escape, but it was not until she went to Poland that she became a secret agent in earnest. Her chief success here was to win the confidence of a young Pole who was confidential aide to Colonel Beck, the Foreign Secretary. Some of her information led directly to obtaining the secrets of a new cipher machine code-named Enigma (q.v.), which was eventually brought to Britain.

'Cynthia' next turned up in Chile and it was at this time that she was summoned to New York and given her code-name by that highly skilled spymaster, William Stephenson (q.v.) head of the British Secret Service in America. War had now broken out and one of the first victims of 'Cynthia's' charms was the Italian admiral Alberto Lais, naval attaché in Washington. She easily persuaded him to let her have the Italian naval code and cipher books and the encipherment tables. This success provided swift results: in March 1941 the Royal Navy won a resounding victory in the Mediterranean over the Italian fleet, solely because the British had been able to read the Italian signals concerning fleet movements. Then Lais told 'Cynthia' of joint Italo-German plans to sabotage ships in American ports. The British passed on this intelligence to the FBI who informed the State Department and Lais was immediately declared *persona non grata* and sent back to Rome.

'Cynthia's' next target was the Vichy Embassy in Washington – a much more difficult operation. Her orders were to obtain information on all correspondence between the Vichy French Embassy and Europe and the keys to the Vichy ciphers. Posing as a journalist, her first target became Charles Brousse, who handled public relations and the press at the Embassy. She soon discovered that he was a former fighter pilot in the French Navy, that he was quite fond of the British and had no love whatsoever for the Germans. Soon 'Cynthia' and Brousse became lovers, and in due course Brousse became her most diligent supplier of intelligence. Obtaining the French naval codes, however, proved a difficult problem. They were locked in a strong-room at the Embassy and even Brousse had no access to them. A solution was found by pretending to the night watchman that they had 'nowhere to go to make love' and this plea plus generous tips did the trick. One night they gave the watchman champagne laced with drugs. While he slept, Brousse and 'Cynthia' let in another British agent, an expert locksmith, who got hold of the vital ciphers (see *Georgia Cracker*, Part III). An unexpected role which 'Cynthia' played in all this was to help disguise the major source of intercepting enemy messages which was, of course, through reading the German signals. In due course news of the Vichy Embassy burglary was leaked to the Germans in a deliberate attempt to mislead them about the vital work of the Bletchley team in reading top-secret German signals.

Later 'Cynthia' was sent to London and attached to one of SOE offices in Dorset Square. Brousse obtained a divorce and in November 1945 came news that Arthur Pack, from whom 'Cynthia' had long since parted, had been found dead in his apartment. He had been in ill health and it was a clear case of suicide. Brousse and 'Cynthia' married the following year and went to live in France.

Further reading
Cynthia: the Spy who Changed the Course of the War by H. Montgomery Hyde (Hamish Hamilton, 1966)
Spy! by Richard Deacon with Nigel West (BBC Publications, 1980)

DANSEY, COLONEL SIR CLAUDE (1876-1944)

One of the worst choices ever made for a senior executive of MI6, Dansey became a deputy-chief of the British SIS before World War II largely on account of his World War I record. He had been stationed in Switzerland before the war and took a personal interest in intelligence from this territory. One worthwhile criticism he made was that everyone throughout the world knew that British Passport Control offices were the regional HQ of the Secret Service, so he successfully urged the creation of the 'Z' network (q.v.). The idea was good in that it was intended to act as a safeguard if the main SIS network was broken, but it depended upon having highly efficient agents, and Dansey's choices were not particularly good. There were therefore two British spy networks in Holland, one headed by Major Stevens and the other belonging to the 'Z' network headed by Captain Payne Best. When World War II broke out it was decreed – foolishly, as it turned out – that the two networks all over the continent should merge. As a result, Best and Stevens were detected by German Intelligence, fed with disinformation and lured to Venlo on the Dutch-German border where they were kidnapped (see *Venlo Incident*, Part III). Thus, two of Britain's key intelligence officers in Europe were made prisoners by the Nazi secret police. Too late did they learn that their German contact man, whom they knew as Schaemmel, was none other than Schellenberg (q.v.) of the Nazi Central Security Agency. As a result SIS networks all over Europe were decisively broken in a single day.

Dansey may have been unfairly blamed for what was basically a good idea, but his choice of agents left much to be desired. He was almost paranoiacally jealous of the Americans and was highly displeased when, later in the war, copies of documents a German brought with him from Berlin reached the SIS via the OSS in Washington. Foolishly, Dansey insisted the documents were fakes and had been planted on the Americans. However, the documents proved to be genuine and the Americans adopted the German agent, obtaining valuable intelligence from him. This slip-up marked the end of Dansey's career. He died in 1944.

Further reading
Colonel Z by Anthony Read and David Fisher (Hodder & Stoughton, London 1980)

DAVIDSON, LORD JOHN COLIN CAMPBELL (1889-1970)

Educated at Westminster and Cambridge, Davidson was called to the Bar in 1913, and after becoming Conservative MP for Hemel Hempstead in 1920, was chosen as adviser on intelligence matters when Stanley Baldwin became Prime Minister. When the British Government succeeded in intercepting and deciphering nearly all the telegraphic traffic between the Soviet mission in London and Moscow, some of these intercepts found their way into Davidson's private papers, though many others disappeared without trace. Davidson's contacts went much further than MI5 and MI6, and he did not hesitate to use informants who were political opponents, if deemed necessary. One such was the Comintern agent in Britain, D.A. Petrovsky, who adopted the name of A.J. Bennet. Petrovsky had managed to infiltrate the Conservative Party Central Office when he was investigating the sale of honours scandal, which in the mid-1920s had become a major political issue in Whitehall. The man behind this was Arthur Maundy Gregory, a former employee of MI5, and though much of the money involved in the sale of honours had originally gone to the Lloyd George Political Fund, Baldwin was concerned that a similar racket was then being operated within the Conservative Party, and Petrovsky proved a useful ally in helping to check this. Petrovsky was interested to discover that Gregory was not only anti-Bolshevik, but also involved in a movement to reinstate the Hetman of the Ukraine and to establish an independent state there. Eventually Gregory was charged with attempting to obtain £10,000 from a Lieutenant-Commander Leake in return for arranging a knighthood. Having pleaded guilty, he was given only two months' imprisonment and a £50 fine.

Davidson, unlike many other Tories, was as anxious to obtain intelligence on Germany and other European countries as on the USSR. Through Petrovsky he obtained some alarming intelligence on the growth of the Nazi Party in Germany and their links with people in Britain. In Davidson's papers there is a note marked 'Secret' which states 'to prevent confusion, but to preserve security, we should forthwith cease referring to AJB, but for his eyes only [the Chairman, whoever this was] spell out the informant as either A.J. Bennett, or A.J. Bennet, taking great care to get the spelling of the surname right ... The same method of reference is being used in communication with Balfour, Remnant and Bogovout-Kolomitzov in Paris'. The last-named was a Russian émigré who enjoyed the best of both worlds, having established close relations with the Soviet government while numbering among his friends many businessmen in London and Paris.

Some years later Petrovsky's contacts with other Russians in London played an important role in events leading up to the abdication of King Edward VIII. One of these contacts was Anatoly Baykalov, a journalist friendly with the White Russians in London, and the USSR. It was Baykalov who reported to Davidson that Mrs Wallis Simpson, the mistress of the then Prince of Wales, was a secret agent of the Germans. Baykalov had noted that Mrs Simpson frequently visited the German Embassy and was a close friend of the German Ambassador, Dr Leopold Gustav von Hoesch. On 4 February 1936, when Edward VIII had succeeded to the throne, Davidson wrote: 'Most Secret memorandum: Mrs S. is very close to Hoech [von Hoesch, the German Ambassador] and has, if she likes to read them, access to all Secret and Cabinet Papers'.

It is possible that Petrovsky paid the penalty for some of the deals he made with the British. He returned to Russia with his English wife, Rose Cohen, and in February 1938 a brief report appeared in the Communist paper, *Militant*, that Petrovsky had been sent to a Soviet prison with his wife.

Further reading
Lord Davidson's Papers (Record Office, House of Lords)

DOIHARA, MAJOR-GENERAL KENJI (1883-1946)

One of the most brilliant of Japan's spymasters between the two world wars, Doihara was at one time dubbed 'Lawrence of Manchuria'. In fact he was far greater than Lawrence had ever been and he had the talents of a diplomat into the bargain. Born into a relatively poor family in 1883, he found a humble background no deterrent to his military progress. He showed outstanding ability at military academy and came first in his class. He spent many years in China, but it was after the Japanese withdrew from Siberia in 1922 that he came into his own. He was reputed to speak nine European languages and four Chinese dialects. He organized a network of renegade Chinese to work for him and used brothels as listening-posts in Mukden and Harben. Thus, by diligent intelligent work he paved the way for the take-over of Manchuria by Japan.

At the age of forty-nine he was promoted to general and created what became known as the puppet state of Manchukuo, at the same time forming *Tokumu Kikau* (Special Service Organization) in Mukden, a body which effectively controlled and collated all intelligence operations in the territory. So thorough was he in his gathering of intelligence that he set up a Refugees' Bureau, exercising authority not only over all White Russian refugees, but their banks, factories and restaurants. The bureau was, of course, a vital instrument of espionage. One of Doihara's most effective secret agents was a woman nicknamed the 'Joan of Arc' of Manchuria (see *Kawashima, Yoshiko*, Part III).

From 1938-39 Doihara was in Shanghai, operating his *Tokumu Kikau* in China and having spies right in the heart of Chiang Kai-shek's entourage. Later in the war with China Doihara was given command of a division in the field. He was one of six senior Japanese officers to be hanged as a war criminal at the end of World War II.

DONOVAN, GENERAL WILLIAM J. (1883-1959)

A modest man, Donovan's nickname of 'Wild Bill' was inaccurate and misleading. He was an Irishman of humble origins, both Catholic *and* Republican, who worked his way through law school. It was in World War I that he earned his nickname when he won the Congressional Medal of Honor. Afterwards he became a lawyer on Wall Street and it was something of a surprise when President Roosevelt asked him to create the OSS in Washington in 1941, mainly on the grounds that the USA lacked any real Secret Service. Prior to this Donovan had been sent to London in 1940 on an unofficial mission at the request of Knox, the Secretary of the Navy, and he quickly made friends with Admiral Godfrey, head of the NID. He returned to Washington urging that the US should have a new Ambassador in London and get rid of the defeatist Joe Kennedy who kept predicting German victory.

Donovan was far from being a brilliant intelligence chief, but he was diligent and forthright, building up a new organization from scratch. He was also limited in his operations as Roosevelt decreed that Nelson Rockefeller and J. Edgar Hoover of the FBI (q.v. Part IV) were to operate in Latin America, and that the OSS was forbidden to engage in any operations within and from Mexico to all places south of that country. Hoover constantly worked against Donovan, both during and after the war, and OSS activities had to be confined mainly to Europe and North Africa. Increasingly, towards the end of the war, Donovan felt that the Americans and the British were giving away too much intelligence to the Russians, and fearing that Russia would be the prime enemy afterwards, he pressed for the creation of a permanent Secret Service for the USA, based on the OSS. Hoover opposed him on this project and in 1945 President Truman dismissed Donovan and ended the OSS. For a brief period he served as Ambassador to Thailand.

Further reading
Donovan of OSS by Corey Ford (Boston 1970)

DOUBLE-CROSS SYSTEM

This system, adopted by Britain in World War II, 'turned' arrested German agents against their masters and persuaded them to cooperate in sending false information back to Berlin. It was controlled by the 'Twenty (XX) Committee' in association with section B1A of MI5, and its head was the late Sir John Masterman (q.v.). Although the system's use is best known in Western Europe, it was actually more skilfully applied in the Middle East, where it deceived the Germans about Allied intentions in both North Africa and the Eastern Mediterranean.

Those agents who were caught and controlled inside the UK totalled thirty-nine in all, most of them with intriguing code names. There was a 'Mutt' and a 'Jeff', a 'Lipstick' and a 'Peppermint', but what was most remarkable was how their code-names rang true to character. There was 'Careless' whose 'personal conduct and the impossibility of controlling him except in prison spoiled a promising case', and 'Weasel' who had to be dropped because he was 'believed to have contrived to warn the Germans'. The absolute gem of them all was Hans Schmidt (q.v.), code-named 'Tate', who operated successfully for more than four and a half years after he was captured when parachuting into England. The Germans lapped up his (faked) radio messages so eagerly that they awarded him the Iron Cross. 'Garbo' (q.v.) was another great success, awarded the Iron Cross by the Germans and the MBE by the British. Sometimes, however, the authorities failed to get the best value from double-agents, an example being 'Tricycle' (see *Popov, Dusko*, Part III). False information fed back to Germany by captured agents included details about where the Allies were likely to land in France, armaments production and the disposition of troops. Some of the manipulated German agents were able to convince their masters in Berlin that more funds should be dispatched to them. 'Tate' was particularly successful in this respect; he was instructed by the Germans to wait at the terminus of the number eleven bus route at Victoria station where he was to get on a bus with a Japanese who would be carrying a copy of the *Times* and a book in his left hand. 'Tate' was to wear a red tie and also carry a newspaper and a book.

Having established his identity in this way, 'Tate' was handed £200.

Security Intelligence Middle East (SIME) achieved even more surprising coups through the double-cross system. Linked with 'A' Force, under Brigadier Dudley Clarke, it proved to be a real war-winner in its use of the system. It was through this that the Germans lost the battle of El Alamein and were deluded as to British plans for the invasion of Sicily and Normandy. Not only did SIME win over German agents, but they also created fictional agents to provide misleading intelligence. Perhaps the most amusing instance of these tactics was the game played by a prostitute named 'Gala', who was actually in jail in Palestine, but for the purposes of misleading the Germans was portrayed as a *poule de luxe* in Beirut with a whole string of imaginary lovers, including Allied officers and an Air Force technician who was supposed to be preparing Turkish airfields for Allied occupation. Two double-agents who were kept in jail were code-named 'Quicksilver' and 'Pessimist', and it was essential that while they were sending out their messages it should appear that 'Quicksilver' was transmitting from Beirut to Athens, while 'Pessimist' was radioing from Damascus (where he was fictitiously established in German eyes) to Sofia.

Further reading
The Double-Cross System in the War of 1939-45 by J.C. Masterman (Yale University Press, 1972)
The British Connection by Richard Deacon (Hamish Hamilton, 1979)
MI5: British Security Service Operations 1909-45 by Nigel West (London 1981)
Master of Deception by David Mure (Kimber, 1980)

DZERZHINSKY, FELIX EDMUNDOVICH (1877-1926)

In December 1917 Lenin gave the task of rebuilding Russia's secret service to one of his fellow Bolsheviks, Felix Dzerzhinsky, the son of a Polish aristocrat who had a long career of revolutionary activity. He had joined the Socialist Revolutionary Party as a student, but grew impatient with their aims and switched to the Social Democratic Labour Party. When the split between the Bolsheviks and the Mensheviks came in 1903, he joined the Bolsheviks and soon attracted Lenin's attention. Ruthless, cold, clear-headed and gifted with organizational talents, he insisted from the start that he must have full authority and not be subject to any supervision. Such was Lenin's regard for him that he agreed without reservation. Dzerzhinsky ordered the arrest of many *Ochrana* officers and agents, but some of them, under threats of death or imprisonment, were forcibly persuaded to work for the Soviet regime. Then he imposed a communications blanket between the Soviet Government and the rest of Russia. Post, telephones, telegraphs and even messengers were banned to all non-Bolsheviks. This was of vital security importance for the first few days after the second revolution, for it meant that many members of the Kerensky administration did not know what was happening, did not, in fact, realize that they were no longer in the government. Dzerzhinsky maintained this secrecy for weeks, sealing off all possibilities of communications between what he termed 'the enemy' and the Soviet Government.

It was at this stage that Dzerzhinsky turned his hastily improvised Security Sub-Committee into the more pretentious sounding title of Extraordinary Commission for the Struggle against Counter-Revolution and Sabotage, usually more briefly referred to as the *Cheka*. In doing this he sought to discredit the *Ochrana* in every possible way, making the brutal declaration: 'We stand for organized terror ... Terror is an absolute necessity during times of revolution.' One should, he urged, shoot first and ask questions afterwards. When the government moved to Moscow the *Cheka* transferred its headquarters to Lyublyanka Street, while its chief office in St Petersburg was moved to Gorochovaya Street, where the section chief was a bloodthirsty tyrant named Uritsky, who was eventually murdered by a Revolutionary Socialist. The men chosen by Dzerzhinsky, though brutal and sometimes semi-educated, were on the whole efficient in carrying out their work. He divided the *Cheka* into two divisions: the Counter-Espionage Section and the Secret Operative Section. By building up a vast army of informers he was able to extend the *Cheka* network to all parts of Russia within a year, while at the same time imposing total discipline upon his officers. While the *Ochrana* simply dismissed unsuitable agents, Dzerzhinsky either had them killed or imprisoned for life.

Censorship on contacts with the outside world was almost total. Yet one must remember that there were plots against Dzerzhinsky's own life, including one by British secret agents (see *Reilly, Sidney*, Part II). On the other hand Dzerzhinsky was equally suspicious of his own colleagues. When Trotsky, the creator of the new Red Army, insisted on developing his own military intelligence organization, the Fourth Bureau (GRU), Dzerzhinsky began to build up a dossier on him, for he saw the GRU as a rival to the *Cheka*. Thus, opposition to Trotsky was slowly built up inside the Communist Party, all stemming from evidence which Dzerzhinsky had circulated. Such was Dzerzhinsky's vigilance in maintaining his own power and authority, as was also evidenced in 1918 when, suspecting an Allied plot against the regime, he ordered his *Cheka* to raid the French Secret Service headquarters in Moscow. The raid was successful and the *Cheka* not only captured a quantity of explosives, but arrested six French agents.

In December 1921 the Soviet government ordered a reorganization of the *Cheka* with the aim of substituting trials for the practice of instant execution. The following year the *Cheka* was abolished by decree and in its place was created the GPU (State Political Administration), retaining the right to screen GRU personnel. It was in this period that Dzerzhinsky set about creating an organization for luring back to Russia opponents of the regime (see '*The Trust*', Part III) and this proved to be one of his most effective operations. Dzerzhinsky died in 1926, but his memory is preserved even today by his bust, the first of any Soviet Secret Service chief, which stands in the middle of the foyer of KGB HQ and around which fresh flowers are placed every day.

ENIGMA

The Enigma encoding device was a major breakthrough in transmitting secret information during World War II. It was a German invention which turned messages into an unintelligible scramble before sending them in Morse. As to who discovered this secret first, there is no simple answer; ultimately, it was team work. 'Cynthia' (q.v.) undoubtedly assisted through her close friendship with an aide of Colonel Beck, the Polish Foreign Secretary, but a number of British agents helped to obtain the secrets of the Enigma encoding device through Polish intermediaries in 1939. It was in that year that Sir Stewart Menzies (q.v.), then deputy head of MI6, went to Warsaw and personally supervised the final arrangements.

One of Britain's most valuable contacts who helped to obtain the Enigma secrets was an anti-Nazi Pole who had worked in the German factory where the Enigma machine had been built. He was Charles Proteus Steinmetz, a Jewish scientist who was forced to leave Germany because of his socialist-democratic views. Nobody else could so ably analyse reports of German scientific developments and then forecast what they would mean in terms of weaponry. The Enigma project was made the vital weapon for fighting the war in the darkest days and it formed the basis for the monitoring team set up at Bletchley during World War II.

Further reading
Most Secret War by R.V. Jones (Hamish Hamilton, London 1978)
Ultra Goes to War by Ronald Lewin (Hutchinson, 1978)

EXAMINATION UNIT

This innocent-sounding title, now almost forgotten, was the name originally given to the Communications Security Establishment in Canada. The Examination Unit was set up in Ottawa early in World War II to deal with signals-intelligence, decoding and cryptanalysis. Some help was acquired from the redoubtable Herbert Yardley, who had established the USA's first signals intelligence unit in 1917. He was first head of the Examination Unit, but was inexplicably removed after only a short time by Lester Pearson, a key man in the Unit and a future Prime Minister of Canada. It is believed there were both American and British objections to Yardley. Sometimes vital information which should have been swiftly passed to the Examination Unit was delayed. For example, a hint of Japanese plans to evacuate official Japanese families from North America was received on 3 December 1941, but was not passed to the Examination Unit until after the attack on Pearl Harbour. A key figure in the Unit was Herbert Norman, the Cambridge-educated Canadian who was in charge of the department decoding Japanese signals in the months before Pearl Harbour. Years later when serving as Canadian Ambassador in Cairo he committed suicide at a time that it was being alleged he was a Soviet spy.

FLEMING, IAN LANCASTER (1908-1964)

The son of an Army officer and Conservative MP who was killed in World War I, Fleming was educated at Eton and Sandhurst, but decided an Army life was not for him. Prior to World War II he had been for a while a Reuters correspondent in Moscow and a stockbroker. When Admiral Godfrey, chief of the NID, was looking for a chief assistant shortly before World War II, he was recommended to take on Fleming by none other than the Governor of the Bank of England, Montagu Norman. With the rank of Lieutenant-Commander, RNVR, Fleming made a distinct impact on NID thinking, for he had imagination as well as administrative talents and became a convenient channel for confidential matters connected with various clandestine organizations outside the Navy. Admiral Godfrey once went on record as saying that Fleming was 'a war winner. I once said that Ian should have been DNI and I his naval adviser.'

The truth is that a number of wartime intelligence coups credited to other people were really manipulated by Fleming. It was he who originated the scheme for using astrologers to lure Rudolf Hess to Britain. Fleming's contact in Switzerland succeeded in planting on Hess an astrologer who was also a British agent. To ensure that the theme of the plot was worked into a conventional horoscope the Swiss contact arranged for two horoscopes of Hess to be obtained from astrologers known to Hess personally so that the faked horoscope would not be suspiciously different from those of the others. All this was connected with a faked revival of the pro-Nazi organization, 'the Link', but it was a cunning hint in the horoscope which helped persuade the astrologically-minded Hess to attempt his one-man mission to Britain. Fleming's other great wartime success was the establishment of No.30 Assault Unit, which first functioned in the Middle East, but later proved its worth in intelligence-gathering and beach reconnaissance in North Africa and Sicily.

Further reading
A History of the British Secret Service by Richard Deacon (Muller, London 1969)
With my Little Eye by Richard Deacon (Muller, London, 1982)

FOOTE, ALEXANDER (1958)

This remarkably cool and level-headed secret agent told his own story (subject to some censorship) in his autobiography (see below). However, a much more interesting and accurate account of his life was made in a statement which he made to a British MP some years later when he was concerned about lapses in the British Security Services. This statement, hitherto unpublished, stated that he 'was recruited into the *Razvedka*, the Intelligence Service of the Red Army, towards the end of 1938, on my return to this country [the UK] after almost two years' service in the International Brigade in Spain. Until the outbreak of World War II, I was active in Germany, subsequently operating from Switzerland against the Axis powers until my arrest by the Swiss Federal Police towards the end of November 1943 ... I had swift promotion, being at the time of my arrest in charge of the sole remaining communications between the Soviet General Staff in Russia and its sources of information "in the heart of the German High Command".'

Foote went on to tell how he was eventually released by the Swiss and arrived in Moscow in January 1945. 'Owing to a peculiar set of circumstances it then appeared to the Soviets that

I had in fact been "got at" by the British Intelligence Service and that certain actions on my part *since* my release by the Swiss in September 1944 were construed in Moscow to be British-inspired with the object of "retarding the advance of the Red Army". I was cleared of this suspicion only after a lengthy scientific interrogation and a check-up on the spot in Western Europe after the end of the war.'

Some still take the view that Foote was actually encouraged to infiltrate the Soviet network in Switzerland by the British Secret Service. He himself simply said that in 1947, when he was still in Moscow, he was told he would be entrusted with the rebuilding of a *Razvedka* network in the USA from a headquarters which he was to establish in Mexico. He then left for East Berlin where he was to establish a German background for a new identity.

'In mid-July 1947 I announced myself to a British Intelligence HQ in West Berlin and subsequently in Hanover ... I spent a total of about ten weeks incommunicado as a "guest" of MI5, one month in Germany and six weeks in a flat in Hammersmith ... I would point out that if, at the time of my defection, I had been persuaded to continue my work with the Soviets, with the secret cognizance of British Intelligence, very possibly the latter would now be in possession of facts and information about *Razvedka* activities which at present they do not have.'

Foote went on to urge that 'the apparent failure of our Intelligence to draw any benefits from my defection should now be studied by the Committee of Privy Councillors set up by the Prime Minister'. He added that his successor in the Hammersmith flat and 'guest' of MI5 was 'a certain defecting Soviet colonel. This individual after only a short stay preferred the risk of death by deciding to return to the Soviet Union. It is reasonable to suppose that this colonel was in the hands of the same people and had been subject of the same cynical treatment that had been accorded to me' (see *Lucy Ring*, Part III).

Further reading
Handbook for Spies by Alexander Foote (Museum Press, London 1949)

X

'GARBO'

'Garbo' is alleged by some to have been one of the most successful double-agents of all time, especially in his use of the 'Double-cross' system (q.v.). But the question still remains unanswered: was there one 'Garbo', or two, or even three? Even more intriguing is whether one 'Garbo' was being run by the British, and yet another different personality by the Russians. According to the official record of 'Double-cross', as given by Sir John Masterman, 'Garbo' started work for the British in April 1942 and carried on until the end of the war. Said Sir John: 'The case was unique in that 'Garbo' himself, rejected by our officials abroad and playing a lone hand, imposed himself upon the Germans and performed the difficult operation of creating and establishing his own trusty and trusted espionage agency ... it was not long before the Germans came to trust his reports.'

Juan Pujol from Barcelona, an unsuccessful hotel manager, first called at the German Embassy in Madrid posing as a Nazi sympathizer after having been a reluctant soldier with the Republican Army in the Spanish Civil War. Prior to this he had called many times on the British Embassy offering his services, but always been rejected. Eventually the British learned how he had fed the Germans some useless information which had caused them to waste much time searching for a British convoy which did not exist. On the strength of this he was eventually brought into 'Double-Cross' and smuggled across to England. He was code-named 'Garbo' on account of his acting ability. Pujol spent much of his time bent over maps and a railway timetable inventing his own network of fictitious agents, concocting the kind of military secret material which he felt would impress the Germans. His imaginary list of agents included a NAAFI waiter, a Welsh fascist, a censor and a secretary in the Cabinet Office.

Keeping total silence for many years after World War II, Pujol reappeared in the early 1980s and told his own story. But his emergence did not solve the mystery of whether there was a second 'Garbo'. Number Two, who is said to have died long since, apparently answered to the name of Luis Calvo. It seems his brother was arrested by the Gestapo when the Germans marched into Paris and Calvo is said to have offered his services to the British in order to avenge his brother. After the war he is said to have gone to Latin America where he snooped on ex-Nazis who had settled there.

As to 'Garbo' Number One, the German cover-name for himself and his network was 'Arabel', which the *Abwehr* divided into three smaller sections: 'Alaric', 'Benedict' and 'Dagobert'. 'Garbo' Number Two was known to the Russians as 'Canary'.

Further reading
The Double-cross System by J.C. Masterman (Yale University Press, 1972)
The British Connection by Richard Deacon (Hamish Hamilton, London, 1979)
MI5 by Nigel West (Weidenfeld & Nicolson, London)

'GEORGIA CRACKER', THE

'Cynthia' (q.v.) has been named as the great heroine of British Intelligence in the USA during World War II. It is only fair, however, that a man who made one of her triumphs possible should also be named, if only by his nickname. When 'Cynthia' needed a locksmith to help her and her lover obtain the Vichy ciphers from a strong-room in the French Embassy in Washington, British Security Coordination gave the job to a Canadian safe-cracker who had been let out of jail after he had volunteered for the dangerous task of cracking enemy safes. He was nicknamed the 'Georgia Cracker', a professional to his finger-tips, and highly regarded by 'Cynthia'. She met him beforehand when he questioned her closely and asked for a sketch of the safe. 'Yes,' he said after a while, 'it's a Mosler with a click-click com lock, probably four wheels. I reckon I can crack it in about fifty-five minutes.'

'THE GIRL WHO NEVER WAS'

The case of 'The Man Who Never Was' (q.v.) is fairly well known, if only because of the book by Ewen Montagu and the subsequent film. It involved a corpse which was floated off the Spanish coast from a British submarine during World War II, the pockets of its uniform filled with fake invasion plans to fool the Germans. Among those fake papers was a photograph of the dead man's mythical girl friend inscribed 'With love from Pam'. The girl was real enough, but she knew nothing whatsoever of the dead man. Her name was Jean and she worked in the War Office. Today she is married to Colonel Gerard Leigh, who for many years was chairman of the Guards Polo Club.

GIULIANO, SALVATORE

Giuliano was a twenty-year-old anti-Fascist desperado in World War II, though not a member of the Mafia. His charm and gifts of leadership suggested he might well play a useful role in organizing a rising to coincide with the Allied invasion of Sicily, and plans were made to give him authority to do this. He went ahead to raise a raiding party and equip it with arms, but for some reason British intelligence officers delayed giving permission for such an operation. Giuliano felt he had been badly let down, especially as at this time he was so strongly pro-British that he actually talked of helping to create a British naval base in Sicily and establishing a government which would recognize the British Crown in return for aid. In frustration he sought American backing, which he got at the last moment. The result was that Giuliano held two German divisions in check with a force of only 100 men in the area of Mount Cammarata. Afterwards he flourished as a Robin Hood-type bandit with Mafia support until eventually they betrayed him. After the war he fought an impudently brave campaign from his mountain stronghold outside Palermo, repudiating all links with the Mafia and claiming he was the only man in Sicily who had fought against Communism effectively. He backed his aims with some subtle propaganda, claiming he only robbed the rich to help the poor, dumping ration gifts on the doorsteps of Sicilian peasants at night and sending money by post to people facing starvation. He was shot dead by the police after defying capture for more than seven years.

GRANVILLE, CHRISTINE (d. 1952)

One of the most accomplished secret agents of World War II was Christine Granville, the daughter of a distinguished Polish family. Born Countess Krystina Skarbek, this tall, attractive and vivacious woman had won a 'Miss Poland' beauty contest in her teens. Her first marriage to the son of a wealthy family lasted only a few weeks. Her second husband was George Gizycki, twenty years her senior, and she was with him in Addis Ababa when war broke out. She immediately travelled to England, offered her services to British Intelligence, was accepted and assigned to Budapest. Living there as a journalist, she repeatedly crossed into Poland to smuggle out Poles and other Allied officers. In this work she linked up with a Polish cavalry officer named Andrew Kowerski, who later, under the name of Andrew Kennedy, became a British agent. On one journey into Poland, Granville was arrested, but managed to escape. When she was again arrested on the Yugoslav border, just after she had smuggled four pilots across, she talked the guards into believing she was on a picnic, persuading them to start up her car which had stalled.

Granville had many lucky escapes. In Cairo she became the first woman parachutist in the Middle East, preparing herself for missions into France. Under the auspices of the SOE she was parachuted on to the Vercors Plateau in Southern France. There she maintained contact with the French Resistance and the Italian Partisans across the frontier, operating as a courier for the Hockey network under the command of François Cammaerts. At this time she was serving in the WAAF and using the code-name 'Pauline'. Lieutenant-Colonel Cammaerts, who later became headmaster of Alleyn's School in London, stated afterwards that Christine Granville 'was perhaps the greatest person I have ever known'. Yet though she was awarded both the George Medal and an OBE, she was churlishly treated by the British Government, being paid off at the end of the war with two months' salary. She was forced to find what work she could, became a stewardess on a liner and

189

had the misfortune to meet a steward who fell madly in love with her and, finding his love unreturned, stabbed her to death. Maybe her shabby treatment had something to do with her claim that she had evidence that the Polish General Sikorski's death in a plane crash was due to sabotage.

Further reading
SOE in France by Foot, (HMSO, London 1964)

GUBBINS, MAJOR-GENERAL SIR COLIN McVEAN (1896-1976)

After serving in the Royal Flying Corps in World War I and winning the MC, Gubbins went on to become brigade major and saw service in Ireland during the troubles of the early 1920s. It was his experience in Ireland which gave him his often rashly expressed enthusiasm for the creation of an SOE, an ill-considered organization with the vague aim of aiding Resistance movements in Nazi-occupied Europe during World War II. Gubbins was an enthusiastic amateur, no more, no less. His only other qualification for becoming chief of SOE was that he had written a pamphlet called *The Art of Guerrilla Warfare*. In the early stages of SOE he was known as 'M' and 'D/CD (0)' and effectively became director of operations and training from November 1940.

Gubbins suffered indifference and occasional hostility from the Foreign Office, especially regarding operations in France; he often clashed with MI6, and to some extent he was hampered by not having automatic access to meetings of the Chiefs of Staff. Overall direction of the SOE was in the hands of Hugh Dalton, head of the Ministry of Economic Warfare, but he had a talent for making enemies easily, usually in the very places where he should be seeking friends. Though many SOE papers have been destroyed or removed out of public reach, nothing can hide the fact that the SOE's record, though highlighted by the bravery of a few individuals, was one of the poorest of the whole war. Some blunders were due to personality clashes, and Cavendish-Bentinck, then chairman of the Chiefs of Staff Committee (see *Portland, Duke of,* Part III), has referred to 'this awful quarrelling between MI6 and Gubbins'. Cavendish-Bentinck is cited by his biographer, David Howarth, as believing that the SOE was a failure: 'SOE would have murdered me if they could. I arranged with Victor Rothschild that, if I suddenly died, he was to carry out an autopsy' (see *Special Operations Executive,* Part III).

Further reading
Intelligence Chief Extraordinary by David Howarth (London 1985)
SOE in France by M.R.D. Foot (HMSO, London 1966)

HEYDRICH, REINHARD (1904-1942)

One of the most evil and ruthless of all the Nazi leaders, Heydrich was the man who created the *Reichsicherheitshauptamt* (RSHA), which in September 1939 brought into a single organization the Gestapo and the State Security Police with the SS. The RSHA, especially the AMT IV A 4B section of it, was largely responsible for the rounding up, transportation and gassing of at least three million people, mainly Jews, during World War II. Heydrich himself was personally responsible for widespread arrests and destruction in Czechoslovakia.

It was Heydrich who used a German agent, F 479, to make contact with the British Secret Service in Holland and so pave the way to luring two key British agents to the German border and kidnapping them (see *Venlo Incident,* Part III). He was strongly opposed to Admiral Canaris and did his utmost to thwart any scheme of the *Abwehr* chief which came to his notice. In December 1941 the Czechs in exile in London decided that Heydrich must die for his appalling treatment of their fellow-citizens. Two Czech agents were smuggled into what was then a German protectorate with the task of finding and killing

Heydrich. On 27 May 1942 they assassinated him, though at an appalling cost in life to the Czechs remaining in the country: 10,000 were arrested and at least 1300 of these were shot, while the village of Lidice was razed to the ground.

HIMMLER, HEINRICH (1900-1945)

During World War II the work of the SS and the Gestapo, both of which Himmler controlled, became the surest weapon in maintaining Hitler's tyranny, but in the end it failed largely through its own excesses. This was because Himmler, however much he may have terrified millions of other people, was himself terrified of Hitler and ruined his health as a result. At one time his father was tutor to Prince Heinrich of Bavaria and the Prince acted as young Himmler's godfather. He was called up for military service at the tail end of World War I and then studied agriculture at the University of Munich.

About this time, as his diaries show, he seemed to develop strong feelings of anti-Semitism through his association with right-wing Catholic nationalists and eventually joined the Nazi Party in 1923. He lost his job as a laboratory assistant and from then on threw himself wholeheartedly into politics. He married a Polish nurse and in 1929 was appointed by Hitler as a Reichsführer SS (*Schutzstaffel*). This organization was little more than Hitler's private bodyguard, numbering less than 300 men. Himmler built it up so that by 1933 it had grown to 52,000. Schellenberg (q.v.), head of the Intelligence and Security Service (SD), declared that 'the SS had been built up by Himmler on the principles of the Order of the Jesuits ... The *Reichsführer* SS – Himmler's title as supreme head of the SS – was intended to be the counterpart of the Jesuits' General of the Order'. It was Himmler who purged the ranks of the SS after the Roehm affair when there were hints of mutiny. It was Himmler again who was so obsessed with racial purity that he set up the *Ahnenerbe* for research into Germanic racial origins, and likewise he planned and supervised the development of the concentration camps, setting up nearly 100 such centres before

Ivan the Terrible, founder of Russia's first secret
service *(Mary Evans Picture Library)*

Benjamin Franklin: a devious operator
(Mary Evans Picture Library)

Chevalier d'Eon: the transvestite spy
who deceived the Czarina
(Mary Evans Picture Library)

General Baden-Powell
(BBC Hulton Picture Library)

Colonel Alfred Redl, who betrayed his country
(BBC Hulton Picture Library)

Sydney Reilly, who spied for at least four nations
(BBC Hulton Picture Library)

Felix Dzerzhinsky, first head of the Cheka
(BBC Hulton Picture Library)

Mata Hari *(Popperfoto)*

Sir Compton Mackenzie, who first revealed the meaning of 'C' *(BBC Hulton Picture Library)*

George Blake on his return to Britain after three years' internment in Korea *(© Sunday Times)*

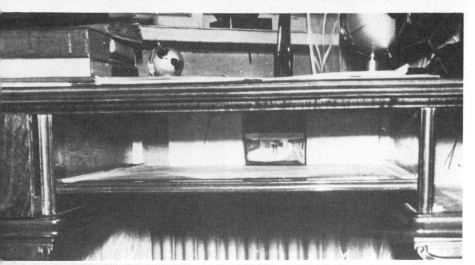

Top: A secret hiding place which, it was alleged, Oleg Penkovsky made in his desk (Topham)

Above: Penkovsky with Greville Wynne in the dock in Moscow, charged with espionage (Topham)

Gordon Lonsdale (alias Konon Molody), Soviet master-spy (Keystone)

Kao Liang, one of China's ablest intelligence officers, arriving at UN headquarters in New York *(Associated Press)*

Kim Philby, the British traitor, walking in a Moscow street *(Popperfoto)*

J. Edgar Hoover, formidable late head of the FBI *(Topham)*

Reinhard Gehlen, late head of West German Intelligence *(Popperfoto)*

Yuri Andropov, the KGB chief who became the USSR's leader *(Popperfoto)*

Allen Dulles, whose World War II espionage successes led to his becoming Director of the CIA *(Popperfoto)*

William Casey, controversial CIA Director of the 1980s *(Topham)*

Top: The vast headquarters of the CIA at Langley, Virginia *(Popperfoto)*

Above: Soviet Secret Police headquarters in Moscow, alongside the Lubyanka Prison *(Popperfoto)*

Century House, home of Britain's Secret Service *(BBC Hulton Picture Library)*

the war. Towards the end of the war he toyed with the idea of founding a new party without Hitler's approval and of making a deal with the Allies jointly to fight Bolshevism. He failed, was dismissed by Hitler, arrested by the Allies and committed suicide in his prison cell.

Further reading
The Schellenberg Memoirs by Walter Schellenberg (André Deutsch, London 1956)

JAHNKE, ERICH

A key man in the German Secret Service in World War II, Jahnke was the son of a Pomeranian landowner, who had lived for some years in the USA and worked in the border police of the US immigration service. Later he made a fortune by finding a hygienic way around the US ban on shipping Chinese corpses back to China. (His solution was to pack the bodies in airtight zinc boxes.) In world War I he helped the German Secret Service (SD) to organize strikes in various East Coast harbours and docks. As a man with extensive contacts in the Far East, he acted as intelligence adviser to Rudolf Hess when he returned to Germany in the years between the wars.

In World War II, as SS-Hauptsturmfuhrer he became a man of great influence in the SD and his advice was frequently sought. However, both Himmler and Heydrich mistrusted him, and Hitler allegedly suspected he was a British agent who was responsible for Hess's flight to Britain. However, he had a strong supporter in Schellenberg (q.v.), head of the SD, who wanted to make full use of Jahnke's Japanese and Chinese connections. It was Schellenberg who arranged for Jahnke to set up a Bureau Jahnke with one assistant to make reports to him personally. Much invaluable intelligence on the Far East was obtained this way, but it was frequently ignored by Hitler and Himmler. Only once was Schellenberg's trust in Jahnke somewhat shaken and that was when he received a secret report that Jahnke had gone to Switzerland to meet a British agent and receive orders. But Schellenberg found no evidence to support this report, and Jahnke continued in his work.

Further reading
The Schellenberg Memoirs by Walter Schellenberg (André Deutsch, London 1956)

K'ANG SHENG (1898-1975)

The first real director of intelligence in the People's Republic of China, K'ang's career in espionage lasted for well over half a century. Born in Chu-ch'eng in Shantung province, he was one of the earliest members of the Chinese Communist Party. He changed his original name of Chao Yun to K'ang Sheng as a mark of opposition to his father who was a wealthy landlord. He went to Shanghai University and became imbued with radical ideas, yet retained a lifelong interest in *I Ching*, the commentaries of which he often quoted. In Shanghai he developed his own spy system and kept the Communist Party supplied with a steady stream of intelligence. While establishing some links with Chiang Kai-shek's Kuomintang, he also extended cautious feelers towards the Soviet Union. He was essentially a pragmatist: while remaining in the Shanghai underground he moved into the French concession of the city where he was safe from Kuomintang interference. In 1933 he was sent to Moscow to study Soviet security and intelligence techniques, retaining his integrity and all his devotion to the Chinese concept of Communism, while having grave doubts about Russian loyalty to the Chinese cause. He also wrote a book, intended mainly for Russian consumption, entitled *Revolutionary China Today*.

In 1934 K'ang was elected a member of the Central Executive Committee of the Chinese Communist Party and a year later was one of the chief Chinese delegates to Moscow. In 1937 he was put in charge of intelligence in the new Communist capital of Yenan in North Shensi, close to the Mongolian border, where he built up some contacts inside Russia without the knowledge of the Soviet government. The *Biographic Dictionary of Chinese Communism (1921-65)* states that 'for reasons of security the Communists [Chinese] have published very little about the chief security organ, the *She-hui pu*, (Social Affairs Department), but it is probable that K'ang headed this department from the late 1930s. What is abundantly clear is that K'ang was an outstanding spy-master over many years: to organize an intelligence service on an efficient scale from a remote province with poor communications was in itself a considerable feat, but K'ang also had to cope with the Kuomintang's blockade of the Communists. In World War II K'ang rectified some of these problems by infiltrating his agents into Chiang Kai-shek's intelligence service. After the war K'ang turned his attention towards checking Soviet infiltration of China. In 1951 he discovered that the Russians had infiltrated the Chinese Institute of Mathematics and, in doing so, had acquired control of electronic computer techniques in engineering, aerodynamics and nuclear physics.'

By this time K'ang was on the board of the Sino-Soviet Friendship Association through which he was able to keep a watch on Russian activities. On visits to Moscow between 1959 and 1960 he made it clear that China strongly disagreed with Soviet policies towards the West, especially on the subject of disarmament. At home he gave orders for a dossier on hostile actions by the USSR towards China to be compiled. Chinese agents were ordered to obtain the latest Russian maps showing the Sino-Russian border. He found that the maps were doctored – first, to claim more Chinese territory than had already been annexed, and secondly, to the Border areas and mislead the Chinese by deliberately altering the location of certain places and installations. K'ang used this information to make further criticisms when he attended the Third Congress of the Romanian Workers' Party in Bucharest in 1960.

Perhaps K'ang's greatest achievements were in the field of nuclear and scientific espionage. While his intelligence-gathering in this sphere took far longer than the Russians',it was acquired efficiently, patiently and largely by legal means. Originally he ordered a register of all known Chinese scientists or scientific students living in the West, acquiring in due course a massive amount of nuclear secrets, and luring back to China some of the more promising scientists. Though K'ang had relinquished his directorship of the office of Social Affairs, he was given overall intelligence authority at the Central Intelligence HQ at 15 Bow Street Alley, in Peking. However, he suddenly seemed to lose much of his authority after the Cultural Revolution of the late 1960s.

KAUDER, FRITZ

Best known under his *Abwehr* code-name, 'Max', Kauder was regarded by the Germans as one of their ace agents in World War II, but was reputedly a Hungarian Jew known as Richard Klatt from Vienna. It should perhaps be mentioned that under Admiral Canaris the *Abwehr* sometimes employed a few Jews in their ranks, though this never applied to other branches of Nazi Intelligence. What is most interesting about 'Max' is that he was also regarded as the most successful agent employed by any Western secret service against the Soviet Union, a view expressed by Heinz Hoehne in his book, *Der Krieg im Dunkeln.* This view is substantiated by the late General Gehlen, who as chief of the *Fremde Heere Ost* was responsible for military intelligence on the Russian front. All this is supported by such people as Walter Schellenberg (q.v.), the director of *Amt VI* (foreign intelligence) of the State Security Central Office, and General Guderian, Chief of the General Staff, who regarded 'Max's' information as 'invaluable'.

Yet the captured records of Foreign Armies East and *Abwehr Stab Walli I* (Main Post East I), now available for study, suggest that 'Max' was a Soviet-controlled agent who sent strategic disinformation to German Intelligence as part of an elaborate deception plan. 'Max's' reports gave information about alleged Soviet intentions gleaned from military conferences in Moscow. One such misleading message in July 1942, was about a council attended by Stalin, Molotov, Voroshilov and others, suggesting a withdrawal by the Red Army across the Volga. This and other reports by 'Max' encouraged the Germans to draw deeper into the Ukraine and to foster over-confidence.

'Max's' prize piece of deception was provided in April 1944 concerning 'Operation Bagration'. The purpose of this was to convince the Germans that the main Soviet summer assault would be launched from the southern Ukraine to recapture the Balkans and not against the German Army Group Centre. But 'Max' made no mention of 'Operation Bagration' either then or at any later dates, and it was this operation which actually destroyed the Army Group Centre when the main Soviet offensive was switched to that front.

The *Abwehr* eventually decided that 'Max' was a Soviet double-agent, but by this stage of the war the *Abwehr* was out of favour in the German High Command and both Gehlen and Guderian accepted his information as being accurate. Yet there is still an element of doubt as to whether 'Max' was a Soviet agent, or merely using this connection to aid the Allies as a whole, or even to help create a new Germany. In 1946 there was an attempt by the Russians to kidnap 'Max' from his temporary billet in the US Zone in Austria.

KAWASHIMA, YOSHIKO (d. 1945)

Kawashima was often compared to Mata Hari and earned herself the nickname, 'Joan of Arc of Manchuria', largely because she had a penchant for dressing up in male clothes. She came from a Manchu family, being the daughter of the self-styled Prince Su who had collaborated with another Japanese Intelligence director, Naniwa Kawashima. After Su's death she was adopted by Kawashima and so became a Japanese citizen. She then became a fanatical supporter of Japan and one of its most ardent undercover agents. She craved adventure and was working as a secret agent, disguised as a boy, in Shanghai in 1933. In response to orders from Doihara (q.v.), head of Japanese Intelligence in Manchuria, she hurried to Tientsin to make contact with the ex-boy Emperor of China, Henry Pu Yi. After Pu Yi was taken away on a Japanese launch, Yoshiko Kawashima had the task of rescuing the Empress. With machine-guns firing in the streets of Tientsin and soldiers interfering with traffic, she disguised herself as a male taxi-driver, drew up outside the Empress's home and calmly told her to get into the cab. Despite being stopped several times, her resourcefulness and calm enabled her to bring the Empress to the safety of a Japanese destroyer.

The American *Literary Digest* once stated that 'whenever a

section of the Japanese Army found itself in difficulties, rumour was that Yoshiko was on her way to join them. When her name was mentioned, it invoked victory and inspired the troops.' In November 1945 a news agency report stated that 'a long sought-for beauty in male costume was arrested today in Peking by the Chinese counter-intelligence officers'. Shortly afterwards she was executed by the Chinese as a collaborator.

KEMPEI TAI

Originally known as the Military Police of Japan, the *Kempei Tai* were founded in 1881, eventually evolving into something very different from the military police of most nations and becoming what could best be described as a combination of Britain's MI5, the Special Branch and the French DST. The Intelligence Branch of the Japanese Army liaised with the *Kempei Tai*, but in due course the latter became a power in its own right. One of its first successes was an investigation of German and British machinations in armaments trafficking. They were largely responsible for discovering the sinister part played by Sir Basil Zaharoff, the chief agent of the Vickers company, in negotiating foreign deals. They fully realized how he had made a fortune for himself from commissions acquired by fomenting wars and selling arms to both sides. Thus they found that Vickers had been remitting large sums to Admiral Fuji of the Japanese Navy.

In 1927 the Japanese Justice Ministry created the Thought Section of the Criminal Affairs Bureau with a staff of thirty-five. This was linked to the *Kempei Tai*, and its purpose was twofold: first, to counter the growth of subversive Radicalism and Communism, and secondly, to make a serious study of the various new political philosophies being propagated. It was a typically Japanese approach to the problem – attempting to sift out any new thoughts worth encouraging as well as those to be discouraged. Whenever the 'Think Tank' caught someone propagating subversive ideas, the aim was to threaten prosecution, but to employ skill and tact in trying to 'turn' the person to more orthodox causes. Figures show that out of

62,000 suspected cases between 1928 and 1941 there were fewer than 5000 prosecutions.

Kempei Tai men normally worked in plain clothes, but they were entitled to wear Army uniforms with the special badge of a star surrounded by leaves. By the end of World War II the US Intelligence teams estimated that there were nearly 75,000 *Kempei Tai* members, of whom around one-third were officers. (It was a *Kempei Tai* report which accused Colonel Lindbergh and his wife of spying when they landed in the Kurile Islands in 1931.) Sometimes they employed female agents, such as Madame Nogami, who was nicknamed the 'Queen Cobra' in the European settlements of Shanghai on account of her dreaded reputation. She held the rank of a captain in the *Kempei Tai*, a very rare honour for a woman. The long arm of the organization extended far beyond the Japanese shores.

The Kempei Tai cooperated with the *Tokko Keitsatsu* (Special Security Police) in World War II in controlling propaganda, including radio broadcasts. All Japanese house servants were enrolled by the *Kempei Tai* to report the conversations and activities of their employers. On 4 October 1945 a comprehensive order was issued by the Allied Occupation authorities for the removal of certain officials, and the abolition of the *Kempei Tai* and the entire network of the 'Thought Police'.

Further reading
Kempei-Tai: A History of Japanese Secret Service by Richard Deacon (Beaufort Books, New York; Muller, London 1982)

KENT, TYLER GATEWOOD (b. 1911)

Born in China, Kent's father was a member of the US Diplomatic Corps who declared that Davie Crockett was one of his ancestors. Kent was educated at Princeton, the Sorbonne, the University of Madrid and George Washington University, and was fluent in a number of languages, including Russian. He joined the State Department in 1934 as a clerk in the Foreign

Service and was posted to Moscow. Returning home briefly in 1939, he was made a code clerk and after a further brief spell in Moscow was posted to London in October of that year. Shortly after this he became acquainted with a White Russian named Anna Wolkoff, daughter of the anti-Soviet Tsarist Admiral Wolkoff who had been a naval attaché in London at the time of the Revolution. The Wolkoffs were already under surveillance by MI5 because of their links with a pro-German organization known as the 'Right Club'.

It was Maxwell Knight of MI5 who took most of the credit for trapping Kent after he was suspected of passing classified material to the Germans by an indirect route. The US Ambassador, Joseph Kennedy, was confronted with proof of Kent's activities and he immediately agreed to waive the clerk's diplomatic immunity, thus allowing the British to arrest Kent. He was charged with seven counts of 'obtaining information for a purpose prejudicial to the safety or interests of the State' under the Official Secrets Act, and on 7 November 1940, after the case had been heard *in camera*, he was sentenced to twelve months' imprisonment. Wolkoff was also found guilty under the same Act. It has been said that Kent passed on to the Germans hundreds of confidential signals including some top secret exchanges between President Roosevelt and Churchill, then First Lord of the Admiralty. There is no confirmation of this claim, however, though there has been some bewilderment as to why Kent was kept under surveillance for seven months before action was taken; it seems likely that his diplomatic immunity posed a problem.

Mystery still surrounds Kent, as there has since been evidence to suggest he was working for Moscow as well as Berlin; as this was the time of the Nazi-Soviet Pact, the issue is somewhat blurred. Kent's contacts in London included one Willy Brandes, who was controlled by the Soviet network in the USA. MI5 also discovered that there was a leakage of information about the American Embassy in Berlin by someone who was referred to as the 'Doctor'. At the same time it was also suggested that there was a link from someone in the British Foreign Office to the German Ambassador in London during the summer of 1939, prior to the outbreak of war. However, he was in no way charged with being a double agent during his trial. Yet when

Kent left Moscow he asked colleagues to forward to him a briefcase by diplomatic pouch. According to records in the National Archives of the US Department of State, this case contained a hand-gun with ammunition, three photographs (one clothed, two nude) of his Moscow mistress, Tatiana Ilovaiskaya, a photograph of a nude Russian actress and another of an unidentified nude male and female.

KRAEMER, KARL-HEINZ ('JOSEPHINE')

One of the least publicized, yet most successful German spies in World War II, 'Josephine' long baffled Allied attempts to track him down. Everybody was looking for a beautiful woman capable of worming secrets out of senior politicians and members of the Forces. It became clear in 1943 that 'Josephine' was somehow sending top-secret intelligence from Whitehall to Germany via Sweden. Having eliminated various women, the finger of suspicion pointed towards the Swedish naval attaché in London who was unjustly suspected of feeding material to a female spy. He was asked to leave the country – a hurt and puzzled man. But the attaché in question was not 'Josephine', nor was he a spy for the Germans. The *Abwehr* had infiltrated a spy under this code-name into the Swedish Foreign Department, a playboy businessman named Karl-Heinz Kraemer, who worked in Hamburg, but had established links in Stockholm which he frequently visited. He seduced pretty Swedish secretaries who worked on the Defence Staff, and they passed on to him, among many other things, the London attaché's invaluable dispatches. Kraemer stayed in Stockholm until April 1945, but was captured by the British in Flensburg and flown to the UK for interrogation.

KRIVITSKY, GENERAL WALTER (d. 1941)

Born a Polish Jew named Ginsberg, Krivitsky was the first top-ranking Soviet Intelligence officer to defect to the West and perhaps because of this, he was the most neglected. Much of the evidence he gave about Soviet infiltration in the highest circles of the British and American establishments was never followed up. He has often been erroneously described as a major-general in the GRU, though he never claimed this title. For some years he was active as a Soviet Intelligence officer in Vienna where he worked with Ignace Reiss (q.v.) but in 1933 he was transferred to Holland as resident director of intelligence with liaison responsibilities for other West European countries, until he defected in 1937. When Reiss was liquidated by the Stalinist murder gang operating in Switzerland, Krivitsky began to realize that his own future might be in jeopardy. By this time he had also realized that Stalin was prepared to 'extend the hand of secret friendship to Hitler', so he broke with the Russians. He defected in Paris and went first to Hyères and then to the USA. For a while he lay low in Canada, living in Montreal under the cover name of 'Walter Thomas'. It was not until 1939 that he was brought to London. Afterwards he complained that 'nobody would listen to me'.

His own statement was that 'in 1923 I was sent to Germany to prepare the world for a German revolution and to organize the manpower for a German "red army". From 1924-26 I worked for the General Staff of the Red Army. In 1925 I became the central Russian chief of the third section of Soviet Military Intelligence. In 1933 I was appointed director of the War Industries Institute and worked in that capacity for a year. In 1934 I returned directly to the intelligence work in the general staff and continued in that capacity until my break in 1937. In 1936-37 I was chief of the Soviet Military Intelligence for Western Europe.' It was Krivitsky who revealed to the USA how the Soviet Government had financed intelligence operations by smuggling gold and jewellery into Britain and the USA in the early 1920s. Before World War II he revealed that 'at least two

202

fully-fledged Soviet spies were in the inner sanctums of the British Government'. He believed one of them was a code clerk named King in the secretariat of the Cabinet. (The name was right, but the man was actually attached to the Foreign Office.) The other worked for the Council of Imperial Defence. Neither the British nor the Americans seemed to take Krivitsky's revelations very seriously. King, who had been a cipher clerk in the Foreign Office, was arrested and imprisoned at the beginning of World War II, but despite being questioned at great length, little was gained from this.

An American member of the Martin Dies Committee who investigated Krivitsky said, 'Sixty-one Soviet agents were described by Krivitsky as working the UK and the Commonwealth and only six of these comprised Soviet citizens having diplomatic status, while eighteen "illegal" agents were operating in Britain alone, providing courier services and setting up "safe houses". Sixteen British subjects were among the full-time Soviet agents and of these, three were members of the Labour Party and one was an Independent politician, four were trade union officials, three were in the Foreign Office, three in either SIS or MI5 (with Krivitsky emphasizing that one was definitely in MI5) and two were foreign correspondents of British newspapers.' One of the most surprising features of this conspiracy of silence by the British establishment is that, at the time of the disappearance of Burgess and Maclean in 1951, Herbert Morrison, then Foreign Secretary, was kept in ignorance of the Soviet defector's evidence. Krivitsky always feared that his movements were being tracked by the Soviet Union. In 1941 he was found shot dead in his hotel room in Washington, and though the verdict was suicide, he is now thought to have been murdered by a hired Soviet killer.

Krivitsky referred in his evidence to one Soviet agent inside the Foreign Office who was 'a Scotsman with Bohemian tastes'. It is now believed that this was not Donald Maclean, but Sir Archibald Clark Kerr (later Lord Inverchapel).

Further reading
I Was Stalin's Agent by Walter G. Krivitsky (Hamish Hamilton, London 1939)

KUCZYNSKI, URSULA RUTH

Ruth Kuczynski was one of the most professional and efficient long-term spies – so efficient, in fact, that even some of the keenest intelligence investigators in the Western World are not sure of the full extent of her successes. Her father was a German Jewish professor of economics who taught at Oxford University. Under her present name of Ruth Werner she published *Sonja's Rapport*, her own story, in East Berlin in 1977. This told how she went out to the USA in the mid-1920s, worked in a bookshop in New York and met 'Rolf' (Rudolph) Hamburger who was finishing his studies as an architect. She went back to Germany and married him in 1929. Already a Communist, when her husband acquired a post as an architect in Shanghai, she went out with him in 1930. Here she met Agnes Smedley (q.v.), the American who worked as an agent for Richard Sorge (q.v.) and others, and it seems certain that Smedley was the person who helped to recruit her into the espionage network.

It seems that Ruth Hamburger undertook espionage work despite the objections of her husband, and that he did not know their flat was used as an illegal meeting place. One of her contacts was code-named 'Fred', and from all accounts he seems to have been Manfred Stern, who was in China as the chief military adviser to the Central Committee of the Communist Party of China, and who later became famous under the name of 'General Kleber' as defender of the Republican Front in Madrid. At some stage it seems certain that 'Sonja', her code-name, was called to Moscow for talks and training after which she returned to China and settled in Mukden. She left China in 1935, leaving her husband behind.

Once again she went to Moscow, this time attending the Wireless Communication School, after which she went to the UK where she was met by her parents. It was at this time that 'Sonja' claims she learnt by accident that she had been promoted 'in the Army [presumably the GRU] from the rank of captain (in China) to that of major'. Later it seems that she was made a lieutenant-colonel. In the UK she established contact with her controller and was given the names of two Britons who would be helpful to her in a new mission to Switzerland. She then made her home in Montreux where she arranged for Alexander Foote (q.v.), whom she calls 'Allen', to be established as the network's radio operator.

By this time 'Sonja' had two children, but this seems in no way to have deterred her from undertaking dangerous work. In her memoirs 'Sonja' mentions 'a second English comrade' called 'Len' whom she met in 1939 when Moscow Centre suggested for reasons of security that she should get a divorce from Rolf and arrange a marriage of convenience with 'Len' in order to get a British passport. How she managed to get out of Switzerland in wartime, surrounded as it was by enemy-controlled territory, she does not say; she merely mentions arriving in Liverpool in 1940. However, there is ample independent evidence that during 1941 and afterwards she was living with 'Len', or Leon Beurton, in a furnished house some distance outside Oxford. She has admitted that during this period she used her transmitter about twice a week, while also passing on intelligence to her Soviet controller in London. 'Sonja' has referred to an important contact she made during this period, an RAF officer who had great respect for the Soviet Union. He had access to details of the latest developments in aeroplane construction. It is now clear that 'Sonja's' father helped his daughter in her mission for the USSR and so did her brother, Jurgen, who was a colonel in the US Army and also cooperating with the OSS.

As a result of information given to MI5 by Alexander Foote when he contacted the British after getting away from Russia, 'Sonja' and 'Len' were interrogated by police officers. In the meantime she had contacts with Klaus Fuchs (see *Nuclear Spies*, Part IV). For some reason MI5 failed to keep a sufficiently close watch on 'Sonja', or to arrest her. Somebody obviously protected her inside the British Establishment, or alternatively there was criminal negligence inside the Security Forces, for 'Sonja' and 'Len' left for a holiday in East Berlin from which they never returned.

LIDDELL, CAPTAIN GUY MAYNARD (1892-1958)

Controversy about Guy Liddell will undoubtedly continue for many years. Was he, as his former colleagues in MI5 and MI6 still insist, an efficient and patriotic intelligence officer, or was he one of the first Soviet agents, even if only as a protector of such agents? The son of Captain A.F. Liddell, he was originally intent on a musical career, being a gifted cellist. He had studied in Germany and, but for the advent of World War I, might have become a professional musician. He served with the Royal Field Artillery from 1914-19, winning the MC. Then he joined Scotland Yard in 1919 where colleagues described him as quiet and secretive, but having a clear mind and a mastery of detail. Later he became the liaison man between Scotland Yard, the Special Branch, the Foreign Office and MI5. A former colleague stated, 'He was involved in an inquiry into the leakage of information about the Arcos raid (q.v.) which enabled the Soviet apparat in the City to burn the most vital papers before the police arrived. Liddell knew all about the raid and it was felt at the time that the leakage could only have come from the Foreign Office or the Yard. Liddell was not suspected at the time, but this incident was remembered years later when he was being investigated.'

In 1931 Liddell was brought into MI5, acting as a liaison man with the Special Branch. During World War II he ran B Division which was concerned with counter-espionage. In this period he made close personal friends of some of the moles inside MI5 and MI6, including Blunt and Philby, both of whom he vouched for in their respective jobs, despite the fact that he knew the pro-Communist background of each. But it was his friendship with Guy Burgess (q.v.) which was later to cost him his post. Liddell liaised with the XX Committee on many matters, including the Japanese questionnaire captured by Dusko Popov (q.v.), which pointed to an attack on Pearl Harbour. Liddell, surprisingly, took it upon himself merely to send Popov to the USA to tell his story to Hoover, head of the FBI, apparently warning Hoover that Popov was also an agent of the Germans. This was, of course, true, but Popov's real loyalty was to the Allies and his value to them was as a double-agent. Hoover disliked Popov from the beginning and regarded him as unreliable; afterwards Popov wrote of Hoover that he was 'the man responsible for the disaster of Pearl Harbour'. But it was more Liddell who was to blame than Hoover. At the very least, Liddell, or the XX Committee, should have seen that the questionnaire was given to the US Office of Naval Intelligence, if not the White House as well.

In his autobiography Philby has written that when Sir David Petric retired as chief of MI5, 'B Division would have voted to a man for Liddell to succeed him'. Ellen Wilkinson, as private secretary to Herbert Morrison, Home Secretary in the Attlee government, had had warnings about Liddell from some of her Continental friends who, like herself, had left the Communist Party before war began. It was partly because of this warning that Liddell did not get the top job, but was made Deputy Director-General. After the war Liddell regularly met Philby, Burgess, Blunt and Tomas Harris (a war-time colleague) at a Chelsea public house. When the Burgess-Maclean scandal broke and suspicions against Philby were voiced, Liddell himself was under investigation, though this was hushed up. Shortly afterwards Liddell was demoted and given the curious job of Chief Security Officer at Harwell. There were those in MI5 who demanded that Liddell should resign at once, but he had powerful friends in both MI5 and MI6 and, though edged sideways into the Harwell posting, nominally he remained with MI5 for two more years, being awarded the CB in 1953. During this period there were totally inadequate vetting procedures at the Atomic Energy Authority at Harwell and several cases of leaked information.

'LONDON CAGE'

One of the most efficient interrogating teams ever established was the 'London Cage', known for a short time as KPM, set up at the end of World War II at 6-7 Kensington Palace Gardens in London. A special intelligence unit of German-speaking interrogators was given the task of questioning German prisoners-of-war. There was also a careful scrutiny of any spies who might have been infiltrated into the ranks of prisoners-of-war and to check disturbing reports (later proved to be unfounded) that the Nazis had gone underground after their defeat and were planning a clandestine organization.

The head of the 'London Cage' was Lieutenant-Colonel Alexander Paterson Scotland, who had actually served in the German Army for a short while. He had spent his early years cattle-farming in S.W. Africa, then under German control, and taken a temporary commission in the German Army when it appealed for recruits to quell a native uprising. On the strength of his fluent German and his knowledge of German military organization, Scotland became an intelligence officer in both world wars and was one of the most formidable of British interrogators. The fact that he had served in the German Army many years previously was carefully disguised. Instead the legend was built up that he had infiltrated the German General Staff in World War II and knew all that had been going on. It was a bluff which worked remarkably well and caused many senior German officers to tell the British a great deal of secret information.

LUCAS, WILLIAM OTTO (1893-1978)

William Lucas is the author's favourite spy, which is the main reason for including him in this book. He was born in St Petersburg to a German father and a British mother named Caroline Yannutsch. Later, while serving in the Russian (Tsarist) Army in World War I, he claimed to be a Finnish citizen. In 1915 he was a member of the Russian Military Purchasing Mission in Paris and New York. What happened after that war is not altogether clear, but it seems that he served on General Mannerheim's staff in Finland, joined General Kornilov's White Russian Army, spent six months in a Bolshevik prison camp and later received protection from a friend high up in the Soviet hierarchy. He went to the USA and became a naturalized American citizen in 1930. In New York he met a man he had originally known in Paris in 1915, Wythe Williams, the editor of a Connecticut paper known as *Greenwich Time*. Under the pseudonym of William van Narvig, Lucas proceeded to give that small suburban newspaper astonishing world scoops of events in Europe between 1937 and the entry of the USA into World War II. He even rigged up a special wireless receiving set, allegedly enabling Williams to have the benefit of intercepted coded messages from the German High Command. So important was Lucas's personal contribution that he shared the credit with Williams for *Secret Sources* a book they co-authored in 1942, which told how 'van Narvig' smuggled out dispatches from his contacts in Germany and even tapped enemy radio communications.

Lucas was believed to be a close acquaintance of Colonel Josef Veltjens, Goering's right-hand man, and to stay on occasions at Goering's hunting lodge at Karin Hall. Yet even during World War II Lucas could equally visit Andrei Zhdanov in Moscow, then regarded by some as a possible heir-apparent to Stalin. As a one-man, freelance spy organization providing scoops for *Greenwich Time*, he was incomparable; sometimes his dispatches arrived by letter from such unexpected places as Rio de Janeiro. When the USA entered the war Lucas became an agent of G-2, the military intelligence branch of the US Army, and was sent on various missions to organize German underground activities and counteract Nazi espionage. Lucas discovered that Moscow's choice for their top agent in the USA was none other than Gerhart Eisler. But Lucas's warnings on Eisler were ignored for far too long. The last news of Lucas was contained in an article he wrote on the war in Korea in July 1953. After that he went down to Florida with his family and disappeared totally. Shortly before this he had been engaged in setting up what he called the Legion of Good Neighbours, a non-political body aimed at preserving world peace and strengthening patriotic causes.

Further reading
With My Little Eye by Richard Deacon (Muller, 1982)
Secret Sources: the Story Behind some Famous Scoops by Wythe Williams and William Van Narvig (Ziff-Davis, New York 1943)

'LUCY' RING

It has been claimed that the 'Lucy' spy network in Switzerland during World War II made all the difference between a Russian victory and defeat. Through this unique secret service, plans and orders of the German High Command on the Eastern Front right down to brigade level were transmitted to Moscow daily. 'Lucy's' identity was revealed after the war as Rudolf Roessler, a German publisher who moved to Switzerland after the Nazis came to power and started up a firm called Vita Nova Verlag in Geneva. He was eventually employed by Brigadier Masson of the Swiss Security organization, in the Bureau Ha (see *Switzerland*, Part I). After the fall of France when the Swiss were temporarily concerned about the possibility of a German invasion, his job was to assess military intelligence relating to Germany. Roessler not only proved to be a highly competent analyst of such information, but to provide extremely accurate forecasts of what the Nazis would do next. At the same time Roessler began to send out information to the Russians, intelligence so valuable that the Soviet Union eventually gave him a retainer equivalent at that time to £350 a month plus various commodity emoluments.

The mystery of Roessler, who is now dead, has always been how he obtained such detailed information of German military plans. Pierre Accoce and Pierre Quet, the authors of *La Guerre a été gagnée en Suisse*, suggest that ten Bavarian officers who served with Roessler in World War I became anti-Nazis, but joined the German Army and, having reached high rank, were jointly able to send to Roessler in Geneva by German Army radio channels intelligence of all operations on the Eastern Front. It only requires a cursory examination of this theory to realize that it defies belief. The ten Bavarians are never named, nor is it explained how they could continue to use official channels for sending such information.

The 'Lucy' ring was, in fact, a Russian controlled organization, employing a number of Soviet agents including Sandor Rado, Ursula Ruth Kuczynski (q.v.) and two Britons, one of whom, Alexander Foote, wrote a book touching on the whole affair, entitled *Handbook for Spies*. The truth is that the

'Lucy' ring obtained intelligence from outside its organization, sometimes from unofficial networks such as PAKBO and INSA (q.v.), but also some material cleverly disseminated by the British from intercepts of German signals at Bletchley. The British knew that the Russians, especially Stalin, still mistrusted them despite the fact that they were allies. Knowing that Germany must be prevented from defeating Russia at all costs, the British used a Soviet spy as their link-agent in passing intelligence to the 'Lucy' ring so that Moscow would not suspect where it came from. Somehow the scheme worked, though on occasions Moscow centre declined even to accept 'Lucy' material as altogether reliable.

Alexander Foote claimed that 'for three vital years of the war' he was 'to a large extent controller of the Russian spy network in Switzerland, which was working against Germany ... I sent back much of the information which enabled the Russians to make their successful stand before Moscow'. The Resident Director of Soviet espionage in Switzerland and mastermind of the 'Lucy' ring was Alexander Radolfi (see *Rado, Sandor*, Part III) who, under the cover of working in a firm of Swiss map-makers, had been in charge of operations since 1937. Roessler's true allegiance was to the Czechs, for whom he worked for a short while after World War II. Only in November 1943, when the tide of war had turned in the Allies' favour, did the Swiss start making arrests of the Soviet spy network, and even then they were extremely lenient towards Foote who had a relatively comfortable time in prison and was released the following year. Kuczynski managed to reach Britain and Rado escaped to France.

Perhaps the final tribute to the 'Lucy' ring should come from Constantine Fitzgibbon, who was involved in deciphering operations at Bletchley during World War II: 'Since the Russians would not accept military intelligence from any but their own sources, Ultra and much else was fed to them via the "Lucy" ring.

Further reading
Secret Intelligence in the Twentieth Century by Constantine Fitzgibbon (Hart-Davis, MacGibbon, London 1976)
Handbook for Spies by Alexander Foote (Museum Press, London 1949)

MACKENZIE, SIR COMPTON (1883-1973)

Born Edward Montagu Compton, educated at St Paul's Scool, London, and Magdalen College, Oxford, Sir Compton Mackenzie originally studied law, but also toyed with the idea of acting. Having already become an author of some distinction before World War I, he joined the Royal Marines, achieving the rank of captain and serving with the Royal Navy Detachment in the Dardanelles expedition in 1915. Invalided during the same year, he was appointed Military Control Officer in Athens in 1916 and later Director of the Aegean Intelligence Service in Syria. During this period Mackenzie was mixed up in a good deal of cloak-and-dagger activities which aroused strong criticism of the British Secret Service among both enemies and neutral parties. He described Secret Service machinations in Greece in his book, *Athenian Memories* (1931). He was appointed head of the Anglo-French police in Athens, accepting this post with considerable enthusiasm, for he had very definite ideas about what British policy should be in the Balkans, and was anxious to see a Greek crusade against both Turks and Germans. As a result some grossly inaccurate and wildly extravagant stories were told about him in Athens. He was even alleged to have made an attempt on King Constantine's life and to have tried to surround the palace with fire so that there should be no possible escape for the inmates.

Mackenzie was always in trouble; unfortunately for him he was often blamed for many of the outrages perpetrated by the thugs employed by Sir Basil Zaharoff, the international arms magnate. As he describes in *Aegean Memories* (1940), on one occasion Captain Sir Mansfield Cumming, 'C', head of the British Secret Service, told him that he had been reported as visiting Maxim's in Paris and talking 'with the greatest indiscretion of diplomatic secrets'. In fact, Mackenzie had never been to Maxim's, and the alleged indiscreet talk could only possibly refer to a dinner party given in the British Embassy. The story was part of a Foreign Office campaign to discredit certain Secret Service agents. Mackenzie landed in even deeper trouble when he revealed in his book, *Greek Memories*, that a former British Intelligence colleague had planned to blow up a bridge near Constantinople. The book had to be withdrawn from publication and Mackenzie was charged under the Official Secrets Act. He was brought to trial at the Old Bailey in 1933 and fined £100. It was a ridiculous charge and a ludicrous sentence. Mackenzie described how the prosecutor condemned him because he had 'revealed the mysterious consonant by which the Chief of the Secret Service is known'. The judge asked the obvious question: 'Why, if C is such a dangerous consonant, is it being used fifteen years after the war?' There was no adequate reply to this.

Mackenzie got his own back on both MI5 and MI6 when he wrote his spoof novel on the British Secret Service, *Water on the Brain*. Blenkinsop, his fictional hero, makes the mistake of referring to his chief, 'N', by his real name of Colonel Nutting, and is swiftly ticked off for doing so. A certain amount of satire directed towards MI5 was contained in Mackenzie's humourous World War II novel, *Whisky Galore*. In that war Mackenzie himself was a captain in the Home Guard. He was knighted in 1952.

THE MAFIA'S ROLE IN WORLD WAR II

Under Mussolini every effort had been made to stamp out the dreaded Mafia secret society because it was feared that it might become a rival to his own Fascist Party. The task of defeating the Mafia was given to the Duce's own chief of police, who arrested suspects by the thousand and shipped them off to penal islands, so that by 1927 Mussolini was able to announce to the Fascist Parliament that the war against the Mafia had ended. When the question of invading Sicily and Italy was discussed, MI6 took the view that it would be extremely dangerous to revive the Mafia and allow it unbridled authority, but it was agreed that some former Mafia members might be cautiously used as agents. The Americans, however, had other ideas. In 1943 'Lucky' Luciano, born Salvatore Lucania in Sicily, and head of the American Mafia, was in prison in the USA, and

American Intelligence, aided by the US Navy, decided to make use of his services to contact the underground head of the Mafia in Sicily. In return for these services Luciano was given his freedom – officially in 1945 – but some claim, he was secretly taken to Sicily and seen in the vicinity of the US Seventh Army's HQ shortly after the invasion.

Extensive Mafia aid was given to the American troops in an area dominated partly by Don Calo, a local Mafia leader. Something like 15 per cent of the US troops were of Sicilian origin, deliberately selected for the operation on orders from US Intelligence. While it would be churlish to detract from the imaginative way in which the US exploited the Mafia in Sicily and so paved the way to a more or less bloodless invasion of the western area of the island, it cannot be denied that the cooperation went too far. Imprisoned Mafiosi were speedily released and within weeks, most Sicilian towns had Mafia mayors. Meanwhile in the area where the British operated, Scotland Yard was asked to send out men to round up the worst of the Mafia gangsters – a stark contrast to US policy. (See also *Giuliano, Salvatore*, Part III.)

'THE MAN WHO NEVER WAS'

This was the title of Ewen Montagu's book which told the true story of the mysterious and mythical 'Major Martin', whose body was washed ashore in Spain in World War II. Montagu, as a lieutenant-commander, RNVR, was in charge of planning an operation by the Naval Intelligence Division aided by the Twenty-Two Committee and MI5. This was named 'Operation Mincemeat' and aimed at deceiving the Germans. When the invasion of Sicily was being planned by the Allies it was essential to mislead the Germans into thinking that landings were being planned in other areas. For this purpose a corpse, supposedly a Royal Marines major carrying plans for an Allied invasion of Greece, was deposited by a British submarine on the Spanish coast in the hope that the Spanish authorities would inform the Germans. This plan, carried out in May 1943, was a resounding success. An obituary of 'Major Martin' was even published in *The Times*. (See also *Spain*, Part I)

What Montagu did not reveal in his otherwise detailed book was the surprising difficulty of obtaining a body in complete secrecy during wartime. He approached his friend, Sir William Bentley Purchase, the Coroner for St Pancras, saying that he needed a body and that his plan (details of which he kept secret) was supported by the Prime Minister. Finally, Sir William found the right corpse, though his biographer, Robert Jackson, stated that 'Purchase's action in providing the body had the sanction not only of the Government, but the man's own relatives, but he was still worried about the effect on public opinion of the unorthodox disposal of a body which had been in his keeping'. All this palaver over finding the right body seems rather ridiculous in view of the grave security risks. Many people must have heard of the quest for a body, even if they did not know the purpose of the quest. One cannot help feeling it would have been safer to have just 'acquired' a body by unorthodox methods without asking questions or getting permission.

The most remarkable feature of 'The Man Who Never Was' operation was the detailed imaginative planning that went with it. 'Major Martin' was not only given a bank statement which showed a modest overdraft, but a photograph of a mythical girlfriend as well (see *The Girl Who Never Was*', Part III). The operation had to be cleared personally with President Roosevelt through William Stephenson (q.v.), who was the SIS's chief link between the British and Americans in World War II.

Further reading
The Man Who Never Was by Ewen Montagu (Evans Bros., London 1953)
Coroner: A Biography of William Bentley Purchase by Robert Jackson

MARCH, DON JUAN (d. 1961)

A multi-millionaire with stakes in banking, oil, shipping and tobacco production, and the owner of half of Majorca, Don Juan March saw some of the espionage action in two world wars. A.E.W. Mason (see Part II), the novelist and a British spy in World War I, has been credited with winning March as an ally. Certainly he became a firm admirer of Britain and British institutions and believed it to be a matter of sound policy for Spain to be on good terms with the British. During World War I he gave considerable assistance to the NID and Admiral Hall. He was a friend both of Sir Basil Zaharoff, the arms magnate, and Admiral Canaris, head of the *Abwehr*. When he escaped from Spain to Gibraltar in 1933 to get away from Republican forces who had sworn he was an enemy of democracy because of his support for General Franco, Juan March was tipped off by the NID about his possible arrest. It was they who arranged his escape from the Alcara de Henares prison where he had been held on charges of alleged tobacco smuggling. Juan March suggested to the British SIS that Canaris was a man who could be won over as — in his own words — 'a sleeping partner of British espionage'. It was advice which was sadly mishandled.

In September 1939 Juan March went to see Admiral Godfrey, then head of the NID, explaining that he had control of all Spanish ports, except on the north and north-west coasts, and would do all in his power to help Britain. He had a rather devious plan which involved the British helping him to purchase fifty-five German ships then in Spanish ports. It was a scheme favoured by Churchill and the NID, but thwarted by the Foreign Office who mistrusted March. Nevertheless March kept in touch with the NID throughout World War II and passed on much vital and accurate intelligence. His control of oil supplies was invaluable.

MASON-MACFARLANE, LIEUTENANT-GENERAL SIR NOEL (1889-1853)

When appointed head of a British military mission to Russia soon after World War I, Mason-Macfarlane not only had his first experience of intelligence work, but developed a deep dislike of Communism, only later matched by his hatred of Nazism. After his death the German periodical, *Der Spiegel*, revealed that he had worked out a plan to assassinate Hitler personally a year before World War II began. Mrs John Hall, his daughter, later confirmed the story, as did others who knew Mason-Macfarlane. The plan failed because it was rejected by both the Secret Service and the British Government.

The Colonel, as he then was, was convinced that the *Führer*'s death would bring about the collapse of the National Socialist regime in Germany. He was well aware that there were forces in the *Wehrmacht* who would have seized the opportunity to overthrow a system they disliked. Mason-Macfarlane had a flat in Berlin which overlooked an area where Hitler and other Nazi leaders frequently reviewed military parades. He was prepared to carry out the killing himself with a rifle from his own window. When he told Ewen Butler, the *Times* correspondent in Berlin, of his plan, Butler protested that 'the murder of the Chancellor by the British military attaché would create a really formidable diplomatic incident. He agreed, but added that nobody in Germany would go to war on that account, whereas if Hitler lived war was certain.'

Mason-Macfarlane was Director of Military Intelligence, British Expeditionary Force, in 1939-40, with the rank of general. Later he was appointed Governor of Gibraltar where he was extremely popular. After the war he stood as Labour candidate in the general election of 1945 against Brendan Bracken and won the contest, much to Churchill's disgust, as Bracken was his protegé.

MASTERMAN, JOHN CECIL (1891-1977)

'Major (Local) and specially employed' was the coy description which Sir John Masterman gave to his World War II service in *Who's Who*. In fact, his work was much more fascinating, and he expressed it much more succinctly in his official report to the Director-General of the Security Service in 1945: 'By means of the double-cross system we actively ran and controlled the German espionage system in this country.'

Masterman, who had been interned in Germany in World War I, spent his life between the wars at Oxford University where he was Censor of Christ Church from 1920-26. In World War II he became chairman of the XX (Double-cross) Committee, which supervised the work conducted mainly by the B 1A section of MI5, which aimed at using pro-Allies posing as German agents and also real German agents captured in Britain to supply Germany with information devised and manipulated by British Intelligence (see *Double-cross System*, Part III). In 1972 Masterman published a history of the whole affair entitled *The Double-cross System in the War of 1939-45*, saying that 'it occurred to me and to others that there might well be a case for publication ... it was also right to give credit for a successful operation to those who deserved it ... Failures are exaggerated, successes never mentioned.'

Masterman told how there were about 120 double-cross agents in MI5 records, though some of the cases either never got off the ground or were not successful. While claiming that the Germans were exploited to a damaging extent by the Double-cross system, Masterman insisted that they 'were at least our equals in all the arts connected with espionage and counter-espionage'.

MATA HARI'S DAUGHTER

This is a convenient title for a character who remains something of a mystery and whose identity has never been confirmed. She has been variously named as Banda Macleod (known by General Sir Philip Christison when he was serving in the Far East in World War II and afterwards Allied Commander Netherland East Indies), and as Banda Gertrud and Wilhelmina Vandereen. Accounts of her life have been given by such authors as Bernard Newman (a highly conscientious source), Kurt Singer and Charles Franklin. Other researches give her name as Margarida Gertrud Zelle Macleod and suggest that she was a seventeen-year-old schoolgirl, living with relatives in Batavia when she heard her mother had been executed in France (see *Mata Hari*, Part II). But she never spoke of her mother; a change of name and her identity was quickly forgotten, except for a few who knew the truth.

She studied hard, went to college and became a teacher. But

when the Dutch East Indies were invaded by the Japanese she listened to those who came to her parties, including Japanese officers, and passed on the information to the Indonesian underground and the Allies. Soon her contacts extended to Allied centres overseas. After the war she met and fell in love with a Malaysian guerrilla named Suleiman who believed the best way of gaining independence for his country was by supporting the Malaysian Chinese Communists. Banda persuaded him that he was wrong and together they worked against the Malaysian guerrillas and bandits and passed information to the British. It is at this stage that any reliable intelligence on Banda becomes scarce. It is said that she went to Washington and was able to convince people there that the Malayan war was not just a question of Britain keeping down the natives, but of creating independence quickly by persuading the Malaysian people to support the British cause. Her husband was by then supposed to have been murdered by the Communists. Another report says that her doom was sealed when she was sent on a secret spying mission to Korea and was discovered by the Communists. She suffered the same penalty as her mother – death by execution squad. It makes a neat end to her story, but alas, there is no proof of this.

MENZHINSKY, VYACHESLAV (d. 1934)

Succeeding the able Dzerzhinsky as head of the GPU, was Menzhinsky, another Pole. He had been a protegé of Lenin who dubbed him 'my decadent neurotic' and this surprising trust was at first maintained by Stalin who called him 'my amiable, but watchful Polish bear'. Menzhinsky not only displayed his contempt for the Communist Party rank and file, but enjoyed luxurious living. He would even conduct interrogations lying on a settee draped in rich Chinese silks, manicuring himself while he put his questions. He surrounded himself with Polish agents and was more interested in counter-espionage than in spying abroad, taking the view that the only worthwhile intelligence overseas was in the field of science. It is not surprising that he was nicknamed the 'Poet of the *Cheka*', as his office was filled with beautiful works of art and he spent much of his time translating poetry.

Despite making enemies easily owing to an impulsive tongue, Menzhinsky remained head of the GPU until 1934, when, according to the *Greater Soviet Encylopaedia*, 'he was atrociously murdered upon the orders of the anti-Soviet counter-revolutionaries'. It should be pointed out that this quotation comes from an encyclopaedia published before the de-Stalinization campaign and was only repeating assertions made in the political trials of the late 1930s. But no explanation of Menzhinsky's death has ever been offered and, though he appears to have got on well with Stalin, it is possible he was liquidated on Stalin's orders.

MENZIES, MAJOR-GENERAL SIR STEWART (1890-1968)

When Admiral Sinclair retired from the post of 'C', Stewart Menzies became the first head of the British SIS who was not a naval officer. Educated at Eton, he had served in the Grenadier Guards in World War I, winning the DSO and MC. During that war he joined Douglas Haig's counter-intelligence division at Montreuil, and as a result of this, was appointed head of the military section of MI6 after World War I. Menzies' meticulously orthodox background was enhanced with a certain mystique because he was reputed to be one of King Edward VII's illegitimate children. He was not only aware of the legend, but sometimes cleverly exploited it because it was the kind of thing that gave him added status with various friends in Germany.

Menzies had a far more sophisticated political sense than any of his predecessors and was admirable in handling politicians. He was equally adept in handling his sovereign, for when King George VI playfully asked him one day who was his chief agent inside Germany, he replied that he could not answer. 'Suppose I said "Off with your head, if you don't tell me"?' enquired the King. 'Then, sire, my head would have to go,' replied Menzies.

His supreme success was in obtaining the secret of the Enigma encoding device (q.v.) through Polish intermediaries in July 1939. Menzies himself went to Warsaw to supervise the final arrangements, being at the time Admiral Sinclair's deputy. Perhaps his biggest disappointment was the lack of success he had in persuading Britain to make an ally of Admiral Canaris, head of the German Secret Service. He believed that MI6 had made a big mistake in not establishing better contacts in that direction years before. Menzies tried to establish such links, but received little encouragement and no cooperation from other Intelligence departments, except the NID. Towards the end of the war he was advised by Cavendish-Bentinck, chairman of the Joint Intelligence Committee (see *Portland, Ninth Duke of*, Part III), to hoard all the money he could because the Treasury would not be very helpful when the war ended. This Menzies did and it undoubtedly helped a British service which has always been made to suffer in peacetime.

NEWMAN, BERNARD (1897-1968)

A grand-nephew of George Eliot and himself an author of spy fiction, Newman was also an enthusiastic amateur spy. He served with the BEF in France during World War I, and the story goes that, because he was unable to stay on a horse, the Army gave him a bicycle. Ever afterwards cycling was Newman's favourite recreation and on his bicycle, which he called 'George', he travelled all over Europe and even behind the Iron Curtain. He entered the Civil Service in 1920 and was once in danger of being sacked when the Foreign Office objected to a book of his, entitled *Danger Spots of Europe*. With the approach of World War II Newman kept an eye open on his travels for any sign of new developments in German arms production, passing on reports to the authorities at home. Quite by chance, he was the first man to make a report on the V2 rocket when, in 1938, he came across some installations built on reinforced concrete and surrounded by barbed wire on the Baltic coast at Peenemunde. A friendly hotel-keeper told him that the place was used for experiments for a new type of rocket. However, the British Secret Service and the War Office both foolishly ignored his report. He was also banned from Italy by Mussolini.

OLDHAM, ERNEST HOLLOWAY (1897-1933)

The London *Times* of 30 September 1933 carried a brief news item stating that 'Kensington police are trying to trace the identity of a man aged about thirty-five, who was found dead in a gas-filled kitchen at 31 Pembroke Gardens, Kensington ... the shirt bore the initials EHO'. After that there was absolute silence in the press, both national and local – no mention of an inquest, no obituary, no indication of the man's identity. A search of wills for 1934 at Somerset House, revealed that the initials EHO stood for Ernest Holloway Oldham, while a search of death certificates showed that he had died from 'coal gas poisoning' and a verdict of suicide while of unsound mind had been recorded. In fact, Oldham was one of the earliest recruits, if not the first, that the Soviet Union acquired inside the British Foreign Office and was known as 'B 3'. He became a clerk in the Foreign Office in 1914, was on active service in the British Army from February 1917 to December 1918, and then returned to the FO. By August 1928 he had been promoted to 'staff officer'. FO records show that he resigned in September 1932, an unusual occurrence at such an early age, especially as he had no other job in view.

Oldham was engaged in handling ciphers and had visited Paris and elsewhere on the Continent. While he was in Paris, using a false name, he called on the Soviet Embassy and offered to sell cipher secrets. From then on Oldham continued to supply the USSR with information in London as well as elsewhere and he also recruited another FO clerk, Captain John Herbert King, as a Soviet agent. Eventually, for reasons which are still not altogether clear, Oldham had a change of mind and told the Russians he wanted to end his arrangement with them. When they insisted he should carry on, he resigned from the FO in the hope that this would strengthen his case. But the Russians knew that if Oldham opted out, their other agents inside the UK, including King, would also be in danger. In view of this, it is possible that Oldham was murdered by the NKVD, rather as happened with Walter Krivitsky (q.v.). Such killings have been a regular technique of Soviet counter-espionage death squads, as testified by Peter S. Deriabin, a NKVD officer who defected to the USA in 1954 (see *Deriabin, Peter*, Part IV).

There is evidence that Oldham did more harm to the USA and Canada than to Britain by providing the names of prospective agents in key positions in those countries. It is thought that he obtained some of these names from a mysterious female agent named 'Leonore'. One of his Soviet contacts was a Russian oilman named Feldman who operated in Britain under the name of Voldarsky and who later started a Soviet network to spy on the USA from Canada. Did Feldman betray Oldham? The question is apt because in 1932 Feldman was arrested and, despite the fact that his activities in Britain had become known to MI5, was fined a mere £5 on a trivial charge and ordered out of the country.

Captain King was eventually tracked down by the British authorities following information provided by the Soviet defector, Krivitsky. He was sentenced to ten years' penal servitude in October 1939 for passing information to the Russian government.

OPERATION 'GREEN'

This was a Nazi plan in World War II for capturing Wales using a combination of paratroops and seaborne divisions which were to be based in Ireland. A subordinate part of this project, code-named 'Whale', concerned the Welsh end of this operation and the diaries of the *Abwehr* (German Secret Service) reveal 'an attempt is to be made to set down the agent, Lehrer, with a wireless operator on the coast of South Wales in order to establish better communication with the Welsh Nationalists'. The Germans had been encouraged in this respect by the fact that there was a tiny but compact and potentially dangerous network of German agents among the Welsh Nationalists, though it should be made clear that the Welsh Nationalist Party had nothing to do with this. In the spring of 1940 a group of Welsh Nationalists lent themselves for this purpose. Hauptmann Nikolas Ritter, former head of the *Abwehr* branch *Ast-Hamburg*, recorded that two German agents were dropped by parachute near Salisbury in the summer of 1940 to 'contact Welsh Nationalist circles who had already expressed themselves willing to help in the event of a Nazi invasion of Wales'.

However, Nazi hopes far exceeded realities and even prior to this, MI5 and the Double-cross Committee had brought Arthur Owens (code-named 'Snow') into their organization. He was to supply the Germans with intelligence under the code-name of 'Johnny'. Owens had volunteered to serve the Germans in 1937 and it was his information on the port area of Swansea that enabled the *Luftwaffe* to deliver a deadly blow against vital targets there. When Owens eventually agreed to serve British interest he became a valuable ally, making the Germans believe he had a network of some fifteen Welsh agents inside the country when he actually had nothing of the sort.

Further reading
They Spied in England by Charles Wighton and Gunter Peis
Vijtde Collone in de Tweede Wereldoorlog by Dr L. de Jong (Amsterdam 1953)

OPERATION 'MAGIC'

In this World War II operation, the Americans broke the Japanese codes by creating the 'Purple Machine'. The man who was originally credited with this was William Friedman, a cryptologist who had been head of the inter-war American Signal Intelligence Service. Certainly Friedman paved the way, but the key man was Captain Joseph J. Rochefort, USN, whose breaking of the Japanese code helped the US win the Battle of Midway. Yet it was not until 1985 that Rochefort, who died in 1976, was posthumously awarded the DSM.

Captain Rochefort was a Japanese linguist as well as a cryptologist and intelligence analyst. In June 1941, as officer in charge of the Combat Intelligent Unit – Station Hypo – at Pearl

Harbour, he built up a skilled team of analysts. Eventually in late May 1942 they succeeded in cracking the codes revealing the time, date and place of the planned invasion of Midway Island. The Japanese had bought a copy of the commercial version of the German 'Enigma' in 1934 and also obtained details of the American M-134-C (designed by Friedman) and the Swedish M-20 (designed by Boris Haeglin), and from these constructed their own machine. They called it the 'Alphabetical Typewriter 97', the number denoting the year 2597 in the Japanese calendar since the machine first came into use in 1937. The Japanese machine did not have rotors like the 'Enigma', but used a series of selector step switches similar to the Strowger selectors used in telephone exchanges, and it took the US teams three years to reconstruct their own copy of the Japanese machine. Their subsequent intercepts were called 'Purple'.

Friedman visited the British decoding station at Bletchley during the war and from about late 1941 onwards there was cooperation between the USA and UK on both German and Japanese decoding. Friedman eventually joined the National Security Agency. Ill health brought on by hard work led to his death in 1969.

Further reading
And I Was There by Rear-Admiral Edwin T. Leyton, with John Costello and Captain Roger Pincau (d. 1985)

OPERATION 'NORTH POLE'

Probably one of the most disastrous operations in the whole history of World War II, Operation 'North Pole', or *'Nordpol'* as the *Abwehr* termed it, was an attempt by the British to build up an espionage network inside occupied Holland. It involved both the SOE and the British Secret Service, but it was fairly swiftly unmasked by the Germans when they arrested an SOE-trained radio operator, Hubert Lauwers, in Holland. After a week of interrogation Lauwers agreed in March 1941 to transmit coded messages, dictated by the Germans, to England. In doing so he managed to omit the pre-arranged security check and also to insert the English word 'caught' into one of his preambles. But the operator in England ignored his warnings and acknowledged the signal. He hoped that the British had noticed his warnings and would cease contact. In fact, through their negligence the *Abwehr* penetrated the whole network simply by continuing radio contact. The operation cost the lives of more than 100 volunteers who, when they landed in Holland, were picked up at once by the *Abwehr* or the *Gestapo*. Apart from this, large quantities of arms, food, clothing and currency were dropped directly to the enemy. The German infiltration of '*Nordpol*' also enabled them to infiltrate SOE networks in France and Belgium (see *Special Operations Executive*, Part III).

PAKBO

A Swiss-based organization founded by Otto Puenter to fight Fascism and aid its victims, PAKBO was one of the most remarkable freelance intelligence services of recent times. It took its name from the first letters of its main contact points: Pontresina/Poschiave, Arth-Goldau, Kreuzlingen, Berne/Basle and Orselina. Puenter had been the chief figurehead in INSA (Information, S.A.) which specialized in disseminating anti-Fascist and anti-Nazi news and had contacts with anti-Fascist movements in Italy, Austria, Germany and Spain. When the Swiss government introduced a law forbidding any Swiss support for either side in the Spanish Civil War, Puenter started PAKBO and made further contacts in Britain and France. He also had some thirty helpers on the frontiers, including railwaymen, customs and postal officials.

PAKBO supplied intelligence to the Russians via the 'LUCY' ring and also gave the British Secret Service plans of the Peenemunde installations long before anyone else. For some years after the war Puenter was director of the Swiss Socialist Press Service and later head of the Press Service of Swiss radio and television.

PETRIE, SIR DAVID (1879-1961)

A Scot, educated at Aberdeen University, Petrie served in the Indian Police from 1900-36, and had at one time been Assistant Director of Criminal Intelligence to the Government of India, finally rising to the post of Director of the Intelligence Bureau to that government. In 1940 he was appointed head of MI5 in succession to Sir Vernon Kell. MI5 underwent a great deal of reorganization at this time with constant changes of personnel that made life far from easy for the new chief. To make his task more manageable, Petrie brought in various experts to form sections for dealing with the different types of agent. This not only made for a tighter liaison inside MI5, but helped to establish closer links with MI6, the Secret Service handling overseas affairs. He retired at the end of the war.

PIGEON POST

The use of 'pigeon post' in espionage work dates back at least as far as the Ancient Romans. Both Frontinus and Justus Lipsius refer to it, and the latter also mentions the training of swallows for use in military espionage. Prior to World War I, when the NID wanted to make use of pigeons for communications in case wireless transmission broke down, the idea was frowned upon by the Admiralty (see *Aston, Sir George*, Part II), but carrier pigeons were effectively used during that war. The French Lafayette Escadrille 'air devils' who dropped spies behind enemy lines relied on carrier pigeons to inform when the spies were ready to be picked up again. Similarly the air-spies who went up in balloons were trained to handle pigeons and used them for sending back reports at regular intervals. Balloon-spies were trained in England, and a Field Intelligence Department was developed by the British Army, using pigeons for swift communications. Even in World War II 'pigeon post' was still used occasionally. The RSPCA's Dickin Medal was awarded to a pigeon named Mercury for an astonishing flight on 30 July

1942, described as 'the most outstanding single performance' of any one pigeon on special service. Mercury flew 480 miles non-stop over the North Sea with a vital message from a Danish Resistance group. For this mission fifty fanciers along the East coast of Britain were asked to present their two best racing birds to be flown over enemy territory and parachuted in crates to waiting Resistance members. Mercury was the only one to return.

In the 1950s pigeons were trained by Israeli psychologists to enable Arab military installations to be pin-pointed. The birds were equipped with electronic signalling devices so that their location in hostile territory could be monitored by technicians in Israel. The pigeons were kept without food until their weight was reduced by around 20 per cent. It was judged that at this weight they would be acutely hungry and desperately eager to spy out food. The theory was that, when released into flight, they would depend for their food supplies on being able to distinguish between natural parts of the environment and man-made camps, presumably close to food stocks. Thus, once a pigeon saw such an installation from on high, it immediately swooped in quest of food, and its flight and movements would be watched on a screen. The scanner could then assume that the pigeon had located something of importance, such as roads being built or missile site developments.

Further reading
RSPCA Archives, London

POPOV, DUSKO (1912-1981)

A Yugoslav, Popov along with his brother, Ivo, was recruited into the *Abwehr* as a German agent in the summer of 1940. Meanwhile both of them had offered their services to the British Secret Service chief in Belgrade. It was, however, Dusko who became the star double-agent, and a success for both the Double-cross operations and for the SIS (see *Double-cross System*, Part III). He loathed the Nazis and took a special delight in posing as one of their agents and passing back information to the British. The *Abwehr* first sent him to Portugal in November 1940 and the SIS gave him the telephone number of their Lisbon station so that he could contact them. In December 1940 he managed to fly secretly into the UK and was interviewed both by MI5 and MI6. Thereafter he became an agent for both, being 'Scout' to MI6 and 'Tricycle' to MI5, who brought him into the Double-cross network. His German code-name was 'Ivan'.

Returning to Lisbon, Popov carried on with his work for the *Abwehr*. He provided valuable military and economic intelligence, but perhaps his most vital item of information was the one which was mishandled. From German sources he obtained details of a proposed Japanese attack on Pearl Harbour, including an actual copy of a Japanese questionnaire on Pearl Harbour. Surprisingly the British did not pass this news on to the White House, nor to the US Office of Naval Intelligence, but MI5's Guy Liddell (q.v.) despatched a copy of the questionnaire to J. Edgar Hoover, head of the FBI, and sent Popov across the Atlantic to see him. Whether Liddell stressed that Popov was a double-agent is not clear, but Hoover took an instant dislike to Popov and denounced him as 'an immoral decadent ... Look at the man's goddam code-name, "Tricycle". It means he likes to go to bed with two girls at once.' What is even more surprising is that, while Hoover doubted Popov's value to the Allies, the *Abwehr* appeared to have no doubts at all. When he returned to Lisbon, they even gave him a new assignment to London. For a double-agent who took such enormous risks it is a measure of his skill that he survived the war, having by general consent provided invaluable intelligence for the Allies.

Further reading
Spy/Counterspy by Dusko Popov (Weidenfeld & Nicolson, London 1974)

PORETSKY, IGNACE (see *Reiss, Ignace*)

PORTLAND, NINTH DUKE OF (b. 1897)

Still generally known as 'Bill' Bentinck, it is doubtful whether Victor Frederick William Cavendish-Bentinck ever expected to become a duke, for he was not even an eldest son. After service as a junior Grenadier Guards officer in World War I, he became an attaché in Warsaw, and then served on Lord Curzon's staff at Lausanne after transferring to the Foreign Office, spending his time decoding Turkish cipher traffic. Later he served in The Hague, Paris, Athens and Santiago, but his career was often upset by his American wife's propensity for quarrelling with his colleague's wives. However, by the time he returned to London in 1939, she had left him and gone back to the USA. From then on his career prospects immediately changed for the better. The Joint Intelligence Committee had hitherto been singularly ineffective in many respects, due to inter-Service rivalries. Cavendish-Bentinck, as he then was, became chairman of the Committee, which consisted of representatives of the three Service Intelligence departments, and as Foreign Office representative and chairman it was his task to advise the Chiefs of Staff about enemy intentions, something he did with shrewdness, tact and firmness.

Everyone in the inner circle of intelligence came to trust him and rely on his judgement. He has rightly been dubbed by his biographer, David Howarth, 'Intelligence Chief Extraordinary'; the fact that the JIC was right in its assessments more often than not is a tribute to this. He had a critical eye for both MI6 and the SOE, regarding the former as being full of 'dead-beats and hangers-on' and the SOE as rather a failure. He was also appalled at the constant bickering between MI6 and Gubbins (q.v.), head of the SOE. After the war Cavendish-Bentinck was spectacularly successful in a business career, becoming a duke in his old age.

Further reading
Intelligence Chief Extraordinary by David Howarth (London 1986)

RADO, DR SANDOR (1899-1981)

Born Alexander Radolfi in Hungary, Rado had served the Communist cause ever since the Bela Kun revolutionaries launched their unsuccessful coup in 1919. He was the mastermind behind the Soviet network in Switzerland during World War II, using the code name 'Dora' (see *Lucy Ring*, Part III). Prior to this he had operated a news agency in France as a cover for his espionage. He was appointed head of the Swiss network by Moscow at the time of the purges in 1936-7.

Rado lived in Geneva with his wife, Helene, and two sons. He had great personal charm which won him many friends, but he had a weakness for luxury and a consequent tendency to play fast and loose with the network's funds. He did not always keep strictly to the rules laid down by Moscow, and he indulged in frequent love affairs. He succeeded for a long time because of the quality of intelligence he provided. When the network was threatened by betrayals within the ranks, Rado panicked and instead of burning his papers and code-books, he put them in the apartment of another agent who was shortly afterwards arrested. Rado wanted to salve what was left of the network by making contact with the British, but Moscow Centre overruled him. When the Swiss moved in on the 'Lucy' Ring and made arrests, Rado fled to France but he was ordered to return to Moscow by plane. When the plane arrived in Cairo Rado immediately tried to defect, as he sensed there would be trouble for him in Moscow. The Russians pressed for his arrest by the British and Egyptians, alleging that Rado was an Army deserter. Foolishly, the British authorities gave way to the Russians and Rado returned to Moscow. He was sentenced to a long term of imprisonment and only released after Stalin's death. He then returned to his native Hungary where he taught geography at Budapest University, and published his memoirs in a book entitled *Dora Jelenti*. On his seventy-fifth birthday he was awarded the Order of the Red Banner by the USSR.

Further reading
Handbook for Spies by Alexander Foote (Museum Press, London 1949)

RAMENSKY, JOHN (1901-1967)

One of the most remarkable crooks ever recruited for spying was John Ramensky, born in a Glasgow slum to Lithuanian parents. Prison life began early for Ramensky when he was sent to Borstal at the age of sixteen. He lived for sixty-seven years and spent more than forty of them in jail. His speciality was safe-blowing and he became something of a legend in the underworld, not least because of his talent for escaping from prison. Despite his criminal record, he was genuinely liked by the police who called him 'Gentle Johnny', as he never used violence.

In October 1942 Ramensky was just finishing one of his spells of imprisonment in Scotland, when he was released, taken to London and brought before Brigadier Laycock, then Chief of the Commandos. Soon he was enlisted in that crack detachment of assault troops and asked to make a series of reports on the techniques of safe-blowing. He was then sent to Italy and assigned a series of missions behind enemy lines acting with the Italian Partisans. When the Allies advanced on Rome he accompanied a raiding party whose orders were to secure the German plans for withdrawal. Ramensky got the plans after breaking open a safe in the German Embassy. In fact he opened four strong-rooms and ten safes within a few hours. When he was demobilized from the Commandos, he was given a signed letter by Brigadier Laycock stating, 'May your gallant service to King and Country be rewarded in the future by peace, prosperity and happiness.' But shortly after the end of the war Ramensky was back in prison again.

REISS, IGNACE (d. 1937)

Also known as Ignace Poretsky, Reiss was a Pole who had been in sympathy with the early Revolutionaries in Russia and was one of the earliest Comintern agents. He joined the Polish Communist Party in 1919, working under Joseph Krasny-Rotstadt, director of propaganda for the Comintern in Poland. His first assignment was to obtain military intelligence for which he was arrested and sentenced to five years' imprisonment. He escaped, made his way to Germany and was brought into the German network of Soviet espionage. Later Reiss worked under Walter Krivitsky (q.v.) in Holland and Vienna. During the time he was in Holland he was ordered to make contact with the Irish Communist Party, as at that time Holland was being used as a base for Soviet espionage against the UK. Slowly he became disillusioned with the Stalinist regime and he virtually signed his own death warrant when he wrote an open letter to Stalin, announcing '... I cannot stand it any longer. I take my freedom of action.' Stalin furiously ordered the immediate assassination of Reiss, but he escaped to Switzerland using a Czech passport in the name of Hans Erhardt, leaving his wife and child in Paris. The Soviet hit-team went into action, first tracking down his wife who had moved from Paris to Switzerland. In September 1937 Reiss's body was found riddled with machine-gun bullets inside a car in Lausanne.

Further reading
Our Own People by Elizabeth Poretsky (University of Michigan Press, 1969)

RIDIGER VON ETZDORF, BARON (d. 1967)

Born to vast wealth, von Etzdorf was a Prussian landowner and former German naval officer who moved in the highest circles and spied for Britain from 1935 to 1945, eventually being given British nationality for his services. In the early 1930s he became convinced that the Nazis were a threat to European peace and that Hitler was planning a second world war, so he offered his services to the British. After the fall of France he was posted to Casablanca, where as 'Mr Ellerman' he created an escape organization to enable British soldiers and airmen to get back to Britain. Many of these had been trapped in France at the time of the French collapse and the Baron provided false papers which identified them as neutrals and got these stamped with Moroccan exit visas and Portuguese transit visas. His activities were eventually discovered by the Vichy police, but being warned in time, he made good his own escape.

His next mission for the British was to spy out the coast and off-shore islands north and south of Dakar in search of submarine hideouts and refuelling depots. His wife described how he had 'a hair-raising journey to Africa in a flat-bottomed Rhine river barge ... His cover story was that he was a coastal trader in coconuts. So at Freetown he filled up the barge with nuts, then sailed for several weeks around the islands and inlets, selling the nuts to native traders.' Later von Etzdorf spied for the British in Chile and the Argentine, being mainly engaged in economic espionage. After the war he undertook a number of jobs, ranging from salesman to chef and language teacher (his wealth had long since disappeared). His later years became rather a tragic struggle, running a working men's snack-bar known as 'Jack's Cafe' in Boundary Road, North London. He kept his past identity a closely guarded secret until he died. His brother was a post-war German Ambassador to London.

SALON KITTY

'Salon Kitty' was a high-class bordello established in a mansion in the Giesebrechtstrasse in the west end of Berlin, rented and controlled by the Intelligence Service (SD). It had nine bedrooms, all of which concealed microphones connected to a monitoring system in the basement. Important diplomats such as Count Ciano of Italy were among its visitors. It was run by Madame Kitty who, after the war, revealed something of what went on there. She said that not all the girls who worked there were professional prostitutes, but some were young society women who volunteered for this service as a patriotic duty.

Salon Kitty was chiefly used to obtain diplomatic secrets, even though von Ribbentrop, the Foreign Minister, was kept in the dark about its purpose. The establishment was controlled by Schellenberg, head of AMT VI counter-espionage service.

SCHELLENBERG, WALTER (1910-1952)

When the Nazis came to power in 1933, Schellenberg was a young man of twenty-two looking for a job. He had just left the University of Bonn where he had studied medicine and then law. Having joined the Nazi Party and the SS, he soon got a job in the Intelligence and Security Services (SD). He was assigned to AMT IV, being given counter-espionage work, and thus created and controlled the notorious Salon Kitty (q.v.) in Berlin, where diplomats' bedroom chatter was monitored. Schellenberg proved to be an able propagandist of his own talents and a shrewd critic of others in the intelligence community. Perhaps because of this he had his enemies inside the Nazi Party, but they failed to destroy him, largely because he scored rather more espionage successes than anyone else.

His first big secret service coup came shortly after World War II began and paved the way to his appointment as overall head of German Intelligence. It was Schellenberg who took the credit for luring the two British spies, Best and Stevens, from The Hague to Germany (see *Venlo Incident*, Part III). Schellenberg himself went to Holland, adopting the name of Hauptmann Schaemmel, and met the British agents. He would have liked to play along with them for a little longer, but Himmler ordered him to arrest them immediately and bring them to Germany. Later Schellenberg was involved in other plots which revealed his imaginative mind, a quality lacking in other Nazi intelligence officers.

In 1940 he was closely concerned with the plan to lure, or kidnap, the Duke of Windsor from his temporary residence in Portugal, being urged by Hitler to win the support of the Duchess because of her influence over the Duke. Schellenberg went to Spain to make plans, arranging for an incident one night in the garden of the Duke's villa when stones were thrown at the windows. He then started rumours that the British Secret Service were behind this, and that they had orders to make things uncomfortable for the Duke until he agreed to leave for Bermuda, where the British Government had nominated him as Governor-General. But Schellenberg always thought that kidnapping was a foolish plan and ultimately persuaded Hitler of this, though Ribbentrop, who was behind the scheme, never forgave him.

In June 1941 Schellenberg was given the task of taking over and reorganizing AMT VI, the Foreign Intelligence Service, and he was largely responsible for hunting down the Soviet-controlled *Rote Kapelle* network which operated all over Europe (see *Trepper, Leopold*, Part III). It is interesting to note that Schellenberg was always a realist and that, unlike Himmler, he was not anti-Semitic. 'When I took over Admiral Canaris's Military Sector,' he wrote afterwards, 'its chief was a German Jew, and he conducted its activities in a manner that was unique … His information network went through various countries and penentrated every stratum of society … The work of this man was really masterly … I had to fight like a lion to preserve this valuable assistant.' It was in the middle of 1944 after the arrest of Canaris (q.v.) that Schellenberg took over all the Admiral's intelligence departments of the *Abwehr*, and within a year he was urging Himmler to negotiate peace through Count Bernadotte of Sweden.

Without doubt Schellenberg was a relatively sane intelligence operator among a bunch of unrealistic Nazi leaders. He was brought to trial in 1948 and the following year was acquitted on all but two charges. Sentenced to imprisonment, he had to undergo a serious operation and was released in 1951 as an act of clemency. He lived in Switzerland for a while, and then Italy, where he died in Turin.

Further reading
The Schellenberg Memoirs by Walter Schellenberg (André Deutsch, London 1956)

SCHMIDT, WULF

The son of a German father who had served in the Luftwaffe, and a Danish mother, Wulf Schmidt was a cosmopolitan who had joined the Nazi Party. He studied law at Lubeck University, but was at heart an incorrigible adventurer and so became a natural target for those seeking secret agents. Having become a minor agent for the *Abwehr*, he volunteered for work overseas. He spoke English, but with a heavy accent. As Agent 3725 Schmidt parachuted from his plane towards the borders of Cambridgeshire and Hertfordshire on the night of 19 September 1940. He was eventually arrested, as his arrival in Britain was not only expected, but interrogation officers had actually waited for him to arrive. He was taken to MI5's interrogation camp 020. Astonished at being arrested so quickly and treated in a relatively polite manner, it was borne in on him that Britain was far from being the defeated and abject nation he had expected to find. He tried to bluff his interrogators that he was Danish, had escaped from Germany and was seeking asylum. It was soon made clear to him that the British knew this was his cover story in the event of capture. Slowly, and mainly through the skill of Dr Harold Dearden, a psychiatrist who was acting as an interrogator at the camp, Schmidt was persuaded to work for the British as a double-agent, being given the code-name of 'Tate' because he resembled Harry Tate, the music hall comedian.

Under close supervision by MI5 he was told to send messages back to Germany at their dictation and even to ask the Germans to send him more funds. The Germans responded by parachuting in another agent with money. This agent was caught, tried as a spy and hanged. On other occasions Schmidt collected funds from such rendezvous sites as the Regent Palace Hotel, the British Museum and (an ironic touch!) the Tate Gallery. Meanwhile he radioed through a mass of disinformation to the *Abwehr* and proved himself to be far and away the best of all 'turned' agents, while the Germans believed he was their best agent inside Britain, and awarded him the Iron Cross, First Class. By the end of the war Schmidt had married a British girl, with MI5's permission, and he sought and was granted permission to stay in the UK. He now has British citizenship, a new identity and is divorced from his wartime bride.

Further reading
SPY! by Richard Deacon with Nigel West (BBC Publications, 1980)

SETH, RONALD (1911-1985)

Possibly one of the unluckiest spies in modern history, Ronald Seth followed his education at Ely Cathedral School and Cambridge by lecturing in English in Estonia. In World War II he joined the RAF and was a Flight-Lieutenant, and as Estonia was the country from which the Germans were getting oil, he was asked by someone in the Intelligence Service to undertake a mission there. Dressed as a civilian, he was parachuted into Estonia with enough explosives in his equipment to blow up a small town. His orders were to sabotage the German-run shale-oil mines, but he landed in the middle of a German patrol with a police dog. The parachutes with his radio and explosives were captured, but Seth managed to escape into the forest. For twelve days he dodged the patrols, then he was captured, jailed and beaten up. Without trial, he was sentenced to death by hanging, but some unknown Estonian patriot had fixed the gallows trap-door so that it wouldn't open. When Seth regained consciousness he was back in his prison cell. He could not explain why he was not taken to the gallows for the second time, but it seems probable that the Germans thought such an experience might 'turn' him to work for them. His mission was accomplished under the auspices of Britain's SOE.

To save his life, Seth offered to help the Germans and they sent him first to Frankfurt to the Intelligence HQ of the Luftwaffe, and then in 1943 to Paris. He was told that the Nazis wanted to use him as one of their own agents in Britain. There he managed to contact the French Resistance, but was discovered and sent to a prisoner-of-war camp. The Germans told him he was to report on his fellow prisoners. Seth refused to divulge any information that might harm his comrades, but he saw no harm in pretending to go along with the German request. However, the officers there suspected him, even though he secretly informed the senior British officer of his orders from the Germans. Some British officers wanted to throw him out of an attic window; in fact, he was given a rough ride by all of them. The Germans had to withdraw him from the camp. Then Himmler (q.v.), chief of the German SS, wanted him to take a personal message to Churchill to the effect that he would seize power in Germany and negotiate peace. Seth agreed, was smuggled across the Swiss border on 12 April 1945 and at once saw the British Minister. In the end the only use made of his escapade was to round up a number of Nazi agents still hiding out in Paris after the liberation.

Further reading
A Spy Has No Friends by Ronald Seth (London, 1961)

SINCLAIR, ADMIRAL SIR HUGH (1873-1939)

Having joined the Royal Navy in 1886, Sinclair spent some time during World War I in the Naval Intelligence Division, and in February 1919 he succeeded Admiral 'Blinker' Hall as Director of Naval Intelligence. Later he was appointed head of the Submarine Service, and in 1923 he was chosen to succeed Mansfield Cumming as head of MI6. He took up residence in a flat at 21 Queen Anne's Gate, which was then the headquarters of MI6. Shortly after this his wife died, and he began to depend upon his unmarried sister, Evelyn, whom he brought into the service of MI6. He was a conscientious man, known by the nickname of 'Quex', but he was never strong enough to withstand the pressures of government economy demands, or to weld the organization into an effective peace-time organization.

In 1921 it had been recommended that the service should be financed from the Foreign Office secret vote. Under Sinclair costs were often reduced or saved by appointing ex-Servicemen who lived chiefly on their pensions. The tragedy was that many of these were either too old, or too inexperienced. Sinclair was much more of an amateur than Cumming. Having brought his sister into MI6, he is said to have shared solely with her the secret locations of 'dead letter boxes' used for communication with agents. Had brother and sister died together in an accident, some sections of the Secret Service might well have been disrupted.

Between the wars there was a tendency for MI6 to become too departmentalized, with each section forming its own policies and plans. The result was that very often one section did not know what another section was doing, occasionally with overlapping complications, sometimes with disastrous results. For a long time intelligence on Nazi Germany was inadequate, with insufficient evidence to back up reports of German rearmament. Sinclair retired owing to ill health shortly after World War II began.

SMEDLEY, AGNES (d. 1953)

An American whose writings on China had attracted wide sympathy in liberal circles in the 1930s, Agnes Smedley gradually became not only a Communist sympathizer, but an agent both for the Russians and the Chinese. She not only arranged for her apartment to be used as a base for the spy network run by Richard Sorge (q.v.), but was primarily responsible for recruiting Ozaki Hozumi, a Japanese journalist. Indeed, for a brief period she was head of the Shanghai Soviet network. She was also a key link between the Soviet and Chinese Communists.

In World War II she was actually appointed by President Roosevelt as one of the advisers to General Stilwell, military adviser to Chiang Kai-shek. She urged Stilwell that the Americans should send military supplies to the Chinese Communists, a plan which Stilwell supported on purely military grounds, despite objections by Chiang Kai-shek. Sorge described her as 'a woman with a brilliant mind ... she was like a man'. One of her oldest friends was Chu-teh, the Chinese Communists' C-in-C, who later fought against the Americans in Korea.

After the war she was driven out of the USA by a campaign launched by the American China Lobby which named her as a Soviet agent. When she died she bequeathed her ashes and her estate to Chu-teh. She was buried in Peking in what was then described as 'the new cemetery for revolutionaries'.

SORGE, RICHARD (1895-1944)

Born in Baku, a Caucasian port on the Caspian Sea, Sorge was the son of a German father and a Russian mother. His parents later moved to Berlin and in World War I Sorge joined up as a private in the German Army and was wounded on the Western Front. After a spell in hospital he re-enlisted in 1916, serving on the Eastern Front. Again he was wounded, and that was the end of his military career. After the war he went to university and became a convert to Marxism, joining the German Communist Party. He was a natural linguist and, while fluent in both German and Russian, he soon learned English, French, Japanese and Chinese. Some time about 1920 Sorge was brought into the Soviet espionage network and in 1921 he married Christiane, the divorced wife of his former professor at Aachen University.

As one of the few Communist agents assigned to the Comintern, Sorge resigned from the Communist Party and was given a trial run in Hollywood with the aim of making contacts inside the film industry. After that he was posted to Scandinavia, Holland and Britain. While in London he was spotted by MI5 as a former member of the Communist Party in Hamburg; as a result his visit was terminated, more or less by mutual agreement. When he reported to Moscow in person he asked to be transferred to the Fourth Bureau of the Red Army Staff as he saw dangers if he remained tied to the much criticized and much observed Comintern organization. By doing so he probably saved his life, as his friend and one-time boss, Ignace Reiss (q.v.), was liquidated in one of Stalin's purges shortly afterwards. Sorge was then sent out to the Far East and given a fairly free hand. His headquarters were in Shanghai and he was allowed to choose his own agents in setting up a spy network which was called 'The China Unit'. He also laid down that the primary task of the Unit was to obtain intelligence on Japan and that espionage concerning China was of secondary importance. In Shanghai Sorge's cover was as a correspondent for *Soziologische Magazin* and his network covered Canton, Nanking, Hangchow, Peking and even Manchuria. He was not merely a conscientious agent, but a good director of intelligence with a flair for picking the right agent. He seems to have avoided using Russians, employing instead a number of Americans, Germans, Japanese and Chinese. One of the Americans he worked closely with was Agnes Smedley (q.v.).

For a while Sorge changed his name and adopted the identity of William Johnson, an American journalist. By the end of the 1930s Russia probably had a highly efficient intelligence service in the Far East. Sorge's reports to Moscow must have impressed the authorities even when they contradicted the reports coming from their agents in Japan, for Colonel Rink, the Soviet military attaché in Tokyo, and Golkovich, the NKVD agent there, were liquidated in 1937. By this time Germany was turning her traditional friendship with China in favour of an alliance to Japan, thus posing a threat to Russia on two fronts, east and west. Sorge was recalled to Moscow for urgent talks and both the Fourth Bureau and the NKVD jointly took steps to improve Far Eastern intelligence, especially on Japan. It was then that Sorge put up the audacious plan that he should return to Germany, establish contacts with leading Nazis, aim to join the ranks of the Gestapo or some other powerful German agency and, in this guise, go to Japan as a Soviet spy inside the German camp. It was a wild gamble because he ran the risk of being tortured and executed by the Nazis and there was always the chance that if he failed, someone in the Soviet hierarchy would dub him a traitor. Stalin is said to have given his personal approval of this ploy. Once he acquired membership of the Nazi Party he became correspondent of the *Frankfurter Zeitung* and the Gestapo failed to find anything wrong with his faked documents or discover that he had once been a member of the German Communist Party. As a correspondent he went to Tokyo and once in the Japanese capital lost no time in building up another spy network.

Sorge secured for himself the post of press attaché in the German Embassy. Each morning he would regale the German Ambassador with gossip and information about Japanese affairs and in return the latter would tell him all manner of things about his own relations with the Japanese. As a result he was able to keep the Centre in Moscow informed on all Japanese plans, though his information was not always believed. Possibly Sorge was pressed too hard to find out too much too quickly, but he soon realized he had to take greater precautions. He insisted on the network's radio set being moved after each transmission and the code was changed monthly. Only the most urgent information was radioed to Moscow, the rest being passed by couriers. By the summer of 1941 the Japanese were certain that a major foreign spy ring was operating in Tokyo. Slowly the *Kempai Tai* closed in on Sorge's network. There is some evidence to suggest that the Japanese had tapped his transmissions long before he was eventually arrested and that it was only when he radioed the Russians about a possible attack on Hawaii that it became imperative for him to be silenced. In October 1941 Sorge was arrested at his home and most of the network were rounded up soon after. Sorge was not executed until November 1944, a delay which raised queries in some quarters about whether he was still alive, or used in an exchange deal, while another man was sent to the gallows in his place. But there can be no doubt that he paid the penalty, as his Japanese mistress traced his grave to a cemetery in Zoshigaya after the war.

Further reading
The Case of Richard Sorge by F.W. Deakin and G.R. Storry (Chatto & Windus, 1966)
SPY! by Richard Deacon with Nigel West (BBC Publications, 1980)

SPECIAL OPERATIONS EXECUTIVE (SOE)

In 1938 a special section of the British SIS called Section D (for Destruction), was set up under Colonel Lawrence le Grand. In the event of a German invasion its aim was to organize subversion and destruction in enemy-occupied territory of the UK. However, all this was overtaken by events when Churchill became Prime Minister and created the SOE in July 1940. It was headed by Dr Hugh Dalton, Minister of Economic Warfare and its purpose was economic sabotage of enemy countries and enemy sources of supply. Dalton was assisted by Gladwyn Jebb (later Lord Gladwyn), Philip Broad and the banker, Leonard Ingrams. Soon the SOE changed its purpose, concentrating on forming links with Resistance movements in France, Holland and elsewhere, and in many instances doing work normally done by MI6. Section D was removed from the SIS and placed under Frank Nelson, a former Conservative MP; George Hill, an old SIS hand, was put in charge of training. For a brief period both Philby (q.v. Part IV) and Burgess (q.v.) were members of the SOE. Later Colin Gubbins (q.v.) took over the SOE.

Recruitment for the SOE was lamentably slack – in some cases disastrous – and its whole organization sometimes lacked credibility. One of its members, Bickham Sweet-Escott, in his book *Baker Street Irregulars* (Baker Street was the SOE's HQ), said, 'Our record of positive achievement was unimpressive. There were a few successful operations to our credit, but certainly not many ... as for Western Europe, though there was much to excuse it, the record was lamentable.' In fact, the SOE was a waste of lives, money and time. Its Dutch section was infiltrated from the very beginning and exploited by two senior *Abwehr* officers. As a result Dutch recruits for the SOE who were parachuted into Holland were captured and the Germans obtained the SOE's secret code signals.

Operations by the SOE in France were doomed from the outset because of rivalries and jealousies between it and MI6. Occasionally each service would mislead the other and this sometimes led to the betrayal and capture of British agents. There was also a high degree of treachery which has never been adequately explained, for many of the vital SOE papers are either destroyed or missing. Almost any history of the SOE is therefore based largely on guesswork. A further complication is that the SOE sometimes used double-agents who passed on information to the Germans. It can only be hoped that this was done in order to feed the Germans with disinformation, but it also resulted in the arrest and torture of genuine SOE agents. There are indications that some of this devious work was done solely to placate Stalin and to keep German troops tied up in the West rather than attacking the USSR. One such disastrous operation was code-named 'Cockade', and involved an enemy agent named Dericourt (working for both the SOE and MI6) who betrayed a number of SOE agents. Someone in either MI5 or MI6 (obviously one of the hidden Soviet agents), tipped off the French Communist Resistance networks that 'Cockade' was a fake, so they laid low and avoided arrest. SOE agents who were supposed to send messages back to London often forgot to give their true identity checks and therefore courted disaster. The Prosper Circuit fiasco, for example, caused the break-up of an entire operational circuit in a single blow and hundreds of arrests.

However, there were heroes in the SOE. There was Wing-Commander F.F. Yeo-Thomas, who had lived in pre-war Paris and been director of a fashion house. He proved to be one of the most resourceful agents the SOE ever put in the field. He was parachuted into France on a number of occasions, until eventually betrayed and captured. He escaped from Buchenwald and was awarded the MC and George Medal. The SOE employed fifty-three women agents in France and some of these, such as Odette Sansom and Violette Szabo, have already had their deeds immortalized in books and films. Then there was Noor Inayat Khan (code-name 'Madeleine'), an Indian princess born in Russia, who had spent much of her life in France and the UK. She escaped from France in 1940, joined the WAAF and transferred to the SOE. An emotional, artistic but unworldly character, she should never have been recruited for such work, yet she was employed as a radio operator. The incredible thing is that this sensitive dreamer revealed amazing courage in adversity. On one occasion she left her code-book on the kitchen table of her room in Paris. Fortunately the landlady gave it back to her. She was eventually betrayed by somebody who sold her address to the Germans for 100,000 francs, and there is some reason to believe that she may have been deliberately liquidated for her lack of security sense. Arrested by the Gestapo, she was taken to Dachau and executed. She was awarded the George Cross posthumously. Of the fifty-three women SOE put in the field twelve were executed by the Germans and twenty-nine were either arrested or died in captivity.

The SOE was one of the most appalling espionage services ever launched and should be a warning for the future.

Further reading
SOE in France by M.R.D. Foot (HM Stationery Office, London 1966)

Madeleine by Jean Overton Fuller (Gollancz, 1952)
The Baker Street Irregulars by Bickham Sweet Escott (Methuen, London 1965)
Duel of Wits by Peter Churchill (Hodder & Stoughton, London 1957)

SPIVAL, JOHN L.

Author of *The Honourable Spy*, Spival personally investigated Japanese espionage in California and Mexico in the years before World War II. He stated that he found 'Japanese engineers masquerading as common railroad workers ... in strategic military areas just south of the American border, and Japanese farmers masquerading as farmers in areas where they could do enormous damage'. This may have been an exaggeration of the facts, but Spival did ascertain that the Japanese had established contact with a member of the Los Angeles police. He found a letter signed by Toship Sasaki, vice-consul in Los Angeles, wanting 'information on communistic movements in coast districts' together with a list of 'Japanese of American and Japanese parents who were suspected of taking an active part in the above'. He believed that the Japanese had been behind the abortive rebellion of General Saburnino Cedillo to overthrow the Panamanian Government because it had banned Japanese fishermen from Panamanian waters.

'THE SPY WHO NEVER WAS'

Not to be confused with the 'Man who never was', this is nonetheless an intriguing story of early World War II. This mysterious character was said to have masterminded the German sinking of the *Royal Oak* at Scapa Flow in October 1939. The story was first published in the *Saturday Evening Post* in Philadelphia in an article by Curt Reiss in 1942. Captain Alfred Wahring, it was said, was a World War I naval officer who had seen the German Grand Fleet scuttled at Scapa and vowed revenge. He went to Switzerland, took out a Swiss passport under the name of Albert Oertel and learned the trade of a watchmaker. In 1927 he moved to Britain, became a naturalized British subject and set himself up with a watchmaker's shop at Kirkwall in the Orkney islands, close to Scapa Flow. At the outbreak of war he somehow sent a message to the Germans, informing them that there was no boom or adequate anti-submarine nets protecting the eastern entrance to Scapa Flow. Thus a German submarine was able to enter the Flow and, according to one report, guided by Oertel's signalling, to sink the *Royal Oak*.

This story became famous in the annals of espionage. The German intelligence chief, Walter Schellenberg, told it as absolute fact, and long afterwards Allen Dulles enthused CIA agents at lecture courses with this example of the long term spy *par excellence*. But in fact there is no trace in any records, German or British, of any Captain Wahring, nor of a watchmaker named Oertel. The only evidence of a possible spy is a mysterious motorist who beamed his full headlights on to Scapa Flow that fatal night. While some reports suggested it was Oertel signalling, there is no real confirmation of an actual signal. British Naval Intelligence confirmed the presence of a motorist, but failed to catch or interview him, and Captain Prien, commander of the German submarine who recorded the incident in his log-book, did not note a signal: 'I must assume that I was observed by the driver of a car which stopped opposite us and drove off towards Scapa Flow at top speed.' It is just possible that some *Abwehr* agent might have been sent there without Prien's knowledge. The motorist may have alarmed Prien and deterred him from sinking other ships before leaving, something he could easily have done. The story of Oertel is undoubtedly a piece of fiction cleverly planted in America by the Germans themselves.

STEIN, GUNTER

A German by birth, Gunter Stein became a Soviet agent while in Moscow as correspondent for the *Berliner Tageblatt*. He arrived in Japan in 1935 and his book, *Made in Japan*, established him as a shrewd authority on Japanese trade and industry. In 1938 he went to Hong Kong and launched an English language paper which was obviously financed by other sources, allegedly Chinese Nationalists. During this period Stein visited China regularly and became a close confidant of Sir Archibald Clark Kerr, then the British diplomatic representative in Chungking. It was Clark Kerr who arranged for Stein to be given British nationality (an unusual privilege because Stein had not even lived in Britain). Afterwards Stein became a correspondent for the *News Chronicle* and the *Financial Times* of London.

A member of Richard Sorge's Far Eastern GRU spy network, continuous radio contact with Vladivostock was maintained from Stein's house in Tokyo. On the arrival of Clark Kerr in Chungking, however, Sorge was ordered to discontinue any relationship with Stein, as the latter's contacts with Kerr were considered of even greater importance to Moscow than Sorge's spy ring. When Sorge was arrested for espionage by the Japanese in World War II he stated that Stein had worked with him, but when he later asked Moscow to confirm Stein as a member of the ring, he received a negative answer. After the war Stein surfaced in New York briefly and then, at the time of the publication of a report on Sorge's wartime activities, he moved to Paris.

STEPHENSON, SIR WILLIAM (b. 1896)

Stephenson was a Canadian, born in Winnipeg, and served in the Royal Flying Corps in World War I, being shot down and imprisoned by the Germans. He managed to escape and it was his extremely detailed reports on what he observed in Germany which first impressed intelligence circles. After the war he became a pioneer in broadcasting and especially in the radio transmission of photographs. By the 1930s he had become an important man involved in broadcasting developments in Canada, in a film company in London, the manufacture of plastics and the steel industry. As a sideline he also won the King's Cup air race in 1934 with a machine which had been built in one of his factories.

Stephenson was alarmed to discover that practically the

whole of German steel production had been turned over to armament manufacture. This not only made him aware of the German threat at a time when the British Government was ignoring it, but persuaded him to carry on a lone campaign of informing responsible people of the need to combat it. Only one man was willing to give him a ready ear and find out more – Winston Churchill. From then until the outbreak of war Stephenson became one of a small, unofficial team who supplied Churchill with intelligence on Germany. In 1940 he was given the job of coordinating an unofficial relationship between the British and American intelligence services, and it was but a short step from some temporary work on behalf of his friend, Lord Beaverbrook, at the Ministry of Aircraft Production to his appointment in New York in the inevitable cover of British Passport Control Officer. There, with an SIS officer from London and recruits of his own choosing, Stephenson set about the difficult task of combining propaganda for the British cause with intelligence work.

Before America entered the war Stephenson had quite a difficult time. A great deal of isolationist sentiment was still around and some lack of faith as to whether Britain could 'go it alone' against the Nazis. Any cooperation with American Intelligence needed to be kept secret even from the State Department where it was at one time suspected there were over-eager plotters working for peace terms with Germany which would have placed Britain in an extremely difficult position. This led to an ex-Army officer, working as a British agent, burgling the safe of Under-Secretary of State Sumner Welles. It was a successful operation that revealed certain German manoeuvres which the State Department had been hushing up and forestalled the sabotage of British ships. The agent was forced to flee to Canada for some months, but he returned to the USA when America entered the war.

Stephenson was as much a diplomat as a spymaster and he worked smoothly with J. Edgar Hoover (q.v. Part IV), and 'Big Bill' Donovan (q.v.), head of the American OSS. His code-name in the war was 'Intrepid' and he continued to use this as his telegraphic address in Bermuda after he retired. His contacts with the film world enabled him to enrol a surprising number of agents in that sphere. The Korda brothers, Alexander and

Zoltan, were two of his recruits; they developed Camp X, a location in Canada where agents were trained and Hollywood make-up artists created disguises for them. Other glamorous names, such as Noel Coward and Greta Garbo, were included in Stephenson's list of agents, though some of them only on the periphery of espionage. Perhaps the most tragic of all was Leslie Howard, who was on a secret mission for 'Intrepid' when his plane was shot down over the Bay of Biscay in 1941. In the latter years of the war Stephenson and Hoover cooled towards each other and this created problems for the intelligence services of both countries. At the end of the war Stephenson was knighted for his services.

Further reading
The Quiet Canadian by H. Montgomery Hyde (Hamish Hamilton, London 1964)

TAI LI, GENERAL (d. 1945)

Reputed to have been born in Chekiang province of China, Tai Li's early life remains a mystery as he took pains to obscure it. He is believed to have worked secretly with the Communists while serving in Chiang Kai-shek's military police, partly to infiltrate the Communist ranks and partly to consolidate his position if Chiang fell from power. A striking personality, full of bonhomie, Tai Li took grotesquely long steps when he walked; people were either terrified out of their wits by him, or fell for his charm. He was a rigid disciplinarian, but believed that two of the most important weapons in the espionage game were women and alcohol. He used both not only to obtain information, but to bring foreigners, especially Americans, on to his side. One of his earlier successes was to lure Chang Kuo-tao, a leading Communist and one of the few ever to defect, to become a supporter of Chiang. To do this he used an attractive female agent.

He disapproved of his agents being married or having permanent mistresses on the grounds that this endangered security. Even General P'an Chi-wu, his deputy commander in the Secret Service which Tai Li headed, was brutally forbidden to marry the girl he loved. When P'an insisted that he was prepared to leave the service in order to marry her, Tai Li shrugged his shoulders. Shortly afterwards the girl was found dead, but whether from natural causes or because she had been killed was never clear.

Tai Li was at the peak of his powers in World War II when as Director of the Kuomintang Secret Service he controlled several secret societies and was on a par with Commodore Miles, who was later to become head of the American OSS. It proved a one-sided bargain, with Tai Li getting by far the best of the arrangement. He certainly overreached himself when he set out to plan the kidnapping of American agents in places as far afield as Calcutta. His aim was to smear some OSS agents in the US Army and he also believed that the kidnappings would be a warning to America not to meddle with other forces inside China. In two instances American officers were kidnapped, while the OSS discovered that two Chinese girls in Calcutta were not only agents of Tai Li, but were relaying information to the Japanese as well. Yet not even this revelation changed the minds of the stubborn men in the Sino-American Cooperative Organization (SAC) who were totally bewitched by Tai Li's charm and magnetism and wouldn't hear a word against him. One day, shortly after World War II ended, Tai Li took off from Nanking in his aeroplane. It exploded in mid-air and some suspected that an OSS limpet bomb might have been attached to an engine of his plane. The evidence of the inquiry into this affair was kept secret and the full truth may never be known.

Further reading
A History of the Chinese Secret Service by Richard Deacon (Muller, London, 1973 and New York, 1979)
A Secret War: Americans in China 1944-45 by Oliver J. Caldwell (S. Illinois University Press, 1972)

'THE TRUST'

Under the skilful leadership of Felix Dzerzhinsky (q.v.), 'The Trust' posed as an anti-Bolshevik organization and thus aimed to lure counter-revolutionaries back to Russia. At the same time it was planned to infiltrate the ranks of White Russians and others to learn details of their plots against the Soviet regime. Two GPU operators, Yakushev and Opperput, were chosen to set up the Moscow Municipal Credit Association as a front for a fake undercover agency assisting the counter-revolutionaries. Gradually, through agents in Finland and elsewhere, 'The Trust' began to win over many unsuspecting anti-Bolsheviks to its network. It even persuaded Boris Savinkov, leader of the anti-Bolshevik crusade, to risk returning to Russia so that he could in due course take over the counter-revolution. Savinkov was imprisoned and in 1925 the Russians reported that he had committed suicide by throwing himself out of a window.

Sidney Reilly (q.v. Part II), an MI6 agent who was then living in America, was the next to be ensnared by 'The Trust', though opinion on this is still divided, some believing that he knew the risks and thought he could trick the organization. Much later 'The Trust' was recreated to combat the Trotskyites in particular, and Stalin's enemies in general. White Russians were again used to spy on both anti-Bolshevik and Trotskyite agents, and to kidnap or kill them as directed. General Eugene Miller, former chief of staff of the Tsarist Fifth Army, who had gone to live in Paris, was chairman of the Union of Russian ex-Combatants, an anti-Soviet White Russian organization. He was lured to the outskirts of Paris, kidnapped and never seen again.

TRILISSER, MEYER (MIKHAIL)

Perhaps the shrewdest and most far-seeing recruiter of talent for Soviet espionage was Meyer Trilisser, an old Bolshevik fighter who in 1921 was given the task of setting up the Foreign Department of the *Cheka*, later known as the INO. Trilisser was given the power to veto any Comintern activities which might affect Soviet security, to infiltrate *agents provocateurs* into the White Russians' ranks, and to recruit spies among them. He proved to be a reliable and skilled INO chief and made it his policy to develop industrial and scientific espionage in the

Western world. He had the utmost contempt for the 'worker-spy' in industry, maintaining that he was too unprofessional and too closely allied to the Communist Party of his own country.

Trilisser decided he must go all out to recruit top scientists, such as Peter Kapitza, the son of a Tsarist general, one of the most brilliantly perceptive moves ever made by any intelligence chief. A hint was passed down the ranks of the Bolshevik hierarchy and Kapitza was awarded an industrial research scholarship enabling this eager scientific student to study at Cambridge University. This marked what was to become a steady infiltration of Cambridge and Oxford universities by Soviet agents over the next fifteen years. Kapitza was not only present at Cambridge when Lord Rutherford first split the atom, but he took back all his secrets to the Soviet Union. Another man recruited by Trilisser was Lev Landau, who had entered Baku University at the age of fourteen. He was later sent to Leningrad University on the instructions of Trilisser, required to learn foreign languages and then sent abroad. Landau made a tour of foreign universities, arrived in Cambridge, contacted Kapitza and later returned to Russia. Trilisser also assisted in directing the organization known as 'The Trust' (q.v.), which lured all manner of anti-Russian opponents into its net. It was Trilisser who started and began to compile the Soviet Index of counter-intelligence which exists to this day. 'Blackmail,' said Trilisser, 'is one of the prime arts of extracting intelligence, and a card-index system that is not intended for this purpose is useless.'

TREPPER, LEOPOLD (1906-1983)

Born a Jew in Poland, Trepper went to Russia, became a Communist and then emigrated to Palestine in 1932. He was expelled by the British during their period of control, and on his return to Moscow offered to set up a spy network in Europe. He proposed to the Soviet authorities that the Moscow Centre should have one senior agent with a radio operator in every country in Europe. On the strength of this he was sent to Brussels in 1938 and built up in a remarkably short time an extremely efficient network, having changed his name to Jean Gilbert, a businessman with offices in many places.

However, for a long time much of his information was either mistrusted or ignored. He warned Moscow of the Germans' plan to launch an attack on the Soviet Union, but evidence suggests this was not believed. German monitoring stations picked up a stream of broadcasts from agents as far apart as Bucharest and Paris, prompting the *Gestapo* to report to Berlin that there was a 'Red Orchestra' (*Rote Kapelle*) network of radio reporters playing direct to Moscow. In this sense Trepper was careless because even if it could not be deciphered, the increasing volume of radio transmissions suggested to the *Gestapo* that they were very important. As a result they organized a special team to trap the broadcasters. Eventually the Gestapo arrested Trepper as he sat in his dentist's chair. He immediately set out to deceive the Germans by agreeing to continue radioing Moscow as though nothing had happened. He not only managed to pass a message through to Moscow warning them of what was going on, but ultimately to escape from the Germans into France and join the Resistance.

When war ended he returned to Russia, believing that he would be accepted as a hero. He was arrested in one of Stalin's purges, accused of working for British Intelligence and spent years in prison and labour camps. After Stalin's death Trepper was allowed out of the Gulag and allowed to join his family in Poland. Once there he devoted himself entirely to Jewish social and cultural life and abandoned Communism. His campaign for a visa to live in the West was not granted until 1973 after a group of British MPs had petitioned the Polish Government for his freedom. In 1974 he returned to Jerusalem where he died in 1983 at the age of seventy-seven.

TSUJI, COLONEL MASONOBU

As chief of Operations and Planning Staff of the 25th Japanese Army in Malaya, Colonel Tsuji was one of the ablest intelligence officers of his time. He had been working for Military

Intelligence ever since 1930 when he had been sent to West Point to study American training methods. He commanded the group of officers who planned Japan's seventy-day campaign for the conquest of Malaya and the invasion of Singapore. In January 1941 he set up the Taiwan Army No. 82 Unit, comprised of only thirty people. Previously he and his team had experienced life in the sub-Arctic regions of Manchuria. Now they had to live and work in tropical jungles under the most primitive conditions. Using all manner of disguises, this team infiltrated British colonial territory and made some of the most thorough topographical and military reports of all time.

Once again it was the courage and discipline of officers in undertaking espionage in conditions of great discomfort which helped pave the way to victory. For example, a spy called Major Asaeda disguised himself as a coolie, went without food and sleep and infiltrated Singapore, Thailand and crossed the Malayan frontier. Another member of the Unit was Sergeant 'Fukui' (this seems to have been his code-name), who was the leader of a special espionage squad to keep Johore Strait under constant surveillance during the ten days before the attack on Singapore. His duties were to obtain details of enemy positions and to study the ebb and flow of the tides, a factor which was always given a high priority by Japanese Intelligence. Later Colonel Tsuji was listed by the British as a war criminal, though there was little hard evidence to suggest he should be dubbed as such. He avoided arrest by disguising himself as a Buddhist monk and in this pose travelled around S.E. Asia for three years after the surrender. He only returned to Japan after the war crimes trials had ended and eventually was elected to the Diet with a large majority as an Independent.

THE VENLO INCIDENT

'The most monumental cock-up in the whole of World War II' was how one British Secret Service executive described the Venlo Incident in November 1939. On the ninth of this month two British Secret Service agents, Captain Payne Best and Major Richard Stevens, set out on a mission which, they optimistically hoped, would end the war. Such was the foolhardy thinking of many Britons in high places at the time that Best and Stevens were allowed to set out to meet an allegedly high-ranking German officer whose name they did not know, but who had led them to believe through intermediaries that he was prepared to defect. Some in London even thought this man might be Admiral Canaris, head of the *Abwehr*. Best and Stevens were lured by car to Venlo on the Dutch-German border and were kidnapped by German intelligence agents acting under orders from the chief of AMT IV, Walter Schellenberg (q.v.). They were imprisoned and interrogated and, as a result, the British Secret Service network in Europe was compromised and destroyed in a single afternoon.

Further reading
SPY! by Richard Deacon with Nigel West (BBC publications, 1980)
The Venlo Incident by S. Payne Best (Hutchinson, London, 1950)

WHEATLEY, DENNIS (1897-1977)

As an author of thrillers and spy novels, Wheatley came into his own in World War II when his talents and imagination were put to some practical use in helping to win the war. It began with a lunch at the Dorchester Hotel in London, three days after the French surrender to the Germans. Sir Louis Grieg, Wing-Commander Lawrence Darvall and a Czech armaments manufacturer were in the party with Wheatley to discuss a paper the author had written, giving his own, unofficial and highly original ideas for repelling a German invasion. He was asked to develop his theme and for the greater part of the war was installed in Churchill's secret underground fortress off Whitehall, the only civilian member of the Joint Planning Staff. Later he was commissioned in the RAF Volunteer Reserve.

Wheatley not only worked out his own projects, but provided some of the background details for two succesful intelligence coups: 'The Man Who Never Was' and the creation of General Montgomery's 'double', who put in appearance at Gibraltar to fox the Germans. 'I made myself think as a Nazi,' said Wheatley afterwards, 'and wrote 12,000 words on a plan for the conquest of Britain as the German General Staff might have planned it.' He then thought up moves to counter this plan. Not all his ideas were accepted, but he had a fair measure of success. One of his pet projects was a plan to invade Sardinia. He remained convinced that the war could have been won at least a year earlier if Sardinia had been invaded instead of Sicily, but 'Operation Brimstone' as the project was called was finally turned down by Sir Alan Brook, the Chief of General Staff, though it was said to have been favoured by Eisenhower.

Further reading
Stranger Than Fiction by Dennis Wheatley (London, 1959)

YAGODA, YENRIK (d. 1938)

When he was introduced to the departmental heads of the OGPU by Menzhinsky, chief of that organization, Yagoda was described as having 'the full confidence of Stalin'. Until that moment he was more or less unknown, a peasant from Latvia, lacking in education, uncouth in manners and speech, but possessed of a ruthless determination not to allow any man who served under him to make a mistake more than once. It was Yagoda who ensured that the Special Division of the Second Directorate was to be devoted almost entirely to liquidating what he called 'the enemies of Stalin', adding, 'for they are the enemies of Russia. The enemies of others are of less account.'

He laid down new rules for espionage overseas, ordering a total reversal of the tactics used by Comintern espionage, which had been based on the belief that agents should be natives of the countries in which they operated. To his credit it must be said that he selected some of the best spies Russia was to possess over the next decade. When Menzhinsky died in 1934, Yagoda took over as head of the relatively new NKVD and it was he who showed an organizational genius by financing Soviet espionage with forged currency. Deciding that pounds sterling were too difficult to forge because of the excellent detective system of the Bank of England, Yagoda concentrated on dollar forgeries, using as intermediaries some crypto-Communist Jewish banks in Germany. One of the chief organizers of this forgery ramp was Walter Krivitsky (q.v.) when he was resident director of Soviet espionage in Vienna. He later declared that nine million forged dollar bills had been passed on to the market.

Stalin constantly interfered in secret service matters, demanding the removal of people who displeased him. Eventually he ordered Yagoda's arrest, possibly because he thought the forgery schemes had compromised Soviet security. Yagoda was succeeded by Yezhov.

YEZHOV, NICOLAI (d. 1938)

During the years between World Wars I and II, Yezhov ran the Special Division of the Third Directorate, the section which liquidated enemies of the regime by murder. Then in July 1936 he succeeded Yagoda as head of the NKVD, being given full authority to purge the Secret Service. Yezhov reacted with both vigour and ruthlessness. He not only appointed more than 300 new heads of departments, executives and agents, but ordered a drastic purge of the overseas networks of the Soviet Secret Service such as had never been carried out before. It was an attempt, mainly inspired by Stalin, to ensure that the last of the old-time revolutionaries with independent views were liquidated. Stalin had developed a phobia against the internationalist, idealist type of Communist and all answering to this description were to be expelled and destroyed. But Yezhov cracked under the strain and in 1938 he was removed to a mental asylum.

YOSHIKAWA, TAKEO

A twenty-eight-year-old ensign in the Japanese Navy, Takeo Yoshikawa was forced to retire from the service owing to ill health, but was assigned to the American desk of Japanese Naval Intelligence. Admiral Yamamoto, quick to spot a potentially brilliant agent in the field, arranged for Yoshikawa's transfer to the Japanese Foreign Office. In August 1941 he was sent to Honolulu under the cover-name of vice-consul Ito Morimura. He was ordered to report in coded messages to the consul and he proved to be a highly efficient spy. He went swimming to get information on beach gradients and the height of tides; he spent his evenings in bars talking to American sailors and trying to obtain information from Nisei girls (born of Japanese parents in American territory). It is true that he was watched by American Intelligence and they learned all about his extremely busy love life by tapping his telephone, but he relied on his flamboyant social conduct as a useful cover, telling one naval colleague that 'a spy without a love life is a spy doomed'.

His reports were detailed to the point of triviality, even including inventories of dustbins. He reckoned to know from such statistics just how many US ships were in Pearl Harbour at any given time. Sometimes he disguised himself as a barefooted Filipino labourer. He organized a system of bonfires and house lights for receiving messages from members of his spy network in Hawaii. His detailed intelligence continued right up to the fatal night before the Japanese attack on Pearl Harbour. Before he was interned by the Americans, as he knew he must be, he burnt his code-book and all compromising material in his possession. Under the arrangements for an exchange of diplomats between the two warring nations he was duly released from internment and returned to Japan where he worked with Naval Intelligence throughout the war.

'Z' SECTION OF THE SIS

It had always been something of a joke to foreign intelligence services that, while Britain always pretended it did not possess a secret service and never admitted its existence, everyone knew it operated from Passport Control offices around the world. But Colonel Dansey (q.v.), deputy head of MI6, sensibly decided that with the threat of war with Germany once more in prospect, it would be wise to have a separate or parallel network of agents working independently under a different cover, but still reporting to the SIS. This was called 'Z' Section and Dansey was its spymaster.

Premises for 'Z' Section were found at Bush House in London and each member or agent of this network was given a 'Z' number, thus Dansey was 'Z' 1, Commander Kenneth Cohen (Royal Navy) 'Z' 2 and 'Z' 3 was Colonel John Codrington. Many commercial and business firms were used as cover addresses for the section, which soon had agents all over Europe, but it was a project which did not commend itself to many SIS personnel. The big mistake was that 'Z' section insisted on being as dominant in The Hague as the larger SIS already based there on the principle that a neutral country was an ideal HQ for an intelligence service network. The result was that when Major Richard Stevens (MI6) and Captain Payne Best ('Z' section) were together lured over the frontier into Germany on 9 November 1939, 'Z' Section was blown and the whole SIS network throughout Europe was put at risk in a single day (see *Venlo Incident*, Part III).

Venlo

PART IV

Spies: 1946–1987

ABEL, COLONEL RUDOLF IVANOVICH (1902-1971)

One of the most professional spies, Rudolf Abel was among the first to be publicized by the Russians when they launched their glorification of Soviet spies in the mid-1960s. He told his own story in the monthly magazine, *Young Communist*. His grandfather had been a minor official under the Tsars and he claimed to have been born in St Petersburg, later proving himself to be a talented linguist who taught English, German and Polish at a Moscow school in his early twenties. In 1922 he joined the Komsomol and at the same time took up radio-telegraphy as a hobby, so that when he was called up for military service he served in a radio unit. When he was demobilized at the age of twenty-five he graduated as a radio engineer and then in 1927 joined the GPU as an agent assigned to the foreign espionage branch.

This much the Russians themselves released about Abel's early days, but they say nothing about his subsequent activities prior to his arrest in the Latham Hotel, New York, in 1957. It is known, however, that his wartime activities were concerned mainly with Germany and he was cited in dispatches for distinguished action as an intelligence officer on the German front. By the time war was over he was a major in the NKVD, and it is said that some of his reports on German military equipment angered Beria, his chief. Once during the war he secured a job as chauffeur with the *Abwehr*, passing back all the information gleaned to Moscow Centre. During the first week of the war with Russia the Germans decorated him and promoted him to lance-corporal. As a result, he was attached to the KGB and promoted to colonel. He was selected to go to the USA as a key agent, first being planted in a displaced persons' camp in Germany under the name of Andrew Kayotis. He applied for entry to Canada and went there in 1947. From Canada he went to the USA and before settling in New York made himself thoroughly familiar with the country by travelling widely. He became Resident Agent in New York around 1950 and controlled not only the local network, but the whole of the North American, Mexican and Central American networks. He had powers never previously given to any Soviet operator in the USA and was regarded in Moscow as the best expert on America they had ever had.

Abel had nerves of steel, an iron self-control and was absolutely self-sufficient and disciplined. Yet he was never a recluse; he liked good food and wine, often cooking excellent meals for a few carefully chosen friends. For ten years he was Russia's masterspy, and when caught, Allen Dulles of the CIA commented with rueful admiration, 'I wish we had a couple like him in Moscow.' He received information, personally analysed it, gave orders to his networks, relayed intelligence to Moscow and managed the finances of the whole outfit more efficiently than any previous spy chief. In the end he was trapped not by any mistake he had made, but because one of his agents, Reino Hayhanen (q.v. Part IV), defected and gave him away.

In New York Abel had taken the cover name of Emil Goldfus and set himself up as an artist, for he could paint passably well. He found the company of unconventional artists a useful antidote to his work as a spymaster. In the world of artists, where routine was detested, his occasional absences went unnoticed. From his studio he radioed information to Moscow, showing caution, even genius, in devising new codes from abstruse mathematical calculations. This enabled a mass of information to be tapped out more rapidly than normal messages. When Abel learned that Hayhanen had defected, he immediately went to Florida with the idea of escaping across the border into Mexico if the FBI seemed to be on his trail. But for a few months nothing happened and Moscow Centre ordered Abel to return to New York. Here he took the name of Martin Collins, but soon afterwards he was arrested. Even then he had the presence of mind to ask to use the toilet and flushed away code details under the eyes of one of the searchers. Charged with conspiracy to transmit military information to the USSR, Abel was sentenced to thirty years' imprisonment in 1957. Later the Americans and Russians agreed to an exchange, Abel was freed in return for the U-2 pilot, Gary Powers, who had been convicted as a spy by the Russians. Abel was awarded the Order of Lenin in recognition of his services.

AGRANIANTS, ILEG

A Soviet agent who had served as a liaison officer to Palestinian guerrillas who were training in North Africa, Agraniants was stationed at the Soviet Embassy in Tunis in 1986. Suddenly he defected to the West, taking with him the names of KGB agents in Algeria, Tunisia, Libya and Morocco. A CIA assessment shortly afterwards was that the Soviet Union would probably have to replace all their agents in North Africa as a result. About the same time Sergei Bokhan, a senior Russian military intelligence officer in Greece, also defected, though there is no known link between the two cases.

AL-TAYEB, GENERAL OMER MOHAMED

Chief of State Security in the Sudan under former President Jaafar Nimeri, General Al-Tayeb, himself a former Vice-President, was given two life sentences and fines of twenty-four million Sudanese pounds in April 1986 for his role in helping Ethiopian Falasha Jews flee to Israel. A state security tribunal sentenced him for ordering security troops to work under the direct control of the CIA and for allowing American planes to land secretly and transport Falashas to Israel between November 1984 and March 1985.

AMIT, GENERAL MEIR (b. 1921)

Born in Tiberias in 1921, Amit was educated at the agricultural college of Givat Hashelosha, becoming a member of the Elonim kibbutz. Later, like many other Israeli Secret Service officers, he was an active member of Haganah, serving as a deputy commander of the Golani Brigade in 1948. After being wounded in action during the War of Independence, he was given command of the brigade in 1950, later becoming head of Operations and serving in Military Intelligence. During this period he paid a long and fruitful visit to the USA. On his return to Israel he was rewarded by being appointed chief of Aman in 1961 and two years later, after the resignation of Harel, became head of the Mossad. Thus he was able to establish superb cooperation between Aman and the Mossad, while at the same time arranging for various highly secret meetings between CIA area representatives in the Middle East and members of the Mossad, with the aim of coordinating policies and intelligence-gathering. Among those who directed these meetings were James Angleton, Ephraim Evron, Meir Amit and Brigadier-General Yariv, Director of Military Intelligence. Yariv and Amit between them played a prodigious part in the preparations leading up to the Six-Day War and it was this highly successful combination which produced the vital information for a swift victory. After that war Amit retired with honour, becoming Director-General of Koor Industries.

ANDROPOV, YURI VLADIMIROVICH (1915-1984)

Just as Semichastny, his predecessor, was Khrushchev's friend, so Andropov was the closest political ally of Brezhnev, Krushchev's successor. An intelligence officer of the modern school, Andropov started life as a telegraph worker in 1930 and his persistence brought him by way of the Petrozavod River

Transport Technical College and Petrozavodsk University to the CPSU Central Committee. From 1936-44 he was officially attached to the Komsomol Central Committee as First Secretary, but during World War II he also helped to organize partisan detachments and was for a time stationed at Murmansk. When war ended he earned steady promotion up the Party ladder, eventually becoming Second Secretary of the Karelo-Finnish Central Committee.

Tactful, efficient, able to avoid Party disputes or personality clashes, Andropov survived the Stalin era and rode the wind of change which followed it. He began to acquire the reputation of a man who was always right. In 1953 he was transferred to the Diplomatic Service and made Counsellor of the Soviet Embassy in Budapest, being promoted to Ambassador in 1954. His advice and brilliant assessments of intelligence reports during the tense days of the Hungarian uprising and the events which followed gave him added weight in the Party. On the strength of this he was appointed head of a special department which was set up to handle relations with Communist Parties in the Soviet-Eastern block. This work further enhanced his status and in 1962 he was made Secretary of the Central Committee which put him on a level with Boris Ponomarev, who was responsible for relations with Communist parties outside the Eastern block. It came as no surprise when in 1967 Andropov was made head of the KGB.

Andropov more closely coordinated the main Intelligence Administration of the Ministry of Defence with the KGB and also, especially in his manipulation of defectors and the arrest of foreigners in the USSR, made his influence felt in the sphere of foreign affairs. Just as the Tsarist *Ochrana* used to publish its own *Ochrana Gazette*, so Andropov's KGB had its own limited circulation *Chekistky Shornik*. One of his first actions as chief of the KGB was to reorganize the whole of the Eastern European Communist bloc's espionage activities into a series of networks centrally controlled from Moscow. He was determined to make greater use of satellite nations in espionage and he ordered a number of their operators, particularly Hungarians, to go to Moscow for special training. He also placed great emphasis on 'disinformation' as a vital weapon in the intelligence game, and the dissemination of this through the KGB has been stepped up ever since. Meanwhile at home, Andropov set out to break the dissidents either by deporting them or giving them 'psychiatric treatment'. When he was head of the KGB the number of 'psychiatric institutions' increased ten-fold.

Such was his power and influence that he became the closest ally of Brezhnev and was closely involved in plans to clamp down on Czechoslovakia in 1968. Almost inevitably he became the next leader of the Soviet Union in 1982, but within two years he was dead.

ANGLETON, JAMES JESUS (1917-1987)

A scholar and an expert on orchids, James Angleton might seem an unlikely intelligence executive, yet history will probably reveal that he was the best counter-intelligence chief the CIA ever had. Educated at Yale University, he served with his father in the OSS in World War II and afterwards in Italy. He not only helped to establish Israel's intelligence service, but was one of the first outsiders to establish a close working relationship with it. This brought him into close contact with Ephraim Evron, Meir Amit and Brigadier-General Yariv. He was one of the first to suspect Philby of being a Soviet mole and he had him watched by CIA agents in Beirut. It was from the Mossad that Angleton eventually obtained proof of Philby's guilt.

As an interrogator and analyst of defectors' statements he was patient, but relentless, believing that sometimes it took years to get an adequate or accurate picture of their value. His opponents (and he had many) thought that too often he believed in the existence of moles among defectors who seemed genuine and that he had a bee in his bonnet about a mole high up in the CIA. However, he was highly impressed by the Soviet defector Golitsin who first mentioned to Angleton the code-name 'Oatsheaf', a Soviet agent who claimed that Harold Wilson was a Soviet agent, and that Hugh Gaitskell had been poisoned to make way for their own man as Labour leader. Dissension in the CIA about the reliability of the defector Nosenko (q.v., Part IV) began in the 1960s, with one side regarding him as invaluable, and the other, led by James Angleton, convinced that he was planted by the KGB to ply the Americans with disinformation. Angleton's theme was that Nosenko had been sent over to protect a top mole in the CIA. It was largely on this issue that, when William Colby became director of the CIA, Angleton lost his battle and was asked to resign. It was a tragedy that the service should have lost one of its ablest officers, but long afterwards Angleton's voice was listened to by some in the CIA. He had a taste for poetry and was a friend of T.S. Eliot. He secured the release of another friend, Ezra Pound, in Italy. He died of cancer in Washington's Sibley Memorial Hospital.

BARNETT, DAVID

Barnett worked for the CIA in the Far East from 1958-63 and was then taken on as a permanent staff officer. During his term of service he was engaged in covert operations in Korea, spent two years at Langley and was then sent to Indonesia. Seeing no prospects of promotion, he resigned in 1970 to start up in business for himself. In 1976, having failed in business and being short of funds, he offered his services to the Russians. The KGB wanted him to rejoin the CIA on a full-time basis, but this he was unable to do. However, he gave the Russians the names of thirty CIA undercover agents, the identities of several CIA collaborators in foreign countries and details of an American operation designed to obtain information about Soviet missiles and other weapons. His intelligence on how the USA proposed to tackle problems posed by the Soviet Styx missile and W-Class submarines was of the utmost value. The Russians paid him $92,000 in all.

In 1979 the CIA hired him as a contract employee. That was probably his fatal error, for it led to his arrest in 1980. The FBI had detected his communications with the KGB and his controller, Vladimir V. Popov, a KGB officer at the Russian Embassy in Washington. Barnett was sentenced to eighteen years' imprisonment.

BEER, DR ISRAEL (d. 1968)

Born in Austria, Israel Beer claimed to have fought in the *Schütbund*, the Austrian Socialists' own armed force, in the uprising against Dollfuss in 1934 and later to have fought in Spain during the Civil War as a battalion commander in the International Brigade. It is almost certain that he was recruited as a Soviet agent in this period. In 1938 after the Nazis took control in Vienna he went to Palestine as a refugee, joining Haganah and being highly regarded by its directors. Serving with the Israeli forces in the War of Independence, he became one of the youngest lieutenant-colonels in the Israeli Army and, having a reputation as a scholar, was chosen to write a history of the war. He became a friend of Ben-Gurion and the principal aide of General Yigal Yadin, Chief of Staff of the Israeli Army, thus gaining access to all manner of military secrets, all of which were secretly passed on to Moscow. He was then made deputy chief of Aman and liaison officer on intelligence to the Defence Minister, a post then held by Prime Minister Ben-Gurion himself. Finally, evidence from defectors and a tip-off from the British SIS led to Beer's arrest in 1962. He was sentenced to ten years' imprisonment for transmitting information calculated to impair the security of the state.

BETTANEY, MICHAEL

Michael Bettaney was a pathetic, inefficient spy who offered secret papers to the Soviet Embassy in London in the clumsiest manner imaginable. His first offer was declined, as no doubt the Russians suspected a trap, so Bettaney made his next approach to the KGB on the Continent. He would hardly be worth mentioning, but for the fact that he was a member of MI5 and an example of that service's appalling vetting procedures (see *United Kingdom*, Part I). Just how mixed up this Oxford graduate was is indicated by his violent swings of interest; at times he wanted to be a Catholic priest, then he became fascinated by Nazism and right-wing politics, and finally converted to Marxism. He was sentenced to twenty-three years' imprisonment on ten spying charges in 1984.

BITTMAN, LADIVSLAV

Bittman served in the Czechoslovak Intelligence Service for fourteen years, including two years as deputy commander of the Department of Active Measures before his defection in 1968. When he was officially the press secretary at the Czech Legation in Vienna (that was his cover), and head of a spy network, he quietly slipped away to a prepared refuge in Switzerland after the Russian intervention in his own country. His departure led to furious rows inside the Czech Intelligence Service and there were even tentative plans to track him down and kill him. His knowledge of the Soviet disinformation machine has been of much value to the West and he has revealed some of this in two books: *The Deception Game* and *The KGB and Soviet Disinformation*. In the first book he states that all around the world Czech intelligence operatives collect the raw materials necessary for the production of forgeries: 'signatures of high-ranking public servants, diplomats and officials of various political, religious or special interest organizations ... The Czechoslovak Intelligence Service developed a very simple and efficient method of enlarging its collection. Intelligence officers abroad send out a large number of Christmas greetings to their foreign counterparts and to important people in general ... Their greetings are duly answered, the answers signed and the signatures sometimes written on letterhead stationery. These papers are carefully sorted ... and sent along to the Centre.'

BLAKE, GEORGE (b. 1922)

Born George Behar, the son of an Egyptian Jew married to a Dutchwoman, Blake was born in Rotterdam. His Communist links date back long before the 'nine and a half years' mentioned by the Attorney-General when he was charged with espionage in 1961. His uncle was Henri Curiel (q.v.), son of a Jewish banker in Cairo, who was involved in the founding of the Egyptian

Communist Party. Curiel kept in touch with his nephew over many years. As a potential sleeper-agent, young Blake was smuggled out of Holland into Belgium during World War II, disguised as a Trappist monk. He joined the Royal Navy as an ordinary seaman and eventually became an officer.

Blake's linguistic ability led to an involvement in intelligence work with the Navy and later with the SIS. Posted to Korea, he was taken prisoner by the North Koreans and released after the armistice of 1953. The story put around that Blake was brainwashed and 'turned' to the Soviet side while in the prison camp was simply a cover-up of the fact that Blake had long been a Soviet agent. It was after this that he was asked by the British to pose as a double-agent, infiltrating Soviet espionage, which meant, of course, giving some information to the other side. Such tactics are always dangerous, but in the case of Blake it was a major blunder. He caused the disappearance (and in some cases deaths) of forty-two Western agents behind the Iron Curtain, and played such havoc with British Intelligence that their networks in East Germany, the Middle East and some Iron Curtain countries had to be rebuilt. Among the most damaging of his coups for the Russians was a warning about the creation of the Berlin Tunnel (see *Operation Gold*, Part IV). After a period of service in the Lebanon he was summoned back to London, arrested and eventually convicted of spying for the Russians. He was sentenced to forty-two years' imprisonment. His subsequent escape from Wormwood Scrubs Prison in London, after serving only six years, was the subject of an inquiry which failed to find adequate answers for lapses in prison security. He went to Moscow where he has remained ever since.

Further reading
Shadow of a Spy by E.H. Cookridge (Leslie Frewen, London 1961)
The Springing of George Blake by Sean Bourke (Cassell, London 1970)

BLUNT, ANTHONY
FREDERICK (1907-1983)

The son of a clergyman who was at one time chaplain to the British Embassy in Paris, and whose mother was related to the present Queen Mother, Anthony Blunt was educated at Marlborough and Trinity College, Cambridge. He was recruited as an agent for Russia in the early 1930s, having made one visit to Moscow, and he also became a talent-spotter for the Soviet Intelligence Services while at Cambridge. From 1932-36 he was a Fellow of Trinity. In 1940 he joined MI5 and was at one time responsible for links with the Supreme HQ Allied Expeditionary Force (SHAEF). For most of the war he was in charge of intercepting diplomatic bags from neutral embassies in London, thus enabling him to pass extremely valuable information to Moscow.

His links with SHAEF gave him the opportunity of informing Moscow about exact plans and dates for the invasion of Normandy, something which the British and Americans were most anxious to keep secret from Stalin. Mr George Young, formerly deputy head of MI6, has stated that 'some of Blunt's wartime knowledge may very well have brought about the deaths of some of our friends in Eastern Europe'. Certainly he was deeply involved in the disgraceful scheme for repatriating many thousands of people to the Soviet Union and other Soviet-controlled territories, some of whom had left even before the Revolution.

At the end of the war he was sent to Germany on a secret mission for the Royal family, the true nature of which has never been fully revealed. In 1945 he left MI5 to become Surveyor and Keeper of the Royal Pictures, but he maintained links with MI5, regularly meeting some of their top personnel at a Chelsea public house at least once a week. Meanwhile his career in the art world flourished and his students at the Courtauld Institute of Art regarded him highly. When George VI died, the present Queen asked Blunt to continue as Surveyor of the Royal Pictures and in 1956 he was knighted.

However, he was not above suspicion. When Burgess (q.v.

Part III) and Maclean (q.v.) fled to Russia in 1951, Blunt was interrogated by MI5 eleven times. Suspicions that he was a Soviet agent remained in the minds of some in the service, but no action was taken. Blunt's links with Buckingham Palace made him impregnable in the minds of some, though it has been postulated that by giving him a knighthood and appearing to be ignorant of his pro-Soviet activities, the British authorities hoped to keep Russia in the dark. However, there is no evidence that such a ploy helped British Intelligence; in fact, rather the reverse. At some time between 1951 and 1964, when Blunt confessed to spying, there is no doubt that sufficient evidence was available to have him charged. Finally, it was evidence from the USA, including a statement from a Cambridge colleague he had tried to enlist as a Soviet agent, which forced a confession from him. Even then he was given immunity in return for a promise of cooperation. He might have remained a deeply respected figure for all time had it not been for the fact that at least two authors finally produced copious evidence of his treachery. In 1979 when the Prime Minister, Mrs Thatcher, was challenged by Mr Ted Leadbetter MP, she was forced to admit that Blunt was a spy. He was then stripped of his knighthood and other honours.

Attempts have been made to suggest that Blunt merely helped the Soviet Union in order to save the world from Nazism and Fascism. The truth is that he ignored the Nazi-Soviet Pact of 1939, which was a prime cause of war, and that he helped the USSR by stooping to sexual blackmail to win more agents and information. (His homosexuality was notorious and he used this quite ruthlessly to win agents for the Russians, threatening exposure if the recruits ever wished to escape the network.) Here was one of the most loathsome spies of all time, a man who wished to have the best of both worlds – Communist and capitalist. He is said to have left an uninspiring memoir of his life to the British Library, though this may not be released for inspection for thirty years. He remained a traitor, despite promises of immunity, for he was in contact with the Russians right up to the end of his life.

Further reading:
Conspiracy of Silence: The Secret Life of Anthony Blunt by Barrie Penrose and Simon Freeman, (Grafton Books, London, 1987)

CASEY, WILLIAM J. (1913-1987)

It was bad eyesight which kept Casey out of direct espionage when he joined the Office of Strategic Services (OSS) in Washington in World War II. Nevertheless as OSS station chief in London in the latter part of the war, he organized a large-scale operation which dropped some 150 agents behind German lines to disrupt Nazi forces and assist the Allied advance. From 1954-71 Casey's own firm, the Institute for Business Planning, helped to instil in him an appetite for digesting information. Then, when he helped President Reagan to his election in 1981 as campaign manager, he became an almost obvious choice for new chief of the CIA. But while he was close to his President – closer than any other CIA chief in the past – Casey was criticized by Congress for failing to keep them fully informed on clandestine operations.

The CIA was in rather a poor state when Casey took over. He had an uphill task in repairing the damage done to the organization during the Carter years of presidency, and even before that. His aim was to give intelligence agents unrestricted authority to spy on Americans at home and abroad. But foremost in Casey's mind was the desire to improve methods of combating terrorism. The new proposals included the use of such techniques as break-ins, physical surveillance and the infiltration of domestic organizations. This was an attempt to overturn many of the regulations imposed on intelligence-gathering by Presidents Ford and Carter in the wake of scandals over the CIA's spying on anti-Vietnam War activists. The view in the Reagan camp was that the CIA had been dangerously demoralized through previous administrations' purges. Casey's task was also to give aid to the counter-intelligence staff of the CIA, which had been seriously weakened after the dismissal of James Angleton (q.v.).

Casey, as a non-professional head of the CIA, was widely criticized for his lack of relevant experience. It was also alleged that, despite his acute analytical mind, he was often inarticulate. Because he so often mispronounced Nicaragua as 'Nicowawa',

275

a group of Democrats said they would not approve plans to 'overthrow the government of any country of which Casey could not pronounce the name'. Constantly under attack from the Democrats, Casey had nevertheless greatly strengthened the morale of the CIA since he took over. He never shrank from tackling problems 'head-on', as for instance when he threatened to prosecute the *Washington Post* in 1986 if they published details of a secret operation to intercept Soviet communications involving American submarines. In this instance he succeeded and publication was withheld. Casey also maintained that the publication of certain material would have totally compromised the means by which Washington decoded transmissions between Libya and its East German Embassy prior to the bombing of a Berlin discotheque and loss of American lives.

At the age of seventy Casey was still a power in the service and government circles, and he was especially forthright in speaking out about the role of intelligence in countering terrorism. He told 900 executives of the American Society of Newspaper Editors that 'Soviet clients like Cuba, Syria and Libya, in reality are waging covert warfare against the USA' and that, though the Soviet connection might seem shadowy, the USSR was attempting to undermine America's security in all strategically important regions of the world.

At the end of 1986 Casey suffered from two seizures after he had been accused of flouting congressional control in waging the secret war against the Sandinistas in Central America, believing that they were about to spread the contagion of communism in that whole area. It was said of him that his mumbling manner disguised a quick and decisive mind: 'He has taken mumbling and turned it into an art form,' commented a CIA colleague. In February 1987, Casey resigned his post after undergoing brain surgery for a malignant tumour. He died the following May, a Catholic who had been educated by Jesuits, but whose policies were denounced by a Catholic bishop at his funeral.

In May 1987, the US Senate approved William Webster, FBI director, as the new CIA chief by 94 votes to one.

CHEBRIKOV, MARSHAL VIKTOR (b. 1923)

A large man with what has been described as a 'steely gaze', Chebrikov joined the Communist Party in the USSR in 1944, making his early career in the party structure at Dnepropetrovsk in the Ukraine, which brought him close to Leonid Brezhnev. After Khruschev's overthrow by Brezhnev, Chebrikov joined the KGB as head of personnel, becoming deputy head of the secret police only a year later. He made a remarkably frank speech in 1981 when he accused the West of using religion, nationalism and ideas of political liberalism to undermine the faith of young Russians in orthodox Communism. For the first time someone in the Soviet hierarchy had actually admitted that Soviet youth was dissatisfied and more attracted by Western ideas, which posed a threat to State security. 'Ideological sabotage' was how he described it.

In 1982 Chebrikov was made head of the KGB in a surprise reshuffle, replacing Vitaly Fedorchuk. Then in 1984 he was promoted to the rank of marshal, the highest rank to be held by a Soviet security and intelligence chief since Stalin. This was interpreted as giving a political boost to the KGB, and it was followed up in 1985 by Chebrikov being promoted to full membership of the ruling Politburo. There was a hint that Mr Gorbachev, the new party leader, needed the full backing of the KGB to purge corrupt, incompetent and some decrepit members of the Central Committee of the Communist Party. The following year a sweeping review of the activities of the KGB was carried out during a secret two-day conference in Moscow. Chebrikov was given the go-ahead to make improvements and he himself went on record as saying that more work was needed 'to ensure that all KGB members were politically steadfast, principled, truthful and self-critical'.

It was about this time that a former KGB official was appointed to take overall control of Soviet radio and television. There was a hint of concern in Chebrikov's warning that Western intelligence services were trying to subvert the State by seeking out 'social misfits' and trying to suborn officials into giving away State secrets. 'They are straining after our political, military, economic and scientific secrets,' he added.

CODES AND CIPHERS

As important today as in the Middle Ages, codes and ciphers are an integral part of all secret services. In fact, the opinion of Antoine Rossignol, Louis XIV's personal adviser on security, holds as true today as in the eighteenth century. Rossignol declared that an unbreakable code was probably an impossibility, but a reliable code should take so long to crack that it would be useless to an enemy by the time this was achieved.

Until 1914 most codes tended to be 'substitution ciphers' and these were relatively easy to break. They involved comparing the frequency of particular letters in a hidden message with the naturally-occurring frequency of letters in the language being used. This may have taken a long time to resolve in the distant past, but now with high-speed technology it can be done much more quickly. A computer, carrying out thousands of operations per second, can very often break a code in a few minutes, especially one based on transposed letters. This is why the NATO decoding centre at GCHQ in Cheltenham has the largest multi-computer system in Europe.

Israeli mathematicians have in recent years made something of a breakthrough in the field of cryptography, notably through Adi Shamir. In 1976 Shamir, together with Leonard Aldeman of the University of Southern California and R.L. Rivest, invented a system by which two people, who had never met or communicated before, could write to each other in a code which only they could understand. The 'ultimate code' (which such a code undoubtedly is), uses extremely large prime numbers like twenty-nine and eighty-three, and which are only divisible by themselves and one. You choose a pair of primes, each preferably longer than fifty digits. The agent multiplies the two numbers, making what is called a prime product. He publicly announces this, but retains the secret primes. Messages can then be sent by people who know the prime product, but which only the person knowing the secret primes can decipher. Of course, like other messages, they can eventually be deciphered, but even with the most up-to-date computer in the world this can take several months, even years, to achieve. By then the information would be outdated. Current concern therefore centres on how long it takes to break secret codes; speed is the essence of the game.

It is perhaps worth recording that in the past the Chinese have relied mainly on memory for transmitting secret messages and they have kept their coding to a minimum. The nature of the Chinese language largely precludes complicated coding, and for this reason a Western alphabet has been used in modern times. The Roman alphabet is extensively used in such communications today, but in top-secret messages destined for the Secret Service hierarchy there appear to be ciphers similar in construction to the eleventh-century ciphers of *Wu-ching tsung-yao*. Although much simplified, these are still extremely difficult to decipher and sparingly used. If the Chinese wished, there is no other language which so lends itself to a limited, but unbreakable, system of coding.

Further reading
The Codebreakers by David Kahn (Weidenfeld & Nicolson, London 1966)
Secret and Urgent: the story of codes and ciphers by Fletcher Pratt (Robert Hale, London 1939)
Machine Cryptography and Modern Cryptanalysis by Cipher by A. Deavours and Louis Kruh (London, 1985)

COHEN, ELIE (1924-1965)

One of the ablest spies of modern times, Elie Cohen was born in Alexandria, the son of Saul and Sophie Cohen, who had emigrated from Syria before World War I. His parents were relatively poor, but Elie had progressed from a school in the Jewish quarter to a French high school and then, with the aid of a grant, to Farouk University. Yet it was not until he started work as a salesman in a clothing store that he first learned Hebrew. When the Egyptians began to take a harsh line with native Jews after the Suez campaign of 1956, Cohen, a dedicated Zionist at heart, emigrated to Israel. In 1960 he was recruited into the Mossad and for several months was given intensive training. He was ordered to make friends with the most influential members of Syrian society when they visited Jerusalem, and he took on a new identity as Kamel Amine Tabet, a Syrian subject, having developed to perfection the Syrian accent of his Arabic. Part of his cover story was that his 'uncle' had emigrated to Argentina immediately after World War II and that he had been asked to take up a post with him there.

Elie's next assignment was to go to Argentina and build up his cover story. Once in Buenos Aires he not only made friends with Syrian Embassy officials, but joined the Baathist Party. In 1962 he went to Syria, smuggling his miniature radio transmitter, codes and other spy-kit across the border from Lebanon with the aid of a friendly Arab. Israel wanted quick results from Elie Cohen who established himself in a luxurious villa in Damascus, setting out to play the role of a fanatical anti-Israeli Syrian patriot, urging the Syrians to build stronger defences against Israel. Senior officers took him into forbidden military areas to reassure him that all was well and he not only obtained Syrian plans, but those of Egypt and other Arab countries as well. He even managed to accompany the Syrian Prime Minister on visits to Cairo and other Arab capitals.

Meanwhile he was asked to give talks on their Spanish programme by the Director of Radio Damascus; these were to be beamed to Syrians who had emigrated. It was a chance Elie was quick to accept, as it not only gave him access to the Ministry of Information, but the chance to slip coded messages to Israel in his broadcasts: The Mossad headquarters in Tel Aviv were soon alerted to this ploy, as well as maintaining contact with Elie through the radio set he kept hidden in his bedroom. Perhaps one of his chief scoops in intelligence was when he learned how the Syrians had built a network of subterranean tunnels in which soldiers were stationed all along the Israeli border. Slowly, however, the Syrians began to suspect a spy in their midst and one morning Elie was arrested at his villa while tapping out messages to Tel Aviv. Through intermediaries Israel secretly offered Syria more than a million dollars, plus army lorries, tractors and medical supplies, in exchange for Elie's life. Never in history has so much been offered to save the life of a single spy. All such efforts failed: Elie

Cohen was hanged in the public square in Damascus, a gallant Israeli patriot whose information eventually helped Israel to win the Six-Day War.

Further reading
Elie Cohen: Our Man in Damascus by Ben Hanan (ADM, Tel Aviv 1967)
L'espion que venait d'Israel by E. Ben Dan (Paris, 1967)

COHEN, MORRIS AND LONA

Two top Soviet agents, Morris Cohen and his wife, Lona, escaped from the network of Russian spies in the USA after it had been rounded-up in the late 1940s. They moved to New Zealand, adopting the names of Peter and Helen Kroger and eventually went to Britain, coming under the Konon Molody network (q.v.). A shop selling rare and second-hand books was opened at 190 The Strand in London in the name of Peter J. Kroger, advertising its speciality as 'Americana from the North Pole to the South Pole'. The Krogers took a bungalow at Ruislip and it was here they were eventually arrested by the police in 1960. A micro-dot reader, hidden cameras and several thousand American dollars were found in a secret compartment in the loft. Police later found cipher pads and several false passports. It was soon clear that the Cohens had been controlling a high-powered radio transmitter for communicating with Moscow Centre and elsewhere. A check with the US authorities revealed that Morris Cohen was the son of East European immigrants living in the Bronx and that both he and his wife had been Soviet agents since before World War II. They were sentenced to twenty years' imprisonment, but were released in 1969 in exchange for Gerald Brooke, a British lecturer who had been gaoled by the Russians for distributing subversive pamphlets.

COLBY, WILLIAM

As a young man Colby was an OSS agent who operated behind the German lines in France and was later put in charge of agents parachuted into Norway. He joined the newly-created CIA after the war and eventually became station chief in Saigon. He was promoted to chief of the Far Eastern Division of the CIA in 1963 and was urged to use his talents gained in earlier years as a covert action operator in Vietnam. He was not entirely successful, for he was probably better in the field than commanding from an office. He returned from Vietnam to be appointed Deputy Director for Operations in 1973, becoming Director later that year. It was Colby, by implication, who was given the task of cleaning up the CIA after Watergate, who provided the Senate Committee of Inquiry in 1973 with ample evidence of what could be regarded as the CIA's more embarrassing activities, something which no other Secret Service chief in the world would be expected to do. But he went further still in clamping down on all manner of legitimate probes within the CIA, especially those which wanted a much more vigilant attitude towards dubious defectors, including men like James Angleton (q.v.). It has been said of him that he allowed his Catholic morals to influence his judgement in his period as Director, though this does not seem to have been the case when working 'in the field' either in World War II or in the Far East afterwards.

CRABB, COMMANDER LIONEL PHILLIP

Starting life in the Merchant Navy, 'Buster' Crabb, as he was usually called, served in the Royal Navy in World War II as a frogman, earning the George Medal and the OBE for his feats. Without question he was one of the Navy's best underwater sabotage experts, and though approaching an age when his diving days were numbered, his services were still eagerly sought in the 1950s. He had successfully carried out a covert underwater examination of at least one Soviet ship, so he was the natural choice for a similar mission on the Russian cruiser, *Ordzhonikidze*, which brought Kruschchev and Bulganin, the Soviet leaders, on a visit to the UK. In April 1956 he dived into Portsmouth Harbour and never reported back to duty.

A parliamentary storm was caused when Soviet Admiral Kotov reported the appearance of a frogman wearing a diving-suit in the vicinity of the *Ordzhonikidze*. There were, of course, the usual denials that Crabb was operating on behalf of British Intelligence or the Admiralty, with some rather snide hints that he might have been a freelance diver for the Americans. Though this 'cover-up story' was ventilated to the press, few believed it. Then it transpired that an SIS officer had removed pages from the register of the hotel in Portsmouth where Crabb had been staying. Later the Admiralty announced that Crabb was presumed dead as a result of trials with underwater apparatus in Stokes Bay. As no body had then been found, this story was not generally accepted either. Fourteen months later a headless body was washed ashore near Chichester and an inquest, on the flimsiest and most inconclusive evidence, recorded that it was Crabb.

With the British having officially put out so many unsubstantiated stories and the Russians giving vent to no more than expressions of indignation at being spied upon during a goodwill visit, it was not surprising that further extraordinary reports about Crabb should appear in the world's press over the next few years. One such report was that he had been seen in the USSR living under a Russian name. One sea captain even brought over a message from Crabb to his fiancée that bore all the marks of being genuine; it said that he was in Sebastopol training frogmen for the Russians. This story was told by Captain R. Melkov, master of the Russian ship *Kolpino*, then in London docks. On 8 May 1968 Melkov was found shot dead in his cabin. Southwark Coroner's Court returned a verdict of suicide.

There is a definite suspicion that Crabb's mission was betrayed in advance to the Russians and that when caught by them, he was taken aboard where he died from a heart attack. Whatever the truth of this affair it caused a row between Sir Anthony Eden, then Prime Minister, and MI6, ending with the resignation of the MI6 chief of the day (see *Sinclair, Major-General Sir John*, Part IV).

Further reading
Commander Crabb is Alive by Bernard Hutton (London, 1968)

CURIEL, HENRI (d. 1978)

An Egyptian by birth and the son of a Jewish banker in Cairo, Curiel was the uncle of the traitor George Blake (q.v.), who worked for Britain's MI6. He was involved in the founding of the Egyptian Communist Part in 1943, which not only remained faithful to Moscow, but retained the closest links with left-wing, revolutionary Arab parties. Curiel claimed to be an orthodox Marxist-Leninist and was imprisoned under Farouk. He was again arrested by Nasser and expelled from the country. In 1951 he settled in France and between 1960-62 was imprisoned for collaborating with the Algerian FLN guerrillas. He had kept in touch with his nephew over many years. Latterly he was suspected of being an ally of the terrorist 'Carlos' (see *Terrorist Spies*, Part IV), of the Japanese Red Army and the *Junta de Coordinación Revolucionaria*. He was shot dead at his home in Paris in May 1978 by two members of the extreme right-wing terrorist group, Delta. About an hour before the killing a French news agency had an anonymous call saying, 'The KGB agent Henri Curiel, a traitor to France, which adopted him, finally ceased all activity today.'

CURWEN, CHRISTOPHER KEITH (b. 1929)

During the past decade or so there seems to have been an unfortunate tendency to appoint elderly heads of MI6 who retire within a few years, and thus have hardly any chance of making their mark. The appointment of Christopher Curwen in the mid-1980s, however, was favourably greeted by the rank and file of MI6 as he was another professional who had been recruited into MI6 in 1952 and had survived dangerous espionage missions in the Far East.

The son of a clergyman, twice married and the father of five, Curwen was educated at Sherborne and Cambridge, served in the 4th Queen's Own Hussars from 1948-49 and in the SIS saw service in Bangkok and Vientiane. His clandestine activities in the Far East did not prevent him from courting a beautiful young lady named Noom Tai, whom he married in 1956. The marriage was dissolved in 1977, and he married Helen Mary Stirling that same year. He was a Counsellor in the Foreign Office in 1980. In 1986 it was reported that burglars had 'stolen a quantity of coins from the home of the head of MI6'.

DERIABIN, PETER

One of the very first top-class defectors to go over to the West, Deriabin, a life-long Communist, had fought against the Germans in World War II. Posted to Vienna as a KGB agent in 1954, he was engaged to spy on the Russian community inside Austria. Surprisingly, within a few months of his appointment he defected to the Americans and went to the USA. His information was of enormous importance. In 1959 he told a United States Committee of Inquiry that he would say that 'the size of the foreign section of the Soviet civilian intelligence is about 3000 officers in headquarters in Moscow and about 15,000 officers around the world'. But even this is a misleading estimate and certainly does not apply to all accredited KGB or GRU agents. However, Deriabin was able to pin-point KGB agents in the West and he was regarded as so important that for five years he was kept undercover.

He told the Sub-Committee investigating security for the US Senate in 1965 that 'murder is an instrument of Soviet policy. As proof of that the assassination department of State security still exists, he added that the State Security office responsible for kidnapping, murder and assassination until Stalin's death was known as the Spetsburo No. 1. 'Nowadays,' he added, 'it is known as Department No. 13, under the Foreign Intelligence Directorate of Soviet State Security ... to my knowledge, say, in 1952, 1953 and 1954, in the Austro-German section we had a few names of wanted people; on the order of the chairman of State Security they were to be assassinated or poisoned or kidnapped or killed.' Deriabin also gave extensive evidence of murders planned in the USA on KGB orders.

Further reading
Murder and Kidnapping As An Instrument of Soviet Policy

(Report of a Sub-Committee investigation into the administration of the Internal Security Act of the Judiciary US Senate, 89th Congress, 26 March 1965)

DUFF, SIR ARTHUR ANTONY (b. 1920)

The son of an admiral, and educated at the Royal Naval College in Dartmouth, Duff served in the Navy from 1937-46. During World War II he was awarded the DSO and the DSC, but he entered the twilight world which covers both intelligence and diplomacy when he joined the Foreign (subsequently the Diplomatic) Service in 1946, serving in Athens, Cairo, Paris and Bonn, before becoming British Ambassador to Nepal in 1964. In 1969 he became Deputy High Commissioner in Kuala Lumpur and from 1972-75 he was High Commissioner in Nairobi. Thereafter he went swiftly up the diplomatic ladder, becoming a Deputy Under-Secretary of State at the Foreign Office from 1975-80, and then Deputy Governor of Southern Rhodesia in the 1979-80 period, prior to independence.

Highly regarded by Mrs Thatcher when she became Prime Minister, Sir Antony became a member of the Joint Intelligence Committee (JIC) and coordinator of security and intelligence in the Cabinet Office. He had the task of implementing some of the changes recommended for the JIC, following the report on that body by Lord Franks, which criticized the handling of the Falklands War. Though over the normal retirement age for civil servants of his rank, Sir Antony became head of MI5 after further administrative criticisms following the trial of MI5 member, Michael Bettaney (q.v.).

DULLES, ALLEN WELSH (1893-1969)

A member of a distinguished family with a long record of service for the US government, Allen Dulles made his name as an OSS operator in World War II. He was head of station in Berne after having been assistant to General Donovan in New York. There he established links with Vanden Heuvel, the SIS head of station. Despite some accounts to the contrary, they appear to have worked well together and Dulles had the advantage of some previous experience of diplomacy, including earlier work in Berne and Vienna. However, there is considerable evidence that Dulles was occasionally baulked by British pig-headedness and a refusal to accept some of his information. This particularly applied to the case of a diplomatic courier named Fritz Kolbe who claimed to be an anti-Nazi and produced a wealth of top-secret documents. The British rejected him out of hand, but Dulles ultimately discovered that Kolbe, given the code-name of George Wood, was a gem among informants. James Angleton (q.v.) then head of an intelligence section in Italy, later described Kolbe as 'one of the best secret agents any intelligence service ever had'. Altogether he supplied Dulles with more than 1500 classified documents over a period of one and a half years.

Dulles went from triumph to triumph, helping the British to unmask the German spy in the British Embassy in Ankara (see *Cicero*) Part III and getting vital information on Germany's V2 weapons. A most unjust smear campaign against Dulles was launched in the USA and Britain, claiming that he was engaged in negotiations to discuss a 'soft peace' with the Germans when Churchill and Roosevelt were committed to 'unconditional surrender'. It was alleged that he had family business interests linked to German companies. In fact, Dulles' links to Admiral Canaris and others in the *Abwehr* could, if accepted by the British, have provided not only an earlier end to the war, but a halt to Soviet imperialist aggression.

When Dulles was awarded the Medal of Merit by the US Government, the citation listed many of these achievements, but doubts about the man remained in Europe and they have since been stirred up by left-wingers more devoted to disinformation propaganda than to truth. He was made head of the CIA in 1952 and he brought all his wartime OSS experience to bear when tackling the problems of the Cold War. He gave the go-ahead for the Berlin tunnel plan to tap Soviet communications (see *Operation Gold*, Part IV), but later ran into trouble when CIA involvement was revealed in the shooting down of Gary Powers in the U-2 operation on the eve of an East-West summit in 1960. Finally, his plan for landing Cuban exiles in Cuba to depose Fidel Castro which ended in disaster forced his resignation as head of the CIA. It was an unhappy end to a distinguished career.

Further reading
The Craft of Intelligence by Allen Dulles (Harper & Row, New York 1963)

EITNER, HORST

In many respects, Eitner was the perfect double-agent, working devotedly for both East and West. Living in East Germany, he contacted British Intelligence in 1950. Some years later he defected to the West and was said to have offered his services to the Gehlen Organization, though only for a short period, it seems. From the mid-1950s Eitner was working for British Intelligence on a part-time basis and also for the Soviet Union. But as with all double-agents, in due course it became almost impossible for either side to know whether what he had told them was true or false. One of his contacts was George Blake (q.v.) who worked closely with him for four years, and somehow during this period Eitner learned that Blake was working for the USSR as well as the UK.

In 1960 Eitner's wife discovered her husband was involved with another woman and she gave him away to the Western side, probably through the West Germans originally. Eitner was arrested without any publicity being given to the affair. Horst Heinz Ludwig, a German naval officer charged with spying for the Russians, mentioned a double-agent code-named 'Victor' who had worked for the British and passed information to the Russians. It was then discovered that 'Victor' was Eitner, who while in prison had told the West Germans that he had become a double-agent who led to Blake's eventual arrest. For his help, Eitner was given a lenient three-year sentence.

ESTRADA, ARMANDO (b. 1933)

One of the shrewdest and most experienced intelligence officers of the Cuban DGI (see *Cuba*, Part I), Estrada fought in a guerrilla group in the Cuban revolution of 1959 and later took part in an unsuccessful terrorist raid into Dominica. When Castro came to power Estrada, known by the nickname of *'Pantera Negra'* (Black Panther), became a key man in the DGI, first of all helping to organize anti-Duvalier revolutionary groups in Haiti (see *Tonton Macoutes*, Part IV). From 1961-71 he was chief of the DGI's African Department, working closely with the KGB, according to Western intelligence sources. He made frequent trips to various parts of Africa during this period, as well as spending some months in the Soviet Union attending a KGB training course in 1968. The following year he arrived in Palestine and went as an observer with the PLO on a night raid into the Sinai Desert. A close friend of Manuel Pineiro, a DGI chief, when the latter was appointed head of a new American Department of the DGI, Estrada joined him and was allotted responsibility for the Caribbean area, though in fact in recent years his sphere of influence has considerably widened.

When appointed Cuba Ambassador to Jamaica in 1979, he continued to indulge in espionage and other undercover activities, making contact with the 'New Jewel' movement from Grenada which eventually succeeded in overthrowing the government of the moderate Eric Gairy. He used Jamaica as a base for all manner of probes throughout the Caribbean, arranging for Haitian revolutionary exiles to set up a government-in-exile in Kingston. While Prime Minister Michael Manley tolerated Estrada's activities, his successor, Edward Seaga, announced that he was no longer welcome as Ambassador, so Estrada returned to Cuba for a spell before being appointed Ambassador to the Yemen in 1982.

FAKE DEFECTORS

It is possible that among allegedly genuine defectors listed in this book there may also be some fakes. This is not the compiler's fault, but arises because the art of fake defection has been developed so skilfully that it is now very difficult, even for professionals, to decide who is not genuine. In recent years, it has got to the point where it is thought to be worth sending two or three fake defectors to the other side in order to make them worry about the supposedly genuine ones. Thus 1983-86 could be called the 'years of the fake defector'. To some extent, this was done to counteract rumours that the KGB had a hand in the attempted assassination of Pope John Paul II. Take the case of Oleg Bitov, an editor of the *Moscow Literary Gazette*, who defected to Britain in 1983, claiming that he was protesting against the lack of freedom in the USSR and the Russian shooting down of a Korean passenger plane. (Bitov's magazine was, in fact, the KGB house organ which published Moscow's version of the plot against the Pope.) The following year Bitov showed up at a carefully staged press conference in Moscow, claiming he had been kidnapped, beaten and held against his will by British intelligence agents. This came some weeks before an Italian judge was supposed to release a report implicating the Kremlin, if only indirectly, in the assassination attempt. What disturbed Western Intelligence Services was whether Bitov was sent on a mission similar to Yuri Nosenko's early in 1964. Were both men fake defectors, or was Bitov simply lured back because he missed his homeland and his family?

In 1985 came the case of the KGB officer, Vitaly Yurchenko, who defected to the Americans and shortly afterwards identified several CIA employees as Soviet agents. The Justice Department denied this, but his defection was nevertheless hailed as a body-blow for Soviet espionage. Then in November 1985 Yurchenko re-defected to the Soviet Embassy in Washington and at a press conference protested that he had been kidnapped, tortured and drugged until he did not know what he was saying. It was later reported from Toronto that Yurchenko had fooled US intelligence agents when he persuaded them to take him to Canada to see a woman he claimed was his former mistress. Canadian intelligence sources said that in reality the woman was a KGB agent who gave him further instructions. Mystery still surrounds the fate of Yurchenko after his return to Moscow. It was reported in July 1986 that he had been executed by a firing squad, but this was later denied by the Soviet Embassy in London.

FEDORCHUK, COLONEL-GENERAL VITALY

It is surprising how many leading KGB men start their careers in the Ukraine. Vitaly Fedorchuk was employed as a journalist in the Ukraine before he joined the NKVD in 1939. He steadily worked his way up the ladder from NKVD to its successor, the KGB, making his reputation largely on his knowledge of operations concerning the Ukraine. For a time he saw service in Germany, as a result of which he was promoted to head of the Third Directorate with responsibility for security of defence and the forces. He followed this by becoming chief of the Ukrainian branch of the KGB where he acquired a reputation for ruthless administration and a certain amount of persecution of dissidents, Christians and Jews.

Fedorchuk was more reactionary than any of his predecessors and this showed in his occasional speeches. He was one of Yuri Andropov's favourites, succeeding him as chief of the KGB when Andropov became head of the Communist Party after Brezhnev's death. His mission – as decreed by Andropov – was to stamp out alleged corruption in the KGB while being groomed to take over the Ministry of the Interior in 1982.

FELFE, HEINZ PAUL JOHANN

One of the most successful double-agents since 1945, Felfe was the son of a Dresden police officer and served in the German Secret Service under Himmler in World War II. For a while after the war he was used by British Intelligence as an informant, but then joined General Gehlen's intelligence bureau in West Germany. He worked his way up that organization until a West German Intelligence Service (BND) was established and he became head of the counter-espionage department. When he was eventually suspected of being a KGB agent and arrested in 1961, it was learned that he had passed a massive amount of information to the Russians, revealing the names of nearly 100 BND agents, as well as helping to discredit General Gehlen (q.v.). In 1963 he was sentenced to fourteen years' imprisonment, but within six years the West Germans agreed to exchange him with the Russians for the release of six other prisoners.

FIGURES, SIR COLIN FREDERICK (b. 1925)

Succeeded Sir Arthur Franks as head of MI6 in 1982, Sir Colin originally worked with the Control Commission in Germany (1953), then went to Aman as first a Third, then a Second, Secretary, served for a few years in Warsaw and in 1966 was appointed First Secretary and Head of the Visa Section in Vienna. He was given the rank of Counsellor in the Foreign Office in 1975. Not without a sense of humour, when asked what his recreations were, he replied, 'Watching sport, gardening and beachcombing.' He retired a few years later.

FRANKS, SIR ARTHUR TEMPLE (b. 1920)

Educated at Rugby and Queen's College, Oxford, Sir Arthur entered the SIS largely on the strength of his wartime service in the SOE. Joining the Foreign Office in 1949, he went to Tehran as Second Secretary the following year at the time of the Iranian coup, and after another spell in London was appointed MI6 chief of station in Bonn in 1962. He succeeded Sir Maurice Oldfield as head of MI6 in 1978, and retired in 1981.

FRANTISEK, AUGUST

A veteran of fifteen years' activity in the STB of Czechoslovakia, Frantisek defected to the free world in 1969, saying, 'I was appointed senior official of the British Section within the No. 1 Administration of the Ministry of the Interior, which then directed intelligence in foreign countries. In my intelligence work I helped direct operations against the British Secret Service (MI6) and the Security Service (MI5) and Czechoslovak emigrés. In 1961-63 I was sent to the Czechoslovak Embassy in London where I worked under the cover of attaché in charge of the consular section.' (This comes from evidence to the Senate Sub-Committee on Communist Bloc Intelligence Activities, November 1975.) Frantisek also stated that when he was in London during the recurring Berlin crisis of the early 1960s the KGB advisers 'instructed us to prepare a list of British intelligence and counter-intelligence facilities that would have to be secured immediately in the case of an invasion of England. Lists were prepared also of persons hostile to the Soviet Union, including members of Parliament and journalists. They were to be arrested immediately upon the occupation of England.' In this period the Czechs infiltrated a group of former Czech officers who came under the control of MI6, located some of MI6's 'safe houses' and set up a number of agents inside the country.

FROLIK, JOSEF

For around fourteen years Frolik, as a member of the Czech Secret Service, worked on what was known as the 'British desk' at STB headquarters in Prague. He was then transferred to the Czech Embassy in London as 'labour attaché', by which title he gave himself the excuse for mixing with trade union leaders and Labour MPs. During this period he supplied the Czechs and, through them, the Soviet Union with all manner of secrets on British foreign and domestic policy and labour relationships. But in 1969, after the Red Army invaded his country, he decided he had had enough; he contacted the CIA and defected. He was rescued, together with his wife and son, in an operation which took him from Bulgaria via Turkey to Washington.

The intensely detailed evidence which Frolik subsequently gave not only to CIA interrogators, but to Senate investigative committees in Washington, resulted in the Czech Intelligence Service being forced to reorganize itself. He revealed that in the mid-sixties Czech Intelligence in London was running thirty full agents and 200 contacts: 'We had our agents in Parliament, the trade unions, the police, the Treasury, government research and private business.' It was on Frolik's testimony that the late Will Owen, Labour MP for Morpeth, was charged in 1970 with passing secrets to the Czechs prejudicial to the safety of the State. Owen was acquitted after a two-week trial, but the revelations made in court about his indiscreet conduct were enough to ruin his career and he resigned his Parliamentary seat. Even his defence counsel told how Owen had admitted receiving a total of about £2300 from officials at the Czech Embassy in London. Other MPs were cited in Frolik's testimony, some of them still alive.

One outrageous Czech plot involved trying to lay a homosexual trap for the former Conservative Prime Minister, Edward Heath, working solely on the principle that a bachelor with apparently little interest in women was wide open to such tactics. According to Frolik, 'organ virtuoso and homosexual, Jaroslav Reiberger, was an agent of Czech Intelligence who was used in an effort to work against the then Conservative leader.' An invitation was extended to Mr Heath to take part in a music festival in Prague, but British Security were able to pass on a warning and the plot was quashed.

Frolik admitted under cross-examination that sometimes, when the Czechs recruited a good agent, he would be taken over by the KGB: 'All the results of the Czech Service are given to the Russians. It is a department of the KGB in a real way.' He told British Intelligence of an occasion when the Czechs were trying to recruit a British trade union official and the Russians stepped in. 'He would have been a prime catch because his union indirectly controlled the publishing industry ... the Russians had taken him over; he was too important for the Czechs.' One other trade union leader Frolik named was the late Ted Hill (afterwards Lord Hill of Wivenhoe), the aggressive and chirpy leader of the Boilermakers' Union.

Further reading
The Frolik Defection (Leo Cooper, London 1975) – US Senate hearing, 18 November 1975, Report of US Government Office 63-061 0

GATES, ROBERT

Appointed early in 1987 temporarily to succeed William Casey as the youngest-ever director of the CIA at the age of 47, Gates immediately faced tough questioning in Senate hearings about his role in the Iran-Contras affair. As deputy director during this earlier period, he was asked why he had withheld suspicions for nearly two months that profits from Iran arms sales were being diverted to the rebels fighting in Nicaragua. Gates joined the CIA in 1966 and spent most of his career in Washington as an analyst of information. He acquired a reputation as a workaholic who had brought about a marked improvement in CIA analysis.

'GARDEN SHED' SPIES

In July 1986 a married couple calling themselves Reinhard and Sonja Schulze were jailed for ten years at the Old Bailey for what the judge called 'very serious offences' against Britain. They had been operating what was an almost foolproof spy system for East Germany from the garden shed of their three-bedroomed semi-detached house in Cranford, Middlesex. Concealed in a blue plastic air freshener in the shed were three items which, if used properly, enabled them to receive or send secret codes never likely to be broken if picked up by the British eavesdropping post at GCHQ in Cheltenham. They used a brevity code to give them a form of shorthand which listed such tell-tale phrases as 'dead letter-box', 'meeting place' and 'cover story'.

Schulze had simply stolen the identity of another man who closely matched his own age: Bryan Waldemar Stunze, the son of a West Country farm labourer. The father had been a former German prisoner-of-war who had stayed on in the UK after the war. The Schulze couple were arrested as a result of a series of East-West defections during the previous year. But the spymaster in charge of this network inside Britain had managed to slip out of the UK three days before the police moved in on the East German couple. The network's target for espionage was the European space satellite Ariane and its capability of being used for NATO. The British network was small and only part of a huge jigsaw of networks seeking the same answers all over Europe (see *Satellite Spying*, Part IV).

GEHLEN, GENERAL REINHARD (1902-1979)

An enterprising and original professional soldier, Reinhard Gehlen became intelligence chief of the German Army in 1942 and a general at the age of forty-three. When surrendering to the American Army at the end of World War II, he had the foresight to bring his files with him. He proved to be helpful, fully communicative and, more important, showed he had a grasp of the whole intelligence problem for the future Germany. The Americans took a risk and put him in charge of an espionage network under the control of, first, their own military officers, and then the newly-created CIA. It was the CIA who in 1953 set up an independent intelligence organization in West Germany and resulted in Gehlen sending agents into East Germany. Finally, the Gehlen organization was brought under the control of the West German Government of Dr Adenauer. Soon the headquarters of the Federal Intelligence Service was created in Munich and employed up to 5000 personnel.

From time to time there was criticism of Gehlen both from within and outside West Germany. He was mistrusted by Dr Otto John (q.v.), the head of counter-intelligence, but Adenauer sided with Gehlen against John. He was also opposed by the American Lieutenant-General Arthur Trudeau of G2, but such criticism in the USA was scotched by Allen Dulles. Some of the warnings about Gehlen should have been heeded; he was a man in a hurry to achieve results, and in doing so he laid himself open to exploitation. In the 1950s Gehlen was the Americans' chief instrument in waging the 'Cold War'. He brought off many coups, such as helping to organize the Berlin Rising of 1953 and the Hungarian revolt in 1956, as well as advising Nasser on his secret service and then infiltrating an Israeli spy into Egypt. He also infiltrated hundreds of spies into East Germany and the Soviet Union. Many of these triumphs he revealed in his memoirs. But what is one to make of a man who first produces 'evidence' that Martin Bormann (Hitler's deputy) was killed in 1945 and then years later claims he was a Soviet spy, still alive in Moscow?

Gehlen does not reveal any of his failures in his memoirs, but the truth is that the arch-infiltrator overreached himself by sending too many agents too soon into East Germany and Russia. The Russians just let them pour in and then, as early as 1951, they quietly 'blew' the Gehlen Organization. They took over many of Gehlen's agents and used them against him. By this means the Russians started slowly but surely to place their key men in vital positions inside that organization. One of the chief men won over was Hans Joachim Geyer, who worked for the East Germans by night and for Gehlen by day. By infiltrating the Gehlen Organization the Russians were also able to infiltrate the CIA and the NTS (the anti-Soviet Russians in exile movement which the CIA had supported). The man who masterminded the infiltration of first the West German and then the Americans' network was Colonel Hans Bormann, the East Germans' counter-espionage expert.

It is true that Gehlen scored many successes, as was shown in East German espionage trials in 1954 when seven people were convicted for stealing patents and documents from an electrical plant. The real clue to Gehlen's early successes was that as head of German military intelligence he had built up a considerable network of informers in the German-occupied territory of the USSR. He was always something of a menace to the Western Allies, plotting against both British and French politicians, including General de Gaulle. He had no hesitation in using former Nazi officers in his service. But his downfall came when it was discovered that Heinz Felfe (q.v.), chief of Gehlen's counter-espionage department, was a double-agent who had been reporting back to the Soviet Union for some twelve years. Even then Gehlen stayed in office until 1966.

Further reading
The Service by Reinhard Gehlen, translated by David Irving
(Popular Library, New York 1972)
The Gehlen Memoirs by Reinhard Gehlen (Collins, 1972)

GERHARDT, COMMODORE DIETER

When South Africa's Intelligence Service was reorganized and renamed the National Intelligence Service, one of its first successes in the early 1980s was the tracking down and arrest of Commodore Dieter Gerhardt of the South African Navy. In 1983 Gerhardt, formerly commanding officer of South Africa's strategic dockyard at Simonstown, together with his wife, Ruth, were convicted at Cape Town Supreme Court of high treason and passing secrets to the Russians. Though these crimes could result in a death penalty in South Africa, they were sentenced to life imprisonment. This was the climax of a sixteen-year quest for the source of leaks about NATO and South African naval secrets, and followed a tip-off from Yuri Loganov, a KGB man caught in Johannesburg in 1967.

Gerhardt was the son of a German architect who, because of his extreme right-wing views, had been interned in South Africa during World War II. His second wife was a Swiss woman named Ruth Johr who was already a KGB agent. The damage caused by the Gerhardt case was widespread. Western maritime intelligence had been seriously endangered by Gerhardt's access to information from the top-secret Silvermines maritime tracking stations. Operated by the South African Navy, Silvermines monitored all shipping movements in the South Atlantic and Indian Ocean, and from the coast of South America to the west coast of Australia. Gerhardt's treachery may also have been responsible for the deaths of dozens of British sailors during the Falklands War, as he used daily intelligence reports from a South African Government listening-post to send the position of the British Falklands Task Force back to Moscow. Worse still, he had also passed on much vital information about Britain's

Polaris programme. Gerhardt visited Gibraltar twice just before Argentina invaded the Falklands and MI5 agents were convinced that he passed on information to Russian contacts from Spain.

GOLENIEWSKI, LIEUTENANT-COLONEL MICHAL

Accompanied by Homer E. Roman of the CIA, Goleniewski defected from the ranks of the Polish Intelligence Service and fled to the West in January 1961. He arrived in the USA on a military transport plane on 12 January. Prior to this – from April 1958 until December 1960 – he had voluntarily served the USA, seemingly at some danger to himself. For a long time he refused to identify himself, but passed on information anonymously, using the code-name 'Heckenschütze'. In his reports he hinted at moles high up in the American and British Establishments, pointed directly at undercover agents in the Royal Navy, to George Blake (q.v.) in Germany and Colonel Israel Beer (q.v.) in Israel. After lengthy debriefings in the USA, Goleniewski was able to provide more information which, on being checked, was found to be accurate. However, there were still a few in the CIA who thought that he might be a highly skilled disinformer, pumping out enough truth to gain confidence and then distilling the kind of disinformation that can do a great deal of damage.

When the US Senate Committee on Internal Security wanted to question him, Goleniewski began behaving very oddly. He declared that he was really Tsarevich Alexei Romanov, the haemophiliac son of Tsar Nicholas II, who had supposedly been shot with the rest of his family at Ekaterinburg in 1918. Goleniewski's astonishing story was that he and his parents and four sisters had escaped from Ekaterinburg, that his mother had died in 1924 and his father had lived on in Poland until 1952. On the face of it this story was monstrously absurd, so much so that it seemed impossible the KGB would sanction disinformation of this nature. The only possible bonus to the KGB would be if his story merely gave the impression that he was crazy and therefore useless as an informant. A likelier explanation was that Goleniewski feared that leakages of any evidence he gave the Senate Committee might do more harm than good and that it could encourage the Russians to hunt him down and kill him. If he claimed to be the Tsarevich, this would seem to make him so unreliable that nobody would take him seriously and at the same time the KGB would think he had gone mad and was not therefore worth the risk of an assassination attempt on US soil. Indeed, there might be every reason why he should remain alive and confuse the Americans.

In an affidavit signed 3 June 1965, Herman E. Kimsey, former chief of research and analysis of the CIA, stated, 'I am convinced that the person referred to as Colonel Goleniewski is in fact the Tsarevich and Grand Duke Alexei Nicholaevich Romanov of Russia,' adding that he had made tests and checks with medical records alleged to be in the British Government's possession and dental records from the late Dr Kostrycki of Paris, formerly the Imperial Family's dentist. Some time after this, when his relations with the CIA were somewhat ambivalent, he set up as 'HRH' in the Kew Gardens area of New York, having married his second wife in the Russian Orthodox Cathedral in 1964. While recognizing that he had provided some first-class intelligence which resulted in the capture of several moles, even the CIA found it embarrassing to cope with so bizarre a claim as Goleniewski had made. Just to add to the mystery, a Free Polish contact in New York states: 'The man in New York may not only not be the Tsarevich, *but not even the real Goleniewski.*' He claims to have known the real Goleniewski, when the latter was chief of Section 6 of Polish Intelligence. His story is that just as Goleniewski was about to leave for Germany in November 1960 he was ordered to Moscow and never returned. Another 'Goleniewski', an impostor, was ordered to defect in his place. There is also a further suggestion that Goleniewski Number Two was murdered on arrival in Germany and that he was substituted by Goleniewski Number Three who was taken to the USA by the CIA. It may be some years before the exact truth of all this is established.

Further reading
The Hunt for the Tsar by Guy Richards (Peter Davies, London 1971)

GOLYTSIN, ANATOLI

Whatever views one may take of him (and there are conflicting opinions), Golytsin is undoubtedly one of the most carefully analysed and widely studied defectors from Russia to the West in the post-war years. Something of his reputation may be gleaned from the fact that, under close supervision, he has been allowed to visit various countries in the Western World to enable their Intelligence Services to track down Soviet agents in their midst. Nevertheless, like Yuri Nosenko (q.v.) he remains rather enigmatic. One SIS executive puts it this way: 'When you get facts from Golytsin, they are indeed impressive. When you get theories, then one begins to doubt.' He defected to the CIA in December 1961 when stationed in Finland. Prior to that he was an executive officer in the KGB in Moscow. He supplied the Americans, and later the British, with the names of scores of Soviet agents in various parts of the world, including such people as Philby. While his factual evidence has proved impressive and satisfied so cautious a man as James Angleton of the CIA, his interpretation of policies has sometimes proved wrong.

GORDIEVSKY, OLEG

On 12 September 1985 the British Foreign Office announced the defection of Oleg Gordievsky, said to have been the top KGB officer in London. Next day newspapers were almost unanimous in claiming that Gordievsky had been a double-agent, working for the British as well as the Russians for between twelve and fifteen years. 'Whitehall sources', however, merely stated that he had asked for political asylum 'several weeks ago' for ideological reasons. It was then that speculation started as to the real reasons for this announcement. Some suggested Gordievsky had been 'brought in from the cold' because British Intelligence feared he might have been betrayed by Hans Tiedge (q.v.), the West German counter-intelligence departmental chief who had defected to East Germany the previous month. It was further revealed that twenty-five Soviet 'diplomats' had been expelled from the UK for undesirable activities. A week later another suggestion was that Tiedge had defected because he feared Gordievsky's information would have involved him. The Soviet Union denied all charges of spying levelled against them, and retaliated by expelling twenty-five British officials from Moscow. Later it was revealed that the Danish Minister of Justice had known that Gordievsky was working against the Soviet Union and it was implied that he had also given information to the Danes some years earlier.

Six more expulsions from Britain were made, followed by the complementary six from Russia. Soon it was clear that the Russians were doing everything possible to discredit Gordievsky, even at first suggesting through roundabout sources that he might have been planted on the West by Moscow. One more recent story from Moscow was that he was smuggled out of Russia when the British kidnapped him in a van with a secret compartment, a very odd story for the KGB to put out.

GOUZENKO, IGOR (1922-1985)

An officer in the GRU, operating under cover of being a civilian cipher clerk in the Russian Legation in Ottawa, Gouzenko caused something of a furore in the Canadian capital in 1945 when he asked to defect. Still regarding the Russians as allies, Canadian officials at first cold-shouldered him and refused to assist. There was even talk of handing him back to the Soviet authorities. Luckily for the Western World, he did in the end defect and went into hiding in Canada. What he told the authorities and the papers he brought with him proved him to be one of the most important defectors of this era. He revealed the extent of the Soviet atomic espionage network inside Canada and the USA. As a result twenty-two local agents and some fifteen Soviet specialists belonging to the Russian mission in Ottawa were rounded up. Later his information led to a number of British scientists being detained for questioning, though in the end only Klaus Fuchs and Dr Allan Nunn May were trapped and sentenced (see *Nuclear Spies*, Part IV). In 1946 a Royal Commission (the Taschereau-Kellock Commission) followed up Gouzenko's evidence. Though this report was left in abeyance for several years, in the mid-sixties a study named 'Featherbed' was instituted by the Canadian Government to probe its findings. The results were so sensational and politically damaging to successive Canadian governments that they were never published.

But did somebody inside MI5 in Britain, or even in the Canadian counter-intelligence, intervene to prevent further investigation of what Gouzenko described in these words: 'The case of the member of MI5 was, in my opinion, much stronger [than those of Rose or Alger Hiss] and there was more to go on ... In the first place I was not told by somebody but saw the telegram myself concerning this person. And then, as a second confirmation, I was told by Lieutenant Lubimov [in Moscow]. With these two pieces of evidence there is not the slightest doubt in my mind that there was a Soviet agent inside MI5 during the period 1942-43 and possibly later on ... This man had something Russian in his background ... The mistake in my opinion in dealing with this matter was that the task of finding the agent was given to MI5 itself ... The results even beforehand could be expected as nil.'

The phrase 'something Russian in his background' was capable of various interpretations, but the identity of this mysterious person in MI5 was never satisfactorily solved, though various theories have been put forward. However, for the record, Gouzenko mentioned one other agent code-named 'Ellie' whom he did not positively identify. He added that, though this was a female name, Moscow had been known to give such names to male agents. Some have tried to suggest 'Ellie' was the mystery man inside MI5, but it is generally thought that 'Ellie' referred to Kathleen Wilsher, who was Assistant Registrar of the Office of the UK High Commisioner in Ottawa. The Canadian Government gave Gouzenko a small pension and in the 1950s he wrote a novel, *The Fall of a Titan*, about life in the

Soviet Union under Stalin, which won the Governor-General of Canada's Prize for Literature. He made no secret of the fact that he believed Western Intelligence Services, especially Britain's, had failed to follow up fully the information he provided. He lived under an assumed name in Ontario and his identity was known only to a few people.

THE GREENPEACE AFFAIR

On 10 July 1985 French Secret Service agents crept into Auckland harbour in New Zealand and, using underwater explosives, sank the Greenpeace vessel, *Rainbow Warrior*, killing a Portuguese photographer on board. Soon afterwards, the police arrested a couple posing as Swiss honeymooners who gave their names as Alain and Sophie Turenge. They turned out to be Major Alain Tourand and Captain Dominique Prieur, agents of the DGSE, and they were subsequently sentenced to ten years' imprisonment.

The *Rainbow Warrior*, belonging to the militant anti-nuclear, conservationist organization Greenpeace, had been planning to sail into the French nuclear test zone in the South Pacific to monitor and protest. After its sinking a vast disinformation exercise was mounted in Paris, including some allegations in the French media that the *Rainbow Warrior* had been sunk by British Intelligence, and a report by the Gaullist Bernard Tricot cleared the French Secret Service of any involvement. But the matter did not end there: soon afterwards the Defence Minister, Charles Hernu, resigned, Admiral Lacoste, head of the service, was sacked, and eventually the Prime Minister admitted that French agents had done the job. France threatened sanctions against New Zealand in an effort to secure the release of the imprisoned agents. In the end the New Zealand Government agreed to transfer them to French military custody and deported them to the Pacific island of Hao.

In 1986 Jacques Chirac, the French Prime Minister, officially saluted the two secret agents for their actions, which, it cannot be denied, was much better than the lies and evasions which the British handed out after the Commander Crabb incident (q.v.) in Portsmouth Harbour. Chirac's justification was that the New

Zealand Prime Minister, David Lange, had said he would spend the French compensation money on improving equipment to monitor French nuclear tests in the Pacific.

GUILLAUME, GUNTHER

Guillaume will go down in history as the man who caused the resignation of Willy Brandt from his post as Federal Chancellor of West Germany in 1974. He was the son of Dr Ernst Guillaume, who had at one time tended Brandt's wounds and saved him from capture. By the mid-1950s Dr Guillaume was living as an invalid in East Germany and his son helped to support him by working as a labourer who crossed into West Berlin each day and worked under the direction of the Allied powers. The KGB and East German Intelligence took note of the fact that young Guillaume was antagonistic to the West, but had a deep sense of obligation to his father. Together they set out to enrol him to their cause, at the same time urging him to ask his father to write to Willy Brandt, reminding him of their meeting in the war and pleading for help for his son. As a result Brandt agreed to take on the young man in 1955.

Gunther Guillaume soon won Brandt's absolute trust not only by his efficiency but because he spent such long hours in his office. Soon Guillaume was supplying East Berlin and the Soviets with a steady stream of top-secret intelligence on the West German Intelligence Service and NATO. West German Security should have screened him much more thoroughly at the start, if only because he had lived in East Berlin and at one time worked in a company used for spying by the East Germans. Eventually evidence from a defector pointed in the direction of Guillaume who was arrested, tried and convicted, together with his wife. After a spell in prison, he was exchanged for some West German citizens held in the East and repatriated in 1982. For his services he was awarded the Order of Lenin.

HAMBLETON, PROFESSOR HUGH

In 1982 Professor Hambleton was sentenced to ten years' imprisonment at the Old Bailey in London for passing on secrets to the Russians over a period of thirty years. Of the hundreds of NATO papers he was said to have given the USSR, more than eighty were classified 'cosmic', containing information 'so important that its disclosure would result in exceptionally grave damage', the jury was told. Hambleton, though born in Canada, was a British subject and was educated in both countries. From 1944-46 he served in the Free French Army in North Africa and later transferred to the Canadian Army where he served in Intelligence. He was recruited as a Russian agent by a KGB officer attached to the Soviet Embassy in Canada in the late 1940s. In 1965, at the instigation of the Russians, he secured a post for himself in the economic section of NATO, based in Paris. After leaving NATO in 1961 he returned to the London School of Economics where he had been a student, and in 1964 became a professor at Laval University.

The 'Mounties' were the first on his trail, and in 1979 he was detained in Canada where a certain amount of sophisticated spying equipment was found in his possession. However, he was not prosecuted until a few years later when he came to London on a British passport. Apparently the laxity of the Canadians in not bringing any charges against him made him over-confident, and he gave the impression of believing he had been given immunity. One interesting revelation from this case was that at his London trial the jury were shown a piece of equipment which, when plugged into the earphone socket of a radio, caused 'the number of the code going over the radio to light up so that the numbers could be read off'. It was a decoder not made in the Western World and entirely a Russian invention.

HAREL, ISSER (b. 1912)

Born under the name of Isser Halperin in Vitebsk in Central Russia, Harel's family were orthodox Jews with a small but

prosperous business which was taken over by the Revolutionaries after 1917. By 1922 the family business was confiscated in
the name of the State and the Halperins moved to Latvia. By the
late 1920s some of the family emigrated to Palestine and Isser
followed in 1931, joining a kibbutz. It was then the family name
was changed to Harel. Young Isser soon proved to be a natural
leader and was sometimes nicknamed 'Napoleon' Harel and
'Isser the Terrible', a reference to his Russian background.
Dismissed from the British Constabulary for insubordination, he
joined the Jewish settlement police. Later he became a member
of Haganah, and it was experience in this underground
movement which served as an apprenticeship for his work in
intelligence. When Mossad, Israel's Foreign Intelligence Service,
was formed Reuven Shiloah became its caretaker in the early
days, but Ben-Gurion, Israel's first Prime Minister and Defence
Minister, chose Harel as the Mossad's first chief, with orders
that he should keep a watchful eye on internal security and
counter-espionage as well as foreign intelligence.

By reason of his close friendship with Ben-Gurion, Harel was
able to get away with many unorthodox actions in his secret
service work. Right from the beginning he thought of Israel's
problems as being global ones and, with this in mind, made the
Mossad respected by the great powers and feared by Israel's
enemies. The master-planner behind the kidnapping of Adolf
Eichmann who was responsible for the mass murders of Jews in
Germany, Harel afterwards admitted that 'my mind was by no
means easy about the need to carry out a clandestine action in
the sovereign territory of a friendly country', but this did not
deter him from tracking down the whereabouts of Eichmann,
who had adopted another name and covered his tracks so well
that many people believed he was dead. It was Harel who
ordered the secret Commando team into Buenos Aires in 1960
to carry out one of the most brilliantly planned kidnappings of
all time. Eichmann was flown to Israel, brought to trial and
executed by hanging in 1962.

It was Harel again who organized the Israeli espionage
campaign against President Nasser's Egypt and even managed
to infiltrate West Germany's Gehlen Organization. He was
rather less lucky in his activities in Switzerland in 1962, when
Swiss newspapers reported that Otto Joklik had been expelled

from Switzerland for trying to induce Swiss scientists to work for the Israelis, with implications that threats against them were used in the process. Publicity surrounding this case created difficulties for Harel who, with Ben-Gurion's backing, had been doing his best in secret diplomacy with the West Germans to get their own scientists out of Egypt. It was unwanted publicity from this and other cases which caused a rift between Ben-Gurion and Harel, with the result that Harel resigned from his post. He had been accused of using letter-bombs as well as threats to German scientists. In the end Ben-Gurion regarded improvement of relations between Israel and West Germany as being more important than any other issue.

Further reading
The House on Garibaldi Street by Isser Harel (André Deutsch, London 1975)

HAYHANEN, REINO (d. 1961)

Hayhanen was one of Russia's most appalling failures as a secret agent, and the KGB's biggest mistake was to send him to America. When Rudolf Abel (q.v.), Russia's senior agent in New York, wanted to conserve time for his cover as an artist, he asked Moscow to send him an assistant director. Their reply was to assign to him Reino Hayhanen, a Finn, who was a lieutenant-colonel in the KGB with a good record. Abel at once spotted that Hayhanen was singularly unprofessional and with very little idea of what security precautions involved. Hayhanen quickly developed a liking for the good life in the USA, began to drink heavily and play around with women. When Abel returned to Moscow in 1955 he expressed his doubts about Hayhanen to the Centre, but they paid no attention. When Abel returned to the USA he was outraged to learn how his deputy had conducted business in his absence. The Finn had continued to use one site for operating his transmitting set instead of moving it periodically, and he had not even collected all the information left at various dead letter-boxes. Possibly because Abel remonstrated with him, Hayhanen suspected he might be in serious trouble, especially when he was told to return to Moscow.

When Hayhanen reached Paris en route to Russia, he asked the CIA station chief for asylum. He was flown back to America where his testimony not only led to the arrest of Abel, but to that of Master Sergeant Roy A. Rhodes of the US Army, who had been recruited as a spy for the Russians while working in the US Embassy in Moscow. In fact, Rhodes had received considerable sums from the Russians in exchange for a mixture of truth and lies, often making his information look more important than it was. Rhodes was convicted in 1958, discharged from the Army and given a five-year sentence. Hayhanen disappeared from view after he gave evidence at Rhodes' trial, and in 1961 it was reported that he had died in a car accident.

HELMS, RICHARD (b. 1913)

Beginning life as a foreign correspondent for the UPI news agency in Hitler's Germany, Helms served in the US Navy in World War II, later joining the OSS. He remained in this service until the CIA was formed, and had first-hand information on the newly created Gehlen Organization (q.v.). He was insistent on the need for secrecy in a secret service, elementary common sense you might think, yet often foolishly challenged nowadays. When attempts were made to computerize the entire CIA employment list he scotched the whole idea on the principle that it was a potential breach of operational security. Eventually he was brought back to Washington, becoming first Deputy Director for Plans, then Deputy Director of the Agency and, in 1966, Director.

Helms was unlucky in not being helped by President Johnson, and he seems to have had unfortunate relations with President Nixon, but much of his troubles stemmed from senators who made impossible demands on him, such as Senator Richard Russell, of Georgia, chairman of the Senate joint sub-committee for overseeing the CIA's activities. Russell wanted the CIA's financial procedures reviewed by an independent body. Although Nixon eventually sacked Helms, he appointed him Ambassador to Iran – but this was not the end of Helms' CIA links. He was summoned back to Washington to answer questions on various matters relating to the CIA, including the

Watergate scandal and various other activities, including many covert operations, such as plots to kill or remove Fidel Castro, bugging suspect American citizens and clandestine operations in Latin America, notably Chile.

Faced with sniping and probing by Senators and Congressmen into sensitive areas of CIA activity, it had been decided to keep the various committees of inquiry in the dark about certain operations. This resulted in giving the code-name 'Family Jewels' to all operations which might damage the Agency if discovered. Astonishingly, Helms was found guilty of misleading the Foreign Relations Committee when he claimed that the CIA had never attempted to overthrow Allende's government in Chile. The Committee made a report to the Justice Department and Helms was charged with perjury, fined $2000 and given a two-year suspended sentence. It was by any sane standards a ridiculous verdict on a man who had done his best to serve his country, and it should be a warning to all other democracies who want their secret services to tell them all they do. Fortunately for Helms, President Reagan made amends in 1983 when he presented him with the National Security Medal and praised him for his services.

Further reading
The Man Who Kept Secrets: Richard Helms and the CIA by Thomas Powers (New York)

HILLENKOETTER, REAR-ADMIRAL ROSCOE H.

Sometimes described as the first chief of the CIA, Admiral Hillenkoetter was, in fact, the third. When President Truman issued an order establishing the Central Intelligence Group (later renamed the CIA) in January 1946, there were three directors in less than two years. The first was Rear-Admiral Sidney W. Souers, the second General Hoyt S. Vandenberg and the third Admiral Hillenkoetter, appointed in May 1947 when the National Security Act changed the Group to an Agency. The Agency was, understandably, not sufficiently advanced or prepared for the Korean War when that burst upon the world, but even prior to this Hillenkoetter had been called upon by a Congressional Committee to explain various failures, most notably the CIA's inability to warn of a revolution in Colombia. Much of this was not Hillenkoetter's fault, for he was an able man, but possibly too cautiously analytical before deciding upon action. While not necessarily a fault in normal times, it nonetheless led to a committee being set up to examine the running of the CIA under his control. The result was that Hillenkoetter was replaced by General Walter Bedell Smith (q.v.) in 1950.

HISS, ALGER (b. 1904)

The case of Alger Hiss has for many years been portrayed as a monstrous miscarriage of justice by liberals all around the globe. Soviet disinformation sources have contributed to the myth that Hiss was a victim of a witch-hunt. The campaign against him had gone on for many years, while those who were sure of his guilt failed to obtain positive evidence against him. The man who named Hiss as a Soviet agent, along with seventy-five other US Government officials, was Whittaker Chambers, an American writer who had joined the Communist Party in New York and become editor of the US *Daily Worker*. He had been a courier for passing information to the Russians, but he quit the Communist Party at the time of the Nazi-Soviet Pact and turned informer on his former comrades.

Hiss was a brilliant law student who had been a favourite with various Supreme Court Justices and became a key figure in the State Department. The first to name him as a Soviet agent was Elizabeth Bentley (see *Ware Ring*, Part IV) in 1945, but nobody would pay much attention. Then it was realized, after Chambers' testimony, that Hiss had been adviser to Roosevelt at Yalta and was Secretary-General at the San Francisco conference when the United Nations was created. It was also discovered that he had appointed at least one known Communist to a key post in the administration. On top of this Chambers claimed that Hiss had passed on to him State Department documents for transmission to the Russians. It was

Hiss's denial of having a close relationship with Chambers which ultimately led to his conviction for perjury before a House of Representatives Committee on Un-American Activities. But it was also established that he had lied about the typewriter on which his wife had typed secret documents for transmission to Moscow. Defectors from Krivitsky to Gouzenko pointed to Hiss as a Soviet agent, even though they could only describe him as 'an assistant to Secretary of State Stetinius'. Chambers died in 1961, bitterly hated by the American Left, but he had his reward posthumously when President Reagan awarded him the Medal of Freedom, more than twenty years afterwards.

Further reading
Witness by Whittaker Chambers (André Deutsch, London 1953)

HOFI, MAJOR-GENERAL YITZHAK

A native-born Israeli, Yitzhak Hofi was a Palmach officer in his late teens and served in the 1948 War of Independence as company commander in the first battalion of the crack Yiftah Brigade of Palmach. After independence he made the Israeli Army his career, becoming the first instructor at the Officers' Training College and then serving under Generals Yigal Allon and Moshe Dayan as Operations Officer, Southern Command. Hofi was eventually given a battalion command in the Sivati Brigade, after which he taught in the new Command and Staff College. Before and during the 1956 Sinai campaign he was deputy commander of the Paratroop Brigade under Ariel Sharon. The two men were about the same age and took a keen interest in the techniques of military intelligence. Eventually he was appointed Paratroops Brigade Commander, a factor of considerable influence in the highly successful Entebbe raid to rescue 100 Israelis from Uganda in 1976.

Prior to the 1973 war Hofi had already become something of an authority on intelligence and he had repeatedly warned of the probability of a Syrian attack. It is said that the Israeli Army desperately wanted Hofi to stay with them, but he resigned in July 1974 and shortly afterwards was appointed chief of the Mossad, as well as chairman of a committee coordinating all intelligence activities. He remained in charge up to 1982, and played an important role in the air attack on Iraqi nuclear-weapon plants in Baghdad.

HOLLIS, SIR ROGER HENRY (1905-1973)

The son of a Bishop of Taunton, educated at Clifton and Worcester College, Oxford, Roger Hollis eventually became head of MI5 and has been accused of being an agent of the Soviet Union ever since his death. Much of this was due to wild allegations by right-wing fanatics and a certain amount of Soviet disinformation. In fact, the more one examines the case against him, the more circumstantial and insubstantial it becomes. First it was alleged that he was a friend of Claud Cockburn, the Irish Communist journalist, while he was at Oxford. But he was also a friend of Evelyn Waugh who could certainly not be described as a Communist sympathizer. Hollis left Oxford without a degree and eventually became a representative of the British-American Tobacco Company in China, having briefly been a reporter on the *Shanghai Post* from 1927-28. There have been suggestions that when he was in China he was in touch with such Soviet agents as Agnes Smedley and Ruth Kuczynski (see Part III), but there is no proof whatsoever of this. Indeed, though Ruth Kuczynski mentions various Western contacts in her autobiography, there is no hint of Roger Hollis.

After developing tuberculosis in China, Hollis returned home shortly before World War II. It has been said that he travelled across China and Russia by Trans-Siberian railways, but the truth is (as revealed in his correspondence home), that he went from China by ship across the Pacific and returned home via Canada. Therefore the theory that he stopped off in Moscow on his way back and was recruited by the USSR can be discounted. After a spell in a Swiss clinic, he returned to London and joined MI5. For a time during World War II he was head of F

Division, responsible for keeping watch on political parties. The Communist Party of Great Britain was his special concern. One of the allegations made against him was that when he went to Canada in 1945 to investigate Gouzenko (q.v.) he made no effort to follow up Gouzenko's allegation that there was a mole inside the British Security Services. In fact, Hollis did not speak Russian and Gouzenko at that time did not speak much English, so he was interviewed by Cyril Mills of MI5. Later Hollis was criticized for his handling of the Profumo case in which a Soviet diplomat named Ivanov shared Profumo's girlfriend, Christine Keeler. However, the Hollis viewpoint was accepted by the subsequent inquiry conducted by Lord Denning. Hollis became Deputy Director-General of MI5 in 1952 and, when Sir Dick Goldsmith White was switched to MI6 in 1956, Hollis succeeded him as Director-General, remaining in this post until 1965.

Hollis may have been ultra-cautious, slow to make decisions and not a favourite with some of the more aggressive members of MI5, but the popular view that MI5 had a poor record in spy-catching during his period of office is not justified by actual results. Many spies were caught in this period and some very important defectors won over. Such was the USSR's anxiety about this that they sent a number of bogus defectors to the USA to sow seeds of doubt about Hollis. In fact, it was from the USA that many doubts about Hollis first emerged, yet in the end even the CIA felt there was no case against him. When Philby escaped from Beirut rather than return to London it was alleged that he might have been tipped off by someone in MI5. This led to an investigation of the Deputy Director-General, Graham Mitchell. When Mitchell was cleared, Hollis insisted that he too should be investigated. Nothing whatsoever was proved against him and he was officially cleared. He was held in high regard by some in the USA, including, surprisingly, J. Edgar Hoover. He was also respected in Australia where he helped to advise on the formation of the Australian Security and Intelligence Organization. He retired in 1965 and died eight years later.

HOOVER, J. EDGAR (1895-1971)

A glutton for self-publicity, Hoover is possibly the best-known counter-espionage chief who ever lived. He was, however, rather more successful at getting his name into the media than in tackling his job, and he will go down in history more as a prima donna than a professional intelligence chief. He first came into the public eye in the 1930s when he was head of the FBI and his agents were tackling American bootleggers and gangsters. Undoubtedly this was a field in which he excelled. When, as war approached, he had to turn the attention of the FBI towards watching German spies, he found this was a totally different game. While it was an investigative agency, the FBI had no intelligence analysts. When World War I broke Hoover cooperated to some extent with British Intelligence, but they found him impatient, often too hasty in making arrests when a longer watch on suspects might have provided more results. He quarrelled with his colleagues in other American Intelligence Services, especially with William Donovan who formed the OSS.

After the war, Hoover belatedly turned his attention to Soviet agents, and eventually, it must be admitted, launched a massive campaign to uncover them, scoring many successes. But he bitterly complained about lack of cooperation from the Roosevelt administration, and even the Truman administration when he wanted to expose treachery in high places. In 1945 he sent Roosevelt a confidential report on twelve government officials suspected of being Soviet agents, including Harry Dexter White, assistant to the Secretary to the Treasury. Nothing happened. It was not until the 1950s that Hoover was able to crush a number of Communist networks in the USA.

Further reading
Master of Deceit: A Study of Communism by J. Edgar Hoover (New York, 1969)

HOUGHTON, HARRY FREDERICK

As a retired Royal Navy petty officer, Houghton went to live in Weymouth and soon found himself a job as an Admiralty clerk at the top-security Underwater Weapons Establishment at nearby Portland. Soon he was posted overseas as clerk to the naval attaché in Warsaw where he soon developed a taste for expensive night life, drinking and Polish women. It proved to be a recipe for disaster. When he returned to the base at Portland he was contacted by a so-called friend of one of his Polish female associates. Before very long he was being asked to provide information from the files at Portland for sums of £5 and £10. It was then that he asked a female friend of his, Ethel Gee, to supply information too. She also worked in the Underwater Weapons Establishment. It was eventually noticed that Houghton was living beyond his means and this aroused suspicion. Scotland Yard's Special Branch kept watch on him and discovered that he was part of the Molody network (see *Molody, Konon*, Part IV). In 1961 Gee and Houghton were arrested in Waterloo Road, London, together with Molody, just as Gee was handing over to Molody no less than 212 pages of technical details about British warships. Houghton and Gee were sentenced to fifteen years each.

HOWARD, EDWARD LEE

In August 1986 the Soviet newspaper, *Izvestia*, announced the defection to Russia of thirty-three-year-old Edward Howard, a former CIA agent who had been given 'political asylum' in the USSR. It was the first such defection since the 1960s by an American, and for the first time the US Government admitted that one of its own spies had gone over to the other side. Howard worked for the CIA from 1981-83, when he was sacked from his post. At that date he had been preparing for a post at the US Embassy in Moscow where his official cover was to be that of 'budget analyst'. Later he worked for the New Mexico legislative finance committee which brought him into close contact with workers at Los Alamos National Laboratory, where top secret nuclear weapons research was carried out. He disappeared in September 1985 and a few days later was charged by the FBI with selling intelligence to Russia. He is said to have escaped under the noses of the FBI agents watching his house by placing a dummy in his car as he made a moonlight getaway. An international search failed to find him, and intelligence chiefs first realized he could be heading for Moscow when his credit card was used in Helsinki.

According to classified documents leaked to the *Los Angeles Times* and the *Washington Post*, Howard showed 'continual and accelerated drug abuse, petty crime and all the bad psychological traits' under a lie-detector test. An examination of the damage done by Howard's revelations to the Russians showed that one of the CIA's best contacts inside the USSR had been executed and ruined other spy operations in that country. 'Howard disclosed virtually every active operation we had and he wiped out our Moscow station,' stated one CIA source. In September 1986 Adolf Tolkachev, a Russian scientific worker was arrested in the USSR on the basis of information given by Howard that he had been guilty of working for the CIA. Later it was announced that Tolkachev had been executed. Greed and anger at his dismissal for bad conduct seem to have been the sole motives for defection in Howard's case.

THE JESUIT CONNECTION

At some stage during World War II it became part of Soviet policy to counter anti-Communism within the Roman Catholic Church, and it was decided that the best way to set about this was to infiltrate the Jesuit order, which had acquired great power over the ages through discipline, organization and secrecy. Soviet agents set about infiltration in a highly professional manner, but it was not until the late 1960s that the full extent of their success was realized. In place of the reactionary, if well educated, Jesuit of an earlier age there started to appear the trendy, theologically liberated young priests of today. Bearing in mind Stalin's eternal query – 'How many battalions has the Pope?' – the Soviet Secret Service attempted to infiltrate the Catholic priesthood, mainly in Spain and parts of Latin America where they actively began to aid revolutionary movements while acting as priests.

The Jesuit Order was not the only one to be infiltrated; not even the Vatican was immune. In 1952 it was announced in Rome that Father Alighieri Tondi, professor of the Gregorian Academy at the Vatican, had been found to be a Soviet agent 'deliberately planted in the Jesuit Order'. Tondi sparked off a nationwide sensation by repudiating his faith and becoming an ardent Communist. As a youth he had been a brilliant scholar in engineering and architecture, then he served with Mussolini's army in Ethiopia, returning to Italy when he was twenty-eight and deciding to become a Jesuit. At what stage of his career he became a Marxist is not clear, but when he officially became a Communist in 1952 he said he had voted for the Party since 1948. He soon put the oratory he had devoted to religious work to the cause of Communist propaganda, delivering speeches at Communist rallies and making violent attacks on the Church. He was given a job in the press office of the Italian Communist Party headquarters in Rome. In 1954 he married Signorina Zanti in a civil ceremony. He was excommunicated on four counts, and yet in 1965 Tondi was not only readmitted to the sacraments as a lay Catholic, but was given a special dispensation which allowed him to continue living with Signorina Zanti, who refused a Church marriage and remained a Communist.

It is estimated that today at least twenty-five Jesuit priests are active KGB agents in various parts of the world and, even though the present Pope has initiated changes in the Jesuit hierarchy, there are probably many others who are involuntary and unconscious agents of the KGB. Just as the Catholic Church in the 1930s sought an accommodation with Nazism and Fascism against Communism, so today it deviously seeks a *modus vivendi* with Communism. Malachi Martin, a former Jesuit priest and a close friend of Pope John XXIII, toured the USA in 1978 and indicated that the Vatican believed future world power would come from a proletarian revolution embracing Italy, Spain, France, Portugal and Latin America and that the Church faced the prospect of making a deal with

Marxism. This 'deal' has been considerably stressed in recent years by the Church's *Pax Christi*, another of the left-wing peace movements.

KAO LIANG

When Peking sent a fifty-two-member team of diplomats to the United Nations in 1971, no effort was made to disguise the fact that two key intelligence officers were among the delegation. The most interesting of these was Kao Liang, who had been in charge of subversive activities in Africa, where he had been one of China's top agents under cover of the New China News Agency. Before joining the NCNA, Kao Liang had been secretary of the Communist Party Committee in Hungchao, a suburb of Shanghai. He owed his rapid promotion to his fluent English.

Expelled from India after being accused of gross interference in India's internal affairs, he went to Dar es Salaam in 1961. He instigated the Chinese-inspired coup in Zanzibar in 1964, providing arms and cash for Sheik Babu, who later became Foreign Minister of Tanzania. He is reputed to have patched up Sino-Congolese relations. He seemed to have influence in many parts of Africa, keeping a close watch on Soviet activities in that continent, while repairing much of the damage created by earlier and more foolishly aggressive Chinese operations in Africa, such as the school for spies in Ghana which resulted in nearly 500 Chinese, including secret agents, being ordered to leave the territory when Nkrumah was overthrown. This extremely active man not only coordinated intelligence activities in New York and at the United Nations, but controlled press relations as well.

KEENAN, HELEN (b. 1945)

Helen Keenan is best described as a spy who was too honest for her own good. Reprehensible though her conduct may have been, she was never unpatriotic. She was twenty-two, working as a shorthand-typist in the Prime Minister's office in Downing Street in 1967, when she suddenly gave up her job because, she said, she was 'bored'. This seemed a rather feeble excuse and security men made further inquiries. Eventually they questioned Keenan who then admitted she had passed copies of Cabinet minutes to a man named Norman Blackburn, who had been working for the South African Intelligence Service. He required details of any moves proposed by the British Government on Rhodesia which had broken away from British rule. As a result Blackburn was sentenced to five years' imprisonment and Helen Keenan to six months. This isolated incident convinced an over-reactive Harold Wilson, then Prime Minister, that South African intelligence agents were behind every kind of incident from bugging his offices to hounding Jeremy Thorpe and other politicians in the UK.

KENG BIAO (b. 1903)

Born in Hunan, Keng Biao graduated at the Whampoa Military Academy and during the Northern Expedition joined the Communists and served with Yeh Ting's troops. In 1949 he was appointed deputy commander of the 19th Army Group; the following year he became Ambassador to Sweden and then in quick succession ambassador to Denmark, minister to Finland and ambassador to Pakistan, before being made a vice-minister at the Ministry of Foreign Affairs in 1960. His exact role in the sphere of intelligence has never been clearly defined, other than that he became head of the CELD and apparently made considerable policy changes towards Taiwan. In 1963 he went to Burma as a special envoy. Whether Keng Biao had anything to do with it or not, it was then that the Chinese had a tip-off from Rangoon that the KGB had set up a new section called 'The Twelfth' specially designed to trap and win over Chinese diplomats and to mount a long-term project to infiltrate the Chinese Embassy in Moscow. 'The Twelfth' appears to have been a dreadful failure from the beginning. It was swiftly nullified by the Chinese themselves.

KHOKHLOV, CAPTAIN NICOLAI

One of the surprise defectors of the mid-1950s was Nicolai Khokhlov, a member of the Division for Terror and Diversion (the 'murder squad' and the successor to *Smersh*) of the KGB. Khokhlov had been selected by Colonel Studnikov, head of the Division, to stamp out the activities of the NTS (q.v.) in West Germany. Khokhlov's orders were to silence Georgi Okolovich, a key NTS figure. He had carried out similar assignments before and was an experienced assassin. Then in 1954 he went to Frankfurt and astounded Okolovich by calling at his apartment, telling of his mission to kill the NTS man, and asking to be put in touch with the Americans. Khokhlov's testimony to the Americans not only revealed how his organization had planned various other killings, but the types of weapons used, all of which were produced at a special laboratory at Kuchine near Moscow. One of the most interesting of Khokhlov's revelations, however, was on the Soviet 'mind-control' programme (see *PSI Espionage*, Part V). According to him, and since supported by independent testimony, the Russians had experimented with psychotronic weapons on a 'large-scale budget'. The heartbeats of animals had been stopped both by telepathy and psychotronic means.

Further reading
In the Name of Conscience by Nikolai Khokhlov (Possev Verlag, Frankfurt 1957)

KROGER, PETER and HELEN
(see *Cohen, Morris and Lona*)

KRUGLOV, SERGEI NICOFOROVICH

When the NKVD was renamed the MVD after World War II, Stalin named Kruglov as head. Beria remained overall head of the Intelligence Services, however, and Merkulov was chief of the MGB. Kruglov had been made an honorary Knight of the British Empire by the British and awarded the Legion of Merit by the Americans, presumably as a token of gratitude for foiling the German plot to kill the Allied leaders in Tehran during the war. Kruglov had one endearing quality: he revealed inside knowledge about all foreigners with whom he came into contact, but would make a social grace out of this information. He informed one astonished American officer that his wife practised ballet steps in front of her dressing-table mirror, something of which the husband was completely ignorant. He was a good public relations officer and did much to publicize the theme that the Soviet Secret Service had saved Roosevelt's life.

Kruglov survived the purge in the Soviet ranks after Stalin's death, though he was demoted by Beria. This state of affairs only lasted a few months, however, and after Beria was executed, Kruglov set about purging the rest of the Beria faction and once again took control of the MVD. He conducted a reorganization within the Intelligence Services and, after he had suffered a heart attack in 1954, Kruglov nominated General Serov (q.v.) as first chairman of the KGB.

KUZICHKIN, VLADIMIR

This young major in the KGB abandoned his car in the centre of Tehran in 1982 and some time afterwards arrived in Britain. There have been various stories as to how and why he defected, including the report that he fell in love with a British female agent, for whom he left his wife. There is also the story that the British made a deal with Iranian Intelligence in handling Kuzichkin, not least because his information exposed a long-term Russian plan for generating chaos in Iran and aimed at taking power when the time was ripe. He revealed the USSR plans for maintaining contact with the Soviet-sponsored clandestine organization of the Iranian Communist Party, Tudeh, and to run the Soviet infiltrators posing as tribesmen who operate among the numerous ethnic groups which straddle the Russo-Iranian border.

LANGELLE, RUSSELL A.

One of the most efficient counter-espionage agents in the Diplomatic Service, Langelle was security chief in the US Embassy in Moscow from 1957-59. He snuffed out various Soviet ploys to penetrate the Embassy and reported attempts to subvert or blackmail American personnel, at the same time sacking a number of Russian employees at the Embassy who were obviously KGB agents. He also prevented a Russian plan to 'bug' the Embassy. An order went out that Langelle must be removed by the most devious and bizarre scheme imaginable – i.e. recruited as a double agent. If that failed, he was to be ordered out of the country on a charge of espionage.

One morning in 1959 he got off a bus in Moscow, was seized by five men and taken to the KGB offices. He was threatened with imprisonment, told he would be arrested for espionage and that his diplomatic immunity would be revoked. Then he was told no charges would be pressed if he agreed to give the Russians certain information. He was eventually released, but given only three days in which to leave Russia. *Pravda* alleged that he had been caught giving money and material for making secret ink to an agent.

LAVINSKI, VYACHESLAV (d. 1960)

Lavinski was one of the most enigmatic spies of the post-World War II period, and even now it is unclear as to who he was spying for and why. Variously described as a Latvian and a White Russian, he hid from the Germans during the war and, according to his own story, was eventually taken by the Bolsheviks and put in an orphanage as a teenager. He escaped to Sweden and somehow acquired sufficient money to buy himself a ten-metre steel-hulled sailing boat named *Frisia*. In November 1950 he sailed from Gothenburg, maintaining that his aim was to seek a new life in South America, which was surprising as he spoke neither Spanish nor Portuguese, though his English was good. He arrived in Guernsey in 1951 and came under suspicion of being a spy, for which reason he was refused permission to stay on the island. Later, radio conversations from the *Frisia* were intercepted and it was learned that he spent some time in Brest, Oporto, Casablanca, Agadir and various ports of Latin America.

In Fortaleza he made friends with a Russian whom he persisted in calling Andropoff (*sic*), though he was no relation to the KGB chief of that name. Once he became stuck on a sandbank after having fallen asleep, and subsisted on fish and birds for several days before being rescued. He was clapped in gaol in Venezuela and, again on suspicion of being a spy, was prohibited from using his radio for some time. The last heard of him by anyone in the UK was a letter to a friend in Guernsey in 1952, asking for a Spanish-Russian dictionary. On 29 April 1960 the Associated Press's correspondent in Caracas issued a story which stated that 'road workers who saw a Venezuela airliner explode in flight said today a survivor told them an apparently demented White Russian blew up the plane with a bomb'. Lavinski was named as the man in question, and he died in the explosion. Tension was high as a result of an unsuccessful revolt the previous week by former General Jesus Maria Castro Leon. Despite widespread enquiries afterwards, nothing further was heard about Lavinski and there was no positive confirmation that he had died in the explosion, though it does seem pretty certain. He was described as 'a freelance spy'. But for whom? Was he being controlled by the Soviet? Or was he anti-Soviet? Among the four foreigners aboard the aircraft were two Poles. Had he been ordered to hunt them down and kill them?

THE LAVON AFFAIR

This incident takes its name from the Israeli Minister of Defence at the time, Pinhas Lavon, who rather unfairly, was blamed for everything. It was a subject which took a long time to live down, as in Israel, even during the 1965 election campaign, Ben-Gurion and Levi Eshkol still fought over this decade-old intelligence scandal. In the 1950s the Israelis were aware that Foster Dulles and the geriatric President Eisenhower had been lulled into believing that President Nasser of Egypt was a bulwark against Communism and must be upheld at all costs. Mossad's aim was to undermine this confidence in Nasser by all means possible. Perhaps fear of being totally isolated suggested that utterly ruthless measures should be adopted, and if so one can sympathize with the Israeli viewpoint. But a plan was launched partly under Defence Ministry planners, but also linking up with Mossad and Shin Beth, to launch terrorist attacks on British and American properties in Egypt and then to blame them on the Egyptians. What gave this crazy plan a sudden impetus was the withdrawal of British troops from the Suez Canal Zone and the failure of two Israeli envoys to the USA to convince the Americans that aid to Nasser was highly dangerous. The project was carried out, but in a blundering and untypically amateurish way which played into the hands of the Egyptian chief of counter-intelligence.

Moshe Dayan, who was then Army Chief of staff, later stated: 'Lavon was anxious to use the Special Services Unit. I thought it should only be used in time of war and remain dormant in peacetime.' It would appear that the man who most strongly supported this sabotage plan was Pinhas Lavon, who had unfortunately not enjoyed the best relations with Isser Harel, head of Mossad. So he turned for support to the Special Services Unit (MLM) and had the silent cooperation of Colonel Benjamin Givli of Aman. The task of masterminding the plot was given to Colonel Abraham Dar, who used the name of John Darling when outside Israel. A team known as Unit 131 was sent to Egypt to plant bombs in the US Information Offices in Alexandria and Cairo, though none of them exploded. Later it was learned that Paul Frank, Colonel Dar's key man in Cairo, had betrayed all details of the operation to the Egyptians. The entire network of Egyptian Jews in both Alexandria and Cairo was rounded up. Two were hanged in Alexandria, while eight others were imprisoned. Worse still, Max Bennett, an Aman operative with great experience as a spy both in Europe and the Middle East, was arrested by the Egyptian police. A committee of investigation produced a report which, though kept secret at the time, resulted in the resignation of Lavon. Ben-Gurion came out of retirement to take over the Ministry of Defence.

Further reading
The Israeli Secret Service by Richard Deacon (Hamish Hamilton, London 1977)

LIE-DETECTORS

Though the lie-detector, or polygraph machine, is merely one modest item of equipment in the world of espionage, it has nevertheless aroused sufficient controversy to be included in this book. The polygraph has four long, thin pens which are attached to highly sensitive instruments measuring breathing, pulse rate and skin moisture. A belt is placed around the subject's chest to monitor respiration, a blood cuff goes around the arm, while electrodes round the first and middle fingers measure sweating. The readings are transferred electronically and trace wavering lines on a moving belt of graph paper. Operators are trained to monitor the reactions of the person being tested to ascertain whether he or she is telling the truth.

The lie-detector has long been used by the American Security Services, but for some years its value has been questioned in Britain and other countries. In recent years there has even been strong criticism of it inside the USA. Dr David Lykken of the University of Minnesota has asserted that 'the best scientific evidence is that the polygraph produces a wrong answer about one time in three, while the results from voice stress analysers are no better than you would get by flipping a coin'. Dr John Beary, assistant Secretary of Defence for Health, in a Pentagon memorandum, stated in 1983: 'I am told the Soviets have a training school in an Eastern bloc country where they teach

326

their agents how to beat the polygraph. Because many of our Defence managers think it works they get a false sense of security ... The hypothesis of the lie-detector is scientifically unsound ... it is an excitement-detector, not a lie-detector.'

All CIA employees are required to undergo a polygraph test, and two members of Britain's MI5 visited the USA a few years ago for training in the use of the lie-detector. In 1983 a pilot scheme for testing lie-detectors on employees at Britain's GCHQ in Cheltenham was given the go-ahead, despite strenuous objections by the Civil Service trade unions. The results were anything but satisfactory. In 1985 Whitehall Security chiefs were impressed by results of secret tests on about 200 members of MI5, the lie-detector showing a failure rate of 37 per cent. Some supporters of the polygraph alleged that the machines had been sabotaged! In a pamphlet distributed to the staff at GCHQ, the Society of Civil and Public Servants claimed that the polygraph had been shown to clear one in four guilty subjects and to brand 50 per cent of innocent subjects as security risks. The UK shelved the whole question of lie-detectors tests for civil servants, despite spending £24,000 on six polygraph machines from the USA, but at the end of 1985 President Reagan ordered such tests for all senior officials with access to top secrets, including members of his own Cabinet. It was trade union interference alone which prevented any British experiment with the lie-detector.

LONSDALE, GORDON
(see *Molody, Konon*)

LOTZ, WOLFGANG
(b. 1921)

Lotz's Israeli colleagues in the Mossad nicknamed him the 'Champagne Spy' on account of his using this drink to loosen tongues. He was half Jew, half Gentile, born at Mannheim in

Baden-Wurttenberg, West Germany, the son of a theatrical impresario who died at an early age. His widow, being Jewish and alarmed at developments under the Nazis, emigrated to Palestine with her son. Lotz joined Haganah at the age of sixteen and learned something of the arts of underground fighting while studying at an agricultural school. In World War II he volunteered for service in the British Army and was accepted and trained as a commando. He rose to the rank of quartermaster sergeant, taking part in the Desert War. By the end of the war he spoke fluent German, English, Arabic and Hebrew. During the War of Independence he joined the Israeli Army as a lieutenant, serving in the crack Golani Brigade. Later he was promoted to major and became Intelligence Officer of his regiment.

Because of his linguistic talents, blond hair and Nordic appearance, the Mossad engaged Lotz as they felt he would easily pass for one of Hitler's perfect Aryan types. Lotz was just the man they were looking for – somebody who could infiltrate the German scientists' colony in Egypt, for the presence of this team, engaged in secret military and aviation work, worried Israel. The Mossad gave Lotz a cover story as an officer in Rommel's Edelweiss Corps because he knew the desert terrain from fighting on the British side. It was a complicated cover and only a consummate actor could have carried it off. Even then it would have been extremely difficult for him to penetrate so deeply into Egypt's top military circles and to have won the confidence of the German scientists without the aid of the Gehlen (q.v.). The Israelis had established first-rate contacts inside Gehlen's organization, which they had initially suspected might be directed against them.

Lotz was given ample funds and he used these to start a riding school and stud farm on the outskirts of Cairo. He gave the impression of having been a fanatical Nazi and a great admirer of President Nasser. In one year he managed to collect quite a lot of information, and returned to Germany to be debriefed by a Mossad officer. Later in Egypt he not only made friends with some ex-Nazi scientists at the rocket and aircraft research stations, but with senior Egyptian Army officers and members of the President's personal staff. To strengthen his hand the Mossad wanted Lotz to have an Aryan-type wife. However, he was already married to a typical Israeli girl by whom he had two children. Secret arrangements were made and back in Israel a faithful and patriotic wife eventually agreed that her husband could be 'married' to an attractive Nordic blonde named Waldraut Neumann. The marriage took place in Munich.

If Lotz's life sounds like a spy of old-fashioned fiction, it was nevertheless hard work, as Israel required and expected quick results. They wanted details of all Egyptian rocket plans and maps of establishments, but enough evidence to be able to launch a diplomatic campaign to force the German technicians out of Egypt. Eventually Lotz was caught in 1964 and underwent interrogation and torture. He kept remarkably cool and the Egyptians did not discover that he was a Jew, nor whether he was spying for West Germany or Israel. He escaped with life imprisonment, while his 'wife' got three years. After the Six-Day War some intensive bargaining went on between Israel and Egypt on the exchange of prisoners. Among those freed were Wolfgang Lotz and his 'wife', Waldraut. An unfortunate result of this affair was that Lotz had fallen in love with Waldraut and she had been converted to the Jewish faith. So he divorced his real wife and subsequently married his German bride for a second time.

Further reading
The Champagne Spy by Wolfgang Lotz (Vallentine Mitchell, London 1972)
The Israeli Secret Service by Richard Deacon (Hamish Hamilton, London 1977; Taplinger, New York 1977)

LYALIN, OLEG ADOLFOVICH

In September 1971, following frequent warnings to the USSR by the British Foreign Secretary, Sir Alec Douglas-Home, 105 Russian diplomats and officials working in London were ordered to return home. Then the KGB's disinformation department gave the London *Daily Express* a scoop by drawing their attention to the defection of Oleg Lyalin, a member of the

Soviet Trading Delegation in Highgate, London. Their object was two-fold: firstly, to suggest the British had been fooled by a minor defector who had been arrested for alleged drunken driving, and secondly, to suggest the Foreign Office had over-reacted. Lyalin's testimony had indeed resulted in the expulsion order because he was no minor defector, but had been a member of the KGB's Department 5. MI5 handled his case adroitly, guaranteeing him and his girlfriend safety, and in return he supplied an alarming catalogue of KGB plans for large-scale sabotage, including a scheme to destroy the NATO radar stations in the UK. The fact that such schemes were envisaged for some distant date in the future in no way altered the dangers of tolerating too many KGB agents under diplomatic cover in the UK.

MARENCHES, COUNT ALEXANDRE DE

Marenches was a huge man who literally stood head and shoulders above everyone else, was for ten years an outstandingly able head of France's Secret Service (SDCE). A gregarious character, the Count was an Army colonel, a member of the Jockey Club and a Knight of Malta, as well as being an old friend of President Pompidou, by whom he was appointed. His mission was quite clear: he was to carry out a purge of the SDECE to eliminate some of the criminal and more violently anti-American members of French Intelligence, as well as removing drug-runners in that service who had in some instances been identified with agents of the KGB. Marenches, who was also a stern disciplinarian, worked wonders in the service within a short time. He maintained the SDECE's reputation for being extremely well informed on all Arab affairs and also developed close relations with China. It was he who arranged with the Chinese Secret Service a regular system of exchanging information. His wartime experience of British and French intelligence services helped him to improve relations with both the CIA and the SIS. However, when Mitterand became President, Marenches was replaced.

MARION, PIERRE (b. 1921)

Appointed by President Mitterand to be head of the DGSE, France's renamed Secret Service, Pierre Marion had worked in the Aerospace Consortium under the President's brother and prior to that had been an executive of Air France. In many respects Marion conducted useful reorganization of the service, especially in his drive to improve the collection of scientific and economic intelligence, and he resisted attempts to close down GEPAN, the UFO-watching agency (see *Ufology Research*, Part V). With the backing of Charles Hernu, the Defence Minister, he brought it under the direction of two engineers of the French National Space Centre. However, in other respects, notably war on terrorism and Middle East intelligence, where France had always been well informed, he was less successful, and he failed to get the cooperation he hoped for from the counter-intelligence body, DST. He resigned late in 1982.

In 1986 Marion told the weekly news magazine, *Le Nouvel Observateur*, that his men in the DGSE had discovered that bombs and guns were being brought into the country in diplomatic bags while the terrorists who were going to use them arrived by plane and train: 'During that period we identified six [terrorist] contacts in Paris. I proposed to M. Mitterand that my service should eliminate them physically. The President refused.' Other contacts were identified outside France, and again the 'elimination' process was refused.

MARKOV, GEORGI (d. 1978)

This man was not a spy, but a well-informed Bulgarian living in exile in London, working for the BBC and Radio Free Europe. He is nonetheless important because he was murdered while waiting for a bus on Waterloo Bridge by methods which suggest that at least one of the world's intelligence services have devised an undetectable method for killing. In the case of Georgi Markov, however, it went wrong. Markov suddenly felt very ill and ran a temperature of 104°F. His wife called the doctor who thought he was suffering from flu. But that night Markov told his wife, 'I have a horrible suspicion that it might be connected with something that happened today. I was waiting for a bus on the south side of Waterloo Bridge, when I felt a jab in the back of my right thigh. I looked round and saw a man drop his umbrella. He said he was sorry and I got the impression that he was trying to cover his face as he rushed off and hailed a taxi.'

The verdict on Markov was that he was killed by a metal pellet containing poison twice as deadly as cobra venom: ricin, derived from the seed of the castor oil plant. The pellet containing it was only fractionally larger than a pin-head. It measured 1.53 millimetres in diameter and two minute cavities of 0.35 millimetres wide had been drilled to accomodate twenty micrograms of ricin. There is no doubt that Markov was murdered because of his anti-Communist broadcasts.

Much research into the use of substances such as ricin has been carried out in Bulgaria, Hungary and Czechoslovakia. In the physiology laboratories of the Medical School at the University of Szeged in Hungary, the effects of experimental intoxication by poisoning have been extensively studied on various animals. This is corroborated by a medical expert of the Chemical Defence Establishment of the British Ministry of Defence at Porton Down. Dr G.A. Balint, of the University of Szeged, was awarded a post-doctorate degree of 'Candidate of Medical Sciences' for this thesis on 'Problems of the Experimental Toxicology of Ricin Intoxication' in 1976, two years before Markov's assassination. Dr Balint was a senior lecturer with the Medical School of Makerere university in Kampala, Uganda, between 1970 and 1974. He recieved a PhD from that university for his thesis, 'Observations on the Pathomechanism of Experimentally Induced Ricin Intoxication in Mammals'. All such research would come under the close examination of the Scientific and Technical Directorate of the First Chief Directorate of the KGB and the intelligence department concerned with chemical and biological warfare of the GRU. Ricin is one of the most potent of poisons and the lack of effective counter-measures makes this substance a potent multi-purpose chemical warfare agent, not least because it is difficult to detect.

Further reading
SPY! by Richard Deacon with Nigel West (BBC Publications, 1980)

McCONE, JOHN (b. 1902)

Appointed as head of the CIA by President Kennedy in 1961 after the disastrous Bay of Pigs operation, McCone was a defence contractor who had been chairman of the Atomic Energy Committee. Initially, he regarded the whole CIA organization with some mistrust, but he soon became enthused with the business of intelligence-collecting, effected a few improvements and helped to build up a detailed picture of the Soviet missiles deployment in Cuba. It was during his period as head of the CIA that the agency introduced a system called 'crate-ology' which was supposed to assess the contents of crates carried on the decks of Soviet ships delivering arms. The system was not well regarded by many intelligence chiefs in the Services, but McCone was able to justify it. By 1965 McCone found himself at odds with both McNamara, Defence Secretary, and the Pentagon, as well as feeling that President Johnson paid insufficient attention to National Intelligence Estimates. Both these things led to his resignation later that year.

McKENZIE, BRUCE ROY (1919-1978)

Born and educated in South Africa, where he went to Hilton College in Natal, Bruce Roy McKenzie joined the South African Air Force on the outbreak of World War II. Seconded to the RAF for the duration of the war, he served in North Africa, Malta, Corsica, Italy, France and Germany, attaining the South African Air Force rank of colonel at the age of twenty-four, as well as being awarded the DSO and DFC. On demobilization he went to Kenya and started farming at Gingalili in an undeveloped area, building it up into one of the best farms in the Rift Valley. McKenzie first entered the Kenya Legislative

Council in 1957, representating farming interests, and later became Agricultural Minister. He was among the first of the Europeans in Kenya to identify himself with the African people's fight for independence, becoming a member of Kanu, the party led by Jomo Kenyatta.

McKenzie's interests in the Kenyan people was absolutely genuine and drew various tributes from Kenyatta and other Africans. Nevertheless, as an intense patriot, he was also active in intelligence-gathering and his services in this field were much appreciated in both London and Israel. He helped in the transport arrangements when the Israeli Secret Services organized the rescue of hijacked hostages from Uganda's Entebbe airport, and for this and other services the Israeli Government awarded him a medal.

A great charmer in his talent for winning over Africans to the Western cause, McKenzie's secret work may never be revealed in full, for in May 1978 he was killed in an air crash while returning from a visit to Uganda. All four aboard the light aircraft were killed when the plane exploded about fifteen miles south-east of Nairobi. It was feared that a bomb could have been slipped into the plane by one of Idi Amin's henchmen while it was parked at Entebbe during a visit McKenzie made to Uganda for talks with President Amin. There were other theories, too: some suggested the PLO was involved, others said enemies of the Amin regime might have planted the bomb to deter foreign businessmen from dealing with the Uganda Government.

The others killed with McKenzie were Gavin Whitelaw, managing director of Lonrho Exports, Keith Savage, a Kenyan businessman, and Paul Lennox, of Universal Aviation Supply, Tolworth, Surrey.

MACLEAN, DONALD DUART (1913-1983)

Probably one of the least competent or justified entrants to the British Foreign Diplomatic Service for many years, Donald Maclean was largely accepted on his Cambridge background and the fact that his father had been a Liberal MP and a

Presbyterian. In fact, Maclean was an alcoholic, a homosexual and frequently mixed up in drunken orgies and violent behaviour, quite apart from the fact that he had committed himself to the cause of world Communism. Yet he was hailed by the British Foreign Office as a potential Ambassador and even a future head of the organization. Frequently, in Paris, Cairo and other postings he was discovered to be inadequate, irrational, violent, drunk at parties, remarkably indiscreet and outspokenly anti-American. Yet he had an American wife whom he married when posted to Paris in June 1940. Long before this he had been recruited as a spy for the Soviet cause. His Russian masters were well aware of his weaknesses and they had obtained various photographs of Maclean in bed with other men, intending to use them as blackmail, if necessary.

To the surprise of many, after he had been recalled from a posting in Cairo for wild behaviour, Maclean was appointed First Secretary in the British Embassy in Washington, and it was while here that he passed vital US documents and decisions on nuclear planning to the USSR, having been given a pass to the headquarters of the US Atomic Energy Commission. He was suspected of being a Soviet spy by the CIA long before the British got around to investigating him. By that time Maclean was back in London and warned that he might be interrogated at any moment. With Guy Burgess, his old Cambridge friend and another Soviet agent (see Part III), Maclean suddenly left Britain and eventually turned up in Moscow. Yet while the British Government was still pretending there was no firm evidence that the pair had fled to Moscow, the FBI had in their possession a curious anonymous letter delivered to the US Embassy in London: 'This is the deposition which Maclean made to me on 24 May: I am haunted and burdened by what I know of official secrets, especially by the content of high-level Anglo-American conversations. The British Government, whom I have served, have betrayed the realm to Americans ... I wish to enable my beloved country to escape from the snare which faithless politicians have set ... I have decided that I can discharge my duty to my country only through prompt disclosure of this material to Stalin.' Maclean, by then a compulsive alcoholic, lived on unhappily in Moscow, eventually separated from his wife and family.

Further reading
The Missing Macleans by Geoffrey Hoare (Cassell, 1955)
Burgess and Maclean by John Fisher (Robert Hale, London 1977)

McMAHON, JOHN

Probably no other intelligence officer was so successful as John McMahon in exposing KGB disinformation tactics against the USA and Americans from the President downwards. His testimony on KGB forgeries to the House of Representatives Permament Committee on Intelligence in 1982 revealed the existence of a steady campaign of what the Soviets call 'active measures'. In July 1982 the US Department of State published a report on the subject, listing such items as a forged letter from President Reagan to the King of Spain in 1981, another forged letter from NATO commander Alexander Haig to NATO secretary-general Joseph Luns in 1982 and many other examples of this kind. McMahon indicated that the USSR was spending vast sums on this kind of fake propaganda.

John McMahon spent thirty-four years with the CIA and was Deputy Director when he resigned in 1986. His resignation was said to be on account of 'personal reasons', but he was believed to be upset that the CIA was spending more on covert operations than on traditional espionage and intelligence-gathering. Certainly right-wing lobbyists in Washington claimed credit for his resignation, and it was said that the White House had received 10,000 letters from Americans demanding his dismissal on the grounds that he had bungled aid to Afghanistan. Whatever the truth of the matter, the indications were that from 1986 onwards there would be a more active policy by the CIA in covert military operations in Afghanistan, Nicaragua, Angola and other Third World areas of East-West confrontation. On the other hand several members of the Senate Intelligence Committee, which oversees CIA operations, have stated that they share McMahon's doubts about some large-scale covert operations, citing the mining of Nicaraguan ports in 1983 as one example.

MILLER, RICHARD (b. 1932)

Miller was the first FBI agent ever to be convicted of espionage, and in July 1981 he was sentenced in Los Angeles to two concurrent life terms of imprisonment for passing secrets to the USSR. The information he provided dealt with FBI efforts to identify and neutralize foreign agents in the USA, and the FBI stated that the Russians had been given a detailed picture of American counter-intelligence. Miller, aged forty-nine, married with eight children and invariably in debt, admitted to interrogators, 'I had a James Bond kind of fantasy that I'd come out a hero in the end,' even suggesting that he was trying at the same time to infiltrate the KGB network in San Francisco. This claim was flatly rejected by the jury.

Miller had worked at the Los Angeles bureau of the FBI as a counter-intelligence agent, and it was then he began an affair with Svetlana Ogorodnikova, a Soviet emigré whose husband, Nikolai, worked in a sausage factory. The prosecution said Miller had agreed to accept $65,000 in cash and gold for passing information. Svetlana Ogorodnikova was gaoled for eighteen years and her husband for eight. What proved most disturbing during the trial of Miller was that his former bosses described him as slovenly, unable to handle complex assignments and that he was prone to lose his credentials and to leave keys in the office door.

MOLODY, KONON TROFIMOVICH (1923-1970)

Better known in the UK as Gordon Lonsdale, Molody was perhaps the perfect example of a long-term 'mole'. Born in Russia the son of a Russian scientist, Molody, was taken to the United States by an aunt at the age of eleven bearing a Canadian passport in the name of Gordon Arnold Lonsdale. Whether or not this was actually planned in the hope that he could later be used as a 'sleeper agent' is not easily confirmed, but it is a distinct possibility, as the real Lonsdale had been born in Cobalt, Ontario, in 1924, so his age matched Molody's to within a year. Young Lonsdale was educated in California until 1938, learning to speak English like a North American. In 1938 he had from all accounts been taken on a visit to Finland and thence to Russia. In World War II he served in the Red Army and had his first experience of espionage when he was parachuted behind the German lines at the age of seventeen. He owed his advancement to Colonel Abel (q.v.), for whom he worked as a radio operator for a while.

Molody returned to North America in the early 1950s, again using the name of Lonsdale, this time as a senior KGB agent. In 1955 Colonel Abel informed Molody that his work was appreciated in Moscow and that as a reward he had been given the appointment in Moscow of Resident-Director in Britain. Molody much preferred Britain to the USA, once admitting that his secret ambition was 'to live like an English country gentleman'. He took rooms at the Royal Overseas League in London and proceeded to build himself up as an extrovert man-about-town, fond of parties, girls and concerts. By the following year he had installed himself in the White House, Albany Street, London, and became a Christmas guest of Major Raymond Shaw, USAF, at the nuclear bomber base at Lakenham in Suffolk. Then, posing as a company director selling, among other things, bubble-gum machines and juke-boxes, he investigated Britain's defences and obtained a great deal of information on the nuclear submarine at Holy Loch, the country's submarine and tracking system, and the location of secret bases. He invented a car burglar alarm which he personally entered in the Brussels International Trade Fair where it was awarded a gold medal as 'the best British entry'.

The story of the Molody network in London and elsewhere is a remarkable one. Among his agents were the Krogers (q.v.) who ran a bookshop in the Strand, and Harry Houghton (q.v.), an Admiralty clerk at the top-security Admiralty Underwater Weapons Establishment at Portland in Dorset. Molody used the Krogers' bungalow at Ruislip for radioing messages to a safe section of Russian Intelligence, possibly in the Embassy in London. Eventually – largely due to errors by his agents – Molody was caught by MI5, arrested and sent to prison for twenty-five years. Later he was exchanged for the British spy,

Greville Wynne (q.v.), who had been captured by the Soviets – a bargain that was greatly in the Russians' favour.

In prison Molody's morale remained high because he seems to have been convinced the Russians would do everything to get him released. During this period he played chess, translated three books into Russian and is said to have started a Chinese-Russian dictionary. Molody himself, speaking on his release, said, 'First my wife, Halina, approached the Soviet Embassy in Warsaw with the idea of an exchange, then she wrote to Mrs Greville Wynne and asked her to approach the British Government on the subject.' On 14 October 1970 it was announced from Moscow that Molody had died at the early age of forty-eight. The circumstances were curious, to say the least: he was said to have collapsed while picking mushrooms in a field near Moscow.

MPAIAC

The initials of this organization stand for 'Movement for the self-determination of the Canary Islands', and it could claim to have the smallest unofficial intelligence service in the world. MPAIAC was founded by Antonio Cubilla, the self-styled 'Castro of the Canary Islands', and it was originally financed by both the Algerian and Cuban governments, as well as receiving subsidies from member countries of the Organization of African Unity. In the late 1970s, MPAIAC was responsible for a wave of terrorist attacks, of which perhaps the worst was the bombing of Las Palmas airport, which caused many deaths. Cubilla's aim was to sabotage the tourist industry and through its Algerian-based radio station, Voice of the Free Canary Islands, it warned tourists, 'Stay away, or you might get killed.' MPAIAC's intelligence service had an office in Algiers, one official car and a small staff and bodyguards, and it had agents in various parts of Spain, Majorca and Morocco.

NATO SPIES

The North Atlantic Treaty Organization (NATO) has long been a number one target for Soviet espionage. It is a continuous problem for the Western World, as the long list of spies caught annually reveals; but more disturbing is the fact that all of these have swiftly been replaced by new agents. In 1969 the Germans discovered that the Russians had obtained details of the radio system for rocket-firing, the navigation system for Starfighter aircraft and NATO radio codes. Evidence pointed to a spy inside the Frankfurt Battelle Institute which led to the interrogation of Josef Eitzenberger, an Austrian-born electronics expert who confessed that he had provided his Soviet controller with both NATO and German *Bundeswehr* secrets. In Italy Soviet agents seeking information about the US 6th Fleet based at Naples have not been quite so successful and Italian intelligence officers claim they have had little difficulty in tracking some of them down (see *Italy*, Part I).

In the UK during the years of Harold Macmillan's premiership, slack British security resulted in one scandal after another involving the betrayal of NATO secrets. The worst of these concerned the Portland naval base where the task of building up NATO's underwater defence programme and the work of detecting enemy submarines was centred (see *Houghton, Harry*, Part IV). The top-secret information which the Russians sought and are believed to have got from Portland included a special anti-submarine device which worked at any depth and was said to have been unbeatable. Houghton might have been caught much earlier if only a probation officer who interviewed his wife in 1958 had passed on her information to the naval authorities. However, it has been in West Germany where the USSR has scored most successes in capturing NATO secrets (see *Rotsch, Manfred* and *Tiedge, Hans Joachim*, Part IV). Much of this espionage has been directed from East Germany and the fact that one out of five West Germans has relatives in the eastern zone constitutes a hazard for the security authorities. It was after Heinz Felfe (q.v.) had penetrated the Gehlen organization in West Germany that it was learned that Colonel Carl Otto von Hinckeldey, a *Wehrmacht* officer, was arrested on suspicion of turning over NATO documents to the USSR.

In this earlier period, though information was passed on, much of it had already become dated. In the past ten years there has been a great emphasis on the need for up-to-date intelligence on NATO matters, and this has involved the introduction of more skilled 'illegals' and more ambitious infiltration. Sometimes plans for obtaining such intelligence were long-term, such as the case of Sergeant Robert Lees Johnson, a US Army NCO stationed in Berlin, who made contact with the KGB through his Austrian wife in 1952. He was the most improbable material for a reliable agent, being apt to get hopelessly drunk, yet he eventually not only brought in a fellow NCO, a secret homosexual, but when posted to Paris, was ordered by the KGB to get wax imprints of the keys to the high-security vault at Orly airport. Johnson succeeded in doing this and in due course was able to remove documents which were handed over to the KGB. This gave the Russians plans for emergency actions in Europe, cryptographic materials and estimates of NATO and Soviet strengths and weaknesses. Eventually, partly due to Johnson becoming depressed and his wife's threats and nagging, he was arrested by the US police and in 1965 was sentenced to twenty-five years' imprisonment.

Towards the end of 1970 Russia and East Germany took the unusual step of offering the Bonn government a major spy swap in an attempt to rescue three of their top-level agents who had been arrested in West Germany. Chief of these was Liane Lindner, a qualified psychologist described by Bonn security officers as 'the biggest fish in the East-West spy net for many years'. Lindner was born in Berlin and her real name is believed to be Ingeborg Weber, but her forged identity documents stated that she was born in the East German textile town of Chemnitz in 1927. Arrested with her were Irene Schultz, secretary to two successive West German Ministers of Science, and an eighty-year-old retired lawyer, Dr Heinrich Wiedemann. Lindner passed on to the USSR many NATO top secrets, including the blueprints of Bonn's space exploration pro-grammes, US Intelligence and Pentagon assessment of Soviet developments and the missile systems developed by the West Germans and the joint Franco-German missiles programme. The Russians went to elaborate lengths to conceal the true identity of Lindner, who held the rank of a lieutenant-colonel in the East German espionage service and was a full colonel with the KGB.

A more recent case of leaked NATO contingency plans

involved the Norwegian diplomat, Arne Treholt, who was arrested in January 1984 in Oslo when about to fly to Vienna to meet a KGB officer named Gennady Titov. Soon after it was announced that Treholt had confessed to spying for the USSR for fifteen years, having passed on many NATO documents. So serious was this case that the Norwegians claimed Treholt had passed on hopelessly outdated plans. Treholt was the most important of Norwegian spies in the Soviet cause, yet since the end of World War II, at least twenty-five of these have been detected.

Of all NATO spies, probably the most damaging at the time was Rear-Admiral Hermann Luedke, who was chief of the logistics department of Supreme Headquarters, Allied Powers in Europe. He shot himself at a hunting lodge in the Eifel Mountains in 1968, shortly before he was to have been arrested on charges of spying for the Russians. There then followed a spate of suicides: first was Major-General Horst Wendland, deputy chief of the West German Intelligence, then a Defence Ministry colonel shot himself, and a civil servant in the Ministry was found drowned. No connection between these suicides and Luedke's was ever admitted, but defectors insisted that they, too, were Soviet moles.

Further reading
The Secret War by Sanche de Gramont (André Deutsch, London 1962)

NE'EMAN, DR YUVAL (b. 1925)

Born in Tel Aviv and educated at Haifa and Imperial College, London, where he took his degree as doctor of science, Yuval Ne'eman also attended the Ecole de Guerre in Paris. He served with the Israeli Defence Force in the War of Independence in 1948 and began to take a keen interest in the technological aspects of military warfare and especially the new science of computerology. He was deputy commander of the Givati Brigade and joined the Aman, the collector of external military intelligence for Israel. Dr Ne'eman found that the methods of Aman were totally inadequate for a young nation without many allies, and he insisted that changes needed to be made. He also stressed that Israel, surrounded by enemies, needed what he called 'instant intelligence' rather more than most nations.

As a result of his promptings Aman's scope was widened and he himself reorganized it so that technologically it would be on a footing with the American Intelligence Services. Ne'eman himself never became chief of Aman, but he was its *eminence grise* and the most brilliant brain associated with it. He insisted that computers were needed for the collection and analysis of military intelligence, believing that Israel needed daily appraisal of enemy military and naval dispositions. In this he was given full backing by Moshe Dayan, then Chief of Staff, who had the imagination to see what computers could do for the defence of the country. He was also concerned with Israel's research into nuclear power and was appointed director of the industrial branch of the Committee of Atomic Energy.

After the 1956 war with Egypt when Israel advanced into the Sinai Peninsula and captured large numbers of prisoners, Ne'eman was able to put his computers to their first major test. Very soon Israel had the most forward-looking *avant-garde* intelligence system in the world. Apart from a carefully analysed computer-bank of instant and up-to-date intelligence, the power of Israel's espionage system lay in mobile electronic watch-systems for probing enemy territory. As for Ne'eman himself, he has carved a special niche for his country in the highest scientific circles. His research work has been admired everywhere. In the USA he has been made a visiting professor at the Californian Institute of Technology and in 1969 he was awarded the Albert Einstein Prize for achievements in theoretical physics, the first time this has been won by a non-American.

Further reading
The Israeli Secret Service by Richard Deacon (Hamish Hamilton, London 1977; Taplinger, New York 1977)

NOSENKO, YURI IVANOVICH

Nosenko has probably caused more anguish, argument and doubts inside the CIA and some other secret services than any other defector in the past thirty years. It was a few months after the assassination of President Kennedy that Nosenko made contact with the Americans in Switzerland and on CIA instructions was helped out of the country to Germany and from thence to the USA. Nosenko had been deputy director of a KGB department concerned with Americans visiting the USSR, but though he undoubtedly provided some accurate and useful intelligence, analysis showed that much of it merely confirmed what the CIA already knew. This could have been a ploy to get Nosenko accepted as a genuine defector.

Most controversial of Nosenko's claims was his insistence that he knew all about Lee Harvey Oswald's visit to Russia. Apparently, the KGB regarded President Kennedy's alleged killer as unreliable and would have nothing to do with him. Some in the USA thought there might be a Kremlin link to the President's death, as Oswald had not only visited Russia, but also had a Russian wife, Marina Prusakova. Nosenko, however, gave an assurance that the KGB had nothing at all to do with Kennedy's killing. The counter-intelligence section of the CIA, led by James Angleton (q.v.), believed that Nosenko had been planted as a disinformer, but unfortunately for them the FBI took a different view for the simple, if cynical, reason that Nosenko let them off the hook. The FBI had been criticized for failing to treat Oswald as a security risk, but if it had managed to show that Oswald was just a lone crackpot unconnected with the Russians, Hoover and the FBI would have cleared themselves. Later the CIA subjected Nosenko to relentless 'hostile interrogation' for several months and, it is understood, during this time Nosenko admitted lying occasionally, but by skilfully supplying other items of accurate information he kept them all guessing.

NUCLEAR SPIES

As the British and Americans were the first to develop and exploit nuclear weaponry and soon established a substantial lead in this field, it is inevitable that most nuclear espionage has been conducted by other nations, mainly the Russians, though the Chinese and Israelis have not lagged far behind. Russia made a drive for scientific espionage in the 1920s, obtaining the services of scientists in the USA, Britain, Germany and Denmark; in this way they were able to build up a picture of possible nuclear developments in the West (see *Trilisser, Mayer*, Part III). When such scientists as Peter Kaptiza and Lev Landau returned to Russia after studying in the West, they were able to supplement such intelligence and analyse it.

Lise Meitner, a Jewish professor of mathematics from Vienna, who worked in Berlin with the nuclear expert, Professor Hahn, was one marked down by the Soviets as someone who should be 'rescued' from Germany, and kidnapped, if necessary. The kidnapping was vetoed on Landau's advice, mainly because Meitner's work was far from complete and it was essential she cooperate with Nils Bohr and finish it off. So there was a compromise: Meitner was helped to escape from Germany by Soviet agents, first to Denmark and then to Sweden. From that day on, details of her research were passed to the Russians. Her Russian code-name was 'Terese', the name by which she was known to the Hungarian branch of her family, but it was a code-name which was never broken either by US Intelligence or the Germans.

The chief planner of nuclear espionage in Moscow was Peter Bukhanov, an MVD colonel who was teaching higher mathematics at the Technological Institute in Kiev when he was asked to organize a special foreign intelligence service in the early 1930s. It was Bukhanov who turned up the names of Dr Klaus Fuchs and Dr Alan Nunn May and gave orders for these men to be sent secretly to Washington and London. Through Douglas Frank Springhall, a Soviet agent recruiter in the UK, they obtained the invaluable information in 1943 that a committee presided over by Sir George Thomson had reported on the feasibility of a bomb dependent on atomic energy and that uranium was being sought from the pitchblende deposits of Canada. Later that year Springhall was sentenced to seven years' imprisonment for passing 'information calculated to be useful to an enemy'.

From then on the drive for nuclear secrets was given absolute priority. Pavel Mikhailov was given the task of spearheading the drive from the Soviet Consulate in New York, but it was not until Colonel Nicolai Zabotin arrived in Ottawa as military attaché in 1943 that new impetus was given to the Canadian network. Within a few months Zabotin had shown exceptional zeal in establishing a specialist network comprising twenty-two local agents and a team of fifteen Soviet specialists in Canada. It was only through the defection of Igor Gouzenko (q.v.) that this network was broken. Meanwhile there were changes in New York too, for Anatoli Yakovlev, under the cover of vice-consul, had been given the task of coordinating nuclear espionage. His key spies were four dedicated Communists: Harry Gold, David Greenglass, and Julius and Ethel Rosenberg (q.v.). By the latter part of the 1940s Soviet Intelligence had penetrated every vital sector of atomic research and bomb development – at the Radiation Laboratory in California, at the Manhattan Project at Oak Ridge, Tennessee, at McGill University and at the US atomic plant at Los Alamos.

In 1942 Britain and America had agreed to pool their scientific knowledge on the production of a nuclear weapon, knowing that it was essential to develop it before the Germans, but it was agreed, mainly on Churchill's insistence, that such knowledge should not be shared with Russia, even though it was an ally. Memories of the Nazi-Soviet Pact helped to clinch that agreement. When the extent of Soviet espionage was realized it came as a severe shock, particularly when so many Britons and Americans were revealed as traitors. It did not take long to track them down from code-names alone. 'Alek' was Dr Alan Nunn May, a British physicist, a Cambridge University man who had been a member of the Communist Party, and sent to Canada to work on the nuclear project. Nunn May's colleague, Enid Klaus Fuchs, had been a member of the Communist Party in Germany before the Nazis came to power and had then, using his Quaker background as a means to an end, been invited to England where he was allowed to study at Bristol University free of charge. He was recruited into the British nuclear research team without MI5 discovering that he had been a Communist, but if they did so later, they ignored the fact. He had been recruited by the Russians while working in Britain during the war. Nunn May was sentenced to ten years' imprisonment, but was released after less than seven, while Fuchs was given fourteen years, but released after nine and went to East Germany where he was given the directorship of a nuclear research institute in Dresden.

One treacherous scientist who eluded capture was Bruno Pontecorvo, who was said to have been warned by traitors inside the British Establishment and so slipped off to his native Italy. Pontecorvo had been a colleague of both Fuchs and Nunn May and, as an Italian physicist, had been enrolled to work in Canada on the nuclear bomb. The Americans suspected him of treachery and informed the British, but incredibly they failed to act and two years later MI5 let him slip through their fingers to go on holiday to Italy with his family. From there he defected to Russia. In 1955 he was paraded at a press conference in Moscow. In 1983 the Russians awarded him the Order of the October Revolution for his work in developing the 'physical sciences' – a neat and ambiguous way of expressing things.

Harry Gold, the Soviet agent who also worked on nuclear espionage, was gaoled for thirty years in 1951, by the US authorities. He was Fuchs' contact, the son of an immigrant family from Russia known originally as Golodnotsky. Before his death in 1965 he was awarded the Order of the Red Star. Another and later nuclear spy was Morton Sobell, who worked under the code-name 'Stone'; he also got a thirty-year sentence in the USA. It must not be forgotten that Donald Maclean (q.v.), the British traitor, had also passed nuclear policy secrets through his membership as a British diplomat of the Combined Policy Committee for Joint Atomic Development in the late 1940s. A much later and less serious case involved Sub-Lieutenant David Bingham, RN, whose wife nagged him so often for more money that he eventually agreed at her suggestion to sell the Russians details of the latest nuclear depth charges, six underwater sonar eyes and information on submarine detectors. This was as late as 1972, when he admitted receiving £5000 from the Russians. He was gaoled for two and a half years and their children were taken into care by the local authority. It was the defection of Oleg Lyalin (q.v.), another Soviet spy, which led to Bingham's detection.

Further reading
The Atom Bomb Spies by H. Montgomery Hyde (Hamis Hamilton, London)
The Traitors by Alan Moorehead (Hamish Hamilton, London 1952)
The Atom Spies by Oliver Pilat (London)

OLDFIELD, SIR MAURICE (1915-1981)

The eldest of eleven children of a tenant farmer at Over Haddon in Derbyshire, Maurice Oldfield made his way by scholarships from the village school to Manchester University. Here he studied medieval history and, but for the advent of World War II, he would probably have embarked on an academic career. During the war he joined the South Staffordshire Regiment and was then transferred to the Intelligence Corps. As a corporal he was sent out to the Middle East where he served at various times in the Suez Canal Zone, in Beirut and Cairo, rising to the rank of colonel. At the end of the war, such was his reputation for intelligence work that he was brought into MI6, first in London and later in the Far East and Washington. Eventually he progressed to deputy head of the service and then to chief, serving under the premierships of Heath, Wilson and Callaghan before his retirement in 1978.

In 1979 he was plucked out of retirement by the new Prime Minister, Margaret Thatcher, and given the extremely difficult task of coordinating security and intelligence in Northern Ireland. During his term as head of MI6, the IRA made at least two attempts on his life, as well as making threats about his family. He achieved some success while in Belfast in his last post, but he became the victim of a trap set by his enemies. Though ill health forced him to retire again in late 1980, in the latter part of his service in Northern Ireland his positive vetting clearance was withdrawn, because according to a statement by the British Prime Minister in 1987, 'in March, 1980, he made an admission that he had from time to time engaged in homosexual activities.' However, the Prime Minister added that 'there was no evidence or reason whatsoever to suggest that security had ever been compromised ... Indeed, he had contributed notably to a number of security and intelligence successes.' His friends and colleagues claim that these homosexual activities referred to a period in his school and university days and not afterwards and that he was deliberately 'set up' by his enemies in Belfast. He died within a year of his leaving Northern Ireland. His was the first example of a chief of Britain's Secret Service rising from humble beginnings to the pinnacle of success, but he proved a highly professional operator, making friends in both American and French Intelligence Services and creating good relations with the Israelis. He loathed what he called 'dirty tricks' espionage, though he was sufficiently realistic to know that unorthodox methods were sometimes necessary. One quirk of his is worth mentioning: for the purpose of character assessment he felt that Chinese astrology was rather better than positive vetting!

Further reading
'C': A Biography of Sir Maurice Oldfield by Richard Deacon (Macdonald, London 1985)

OPERATION 'BLUEBELL'

This was the code-name of a CIA operation undertaken shortly after the Korean War started. To obtain information about the North Koreans' movements and plans, thousands of Korean refugees were sent behind the North Korean lines with instructions to return with information as and when they could. Some valuable intelligence was obtained through this operation, even though many were caught and unable to return, but the lesson the CIA learnt was that, surprisingly, the best and most accurate intelligence came from children.

OPERATION 'GOLD' (THE BERLIN TUNNEL)

This was a joint Anglo-American operation in 1953 for creating a tunnel underneath East Berlin in order to tap Soviet and East German military communications. The idea for the tunnel came from a CIA communications expert who happened to discover that the major trunk telephone cables between East Berlin and Leipzig passed underground only about 350 yards from the American sector of Berlin. Through his knowledge of communications, the expert deduced that these cables would carry messages from the East German Army HQ. The Americans and British pooled resources and the tunnel was built in total secrecy. It started in a suburb of Berlin near a cemetery, and ran for about half a mile under the barbed-wire fences of the border into Alt Glienicke in East Berlin. Messages were regularly tapped without interruption until 1956, when it was discovered by the Russians. Scouts employed to watch the road above the tunnel saw a Russian telephone repair team arrive and start digging. Knowing that discovery was imminent, agents were able to warn their people in the tunnel and get them back to the American zone in time.

OPERATION 'NOAH'S ARK'

Yet another daring Israeli coup sponsored by the Mossad, this operation came to be known as the 'case of the Israeli gunboats'. It was Israel's swift and secret response to the irksome arms embargo imposed by France on Israel in 1968. Israel had ordered the purchase of five gunboats which were to be built in the naval base on the west side of Cherbourg's inner harbour, but the ban prevented the ships from being collected. Various plans were considered by the Mossad for the removal of the ships, including one for a quick dash to a British port, but this was ruled out because of pro-Palestinian influences inside the Wilson Government's Cabinet. There is a suspicion, however, that despite approving the ban, de Gaulle was prepared to turn a blind eye to any Mossad action provided it was carried off efficiently.

The harbour was one of the most difficult in Europe from which to escape and it was closely guarded by police, the Army and trained dogs. First of all the Israelis sold the ships to a 'Norwegian' oil exploration company called Starboat Oil of Panama through London solicitors and with only an accommodation address in Norway. This ploy was adopted to let the French off the hook when the ships were eventually smuggled out of Cherbourg at 2.30 on Christmas morning, 1969. The normal route out to sea would have exposed the ships to observation from French naval gun batteries, so they took the shorter, less exposed but far more dangerous course straight across the outer harbour, a much narrower exit with less than two fathoms of water in which to navigate. They arrived safely in Israel.

Further reading
The Israeli Secret Service by Richard Deacon (Hamish Hamilton, London 1977; Taplinger, New York 1977)

OPERATION 'PLUMBAT'

Directed by the Israeli Secret Service, this was a 1968 Mossad operation to surreptitiously acquire 200 tons of uranium for its nuclear reactor – the same type of uranium required for making nuclear weapons. A German registered ship, *Scheersberg*, arrived in Rotterdam in November 1968 and the captain took a new crew aboard. The ship went on to Antwerp where it collected the uranium, supposedly bought by a West German company from the Belgian *Société Générale des Mineraux*, and destined for an Italian company. However, the ship and the uranium disappeared. Later the next month the uranium was offloaded to an Israeli freighter between Cyprus and Turkey.

Further reading
The Israeli Secret Service by Richard Deacon (Hamish Hamilton, London 1977; Taplinger, New York 1977)

PAK NO-SU (d. 1970)

In the post-World War II period there was a small network of Chinese students at Cambridge University providing intelligence for Peking. One of these was Pak No-su, who was arrested by the South Korean secret police soon after he returned from Cambridge in 1969. He was accused of masterminding a spy ring at Cambridge and recruiting Korean intellectuals in Europe for the North Korean cause. Pak was rounded up with thirty-two others after he had been lured home to South Korea with the offer of a job in the President's office. One of the tragedies of this case was that Pak's wife cooperated with the prosecution against her husband and thus got off with a very light sentence. Pak himself was executed (see *South Korea*, Part I).

PAQUES, GEORGES

It was partly as a result of a novel called *Topaz* by American author, Leon Uris, which hinted at the existence of a Soviet spy-ring in the French President's entourage that General de Gaulle ordered an inquiry into the possible existence of NATO spy rings in the early 1960s (see *De Vosjoli, Philippe T.*, Part IV). In the meantime de Gaulle had a warning from President Kennedy on the same subject. Georges Paques, a French press attaché with NATO, was arrested and sentenced to life imprisonment for spying for the Russians. He had been recruited as a Soviet agent in Algiers around the end of World War II, but it was not until he was appointed as an official in the French Defence Ministry in the late 1950s that he was able to offer them much. Paques made his own terms for passing on top NATO secrets to the USSR. He regarded himself as an 'adviser' rather than a spy – one who believed that Russia and France together could unite Europe. He refused to photograph documents for the Russians, but he did accept their money, his reason being that it was the only way of making the Russians believe his intelligence was genuine. His sentence was later reduced to twenty years.

PATHÉ, PIERRE-CHARLES

The son of an early film pioneer, Pathé was a journalist who worked in the UNESCO headquarters in Paris. The Russians have always regarded UNESCO as a useful operating ground for spies and agents abroad. Nearly one-third of the seventy-two Soviet officials who worked permanently in UNESCO at one time were full-time members of the KGB or GRU. These people sought out agents in the various cultural bodies linked to UNESCO, and Pathé proved himself invaluable to the KGB over a period of twenty years. His forte was not actually spying, but putting out disinformation and using it not merely to provide propaganda for the USSR, but also to sow seeds of dissension between other countries, particularly in the late 1950s. Pathé was arrested in 1979 and charged with what amounted to the 'continuous process of disseminating Russian disinformation'. For nearly twenty years he had been cunningly inserting Soviet-produced material into articles he wrote for the French press, making special use of the newsletter, *Synthesis*, which he personally directed. The newsletter was funded by Soviet money and its subscribers included French Senators, members of Parliament and Ambassadors. It was a most unusual case. Pathé was sentenced to five years' imprisonment, while Alexander Kuznetsov, his case officer, was expelled from France after claiming diplomatic immunity.

PELTON, RONALD W.

In June 1986 a Federal jury convicted Pelton, a former employee of America's top-secret NSA, on four counts of spying for the USSR. One of the secrets he was alleged to have sold to the Russians was an intelligence operation in which American submarines reportedly eavesdropped on the USSR while lurking close to Russian shores. The *Washington Post* said the operation, referred to in court only as Project A, involved the use of US submarines stationed in the Sea of Okhotsk between the Kamchatka Peninsula and the Soviet Asian mainland. Pelton was further accused of selling vital data on the

NSA's interceptions and decoding for $35,000. Before the trial some authorities favoured not prosecuting Pelton because of the adverse publicity.

PENKOVSKY, COLONEL OLEG (1919-1963?)

'The answer to a prayer,' was how Sir Maurice Oldfield, then MI6 liaison officer in Washington, described the intelligence provided to the British by Penkovsky in 1961. 'What he provided seemed like a miracle. That is why for so long he was mistrusted on both sides of the Atlantic.' Penkovsky, a GRU officer, was born in the North Caucusus and joined the artillery school in Kiev, passing out as a lieutenant in 1939. He fought in the Soviet-Finnish War, joined the Communist Party and at the end of World War II was a lieutenant-colonel. In 1955 he was appointed assistant military attaché in Ankara, at which time he was first marked down by the British Secret Service as a potential defector or informant. A clumsy attempt by him to make contact with the Americans had been rejected because it was suspected of being an attempt at provoking trouble by the Soviet police. Meanwhile, Penkovsky had been appointed to the State Committee for the Coordination of Scientific Research, where he became deputy head of the foreign department. Eventually he was accepted by the British as a supremely important informant on an official visit to Britain in April 1961. From then on he turned over a wealth of intelligence, not merely about Russian military technology, but the deployment pattern for missile sites. He revealed how Khrushchev's 'secret weapon' had blown up on the launching pad, killing the chief of the USSR missile forces and 300 officers. He revealed that Russia was in no position to make good its boasts of being able to threaten the USA.

The problem for the British was to persuade the Americans that Penkovsky was genuine and not an infiltrator. Much of his information was highly technical and it had to be analysed by scientific experts; sometimes he even produced original documents rather than photocopies. He did not defect, but remained in Moscow, taking tremendous risks and passing material out through his British contact (see *Wynne, Greville*, Part IV). Penkovsky's reports undoubtedly enabled President Kennedy to call Khrushchev's bluff at the time of the Cuban missiles crisis and thus won the day for the West. However, the true value of Penkovsky's evidence and testimony may not be known for many years, and arguments as to what extent he was a double-agent will continue, especially among those who felt his actions on behalf of the West were too good to be true. One of his chief tasks had been to collect and assess information on NATO rocketry for the Russians. The Russians were certainly incredibly slow in catching him, but, judging from the number of dismissals which followed his arrest, this was simply carelessness on their part. Penkovsky was charged in 1963 and reported to have been executed that year. Later it was suggested that he had been used by the Russians to mislead the West and that he was living in retirement. Similarly these same critics cast doubts on the *Penkovsky Papers*, published with approval of the CIA. On balance it is almost certain that the Russians pumped out massive disinformation to try to discredit Penkovsky and to cover their own failure in not catching him sooner.

Further reading
The Penkovsky Papers by Oleg Penkovsky (Collins, London 1965)

PETROV, VLADIMIR Defect (w)

Petrov became a KGB officer after serving in the Soviet Navy as a cipher expert and eventually achieved the rank of major. Long before he defected to the Australians in April 1955, he was known to the author of this book as an authority on Australian football teams with a knowledge unmatched by any Australian journalist working for British newspapers. Some people still say that it was an interest in Australian soccer which helped to lure Petrov into defecting. However, as a member of Beria's team, Petrov became afraid of what might befall him in Moscow after Beria was ousted. Petrov's wife was also a KGB officer and when he defected she was held under guard at the Embassy. The

Russians attempted to remove her swiftly from the country by air, but this was checked at Fort Darwin when she told the crew of the aircraft that she wanted to stay in Australia. After a brief tussle the Soviet guards on the plane were disarmed and she was reunited with her husband. This defection was a triumph for the Australian Security Intelligence Service as they had observed Petrov's love of Australian life over a long period and had put him in touch with Dr Michal Bialoguski, a Polish refugee who had been employed to pose as a Communist sympathizer. It was Petrov who first pointed to 'Kim' Philby (q.v.) as a Soviet agent, but his evidence was not admitted and even as late as 7 November 1955 Prime Minister Macmillan shocked counter-intelligence agencies in the UK and USA by telling the House of Commons that, 'I have no reason to conclude that Mr Philby has at any time betrayed the interests of this country.'

Further reading
Empire of Fear by Vladimir and Evdokia Petrov (Praeger, New York 1956)
The Case of Colonel Petrov by Michal Bialoguski (McGraw Hill, New York 1955)

PHILBY, HAROLD ADRIAN RUSSELL (b. 1912)

Nicknamed 'Kim' after the Indian boy-spy in Kipling's stories, Philby was the son of the eccentric St John Philby, formerly of the Indian Civil Service but latterly an unofficial adviser to various Middle East potentates and living in Arabia. With this background his son may well have felt that he was a cosmopolitan and did not belong to any one country. Educated at Westminster School and Cambridge University, Philby soon made friends with the pro-Communist network at Cambridge and was recruited as a Soviet agent in the early 1930s. He went to Vienna and married Litzi Friedman, an Austrian Communist who had just secured a divorce from a fanatical Communist. She was herself in some danger of arrest, so in marrying her Philby provided her with a British passport so that she could return with him to England. Philby has stated in his book, *My Silent War*, that he was 'given the job of penetrating British Intelligence and told it did not matter how long I took to do the job'. Marrying a foreign Communist just to give her a British passport seems an odd way of setting about such an assignment. But, once he had returned to Britain, Philby set about repudiating any Communist opinions he may have held and gave the impression of having veered to the right politically. He became a member of the Anglo-German Fellowship, a society having friendly relations with the Nazi regime, and when the Spanish Civil War broke out got himself accepted as the *Times* correspondent with the Franco forces in Spain.

It was in 1939, he declares, that he was recruited for intelligence work on behalf of the British by Marjorie Maxse (later Dame, chief organization officer of the Conservative Party Central Office). He was given a security clearance by Captain Guy Liddell of MI5 (q.v. Part III). He progressed in the Secret Service from one department to another, eventually being linked with the SOE and then becoming a highly influential operator in Section V which dealt with operations on the Iberian Peninsular. He had great personal charm, was popular with Stewart Menzies, the head of MI6, and towards the end of the war was being spoken of as a possible future head of the Service. He was then made chief of Section IX, which was intended to keep a watch on Soviet espionage, as well as direct espionage against that country. Thus Philby was able during the last stages of the war and for some time afterwards to check or destroy any moves by MI6 which compromised the USSR. Once the war had ended he did his utmost to sabotage all anti-Soviet activities coming within the orbit of Section IX. Then came the news that a minor Russian diplomat, Constantin Volkhov, had made a secret approach to the British vice-consul in Istanbul asking for asylum and intimating that he could supply details of two Soviet agents who were working in the Foreign Office in London and a third who was a senior member of MI5. Philby suggested he should go to Istanbul to investigate and his offer was approved. Presumably he tipped off the Russians in the meantime because by the time he arrived in Istanbul a perplexed British Consulate official reported that Volkov, heavily bandaged, had been taken aboard a Russian aircraft and returned to Moscow.

In the next few years Philby helped betray the CIA-MI6 project for landing members of the clandestine Albanian Resistance movement by sea and parachute into Albania. Then he was appointed as a liaison officer to Washington, in which period some perceptive American intelligence officers began to suspect him. When Burgess and Maclean defected in 1951, Philby came under interrogation from the British. But while some in MI5 had grave doubts about him, his colleagues in MI6 tended to trust him. It was only because of pressure from the Americans that MI6 reluctantly agreed to withdraw him from his Washington post. Yet because MI6 gave the impression of still trusting him and even maintained close relations after arranging for him to have a journalistic post in Beirut, the Russians took quite a long time to convince themselves that Philby had not betrayed them.

In the meantime Philby was divorced from his first wife, Litzi and married a girl named Aileen Furse, whom he left behind in England when he went to Beirut. When she was found dead in bed in an empty house, he married Eleanor Brewer, the ex-wife of an American journalist. Slowly, reports from defectors and others filtered back to London, all suggesting that Philby was a Soviet agent. An emissary from London called on him in Beirut and urged him to return home to answer some questions. Then Philby received news from the Russians that a CIA hit-man was on his trail. On 23 January 1962 Philby disappeared and, with Russian help was smuggled into the USSR. His arrival in Moscow was not announced to the world until six months later. In July 1980 *Izvestia* stated that Philby had been awarded the People's Friendship Order, designated for foreigners who have helped Russia. When his third wife died he married a Russian girl, Nina, who worked as an interpreter at Moscow's Scientific Institute.

Further reading

My Silent War by H.A.R. Philby (Grove Press, New York 1968)

The Spy I Married by Eleanor Philby (Ballantine Books, New York 1968)

The Philby Conspiracy by Bruce Page, David Leitch and Philip Knightley (Signet Books, New York 1968)

Escape by Richard Deacon (BBC Publications, 1980)
Philby: The Long Road to Moscow by Patrick Seale and
Maureen McConville (Hamish Hamilton, London 1973)

POLLARD, JONATHAN JAY

Shortly after the arrest of Pollard, an American intelligence
analyst, on charges of spying for Israel in 1985, allegations were
made in the *Los Angeles Times* of a spy network run by Israel
inside the USA. It was suggested that this network was directed
by an obscure Israeli scientific officer known as Lekem and run
by a career intelligence officer known as Rafael Eitan. The day
after Pollard's arrest two Israeli scientific attachés returned to
Israel from Washington and Eitan was moved to another post.
The Israelis denied the newspaper allegations and issued a
statement after a Cabinet meeting, declaring that it was
inconceivable that attempts to 'foul the atmosphere' between the
USA and Israel should succeed. Israel was particularly
disturbed by one story that the Mossad, its intelligence service,
had organized the theft of uranium sufficient to manufacture six
nuclear bombs from a Pennsylvania plant. Israel also claimed
that the espionage conspiracy in which Pollard was paid
$30,000 for delivering US naval and military secrets was 'a
rogue operation' unknown to the Israeli intelligence community.
It was revealed, however, that Pollard's controller in the USA
was an Israeli Air Force general, Avian Sella.

In June 1986 Pollard pleaded guilty to spying for Israel, and
admitted that both he and his wife belonged to an Israeli
espionage network and that he had sold documents to Israel.
According to declassified FBI documents released in 1986,
Brigadier Eitan, former chief of operations for the Mossad,
travelled to an American nuclear plant in Pennsylvania in 1968
and arranged for quantities of weapons-grade uranium to be
illegally diverted to Israel. In March 1987 Pollard was sentenced
to life imprisonment for passing thousands of pages of top secret
US military material to Israel.

PONOMAREV, BORIS NIKOLAEVICH (b. 1905)

Ponomarev's main claim to fame is that he largely masterminded the development of 'disinformation' as a highly skilled modern tactic of Soviet policy both within and without the KGB. For a long time he was responsible for relations with Communist Parties outside the Eastern bloc, as well as being a favourite to become head of the KGB. It was he who persuaded the British TUC, once so resolute in refusing to have links with any bogus trade unionism behind the Iron Curtain, to have talks not only with him, but with Soviet 'trade unions'. He was received by the TUC in London in 1976.

PRAEGER, NICHOLAS (d. 1981)

Born a Czech, Praeger inherited British nationality from his father who, having worked in the British Embassy in Prague, became a British citizen in retirement. He joined the RAF and as a sergeant worked in a special radar unit as an electronics engineer. He was recruited as a spy for the Czechs by an agent who had had an affair with his wife. In due course he supplied the Czechs with photographs of the entire documentation relating to a new anti-radar system. Shortly after he ended his work with the RAF, Praeger joined the English Electric Company, working on electronics. Under the code-name 'Marconi', Praeger went on spying for some years until he was caught and charged in 1971, being sentenced to twelve years' imprisonment. He was released on parole in 1977 and deported from Britain. The Czechs refused to accept him and he was classified as stateless.

PRIME, GEOFFREY (n. 1938)

When Geoffrey Prime, who worked at GCHQ, was sentenced to thirty-eight years' imprisonment for spying in 1982, there was a real fear on both sides of the Atlantic that he had already been replaced at Cheltenham with several other moles. Prime had passed secrets to the Russians over a lengthy period. Jock Kane, a former radio supervisor who left GCHQ after his repeated warnings about lax security at the base had been ignored, stated: 'The mole still inside GCHQ has got to be much nearer the top than Prime ever was!' Kane joined GCHQ in 1946: 'In thirteen years I alerted my superiors to frightening lapses.' Prime was caught in the end, not directly through his spying activities, but because of his sex attacks on little girls. It was after he had confessed to three such attacks that police searched his home and found a code-pad, a document explaining how to handle microdots and a top-secret memorandum. Eventually he admitted passing secrets to the USSR in London, Berlin, Vienna and Potsdam over a period of fifteen years.

After joining the RAF Prime took a Russian language course and was subsequently placed on interception work on Eastern bloc military communications; he was promoted to sergeant. He started passing information to the Russians while still in the RAF and when he left the service in 1968 he joined GCHQ where his knowledge of Russian and German came in useful. Despite the fact that while serving at GCHQ he reported to his Soviet control not only in London, but on trips to Vienna, he was cleared by four vettings. Once he was even taken to a Russian cruise ship on the Danube for two or three days and questioned by the Russians about the material he had brought with him. However, Prime still found time to keep an up-to-date card index of young girls aged 10-15 years old; at the time of his arrest he had 2287 such cards.

In a statement to the House of Commons after Prime's conviction, the Prime Minister admitted that from 1968 'at least until 1980, Prime had access to information of the utmost secrecy'. Eight days after Prime's conviction Jack Wolfenden, a communications expert at GCHQ, crashed his glider into a hill and, though the coroner returned a verdict of 'accidental death', security agents carried out an investigation in case Wolfenden had committed suicide through fear of being exposed as a spy. As a result of the Prime case and fears of other moles in GCHQ, tougher vetting procedures were demanded, and it was also suggested that vetting officers might be more carefully chosen.

RABORN, ADMIRAL WILLIAM T. (b. 1905)

Raborn was yet another CIA chief who was both a naval officer and a failure. While serving in the Navy he had been concerned with developing the submarine Polaris missile force, but he was chosen as head of the CIA in 1965 by President Johnson because he had supported the President's election campaign and was a fellow Texan. All that can be said of Raborn is that he was totally out of his depth in this job. Even the CIA was glad to see him go.

RAFAEL, SYLVIA (d. 1985)

One of the Mossad's best and most courageous female agents, Sylvia Rafael was a member of the Israeli hit-team sent to Norway in 1973 in what proved to be a disastrous attempt to kill Ali Hassan Salameh, the Black September gang chief responsible for organizing the massacre of Israeli athletes at Munich and for various murders and plane hijackings. The man who was mistakenly killed turned out to be a Moroccan waiter. It is claimed that Norwegian intelligence officials actually aided the 'avenger squad' and helped some of the hit-team to get away after the killing. However, the Norwegian police found two people in possession of Canadian passports with the names of Leslie and Patricia Roxburger and noticed among their possessions the ex-directory telephone number of the Mossad's man in Oslo. The 'Canadians' proved to be Sylvia Rafael and Abraham Gehmer and they were sentenced to five and a half years in prison, a remarkably tolerant sentence. Rafael was released after twenty-two months, retaining her post with the Mossad.

A Norwegian who interviewed her on a number of occasions said, 'Sylvia Rafael was not so ruthless an operator as the hit-team's chief female killer – the one we did not capture. But I am willing to bet she was a better all-rounder, a shrewd digger of information and in the long run a more efficient spy. She was chic, attractive, with a terrific personality.' She was feted on her return to Israel, but in 1985 was one of three Mossad agents killed by PLO men in Cyprus.

RENNIE, SIR JOHN OGILVY (1914-1981)

Educated at Wellington and Balliol, Rennie worked with the firm of Eckhardt, Inc., in New York from 1935-39. From 1940 he was Vice-Consul in Baltimore, and then took various appointments in Warsaw, Washington and Buenos Aires through the British Information Services in New York. After a spell at the Foreign Office from 1946-9, he eventually became an Under-Secretary of State. Rennie was never an Ambassador but, when he became head of MI6 in succession to Sir Dick White, he was officially described and listed as the Superintending Under-Secretary of the Planning, Research and Library Records of the Foreign Office. It was a surprise choice and due to Foreign Office influence, as some of its senior members wanted to bring MI6 more under their control.

Rennie was originally a painter who had found early recognition of his talents in the Royal Academy and the Paris Salon. Surprisingly, one of his hobbies was electronics, and this came in useful when he was chairman of a number of committees dealing with defence matters. Rennie was to some extent out of his depth as head of MI6, being painfully slow in making decisions. His cover was blown when his son was imprisoned for drug offences and the foreign press referred to the father as 'C'. Shortly after this he retired.

ROOSEVELT, KERMIT

Probably one of the ablest officers 'in the field' the CIA ever had, Kermit Roosevelt, grandson of President Theodore Roosevelt, was a cultured, cosmopolitan American who became CIA station chief in Tehran in the turbulent days immediately after World War II. This was the time when the Iranian Prime Minister, Mohammed Mossadegh, with the aid of the Tudeh Communist Party and some backing from the Soviet Union, had nationalized the Anglo-Iranian petroleum company and was actually aiming to arrest the Shah, having already overthrown him. To combat this there was a joint CIA-British SIS operation code-named 'Operation TAPJAX/Boot', aimed at restoring the Shah in 1953. This whole operation was marked by an excellent relationship between the US and British Intelligence Services. MI6 planned the initial details of the coup, in the early stages of which the Americans had shown a strong disinclination to become involved, believing that Britain might be branded as an aggressor at the United Nations. Fortunately, the CIA took a different view from the US Government and Kermit Roosevelt proved a key figure.

Even though the number of CIA operatives in the area was not more than forty at this time, the coup succeeded brilliantly. The beginning of the end came when Mossadegh's chief of police, General Ashfar-Tus, was kidnapped, and pro-Soviet agents inside the police and army were removed. Perhaps the true key to success was that Roosevelt got $2 million for the covert mission. But he used imagination in recruiting all manner of unlikely people to arouse the population of Tehran in the Shah's favour. He deserved the recognition he received from President Eisenhower, though the British who had initiated the scheme got no thanks whatsoever. Roosevelt carried on as a Middle East expert in the CIA, but he never gained much from attempts to woo Nasser. He retired in 1958.

ROSENBERG, JULIUS AND ETHEL

The Rosenbergs were responsible for a change in American law which eliminated the ten-year statute of limitations in espionage cases. Their trial alerted the whole American nation to the perils of espionage in peacetime. This was the period when America discovered the appalling extent of internal espionage, so the Rosenbergs became scapegoats for all the others who were caught, most of them guiltier.

The Rosenbergs were children of Jewish immigrants, who became members of the Communist Party and were then recruited as spies by Anatoli Yakovlev, the New York KGB officer. Julius Rosenberg had recruited other spies and there is no doubt that his wife assisted him in this work. It was largely because they proved to be rather ineffective spies that a world-wide howl went up when they were sentenced to death under the old law because it was proved that their offences were committed in wartime.

ROTSCH, MANFRED

A department head at the aerospace concern, Messerschmitt-Boelkow-Blohm, Rotsch was sentenced to eighteen and a half years in prison in July 1986 for spying for the KGB over a period of thirty years. Rotsch was a highly skilled aerospace engineer who had been involved in the joint West German-British-Italian Tornado fighter aircraft project and he had been passing top-secret information on a number of projects to the Russians. About the same time, Professor Herbert Meissner, a prominent East German, took shelter in the East German mission in Bonn after the West German Federal Public Prosecutor announced he was dropping an investigation into suspected espionage against the Professor in the national interest. The Meissner affair strained East-West relations until it was mutually agreed that the professor, who was deputy chairman of the East German Academy of Science, could return home after an arrangement was made between East and West Germany's two chief spy-exchange operators, Herr Wolfgang Vogel of East Germany and Ludwig Rehlinger of the Bonn Ministry for Inner German Relations.

SATELLITE SPYING

Each year satellite espionage becomes increasingly vital to all national security systems, and as probes into outer space continue, so satellite competition between the great powers will increase. Certainly in wartime, even in a minor war such as the Falklands in 1982, satellite intelligence can make all the difference. The 'spy-in-the-sky' satellite code-named SAMOS (satellite and mission observation system), photographs enemy territory while in orbit and was first launched in California in 1961. In theory SAMOS could photograph an entire continent; it is a five-ton satellite launched by rocket, and photographs are automatically developed on board the craft. Its vital partner is the satellite MIDAS, which carries infra-red detection equipment which gives out warnings when missiles are launched.

Since the inception of satellite intelligence-gathering, all the great powers have adopted it, with the USA, Canada, Australia and Britain forming an effective global network. Recently there has been criticism of links between the US-UK satellite networks and Silvermine, the South African installation near Cape Town. This arose after reports that the USA and Britain have provided the South African Government with intelligence about its leading internal enemy, the African National Congress. One report claimed that in the 1980s South Africa depended on Britain and America for communications intelligence from Black Africa in return for information from the South African Directorate of Military Intelligence about Soviet shipping. The Russians have stepped up their drive for satellite manufacture intelligence in recent years, concentrating especially on all connected with the European space satellite, Ariane. A network of East German agents has been despatched throughout Europe with the task of seeking out all details of Ariane (see *Garden Shed Spies*, Part IV). More recently it was claimed that Christopher Boyce, who was sentenced to forty years' imprisonment in the USA in 1977, had passed on to Soviet agents 'documents and a package containing the KH-11 manuscript'. KH 11 is the CIA name for the 'keyhole' satellite, a device capable of making observations on Russia, as if through a keyhole. Boyce had worked in the code room of a Southern California firm which supplied and operated top-secret satellites for the CIA.

No power guards its space research secrets more carefully than the USSR, even to the extent of giving out a certain amount of disinformation on their own space achievements. At one time the Russians were giving so much publicity to their Venus probes that it was suspected the KGB were using these to distract attention from other space operations. The last landing of a spacecraft on Venus by the Russians was in 1970. A year later came an announcement that Russia's Venus-7 had sent back signals to Earth for twenty-three minutes after landing and that 'scientific information had been derived from it'. It was not stated why the spacecraft stopped transmitting after twenty-three minutes, nor was there any explanation for the delay of nearly six weeks before issuing this statement. One reason for space probe disinformation may be that the Russians are far more preoccupied with satellite espionage and military domination of outer space than in putting men on the Moon or other planets.

China launched a military satellite in 1975 for the purpose of providing 'rudimentary information on major Russian military activities in Mongolia and on the Sino-Soviet frontier', according to American experts in Hawaii. This satellite had no camera, but sufficient electronic equipment to monitor the number of active operational aircraft in any given area, as well as intelligence on tanks and mobile artillery. Since then China has made considerable advances in this sphere of operations.

Of equal importance to the sky satellite system is the round-the-world oceanic watch. In a huge concrete bunker under Northwood Hills in London a perpetual watch is now being kept on Soviet ships, submarines and aircraft around the world, using both satellite and other methods of observation. This is OPCON, or Operational Control, which operates on behalf of the Royal Navy, but is linked to other NATO defence systems. The system uses computers and other components which make it more advanced than anything the US Navy yet has. This is a £12 million system, partly paid for by NATO, which has taken twenty years to perfect, and it can also be operated at sea.

SCHOUTERS, GEORGE

Convicted of the murder of a nightwatchman and sentenced to twelve years' imprisonment by a Canadian court, Schouters, a Belgian, was released in 1967 on condition that he left Canada and did not return. Police officers were anxious to see exactly what he would do and where he would go, so they tracked his movements, with some help from European security services. First he went to Brussels, then to Prague, Paris, Geneva and Stockholm before finally being found working as an instructor in a guerrilla training school run by the East Germans. Schouters, along with François Schern, a Hungarian who had served in the French Foreign Legion, emigrated to Montreal in the late 1950s. They were among the original founder-members of the Quebec Liberation Front (FLQ), which launched a terrorist campaign in the province. Both men were believed to have been active in Communist-directed resistance movements in Europe in World War II.

SCHULZE, REINHARD AND SONJA (see Garden Shed Spies)

SEJNA, GENERAL JAN

Defer (w)

When General Sejna, who had been Deputy Minister of Defence in Czechoslovakia, defected to the USA in 1968, he took some sensational intelligence with him. He was able to supply the Americans with Russia's plans in collaboration with some of her Eastern allies to conduct large-scale sabotage in the West, not merely in the event of war, but, if deemed necessary, as a preparation for war. Later he stated in an interview published in a French magazine that he had been present at top-level Warsaw Pact meetings in which plans 'to paralyse totally the economic and political life' of Britain, Western Europe and North America had been discussed. One plan, submitted by the Czechs and approved by the Russians, was to close down the London Underground railways system by a plan which involved using agents of influence in the trade unions and Communist front organizations. He disclosed that similar plans had been drawn up to cut off London's water supply. Later this report was confirmed from other sources.

SEMICHASTNY, YEFIMOVICH (b. 1924)

Like Shelepin, his predecessor as head of the KGB, Semichastny, who took charge in 1961, was also a former director of the Party Youth organization, and his influence in this direction soon showed. Until this time the Soviet line in propaganda had always been that espionage was something which only capitalist states indulged in. Semichastny changed all that by attempting to publicize an heroic image of the KGB. Shortly after his appointment he inspired an article in *Izvestia* which included an interview with 'a senior KGB officer' (Semichastny himself) who stated, 'many young Party and Komsomol workers have joined the KGB and none of the people who, during the time of the personality cult, took part in the repressions against innocent Soviet people is now in the Service.' Semichastny went further than this, urging that the KGB had another side to its character – 'the rehabilitation of people unjustly accused during the personality cult' [i.e. in Stalin's time].

Soon there were articles and books appearing in the USSR glorifying Soviet spies – men like Richard Sorge (q.v. Part III), 'Kim' Philby (q.v.), Colonel Rudolf Abel (q.v.) and Gordon Lonsdale (q.v.). Ultimately Semichastny first, and later Khrushchev himself, were dismissed from their posts as a result of a series of set-backs for the USSR in their relations with the

West. The discovery that Oleg Penkovksy (q.v.), one of Semichastny's senior officers, was passing secrets to the West was the final ignominy.

SEROV, GENERAL IVAN ALEXANDROVICH (b. 1905)

Formerly a member of the *Cheka*, Serov was the son of a peasant, born in the Vologda province of Russia. At the age of eighteen he was head of his native village council and shortly afterwards joined the Red Army, rising to be chief of staff of an artillery regiment. In 1939 he was assigned to the NKVD, serving as a deputy commissar for State Security and as such was responsible for the mass deportations from the three Baltic states which began after their occupations by the USSR in June 1940. He was very close to Khrushchev, who was undoubtedly responsible for his advancement. Serov rose steadily in the Soviet hierarchy and in 1945, working under Marshal Zhukov in Germany, had directed the deportation of German atomic and rocket experts to Russia. A tough, rather brutal-looking man, Serov was efficient and ruthless, but occasionally charming, and gifted with a macabre sense of humour laced with sarcasm. He was in charge of the security arrangements when Khrushchev and Bulganin visited Britain in 1956. While Serov's visit to Britain was heralded by much criticism in the press, he nevertheless ingratiated himself with some in British intelligence circles, hoping to secure an exchange of facilities in the Far East. Just how genuine this request was it is impossible to tell, but it was nonetheless declined.

In 1958 Serov, who had been made head of the Soviet Secret Service in 1956, was dismissed from the KGB for reasons which are still not altogether clear, though they were said to be partly due to the Hungarian uprising. It has also been said that he failed to detect a plot against Khrushchev. There were rumours that he had been given another equally important job, but from about 1960 onwards Western intelligence services lost all track of him.

SHELEPIN, ALEXANDR (b. 1918)

A former Komsomol (Soviet youth) adviser with no previous experience in security or intelligence work, Shelepin was nominated to succeed Serov as head of the KGB largely to protect Khruschchev's interests. He was described as one of the Communist Party's Puritans, remorseless in his campaign against drunkenness, hooliganism and 'decadent Western pleasures'. To some extent Shelepin's work was to improve the image of the KGB, but also, some opined at the time, to encourage youthful recruits to the service. There is some evidence that he actually made improvements in the organization and raised the quality of intelligence. But he was made a scapegoat for the Cuban crisis disaster – curiously, more for his warnings on the American 'Bay of Pigs' invasion plan than for anything else. Shelepin warned that Khruschchev was making a dangerous mistake in seeking a nuclear confrontation with the USA, for which advice he was sacked in November 1961.

SHEVCHENKO, DR ARKADI

Defects (w)

Shevchenko graduated from the Institute of International Relations in 1954, joined the Soviet Ministry of Foreign Affairs and soon became a close associate of Andrei Gromyko, the Foreign Minister. With ambassador's rank, he was given the post of Under-Secretary General of the United Nations in New York in 1973. He succeeded so well in Soviet eyes, and his judgment was so greatly regarded, that when his five-year term ended, the Russians readily agreed to his staying on for two more years. Yet during this period Shevchenko apparently believed that his advice was not sufficiently heeded.

Between 1977-8 the Russians seemed surprised at the Americans' ability to predict their policy-making changes on arms limitation, but then began to suspect Shevchenko of passing them information. Early in 1978 a cable from Moscow informed him that he was doing a splendid job in New York, but that he should return to Russia for talks. At first it seemed that he would go to Moscow, but then, either from a tip-off or through his own astuteness, he decided against it and announced that he would defect. There was consternation in Moscow and the Russians immediately alleged that the CIA had set him up. Shevchenko had developed a taste for the good life, and it seems that he had been spending freely for some years before his defection. Indeed, sometimes his outgoings were greater than his salary of £50,000 a year. This was how he came to be a controlled agent of the American Intelligence Services prior to his defection. The information he passed on to both the CIA and the FBI was invaluable, especially in revealing KGB infiltration at the United Nations, and in helping to check and double-check the reliability of other earlier defectors from the USSR. Yet when his best-selling book, *Breaking with Moscow*, was published it was denounced by Edward Jay Epstein, a writer on intelligence affairs, as 'a CIA fabrication', alleging that it was the story of 'the spy who came in to be sold'.

Further reading
Breaking with Moscow by Dr Arkadi Shevchenko (1985)

SILLITOE, SIR PERCY (1888-1962)

Joining the British South African Police Force in 1908, Sillitoe was gazetted in the Northern Rhodesian Police in 1911, served in the German East African campaign in World War I, then returned home to embark on a spectacularly successful police career in Britain. As Chief Constable of Sheffield he set up Britain's first forensic science laboratory in 1929, and later as Chief Constable of Glasgow became famous as the most effective gang-buster which that crime-torn city has ever known. From 1945-6 he was Chief Constable of Kent, and being situated in an area where wartime security was more predominant than in other parts of the country, he learned to work closely with civil and military intelligence.

Sir Percy became head of MI5 on 1 May 1946, the day that Allan Nunn May was charged at the Old Bailey with passing secrets to Russia. He was a surprise choice for the job, but both Attlee and the Home Secretary, Herbert Morrison, had been urged not to promote anyone from within the ranks of MI5, partly through lack of suitable candidates, but also because of hints that some senior officers were suspected of being pro-Soviet. From the beginning Sir Percy's task was made difficult by those immediately under him, and in an article he wrote for the *Sunday Times* on 22 November 1953 he said, 'I cannot deny that during my first few weeks as head of MI5, I found it so extremely difficult to find out precisely what everyone was doing that I felt its popular reputation for excessive secrecy was in no way exaggerated. The men I was attempting to direct were highly intelligent, but somewhat introspective, each working ... in a rather withdrawn isolation ...'

Sir Percy held the post from 1946-53 and was a rather underrated chief, largely due to the disloyalty of some of his senior colleagues who did their best to discredit him. Of all the heads of MI5, he made no pretence of ridiculous secrecy, even disclosing the exact position of his office in *Who's Who* – 'War Office, Room 055'. Sillitoe had very little cooperation from either MI6 or the Foreign Office, especially on the affair of Burgess and Maclean. After his retirement he took an appointment with the De Beers company in South Africa to track down diamond smugglers.

SINCLAIR, MAJOR-GENERAL SIR JOHN (1897-1977)

Known as 'Sinbad' Sinclair because he had served as a midshipman in the Royal Navy after being educated at Winchester and the Royal Naval College, Dartmouth, John Sinclair switched over to the Army. He entered the Royal Academy, Woolwich, in 1918, and was commissioned in the Royal Artillery the following year. In World War II he was made Deputy Director of Military Operations. Sinclair lacked the experience and knowledge of his predecessor, Menzies, nor had he the same political instincts. However, it is doubtful whether he was to blame for the incident which led to his retirement, or even put fully in the picture. It concerned Commander Lionel Crabb, one of the Royal Navy's best underwater sabotage experts, who dived into Portsmouth Harbour in April 1956 on a secret mission for MI6 to investigate the Russian cruiser, *Ordkhonikidze*. When this story broke in the press there were, of course, denials that the British were involved, and the Prime Minister of the day, Sir Anthony Eden, was furious, as the Soviet cruiser had brought over Marshal Bulganin and Nikita Khrushchev on a goodwill mission. First to be sacked was the Foreign Office adviser to MI6, and shortly afterwards Sinclair himself was replaced.

SMITH, GENERAL WALTER BEDELL (1895-1961)

Having achieved a reputation for himself as General Eisenhower's Chief of Staff, Bedell Smith was appointed head of the CIA in 1950, following strong criticisms of the new intelligence service. From 1946-49 he had been Ambassador to Moscow, and it was felt that this experience alone should be a strong qualification for his new job. He brought something like military discipline to bear upon the CIA, and proceeded to get rid of the misfits and many of the OSS leftovers. Apparently he was alarmed at much of what he saw in the CIA, for he told the House of Un-American Activities Committee in 1952 that he believed 'there are Communists in my own organization. In the past we have discovered one or two, and I believe that in the future we will from time to time discover them.' Bedell Smith brought in Allen Dulles as his deputy, and he also tightened up on the screening of recruits for the CIA. Before he left the agency to become Under Secretary of State of Political Affairs he made it clear to the SIS that the CIA would have no further relations with 'Kim' Philby (q.v.), who had been liaison officer with the service in Washington.

Further reading
My Three Years in Moscow by Walter Bedell Smith (Lippincott, New York 1950)

SPIES FOR PEACE

In April 1963 various anonymous 'Spies for Peace' documents were distributed among Aldermaston marchers against nuclear warfare. These claimed to give details of the system of government planned for Britain in the event of nuclear attack, naming the locations of regional seats of administration. The information contained in the documents was believed to have been compiled from official papers issued in connection with a NATO exercise the previous autumn. A leak from inside the Civil Service was suspected, but the Spies for Peace were not discovered.

SPRY, BRIGADIER SIR CHARLES CHAMBERS FOWELL (b. 1910)

Educated at Brisbane Grammar School and graduating through the Royal Military Academy, Duntroon, Sir Charles served in World War II as a colonel in the Australian Imperial Force in the South West Pacific and the Middle East, being awarded the DSO. From 1946-50 he was Director of Australian Military Intelligence, and was therefore a natural candidate for chief of the newly-created Australian Security and Intelligence Organization when it was formed after the war. He made an excellent chief and swiftly established a rapport with the SIS and the CIA, as well as being an astute analyst of numerous Soviet defectors. Says one CIA executive: 'Spry's views on defectors were always good value, sometimes worth pure gold.'

Assacin + Defector (w)

STASHINSKY, BOGDAN (b. 1931)

A Ukrainian employed by Soviet Intelligence to keep watch on Ukrainian exiles in West Germany, Stashinsky was told to report news of any anti-Soviet moves they might be making. He carried out this work diligently, reporting that one exiled Ukrainian politician, Lev Rebet, was actively plotting against the USSR. In September 1957 Stashinsky was ordered to meet a KGB man in Karlshorst in East Berlin. There the KGB man showed him 'the weapon which is to do the job for you – the perfect weapon for the perfect murder. This is what you will use on Rebet.' The weapon consisted of a slim metal tube; in the bottom of three sections was a firing pin which ignited a powder charge. This caused a metal lever in the middle section to move and crush a glass ampoule in the mouth of the tube. This contained a poison that resembled water in appearance and escaped from the front of the tube in the form of vapour. The KGB man gave a demonstration with the gun and then warned Stashinsky that, as a safeguard, he must swallow an antidote pill to guard against any ill effects the vapour might have on him as well as his victim.

Stashinsky kept watch for Rebet and used the weapon on him as he was entering his Munich office. The subsequent autopsy did not reveal the truth and a verdict of death by heart attack was returned. On another occasion Stashinsky was ordered to kill Stepan Bandera, another leader of the anti-Soviet Ukrainians. Stashinsky worked for a branch of the KGB called *Otdely Kontrrazvedki* (OKR), the greatly feared counter-espionage killer brigade, and for his services he was awarded the Red Banner decoration. Stashinsky however, was far from happy with his lot. He had planned to be a doctor, but was lured into the Soviet organization with a mixture of threats and promises. Meanwhile he had fallen in love with a German girl, Inge Pohl, and it was her influence which eventually caused him to escape to the West, surrendering to the American authorities. He was tried by a West German court, but won their sympathy to the extent of being sentenced to only eight years as an accomplice to murder. In this trial he gave details of other Ukrainians he would be expected to kill, including Raoslav Stetskow, who had been Prime Minister of the Ukrainian Republic in 1941, and was living in exile in Munich. In 1969 it was announced in Bonn that Stashinsky had been secretly released from gaol on New Year's Eve in 1966 and that he was living in America.

Further reading
SPY! by Richard Deacon with Nigel West (BBC Publications, 1980)

TERRORIST SPIES

While terrorists hardly qualify as spies, the fact is that, especially in modern times, some of them indulge in espionage and are even spymasters. One such was Dr Wadi Haddad, the most ruthless of the Palestinian terrorist leaders, who eventually died of cancer in East Germany. Haddad, who came from a Greek Orthodox family, became involved in politics when studying medicine at the American University of Beirut. With George Habash he formed the Popular Front for the liberation of Palestine and it was he who sent three Japanese Red Army fanatics to carry out the massacre at Lod airport, and Leila Khaled was acting under his orders when she tried to hijack an El Al flight but was captured and arrested at Heathrow. Haddad was behind the hijacking of four aircraft in a mass operation, the mastermind behind the Entebbe and Mogadishu hijacks. He swore he would never make peace with the Israelis, and through him funds flowed to such gangs as the Baader-Meinhof group in Germany, the Red Brigades in Italy and the Japanese Red Army. He had his own intelligence organization and relied upon this to keep him guarded after an Israeli rocket attempt on his home in 1969.

Another terrorist-spy with whom Haddad had links was the international terrorist, Illych Ramirez Sanchez, more generally known as 'Carlos the Jackal'. The son of a Venezuelan doctor, 'Carlos' was a hard-line Communist, educated at the Patrice Lumumba University. After graduating in 1971 he went to Paris and was assigned to the Palestinian terrorist organization known as *Parisienne Orientale*. He made his name in 1975 when he shot a Lebanese informer and three French security agents while trying to escape. Later that year he led a raid on OPEC headquarters in Vienna. He maintained links with the KGB, all sorts of terrorist and underground organizations from the PLO to the IRA, and was the European contact for the Japanese Red Army, sometimes using the names 'Hector Hirodikon', 'Adolf Granel' and 'Carlos Martinez'. George Habash, on Moscow's recommendation, appointed Carlos as head of European operations and he renamed the *Parisienne Orientale* the Budiea Commando. Both the British SIS, the French security service and Israel's Mossad have attempted to track down and capture 'Carlos' but with no success. Later he developed links with both Cuba and Libya. Many of his attacks on planes were aimed at prominent Israelis. He was liable to go into hiding in almost any country and get away with it. In London he used his girlfriends' homes as 'safe houses', though they usually had no idea what his occupation was. He engineered a raid on the Tel Aviv Chen cinema from Nicosia. He picked up a suitcase carrying a time-bomb from the KGB in Athens and airfreighted it, causing the plane to blow up over Corfu. In February 1986 it was reported from Tel Aviv that Israeli intelligence officers had learned that 'Carlos' had been killed by his Libyan 'sponsors' and was buried in the Libyan desert. The report was that he 'knew too much. His up-to-the-minute knowledge about the involvement of Arab leaders and their intelligence services in international terrorism had become too dangerous for them.'

The combination of terrorism and espionage has had a devastating effect all over the world. In the 1970s France and Italy made secret deals with Libya to spare their citizens from attack in return for freedom for terrorists sponsored by Colonel Gaddafi to travel through Europe; the French were said to have made a similar arrangement with the PLO. At the same time Mr Schultz, the US Secretary of State, told the American Jewish Committee that the CIA should be given Congressional backing to wage secret war against terrorism. Then in 1986 the University of Aberdeen announced the compilation of the world's first 'Who's Who' of international terrorism on a computer data-base. This was developed jointly by Professor Paul Wilkinson, head of international relations at Aberdeen

University, and Dr Edna Reid, a computer expert from the University of Maryland. The aim of the register was to help government and private organizations facing terrorist problems by providing up-to-date information on suspects.

Meanwhile the title of the world's most wanted terrorist now goes to Abu Nidal, the man held responsible for the attacks on Rome and Vienna airports in 1985 in which fourteen people died and 121 were wounded. Apart from maintaining offices in Libya and Syria, Abu Nidal also has a training camp in South Lebanon. In October, 1986, a record 45 years' jail sentence was given at the Old Bailey to the Jordanian terrorist Nezar Hindawi, for trying to blow up an El Al jumbo jet – using his pregnant Irish girl friend as a human time bomb. At the same time diplomatic relations between Britain and Syria were severed after the British Foreign Secretary had declared that Britain had independent evidence of the Syrian Ambassador in London, Dr Haydar's, personal involvement in planning the El Al bombing.

Further reading
Carlos: Terror International by Dennis Eisenberg and Eli Landau (Corgi Books, London 1976)

TIEDGE, HANS JOACHIM

West Germany's goverment and intelligence services were considerably shaken in 1985 when it was reported that Tiedge, a departmental head in the counter-espionage organization (BfV), had defected to East Germany. The news was contained in a note from Tiedge which stated that he had defected because he was 'in a hopeless situation'. He had fled to East Germany with only his electric shaver, false personal papers and a railway ticket. The Minister of the Interior said attempts had been made to persuade Tiedge to return, but he had refused to talk to his former colleagues. 'Significant things will have been betrayed by Tiedge and as a result, a whole range of operations have had to be broken off,' Herr Zimmerman, Minister of the Interior, told an emergency session of the Bonn Defence Committee.

It transpired that Tiedge had long had a drink problem and was being hounded by debt collectors, yet despite his senior colleagues knowing all this, no action had been taken. Fears were immediately expressed that Tiedge's defection put American and British agents at risk. To make matters worse, Tiedge had actually been concerned with counter-espionage operations against East Germany so he had details of all these and knew the strengths and weaknesses of their spy network. It remains a mystery why he was allowed to continue working, not simply because of his alcoholism and mounting debts, but because he had lost his driving licence through a drink-driving offence.

TONTON MACOUTE

For many years this strange organization was, in effect, the combined secret and security service of Dr François ('Papa Doc') Duvalier, ruler of Haiti in the 1950s and '60s. Unable to trust the Army, Duvalier built up the Tonton Macoute, giving new status to what had previously been merely a semi-secret society, and making Clement Barbot head of this sinister force. The Tonton Macoute acted as a ruthless secret police, stamping out every manifestation of opposition to or criticism of Duvalier. Sometimes this meant imprisonment without trial, sometimes sudden death by unknown killers. When information was required, torture was unhesitatingly used to obtain it. Barbot was rarely to be seen without his sten-gun and bullet-proof vest, but even he fell into disfavour and in 1960 was arrested by the Presidential guard.

After this, a trio of tough men took over the Tonton Macoute – Elois Maître, Luc Désir and Major Jean Tassy. A large number of government employees were members of the organization, some receiving a monthly payment for services, others operating for nothing because of the unwritten licence to steal and kill which membership gave them. When the British Ambassador, Gerald Corley-Smith, protested about the fear which Tonton Macoutes were instilling into the Haitian people, he was ordered out of the country and Haiti withdrew its ambassador from London. Through the Tonton Macoute, Duvalier cunningly employed voodoo priests to enforce his will, especially in the rural areas. Voodoo drugs were used to turn some malefactors into zombies. Nevertheless the organization had countless failures, a notable one being an inability to track down Armando Estrada (q.v.), a Castroite from Cuba who took charge of running revolutionary networks inside Haiti and adopted the patronymic of 'Lescaille' in order to suggest to his agents that his mother had been Haitian.

Further reading
Papa Doc: Haiti and its Dictator by Bernard Diederich and Al Burt (Bodley Head, London 1970)

TURNER, ADMIRAL STANSFIELD (b. 1923)

A former naval classmate and friend of President Jimmy Carter, Admiral Turner became CIA chief in 1977, and inevitably the way he ran the service was linked to the indecisiveness of Carter as a national leader. Turner was a tough taskmaster, but in the wrong way. His over-zealous purge of the service resulted in the dismissal of more than 2000 personnel. His excuse was that he wanted to axe the old hands to make room for new blood. There is no doubt, however, that the purge did considerable harm and robbed the service of some first-class brains. Morale declined and many people felt he had ruined the Clandestine Service. He also interfered in the affairs of other intelligence services, urging that they should all come under one chief. Only the FBI escaped from his authority. When Reagan became President, Turner was dismissed.

VANUNU, MORDACHAI

After weeks of silence the Israeli government announced in November 1986 that they were holding Mr Mordachai Vanunu, their nuclear scientist who had been accused of leaking details of his country's nuclear arms capability. This terse statement that he was 'under lawful detention' ended weeks of speculation that Mr Vanunu had been abducted from his London hide-out by Mossad agents. All that was known until then was that he had left his hotel in Bayswater, London on 30 September 1986, and had not returned. It transpired that Mr Vanunu had been active as a university student in campaigning for a Palestinian state and Arab rights and that he had carried on these political activities even when he was employed at the Dimona nuclear plant in Israel. A month later it was stated that Vanunu had claimed he was captured by Israeli secret service agents in Rome after taking a British Airways flight from London. This claim was disputed by the Italians and a British Embassy official in Rome declared that 'Israeli agents captured him in Paris.'

VOSJOLI, PHILIPPE THYRAUD DE

A serious blow to French prestige was struck by revelations in 1968 from Philippe de Vosjoli, former head of French Intelligence in Washington, and chief liaison officer between the French and the CIA. It all started with the publication of a spy novel entitled *Topaz*, by the American author, Leon Uris. It told how the head of the KGB's anti-NATO bureau defected to the Americans and revealed the existence in Paris of a Soviet spy ring code-named 'Topaz', of which the two key members were a senior French official and a close adviser of French President de Gaulle. *Le Canard Enchaîné*, the French satirical weekly, suggested that *Topaz* was based on fact. Then it was realized that de Vosjoli was a friend of Uris. De Vosjoli had also incurred the wrath of his French employers by being a little too enthusiastic in his collaboration with the CIA whose favourite Frenchman he was. He was ordered to return to Paris, but refused to go and resigned from the service. Then he made his revelations, published in the USA and Britain, that not only was the French Secret Service infiltrated by Soviet agents, but that there was a spy inside de Gaulle's own entourage. A subsequent inquiry ordered by de Gaulle resulted in the arrest of Georges Paques (q.v.), a French press attaché with NATO.

There were two views about these revelations at the time: some thought they were part of a CIA plot aimed at embroiling de Vosjoli and discrediting de Gaulle, while others thought they were based partly on de Vosjoli's own researches and disinformation pumped out by Soviet defectors. Certainly the whole incident upset Franco-American relations at a time when they were improving, and only the USSR benefited. Undoubtedly the KGB exploited the whole situation to the maximum, not least in a disgraceful attempt to smear one of de Gaulle's closest advisers, Jacques Foccart, the ablest intelligence analyst in Paris, and pin the blame on the CIA. As a matter of interest, there *was* a Soviet spy ring in Paris at this time, but it was code-named 'Sapphire', not 'Topaz'.

WALKER FAMILY SPY RING

The Walker family spy ring was a case which the US Government regarded as one of the most damaging for several decades. The material supplied to the Russians by the ring was so sensitive that, according to Navy Secretary John Lehman, it had cost $100 million just to re-secure radio and communications channels in the US Navy, while actually fixing the damage would take years. John Walker, head of the ring, a former Navy man, was sentenced to life imprisonment in 1985 after pleading guilty to spying for the Russians for seventeen years. His son Michael, a former Navy yeoman, received twenty-five years, and his brother, Arthur, was also convicted of espionage. But the affair of the Walker spy ring was not cleared up until 1986, when former naval Petty Officer Radioman, Jerry Whitworth, was found guilty on seven spying charges and five counts of tax fraud. Whitworth was a key man in the whole ring who failed to report on his income tax returns that he had received $332,000 from the Russians for stealing vital code and communications secrets. The KGB had given Walker a miniature camera which Whitworth took with him when he served at communications centres aboard two aircraft carriers, a supply ship and a shore relay station. He had virtually unlimited access to codes and messages. Whitworth was given a 365-year gaol sentence plus a fine of $410,000 which means that he must serve at least sixty years before being eligible for parole.

Caspar Weinberger, US Defense Secretary, stated at the end of this case that the KGB deciphered more than a million secret

American messages as a result of the Walker family spy ring, and that the flow of stolen documents was so great that KGB officers were posted to the Soviet Embassy in Washington solely to handle them.

WARE RING AND OTHER SOVIET SPY NETWORKS IN THE USA

It was from bases in London and Montreal that the USSR infiltrated the USA in the 1930s and began to build up a series of spy networks. Of these, the first and most effective was that established by the late Harold M. Ware, who when he came to Washington, described himself as an 'agricultural engineer'. Six members of the Ware Ring worked for the Agricultural Adjustment Administration – Alger Hiss (q.v.), Lee Pressman, John Abt, Nathan Witt, Nathaniel Weyle and Charles Kramer. Long before the end of World War II, the Russians had infiltrated some of the highest administrative positions in the USA and Canada (see *Gouzenko, Igor*, Part IV). Key manipulators in the US Treasury Department included Harry Dexter White, Frank Coe, Harold Glasser, Victor Perlo, Irving Kaplan, Sol Adler, Abraham George Silverman and William Ludwig Ullmann. Within the four major rings of Soviet espionage in the USA were also sub-sections such as the Silvermaster Ring and the Perlo Group. Two key Soviet spymasters handling these groups were Jacob Golos, head of a 'cover' company called World Tourists, Inc., who died in 1943, and Anatole Gromov, First Secretary at the Soviet Embassy in Washington. It was Gromov whom Elizabeth Bentley identified as her Soviet control, 'Al', when she defected from the Communist Party in 1946. Gromov's real name was Anatoli Gorsky, who originally controlled Anglo-American recruitment of agents from London when he was operating there between 1936-44. It was he who recruited five wartime members of the OSS into a Soviet spy network. How many priceless American secrets were conveyed to Moscow through these rings may

384

never be known, but a discovery by OSS agents in 1945 at the office of the magazine known as *Amerasia* suggested that these were considerable. According to Frank Bielaski, who conducted investigations for the OSS, 'there was a lengthy document detailing the location of the units of the Nationalist Army in China, their strength, how they were armed ... the total number of documents involved exceeds 1000 ... and I think the FBI seized 467 in Jaffe's office later.'

This was a reference to Philip Jacob Jaffe, *Amerasia*'s managing editor. Born in the Ukraine in 1897, Jaffe had emigrated to the USA and was naturalized when he was twenty-six. He had organized a group calling itself 'American Friends of the Chinese People' and was also affiliated with the American Council of Soviet Relations. When *Amerasia* offices were raided, papers were found from British Intelligence, G-2 State Department and the OSS. Neither Jaffe, nor any of his assistants, were charged with espionage, but simply with being in illegal possession of Government documents. Clearly, warnings of Soviet infiltration were ignored for a long time by the US Government and especially the State Department. Gouzenko, Whittaker Chambers and Bentley had all given evidence pointing to Hiss's involvement, in 1945-6, but the real facts did not emerge until the House Un-American Activities Committee had its hearings in 1948, and the Judiciary US Senate received the report of the Sub-Committee on interlocking subversion in government departments in 1953.

In 1948 Elizabeth Bentley made her first statement under oath showing how the OSS had been penetrated: 'All types of information were given, highly secret information, in what the OSS was doing, such as, for example, that they were trying to make secret negotiations with governments in the Balkans bloc in case the war ended, that they were parachuting people into Hungary, that they were sending OSS people into Turkey to operate in the Balkans ... the fact that General Donovan, head of the OSS, was interested in having an exchange between the NKVD and the OSS.' It was also pointed out that Silverman had been Chief of Analysis and Plans for the Assistant Chief of Air Staff, while Ullmann had been employed in Air Corps HQ in the Pentagon. The final conclusions of the 1953 Committee were that 'the Soviet International organization has carried on a successful and important penetration of the US Government and thus penetration has not been fully exposed ... Thousands of diplomatic, political, military, scientific and economic secrets of the US have been stolen by Soviet agents in our Government and other persons closely connected with the Communists.'

Further reading
'Interlocking Subversion in Government Departments' – report of the Sub-Committee to the Committee on the Judiciary, US Senate (30 July 1953)
Congressional Record (22 May 1950)
'Report of Senate Committee on Foreign Relations' (1950, pt.2, pp 2502-5)

WATKINS, JOHN (1902-1964)

A Canadian diplomat who eventually became Ambassador to Moscow, Watkins was marked down as a prospective agent by Anatoli Gorsky many years before when it was realized that he was a notoriously promiscuous homosexual. Watkins was successfully entrapped, 'set up' and then blackmailed. After that it was easy for him to be manipulated as an agent of influence. Eventually defectors informed the US authorities about Watkins having been seduced by another man while KGB photographers took pictures of the incident with hidden cameras. This information was passed on to the 'Mounties' and one of their officers confronted Watkins, who by this time had retired and gone to Paris. Watkins died of a heart attack before inquiries could be completed.

WENNERSTROM, COLONEL STIG ERIK COMSTANS

A pilot in the Swedish Air Force, Wennerstrom became friendly with Archibald Clark Kerr (later Lord Inverchapel) when the latter was a diplomat in Stockholm. It was Clark Kerr who encouraged him to become an air attaché, as from all accounts

Wennerstrom was not a very good pilot. As a result in 1933 he got a language scholarship in the Swedish Defence Department and was sent to Riga to stay with a Russian family and learn the language. He was also trained for intelligence work. Yet even in this sphere of activity Wennerstrom does not seem to have been highly regarded by the Swedes, and when he became a middle-aged colonel denied further promotion, he was angry and frustrated. The Russians learned of his bitterness towards the Swedish authorities and made cautious efforts to establish contact. There were invitations to parties and dinners, some flattery and hints that his services could very well be appreciated by Russia.

Wennerstrom's recruitment was one of the cleverest jobs the KGB pulled off and he provided them with a mass of information, not merely on Sweden, but on Norwegian and NATO secrets as well from 1948 until 1963. The Soviet plot was to feed his vanity by giving him promotion inside the Russian Secret Service that he had been refused in Sweden; he was made a major-general in the GRU and even presented with a series of secret decorations. In the end he was caught and given a life sentence by a Swedish court. As a concession he was later moved to an open prison at Skenaes where he taught languages. Despite the fact that the GRU paid him handsomely there is evidence that Wennerstrom passed on intelligence about the USSR to both the American and West German Intelligence Services, though whether this was at the behest of the Soviet Union is not altogether clear. There are also indications that in the 1930s Wennerstrom may have done some jobs for British Intelligence in Latvia and Sweden.

Further reading
An Agent in Place: the Wennerstrom Affair by Thomas Whiteside (Heinemann, London 1967)

WHITE, SIR DICK GOLDSMITH (b. 1906)

Educated at Bishops Stortford College, Christ Church, Oxford, and the universities of Michigan and California, Dick Goldsmith

White was originally a schoolmaster who joined MI5 with a view to making a permanent career in intelligence. He succeeded in the sphere of counter-espionage by his capacity for sheer hard work. Under Sir Percy Sillitoe (q.v.) he had been in charge of B Division of MI5 (the counter-espionage section), and then in 1953 he succeeded Sir Percy as head of MI5. His reputation was so high during his stay at MI5 that it came as no surprise to many in intelligence circles when he was made head of MI6 in succession to Major-General Sir John Sinclair, though the idea of someone from MI5 being made their chief was anathema to some of the older members of MI6. This was the first time the appointment had gone to anyone other than a naval or military officer.

Sir Dick was a thorough professional and he made a number of changes to improve the service, as well as playing a diplomatic role in smoothing relations between MI5 and MI6 after the scandals caused by the defection of Burgess, Maclean and Philby, and the unpublicized cases of other traitors within the ranks of both services. He had no easy task and for a long time his presence was resented by the pro-Philby faction in MI6 who believed that the new chief had been appointed to take a closer look at their own activities. This was indeed the case. But it was a long time before the Philby problem was resolved and even then, at the last moment, Philby slipped out of reach and went to Moscow. The late Lord Wigg, who as Paymaster-General in the earlier Wilson governments kept a watch on intelligence matters, regarded Sir Dick very highly indeed, even urging that he should become an intelligence overlord with control of both MI5 and MI6. Sir Dick retired in 1968.

WOLF, MARKUS

Born in Baden-Wuerttenberg in 1923, the son of a communist Jewish doctor and playwright, Markus Wolf moved with his family to Switzerland when Hitler came to power. Later he went to live in France and in 1934 left for the USSR where he studied in Moscow's Comintern School for international emigrés. After World War II Wolf returned to Germany to assist the Russians in turning the Soviet zone into what eventually became East

Germany. Before joining East Germany's diplomatic service he worked as a radio commentator. Then, until 1951, he was first counsellor at his country's mission in Moscow. He largely developed and expanded the *Hauptverwaltung Aufklärung* from the undercover organization of the Institute of Economic research, becoming its head in 1958. As East German intelligence chief he soon established the reputation of being among the world's most efficient spymasters, rising to the rank of lieutenant-general. His outstanding achievement was his recruitment of Guenter Guillaume whom he coached for the role of senior aide to the West German Chancellor, Willy Brandt. It was Guillaume's arrest in 1974 which led to Brandt's resignation. In 1987 Wolf retired at his own request on health grounds, and was replaced by Werner Grossman.

WU-TAI CHIN, 'LARRY' (1923-1986)

For thirty years this versatile character worked for both the CIA and the Intelligence Service of the People's Republic of China, and was decorated by both powers for his services. Born in Peking, he first served as an interpreter and translator for the US Army Liaison Office in Fukien Province in 1943-4. Later he attended classes at Yenching University, where he was actually recruited as an agent by the Chinese. Then, as an infiltrator, he secured a job inside the US Consulate in Shanghai and in 1952 started work with the American Broadcasting Information Service, monitoring Chinese radio broadcasts for the CIA. During the Korean War he collected reports of interviews with Chinese prisoners conducted by US intelligence officers. These he passed on to the Chinese and was paid $2000 for his services. In 1952 he worked for the American Foreign Broadcast Information Service, monitoring Chinese radio broadcasts for the CIA, first in Okinawa, then in Santa Rosa, California, and finally in Virginia. In 1965 he became an American citizen.

In 1986 after a six-week trial, a US federal court at Alexandria, Virginia, found him guilty on seventeen counts of espionage and unauthorized disclosure of classified information.

He was sentenced to a prison term of two life sentences and fines totalling more than $3 million. Investigations revealed that he had $200,000 on deposit in Hong Kong banks and owned property worth $700,000. Chin was given away to the FBI by a defector, but he committed suicide three weeks before sentence was to have been formally passed on him.

WYNNE, GREVILLE MAYNARD

Recruited by MI5 in 1939, Wynne became a civilian businessman after World War II, selling electrical equipment. This became a first-rate cover for him when some years later he was asked to join MI6. While visiting Moscow when East-West trade was becoming rather more popular, he came into contact with the State Committee for the Coordination of Scientific Work and, through this, met Colonel Penkovsky (q.v.). In 1959 he was sent to Odessa to help a Russian intelligence officer, Major Kuznov, to defect to the West. Wynne later became an intermediary for top-secret information passed by Penkovsky to the British. In 1962 Wynne was again asked to contact Penkovsky in Russia and, if necessary, to try to bring him safely out of Russia. By this time, however, it was clear to both men that they were being watched by the KGB and the plan was abandoned.

Wynne moved on to Budapest but was arrested and flown back to Russia after Penkovsky was arrested in Moscow. Wynne was eventually sentenced to imprisonment, but later released in exchange for the Soviet spy Gordon Lonsdale (q.v.). In a BBC broadcast in October 1981, Wynne claimed that misinformation about the supersonic aircraft, Concorde, was fed to the Russians after a Soviet mole had been discovered within the British Aircraft Corporation in the late 1960s. Four years later the giant Russian Tu-144 airplane crashed at the Paris air show, killing fifteen people. It was afterwards suggested that this might have been caused by misinformation from the British.

Further reading
The Man From Moscow by Greville Wynne (London 1967)

ZAISSER, WILHELM

The first head of East German Intelligence (SSD), Zaisser had worked for the Communist cause when he joined the Spartacus Bund and involved himself in the 1923 revolt in Germany which ended in failure. After that he became a naturalized Soviet citizen and was trained for intelligence-gathering duties in the USSR. He first served in China under the GRU and in 1936 was sent to Spain as a commander of the XIII Brigade of the International Brigade. From all accounts his military career was not very successful, as his brigade lost almost half its troops as casualties. Towards the end of World War II Zaisser, together with Walter Ulbricht, was consulted on plans for the Soviet occupation of Germany. At the end of the war he was moved into East Germany and held office as chief of the SSD until 1953 when he failed to warn of the sudden revolt which nearly ended the Ulbricht regime. For this he was dismissed.

ZAMIR, MAJOR-GENERAL SVI (b. 1925)

Zamir arrived in Israel from Poland before he was a year old. When he was seventeen he joined Palmach and in 1946 was arrested by the British police in Palestine for his part in aiding the landing of so-called illegal immigrants. Eventually he joined the Israeli Army and in 1951 was given command of the Givati Brigade. A jovial man off-duty, General Zamir is very much the dedicated Army officer who briefly describes his education in *Who's Who*: 'Staff colleges in Israel and the United Kingdom'. He succeeded Amit as head of the Mossad after the Six-Day War and under his direction this service became a far-ranging and versatile organization, covering not only intelligence from abroad, but the strange new world of electronic and computerized espionage. It also has a special section devoted to intelligence on nuclear developments.

Zamir kept a much lower profile than either of his predecessors and he frequently 'went into the field' himself to

391

make personal assessments, thus learning a great deal about Arab guerrilla tactics. It is thanks to him and his appointment of scientific advisers that the Mossad is currently as scientifically-minded as any secret service in the world. He personally directed a number of 'avenger squad' actions, starting with the retaliation for the attack on Lydda airport. Although these squads now operate with clinical efficiency, their early actions were the subject of as much criticism inside Israel as outside, particularly when they went wrong. A squad operation involving Sylvia Rafael (q.v.) resulted in the wrong man being killed in Norway. Shortly after this incident General Zamir retired.

GLOSSARY

A list of abbreviations, titles, jargon and esoteric subjects linked
to the world of espionage

Ag and fish British Ministry of Agriculture, Fisheries and Food, which in World War II was sometimes used as a cover address for 'resting' intelligence operatives. Alexander Foote, the double-agent who worked for Russia and Britain, had a desk there for some period. 'Ag and Fish' came to mean 'gone to ground' in the early 1950s.

Agent of influence An agent who is employed to change and influence opinion in the country where he operates.

Agent provocateur An agent employed to stir up trouble, create chaos and generally make mischief.

Anpo Kenkyu The code research section of the Japanese Navy.

Apparatchik In the West this has come to mean a secret agent or unit of such agents. In the USSR it simply means an official who has administrative powers.

ASIO Australian Secret Intelligence Organization.

AVB (*Allami Vedelmi Batosag*) The Hungarian Intelligence Service, formerly known as the AVH.

BfV (*Bundesamt fur Verfassungsschutz*) West German Federal Internal Security Office.

Biographic leverage CIA jargon for blackmail.

Black-bag jobs Agents' work, which ranges from bribery to burglary.

Black operations This covers several illegal operations, such as murder, blackmail, extortion and kidnapping, carried out by intelligence agencies.

Black trainees The nickname given to foreigners recruited for CIA undercover training at the hush-hush 'farm' in Virginia. At one time these trainees were allegedly not supposed to know they were on US territory.

Bleep-box Used by some agents both for telephone tapping and placing calls to anywhere in the world without paying. In its primitive form this has been extensively used by agents in Europe, especially Britain. The Chinese have developed a more sophisticated device called a multi-frequency-simulator, a machine for generating tones or frequencies used on various telephonic networks. With this they have cracked the secret numbers of various organizations round the world and thus gained much useful information. This device has been adopted by almost all top-ranking intelligence services.

Blown The phrase used to describe an agent whose cover has been broken, or a network of spies which has been infiltrated. When an agent deliberately gives away to the opposition details of his sub-agent, wife or mistress for some devious reason, he is said to have 'blown his own strumpet'.

BOSS Bureau of State Security of the South African Government. These initials are still used, despite the fact that the organization's name has been changed to the National Intelligence Service.

BPR A joke reference for many years to CIA headquarters in Langley, Virginia. The only indication as to its location in that area was a signpost bearing these initials which were supposed to signify Bureau of Public Roads. Eventually the signpost was substituted by one stating 'Fairbanks Highway Research Station'. But the CIA has many establishments elsewhere: Washington, New York, Chicago, San Franciso, New Orleans and other US cities.

Bugging All manner of eavesdropping, from telephone tapping to electronic devices.

Burnt The word applied to an agent who has either been discovered or so severely compromised that he is no longer useful.

'C' The initial denoting the head of the British Secret Service. The full initials are CSS.

Cacklebladder Secret Service slang for the method of disguising a live body to look like a corpse after having induced an enemy agent to hit or shoot a 'dummy' corpse. As a general rule, the blood of poultry is used for smearing over the 'corpse'. Though this may sound like a complicated and obscure operation belonging more to spy fiction than fact, it is a ploy frequently used for blackmail or for forcing a confession from an agent.

Cannon Name given to a professional thief employed by an intelligence agency whose sole purpose is to steal back the 'inducement' given to enemy agent or target in exchange for information. Often practised by intelligence units short of funds, especially in wartime.

CASMS Computer-controlled Area Sterilization Multi-Sensor System, a highly sophisticated area of the modern intelligence game and a revolutionary development in electronic eavesdropping which was tried out in Vietnam. Hundreds of small, self-contained bugging devices are dropped by aircraft in a certain area. They can pick up the movements of troops, tanks or individuals hidden in the jungle.

CAT Civil Air Transport, the CIA's private air service. Founded in 1946 in China and later based in Taiwan from where it supported clandestine air operations in Korea, Vietnam and other Asian states. CAT operations are described in *Perilous Missions: Civil Air transport and CIA Covert Operations in Asia*, by William M. Leary.

CELD Central External Liaison Department, an important branch of the Chinese Secret Service which is concerned with the analysis of foreign intelligence.

Centre KGB headquarters in Moscow.

CESID (*Centro Superior para la información de la Defensa*) Spain's intelligence service.

Cheka (*Chrezuvychainaya Komissiya po Borbe s Kontr-revolutisnei i Sabottazhem*) Extraordinary Commission for the Struggle against Counter-Revolution and Sabotage, predecessor of the KGB.

Chekist derived from the *Cheka*, the former name of the KGB, and sometimes used to describe KGB members.

Cheng Pao K'o Chinese counter-espionage service employed against foreign agents and to keep watch on the Chinese overseas. Not to be confused with with *Chi Pao K'o*, the Internal Security Section.

CIA American Central Intelligence Agency. South Korea also has its own CIA.

Cobbler A forger of passports.

Company Nickname of the CIA.

Condemned spy A Chinese Secret Service term which has sometimes been wrongly interpreted in English. Literally, it means: 'Ostentatiously doing things calculated to deceive our own spies, who must be led to believe that they have been unwittingly disclosed. Then, when these spies are captured in the enemy's lines, they will make an entirely false report, and the enemy will take measures accordingly, only to find that we do something quite different. The spies will thereupon be put to death.'

Control questions A system of checking used by the KGB. These questions are known only to the Centre, the Resident Director and the agent concerned and are employed to verify his identity, should he appear in an unexpected place.

Counter-spy An agent put in a place where he can betray or mislead opposing spies.

Cousins British SIS members' nickname for the CIA.

Covert action CIA jargon for attempting to influence the affairs of another country.

CSIS Canadian Security Intelligence Service.

Cut-outs Intelligence officers who come directly under the area Chief Intelligence Officer (or in the case of the Russians, the Resident Director). They are talent spotters and recruiters and act as go-betweens for agents and the Chief Officer or Resident Director. Their aim is to protect the identity of other agents.

Defectors Those who desert their cause or country. The 'walk-in defector' arrives unannounced, bringing information with him. The 'defector-in-place' plays the part of a defector, but in reality is an undeclared agent who continues to work for his cause or country.

Demote maximally To purge by killing.

DGI (*Direccion General de Intelligencia*) Cuba's secret service.

DGSE (*Direction Général de Sécurité Extérieure*) This is the new title for the French Secret Service, replacing the SDECE. Many writers have fallen into the error of calling the *Deuxième Bureau* the French Secret Service, and Ian Fleming even described it as the French counter-intelligence agency – wrong again. The *Deuxième Bureau* began as a branch of military intelligence within the French Army. Today it is still a military service, but one which coordinates all intelligence services concerned with national defence.

DI5 The new title for MI5, though almost everyone uses the old title.

DI6 The technical name for MI6, but rarely used. It refers to the British Secret Service controlling overseas agents, also known as the SIS.

Dirty tricks Usually applied to the 'black operations' of the CIA and covering a wide range of espionage and counter-espionage skulduggery. It sometimes applies to breaking into premises illegally to install bugging devices, also called 'dirtying'.

Disinformation Manufactured evidence, smear tactics or forged documents used to discredit opponents. The KGB actually have a department of disinformation, known as Department D.

Doctor A name sometimes given to the police.

Double-agent In the past a double-agent was usually a freelance intelligence operative working for two sides without either knowing about the other. In recent times a double-agent often appears to be working for two sides, but is actually working for only one side, the aim being to obtain intelligence and to fob off false information on the opposition. Sometimes, though more rarely, there are treble- and even quadruple-agents, but their careers are usually brief.

Drop This word has two meanings. In the CIA it denotes success in a 'black operation'. In the KGB it refers to a 'letter-box' or hiding-place for secret messages, sometimes a crevice in a wall (see *Dubok*).

DS (*Darjavna Sugurnost*) Bulgaria's State Security Service.

DST (*Direction de la Surveillance du Territoire*) The French Internal Security organization.

Dubok A secret hiding-place for agents' messages in the GRU and KGB. Curiously, for a nation so sophisticated in espionage, Soviet agents sometimes adopt the kind of hiding-places used by schoolboys for their secret notes. For example, a Soviet sub-agent involved with Colonel Rudolf Abel (see Part IV), told the Americans he had been using a hole in a flight of steps in Prospect Park, New York. An alternative place had to be found when park workers noticed the hole and filled it in with cement.

ECM Electronic counter-measures. Special gear for producing these measures is installed in NATO power submarines engaged in round-the-clock anti-submarine warfare watch – currently the front line of espionage.

E & E Escape and Evasion. Specialist agents in the CIA are used for such tasks as sending a man in to rescue a captured agent, or preparing an escape route. MI9 operated on these lines for Britain in World War II.

Elint Electronic intelligence. Information obtained by planes, ships, submarines, space satellites, electronic intercept stations and radar. This is handled and interpreted by 'squawk hawks', officially known as substantive intelligence analysts.

Etsiväkeskus Former name of Finland's secret police (now *Suojelupoliisi*).

FBI Federal Bureau of Investigation. The USA's counter-espionage organization.

FIA Federal Intelligence Agency. The NATO powers' name for the West German *Bundesnachrichtendienst* (BND).

Field Foreign territory in which an agent is actually on assignment.

Firm, the The name sometimes given to the British Secret Service by its agents.

Fix CIA word meaning to compromise, blackmail, or simply con. Agents exploring 'fix' possibilities talk of a 'low-key' fix, or an OK fix (blackmail).

Fluttered To be examined by a polygraph lie-detector.

Fortran Formula Translation Language. A computer language with special reference to engineering and scientific matters.

Footwarmer A linear amplifier used in radio transmission.

Fumigating Checking premises for listening and other espionage devices, and removing them.

Fur-lined seat cover oblique reference to an agent who has a female passenger.

Game, the A person who works in intelligence is said to be 'in the game'. Not to be confused with 'on the game' (prostitution), though sometimes the two are combined!

GCHQ Government Communications Headquarters. The communications monitoring and listening post of the British Government, stationed at Cheltenham. It is linked to a world-wide network of spy bases, ships, planes and satellites and part of the four-nation UKUSA network which shares out intelligence and divides the world into different areas to be monitored by each participant, including the USA, Canada and Australia. Large listening stations with more than 1000 staff are operated in Cyprus, Hong Kong and Berlin, but there are also smaller station links in the Ascension Islands and Oman, while British GCHQ bases are to be found at various places in the UK, from Brora in Scotland to Morwenstow in the south-west. GCHQ itself operates from two large sites at Oakley and Benhall on the outskirts of Cheltenham (see *HMCC*).

Going private Leaving the Secret Service; this applies both to the Americans and British, but not, of course, to the KGB or GRU!

GPU (*Glavnoye Gosudarstvenno Politcheskoye Upravleni*) The Soviet Union's predecessor to the KGB.

GRU (*Glavnoye razvedyvatelnoye Upravlenye*) Soviet Military Intelligence.

Harmonica bug A tiny transistorized eavesdropping gadget which can be placed inside an ordinary telephone.

Hauptverwaltung aufklärung East Germany's intelligence service (part of MfS).

HMCC Her Majesty's Government Communications Centre. A separate organization from GCHQ sited at Hanslope Park, north of Milton Keynes, which is responsible for the British Government's own communications. It brings into the UK all radio signals intercepted at small listening posts throughout the world. These are transmitted directly to GCHQ at Cheltenham.

Hospital Prison.

Illegals Elite Soviet espionage agents usually sent under false passports into foreign countries where there are severe penalties for espionage. They are mainly deployed by the GRU. Referred to in intelligence circles as 'singles' or 'doubles', the latter meaning married couples who are 'illegals'.

KGB (*Komitet Gosudarstvennoy Bezopasnosti*) The Soviet Committee for State Security, but actually an organization of vast ramifications covering both espionage and counter-espionage, as well as border guards.

KISS Korean Intelligence and Security Service.

Ladies A euphemism for female members of an intelligence team out to compromise one of the opposition. They aim to ingratiate themselves with the male 'target' for treatment, sometimes, but not always, seducing him. As the name implies the 'ladies' are often out of the top drawer of society.

Legend The faked biography of a spy to provide him with a cover.

Lion-tamer When an agent is sacked, he sometimes goes berserk and makes threats. One of the agency's muscle-men, referred to as a 'lion-tamer', is then called in to soften him up. The 'lion-tamer' is also used to cope with recalcitrant or double-crossing 'ladies' or 'sisters'.

'M' the initial given to the head of the British Secret Service in James Bond fiction, but not in real life. However, the head of the SOE in World War II was known as 'M' for a brief time (see *Gubbins, Major-General Sir Colin*, Part III).

Magpie board A small board or pack of keys, wire, knives and other odds and ends for aiding escape. In more sophisticated packs benzedrine tablets, compasses, maps and even miniature radio transmitters are included.

MGB (*Ministerstvo Gosudarstvennoy Bezopasnosti*) The Soviet Ministry of State Security.

Measles A murder carried out so efficiently that death appears to be accidental or due to natural causes..

MfS (*Ministerium für Staatssicherheit*) East Germany's Ministry for State Security.

MI1C The original initials of the British Secret Service before they were changed to MI6 – hence the use of 'C' for the head of the Service.

MI5 Britain's counter-intelligence service, operating primarily at home.

MI6 Britain's Secret service, operating mainly overseas, but with its headquarters in London at Century House.

MI8 Entirely an American organization set up after World War I by the cryptographer, Herbert O. Yardley. It was, in effect, the cryptographic bureau of military intelligence and was the precursor of the National Security Agent.

MI9 Initials of the World War II organization set up by the British for planning escapes and escape routes for Allied prisoners-of-war and others. Its most celebrated executive was the late MP, Airey Neave, who paved the way by escaping from the German prisoner-of-war camp at Colditz in 1942. 'You cannot escape,' said Neave afterwards, 'unless you prepare with meticulous detail. In my experience it is the modest and practical person who survives.' See *Saturday at MI9* by Airey Neave (London, 1969)

Mokrie dela In Russian this means literally 'wet or bloody affairs' and refers to espionage missions involving bloodshed, violence or death. The CIA refer to a killing in the course of business as 'wet work'.

Mole An agent ordered to infiltrate the services of the enemy in order to send back information.

Mossad (*Mossad Le Aliyah Beth***)** Israel's Institution for Intelligence and Special Services.

Mozhno girls Mozhnos, or 'permitted girls', are recruited and trained by the KGB to seduce Western officials and agents and to report back what they learn from them. This practice was somewhat curtailed after Stalin's death because a few *Mozhnos* actually married the person they had been told to seduce. One such *Mozhno* was Nora Murray who wrote a book called *I Spied for Stalin*.

Mukhabarat Libya's intelligence service.

Mukhabarat el-aam (General Intelligence Agency) Egypt's secret service.

Music box A wireless transmitter.

Musician A radio operator.

MVD (*Ministerstvo Vnutrennikh Del***)** The Soviet Ministry of Internal Affairs.

Naked Operating entirely alone and without any assistance from outside.

Nash A person belonging to one's own side. This is a horrible corruption of a Russian word used by Western operatives.

Neighbour A Soviet word for the local Communist Party or a member of it. Westerners would call a 'neighbour' a 'fellow traveller'. Occasionally the word is used to denote another branch of the same intelligence service.

Neighbours A name sometimes given to the Warsaw Pact powers in Moscow.

News News in the intelligence game is usually bad, and this word is used to tell a contact or 'target man' that he is on the spot, i.e. he must either deliver the goods, which can mean anything from revealing information to carrying out a mission, or face exposure or blackmail. The 'news' is usually conveyed subtly so it will slowly sink in and the victim can ponder the alternative. Occasionally this is done merely to keep a 'target man' on ice – a hint that he may eventually be required to perform a task for his mentors or tormentors – in CIA language be 're-activated'.

NID Naval Intelligence Division (British). Once the equal of MI6. Now, alas, deplorably reduced in size.

NKGB (*Narodnyi Kommissariat Gosudarstvennoi Bezopasnosti*) The Soviet People's Commissariat for State Security.

NKVD (*Narodnyi Kommissariat Vnutrennikh Del*) The People's Commissariat for Internal Affairs.

NSA National Security Agency of the USA.

NTS (*Natsionalno Trudovoy-Soyuz*) The Society of National Unity, founded in 1930. Roughly translated, it means the 'Producers' Party', embracing technicians, labourers, artists, farmers, engineers, professional men and producers of all kinds. It aimed to be a constructive movement to combat Communism with a definite political and social programme. The object was to improve the life of the Russian masses and to offer a worthwhile alternative to Communism. The NTS was not a Tsarist movement and made no mention of restoring Tsardom in its programme, so it was unpopular with Tsarists of the old school. For years it slumbered as an ineffectual society, but the war and subsequent creation of satellite states gave it something of an impetus. The NTS needed funds and during the war years these came in the shape of assistance from German Intelligence. Despite this, more than 200 NTS were incarcerated in Nazi concentration camps during World War II, including some of the leaders. After the war the NTS was linked to the American CIA through one of its members, K. Boldyreff, and having acquired funds from American sources, set up cells in Yugoslavia, Hungary, Romania, Poland and Czechoslovakia and also gained some ground inside Russia, especially in the Ukraine. Later it was infiltrated by the KGB and manipulated in much the same manner as 'The Trust' (see Part III).

Ochrana The Tsarist Intelligence and Security Service, succeeded by the *Cheka*.

OKW (*Ober Kommando Wehrmacht*) The German Military Intelligence organization in World War II.

One-man Bay of Pigs A phrase used to describe an incompetent agent who has made a hash of things, but more specifically to describe Richard Bissell who sanctioned the CIA's catastrophic Bay of Pigs operations against Fidel Castro during President Kennedy's term of office.

ONI Office of Naval Intelligence (USA) (see *Office of N.I.*, Part II).

Orchestra A term coined by Lenin referring to the creation of a team of potential long-term agents, people selected without being told and allowed to remain dormant until ultimately they could be bullied, blackmailed, cajoled or compromised into collaboration. Usually those chosen had access to secret information or to important individuals or offices; this would apply as much to cleaners or caretakers as to highly placed people inside the Establishment, as long as they had weaknesses which could be exploited, such as perversions, homosexuality, alcoholism and marital infidelity. Sometimes 'orchestra' is applied to a network, but this is mainly because in the Second World War the Germans nicknamed the Soviet espionage network in Belgium *Rote Kapelle* (Red Orchestra) when they discovered that a radio operator in Soviet espionage terminology was a 'musician'.

OSS Office of Strategic Services. Set up in the USA in World War II under General 'Big Bill' Donovan, this was the forerunner of the CIA.

Pavement artists A surveillance team, or an agent keeping watch on a house. Though the phrase is used today in intelligence circles, there is a slight suspicion that it was actually invented by John Le Carré.

Peep A name given to an espionage photographic specialist who can take good pictures in conditions of great difficulty, and to someone who plants secret cameras.

PFIAB President's Foreign Intelligence Advisory Board (USA).

Piano concerto Message. e.g. 'See my forty-third concerto.'

Piano study Radio operating.

Piscine Nickname of the French Secret Service headquarters which is situated close to a large swimming-pool.

Place of conspiracy A Soviet term for a secret meeting-place, usually in a nearby country where an agent may in certain circumstances make contact with his 'side' on fixed days.

Playback This occurs when an agent is captured and forced to continue transmitting back home, usually including false information.

Plumbing The work undertaken to prepare for a major operation, though it can also refer to reconnaissance of a building and the planting of 'bugging' gadgets. This work is undertaken by 'plumbers'.

PSI espionage Inexplicable psychic phenomena which may be new manifestations of espionage, or lend themselves to such purposes. These phenomena include not only ESP and 'brain manipulation', but all sorts of paranormal experiments, including mind-control by long distance hypnotism to 'psychic warfare' and psychokinesis. The Israelis have first-hand knowledge of such experiments carried out under military control in seven Russian cities and at least four other East European capitals. In Bulgaria, for instance, the secret police have used clairvoyants to assist them in crime detection and have set up Institutes of Suggestology and Parapyschology in Sofia and Petrich.

One of the first defectors to throw light on Russian PSI espionage experiments was Nikolai Khokhlov (see Part IV), a former KGB agent. He testified that the Soviets had a 'mind-control' programme backed by the military as well as scientists, and that they had experimented with psychotronic weapons. Since the early 1970s the CIA have taken a positive interest in searching for evidence of psychic warfare development in the Eastern bloc. The KGB keeps quiet about its psychic research establishments, but has deliberately fed false information to the West about its paranormal investigations. This claim made by former Novosti Press Agency employee, Tomas Schuman, appeared in a supplement to *PSI Research*, a psychic magazine published in the USA and edited by the highly reputable Larissa Vilenskaya, also a Russian refugee, who has arranged seminars on parapsychology in Israel. In 1977 the *New York Times* revealed that parapsychology research was undertaken by the Soviet military in a special laboratory of Siberia's Science City. One of the researchers, now living in Paris, was Dr August Stern, who later identified the centre as a branch of the Institute of Automaton and Electrometry, designated 'Special Department No. 8' and established in 1966 under the direction of a naval officer, Vitaly Perov. The laboratory was unexpectedly shut down in 1969, but it is believed that a new KGB-controlled laboratory has since been established in Moscow to carry on the work.

Further reading
With My Little Eye by Richard Deacon (Muller,London 1983)
PSI: Psychic Discoveries Behind the Iron Curtain by Sheila Ostrander and Lynn Schroeder (Sphere Books, London 1973)
Sovjetspionage i Sverige by Dragan Jovius (Stockholm 1979)
'*The Third World War*', by Guy Playfair (*The Unexplained*, no. 64, vol.6, 1981)
Soviet Military Review (November 1973)

Pudding A sarcastic term applied by intelligence agents in the West to the United Nations. 'In the pudding club' means inside UN headquarters.

Puzzle palace NSA headquarters at Fort Meade, an agency which was for years so hush-hush that its initials were jokingly interpreted as 'No Such Agency'. It was created by a Presidential memorandum signed by President Truman, is several times larger than the CIA and receives and analyses massive amounts of data picked up by land-based listening posts, submarines and satellites. It is a twelve-acre underground warren packed with computers, surrounded on top by a ten-foot high fence topped with barbed wire, inside which is a five-strand electrified fence, while a third fence inside is patrolled by guards with dogs.

PZPR Polish Secret Police and Intelligence Agency.

Quick trip around the horn An agent-radio operator's check on activity in communications.

R-12 Sometimes called the 'Buzby Bug', this can be inserted in a telephone and then called up from anywhere in the world to eavesdrop on conversations. The bug was invented by the Special Investigations Divisions of the Post Office – code-named R-12 – and based at the Post Office's research centre at Martlesham Heath near Ipswich in Suffolk.

Rabcor An abbreviation of the Russian name of a system of 'worker-correspondents'. This was one of the first forms of

Soviet espionage, set up in France before World War II and revised afterwards. It was based on developing a system of industrial espionage in factories and elsewhere. During the early 1950s there were said to be more than 800 *rabcors* in France, all supplying intelligence to the USSR.

Radar button A gadget which can pin-point its carrier's position back to base at any given time, which means that the agent can be shadowed by the controller who can send help, if necessary.

Raven A male agent employed to seduce men or women who could be of value to his agency.

RCMP Royal Canadian Mounted Police.

Resident director The head of a Soviet Secret Service spy network. May be resident in the country against which the network is directed, or based in adjacent territory. The Director usually had diplomatic status, but not always.

Residentura Spy network controlled by a Resident Director.

Safe house A hideaway, where agents and defectors can be accommodated. More often the term applies to a place where agents and suspects can be interrogated.

Sanctification An American term bluntly described by Miles Copeland (former CIA executive), as 'blackmail for the purposes of extracting political favours from a victim, not money'. A Russian translation of this word is applied to tactics of the KGB and GRU in winning defectors from the Roman Catholic priesthood. When they secure a priest as an agent, the KGB say he has been 'beatified'.

Sanction Intelligence agency approval for a killing (usually for revenge or other counter-measures). The phrase is sometimes used in CIA circles.

411

SB (*Sluzba Bezpieczentstwa*) The Polish Intelligence Service (see *PZPR*, Part V).

Scalp-hunters Specialists in the subject of defection and experts in telling genuine defectors from fakes. Their job is to keep their eyes open for news of any diplomat or priority 'target' in the enemy camp who seems anxious to defect. They are given top priority in such instances over their intelligence operators.

SDECE (*Service de Documentation Extérieure et de Contre-Espionage*) Formerly the French Secret Service (see *DGSE*, Part V, and *France*, Part I).

Setting-up Framing or trapping an individual by secret agents. A diplomat, for example, is said to be 'set-up' when he is lured into a bedroom fitted with hidden cameras and microphones and seduced by one of the 'ladies', 'sisters', or even a male 'raven'. The KGB are past masters at 'setting-up', but these tactics have been used by other intelligence services as well.

Shoe A false passport.

SIFAR The Italian counter-intelligence service.

SIS Secret Intelligence Service (British). Another title for MI6 or DI6. Also Security Intelligence Service (New Zealand).

Sisters The lower ranks of the 'ladies'. They usually get the tougher assignments and invariably find themselves bedding down with the opposition, regardless of their inclinations.

Sleeper A deep-cover agent planted in opposition territory with orders to lie low and work up contacts over a period of years. Gordon Lonsdale (see *Molody, Konon*, Part IV), the Soviet spy caught in London in 1961, was a typical 'sleeper', having been planted in Canada in the 1930s.

Soap Nickname for the truth drug, specially treated sodium pentathol, known for short as 'so-pe'.

Smersh An abbreviated combination of two Russian words, *Smyert Shpionam* (Death to Spies), used to describe a Stalinist military counter-intelligence unit. An organization of this name existed in the 1940s, but was incorporated into the *Otdely Kontrrazvedki* counter-espionage service in 1946.

SOE Special Operations Executive. A World War II British-sponsored organization for aiding and collaborating with Resistance movements in occupied Europe (see *Special Operations Executive*, Part III).

Software Programmes and systems for use in computers in intelligence.

Son et Lumière This is the amusingly apt description of evidence from a 'setting-up'. It means that the seduction of a victim is recorded by hidden cameras and microphones.

Special projects A CIA name for the tougher and more unpleasant side of the intelligence game, including anything from murder to para-military operations, but sometimes this covers illegal bugging as well. Watergate was a 'special project'.

Spoofing Post-World War II aerial reconnaissance. The name was conjured up by the British when they sent out planes skirting the borders of the USSR, sounding out radar installations and collecting intelligence. 'Spoofing' was usually limited to flying across the Soviet borders and back again, sometimes provoking intervention by Soviet planes. It was eventually replaced by U-2 operations which were launched by the USA in 1956. The U-2 was then regarded as the perfect weapon against an unexpected Soviet attack. Gary Powers carried out U-2 'spoofing' until 1960 when he was ordered to fly over Russia and given various key points to survey, including the Sverdlovsk rocket-launching pad, and other naval and air bases. Powers was fired on and parachuted on to Russian soil, being captured and publicly interrogated before being gaoled for three years. Eventually he was exchanged for the Soviet spy, Rudolf Abel. When he returned to the USA he was subjected to a court of inquiry for having failed to push the destruct button on the U-2 before bailing out. Powers was killed in a helicopter crash working for a Los Angeles TV station in 1977.

Spook A professional intelligence executive or agent.

SSD (*Staatssicherheitsdienst*) The East German Intelligence Service.

Stable The list of 'ladies' and 'sisters' available for 'setting-up' operations in an allotted territory. This sometimes includes 'taxis' and 'fairies'.

Station chief CIA official under diplomatic cover in a USA embassy.

Stepped on Signal and radio interference.

Stroller An agent operating with a walkie-talkie set.

STB (*Statni Tajna Bezpecnost*) The Czech Intelligence Service.

Sweetener Any method used for softening up a 'target', either by gifts or inducements.

Taxi Cover word for 'jacksie', a homosexual member of the 'stable', but now rather dated, as even 'taxis' tend to be called 'ladies', 'sisters', or 'swallows'. As one SIS executive told a British minister during a sex scandal of the 1970s involving another Minister: 'We all have to talk and think in bisexual terms these days, and when our stablemates say that they have "got the whips on", they aren't talking in Parliamentary language.'

Target Someone selected for 'sanctification' by the Americans, and in British parlance for 'special treatment', in other words a person usually in the enemy camp on whom incriminating evidence is needed so that a hold on him or her can be acquired. But it can also refer to someone marked out as a likely defector who needs just a last push to be lured across.

Thermal detector A gadget which makes it possible to discover where people have been sitting or lying, and even how many clothes they have been wearing.

Thirty-threes An emergency.

Tiger in the tank A linear amplifier.

Turned agent An agent of an enemy power who is either captured or goes voluntarily to the other side and is used by that side to feed false information to the enemy and obtain information from them.

Ufology research Many countries investigate UFOs, but few will admit it. Such research aims to identify all sorts of terrestrial sightings that cannot be easily explained. The British frequently deny that they have ever done such research, but occasionally have gone to the trouble of covering up all evidence of anything unusual. Such a case happened at an East Anglian airfield on 27 December 1980, but the American deputy commander on the base at Woodbridge eventually gave details of this UFO sighting. Yet Dr J. Allen Hynek, who for twenty years was scientific consultant to the US Air Force's UFO investigation team, has stated that 'there's no doubt that the US Air Force has not played clean pool with the public ... The UFO reports have been played down.'

The French set up an organization named GEPAN under President Giscard d'Estaing, exclusively to monitor reports on UFOs. GEPAN worked closely with some 15,000 police stations, to which it delivered advisory manuals. Later there were attempts to close down GEPAN, but on the insistence of the French Defence Minister the research was continued and GEPAN brought under the direction of the French National Space Centre. There are two secret UFO study centres in the UK, one in West London and the other at Rudloe Manor in Wiltshire.

Walk-in One who volunteers information or offers his services.

War of diversion This is a Soviet term for carefully calculated sabotage of Western installations and factories. This is hardly ever indulged in on a large scale, but is intended mainly as a 'diversion' and a probe. Sometimes such work is carried out under cover of terrorist movements like the IRA and the Red Brigades. It used to be controlled by the Ninth Section for Terror and Diversion of Soviet Intelligence.

WEB West European Bureau of the Comintern (USSR).

What's your twenty? Where exactly are you?

XX Committee The double-cross (usually referred to in code as 'The Twenty') Committee, set up in World War II to control and exploit double-agents or turned agents (see *Double-cross System*, Part III).

Y-Service Wireless deception.

Zoo Police station.

Ze-2 Polish Military Intelligence.